Jack the Ripper Suspects: The Definitive Guide and Encyclopedia

by Paul Williams

Contents

Michael Kidney.

Edward Watkins.

George Morris.

Thomas Conway.

John Kelly.

Joseph Barnett.

Daniel Barnett.

Joseph Fleming.

Thomas Bowyer.

John McCarthy.

George Neating.

George Hutchinson.

James Thomas Saddler.

Arrested on Suspicion

John Leary.

Private Law.

Corporal Benjamin.

Corporal George.

Skipper.

John Pizer.

Julius Lipman.

William Piggott.

Jacob Isenschmid.

Friedrich Schumacher.

Edward Mc Kenna.

Charles Ludwig.

Edward Quinn.

Frank Raper.

John Langan.

George Richard Henderson.

William John Foster.

Andrews.

George Compton.

Sir George Compton Archibald Arthur.

Thomas Murphy.

Arthur Henry Mason.

Nikaner Benelius.

Oliver Matthews.

Charles Akehurst.

Douglas Cow.

James Connell.

Van Burst.

Alfred Parent.

James Shaw.

John Moynihan.

Stewart.

Joseph Isaacs.

Joseph Lis.

Edwin Burrows.

Joseph Denny.

Pierce John Robinson.

John Larkin Mills.

John Sullivan.

Charles Evison.

John Connors.

Arbie La Bruckman.

Accused During the Terror.

John James.

George Cullen.

Thomas Mills.

John Lock.

Doctor MacDonald.

John George Donkin.

John Davidson.

Doctor Hartley.

James Malcolm.

Alaska.

Maurice.

Bertram Knutson.

Robert Louis Stevenson.

Richard Mansfield.

Lyttelton Forbes-Winslow.

Dick Austin.

Willie Boult.

Doctor Sass.

Doctor Straus.

Henry Taylor.

Hans Bure.

Mac Sweeney.

James David Lampard.

Johann Stammer.

William Arthur Wills.

Crossley.

HC Kromschroeder.

General Brown.

John Davies.

Charles Stuart Parnell.

Louis Solomon.

William Onion.

Accused after the Terror

Manuel Cruz Xavier.

Jose Laurenco.

Joao de Souza Machado.

Joachim da Rocha.

Antoni Pricha.

Joseph Turner Ward.

Wolf Levisohn.

Henry Edward Leake.

Gersie Somo.

Samuel Graham.

Robert D'Onston Stephenson.

Morgan Davies.

Julius Wirtkofsky.

William Barrett.

James Farrow.

Jack Irwin.

Robert Hiron.

William M'Kellick.

G Wentworth Bell Smith.

Herbert Freund.

Cornwall.

Edward Hamblar.

William Thick.

Frank Castellano.

Jean Tomplier.

William Magrath.

O'Brien, William.

Wilson.

James Wilson.

John Alexander Fitzmaurice.

Mr Churchill.

Mad Confessions

Joseph Woods.

John Fitzgerald.

Augustus Nochild.

William Bull.

Alfred Napier Blanchard.

William Stanley.

Frederick White.

John Williams.

John Murray.

Henry Skinnerton.

John Foy.

Benjamin Graham.

Holt.

John Avery.

John Perryman.

Michael Hertzberg.

John Lewis.

Benjamin Isaacs.

George Pierelli.

John Tyson.

William James.

Theophile Hanhart.

William Petitt.

John Davies.

William Broder.

William Sheals.

William Jones.

William Gilbert.

James Glen.

Henry Denker.

John Henry Thompson.

Charles Corbett.

Charles Bond.

Samuel Scar.

Charles McClintock.

John Hill.

James Malone.

Gee.

Charles Y Hermann.

False Confessions

Anderson.

John Sanderson.

Doctor Stanley.

James Maybrick.

Michael Maybrick.

Frederick Abberline.

John Pavitt Sawyer.

Lister.

Hotham

Duberly.

James Carnac.

Contemporary Killers

William Bisgrove.

James Kelly.

Thomas Lott.

William Waddell.

William Henry Bury.

Thomas Harding.

Thomas Neil Cream.

Frederick Bailey Deeming.

Alois Szemeredy.

Later Killers

Hendrick de Jong.

Carl Feigenbaum.

Ernest Schulz.

Almeda Chatelle.

Reginald Saunderson.

HH Holmes.

George Robertson.

Sampson Silas Salmon.

Severyn Klosowski.

Emil Totterman.

Other Criminals

Mary.

James Johnson.

Collingwood Hilton Fenwick.

Alfred Gray.

John Royal.

Knightley Bazeley.

Thomas Jones.

John Batterson.

Leonard Harting.

Charles Le Grand.

Thomas Cutbush.

Daniel Gavan.

Percy Greathead.

James Farley.

William Grainger.

Jim McDermott.

Macnaghten's Memorandum

Montague John Druitt.

Aaron Kosminski.

Martin Kosminski.

Michael Ostrog.

Recollections

Thomas Molin.

Henry Dalkin Robertson.

Donald Robertson.

John Norton.

George Robert Sims.

John Hewitt.

Ernest Dowson.

John Barlas.

Francis Thompson.

Mr Taylor.

Frederick Chapman.

Thomas Dutton.

Alfred Hinde.

Alonzo Maduro.

Frank Edwards.

Denis Halstead.

Bransby Williams.

Doctor Cohn.

Clarence Simm.

Walter Thomas Porriott.

Leonard Thornton.

Littlechild's Letter

Francis Tumblety.

Lunatics

Oswald Puckeridge.

Nikolay Vasiliev.

Alexander Pedachenko.

Levitski.

Winberg.

Nathan Kaminsky.

David Cohen.

Hyam Hyams.

Jacob Levy.

Cornelius Bruyn.

George Hutchinson.

Newland Smith.

John Sanders.

George Borrett.

Fogelma.

George Bloombein.

George Miles.

Women.

Elizabeth Ashworth.

Elizabeth Halliday.

Olga Tchkersoff.

Mary Pearcey.

Helena Blavatsky.

Constance Kent.

Rose Mylett.

Lizzie Williams.

John Williams.

Doctors and Surgeons.

Morford.

Thomas Barnardo.

John Sanders.

James Gloster.

Arthur Conan Doyle.

Septimus Swyer.

13

Stephen Appleford.

William Westcott.

Nigel Torme.

Charles Hebbert.

William Thomas.

Frederick Treeves.

Joseph Merrick.

Aristocrats and Royals

King Edward VII.

Prince Albert Victor.

Francis Russell, Duke of Bedford.

George Russell, Duke of Bedford.

James Stephen.

John Netley.

William Gull.

Robert Anderson.

Charles Warren.

Lord Salisbury.

Walter Sickert.

Lord Euston.

Lord Arthur Somerset.

John Courtenay.

Randolph Churchill.

Lord Blandford.

Frederico Albericci.

Herbrand Russell.

William Humble Ward.

Alfred Pearson.

Harold de Walden.

King Leopold II.

William Gladstone.

Other Men

George Gissing.

Algernon Swinburne.

Thomas Vere Bayne.

Lewis Caroll.

Melville Macnaghten.

James Monro.

Claude Conder.

Henry Wellcome.

Vincent Van Gogh.

Henri de Toulouse Lautrec.

Henri Bourges.

Jose Protacio Rizal.

Antonio Regidor.

Reinhold Rost.

Robert Mann.

Edward Buchan.

Richard Brown.

George Lusk.

John George Gibson.

Samuel Barnett.

Moses Eppstein.

Walter

Francis Spurzheim Craig.

William Belcher.

Albert Bachert.

Introduction

In the autumn of 1888, a serial killer known as Jack the Ripper stalked the East End of London. He was never identified but hundreds of people were accused. Some were known to the authorities at the time and others were named by later researchers. The truth about them, and the reasons why they came suspicion, is often lost in a plethora of opinions and misinformation.

For the first time this book presents the evidence against 333 suspects. They include the publican who painted his dog, the first woman sentenced to the electric chair, the writer of the Red Flag, the man with a thousand convictions, Britain's oldest Prime Minister, and many others. People from all walks of nineteenth century life, representing many different nationalities and professions. United by a link, however tenuous, to the most famous murderer in history.

The Murders

Before looking at suspects we need to establish what they are accused of. There is no agreement on the number of murders committed by Jack the Ripper, but it is sensible to exclude any crimes not mentioned in the contemporary police files, unless relevant to specific suspects. Those files begin with the murder of Emma Smith, a 45-year-old prostitute on Tuesday 3 April 1888, the day after a bank holiday. She returned to her lodging house in George Street, between 04:00 and 05:00, saying some men had robbed and ill-treated her. On the way to hospital she pointed out the place where the assault took place, near a cocoa factory on Osborne Street. She told Doctor Haslip, the house surgeon, that she crossed the road at about 01:30 to avoid some men who followed her, assaulted her and took her money. She might also have been raped. There were two or three men, one of whom appeared to be a youth of nineteen. A portion of her right ear was torn and there was a rupture of the peritoneum and other internal organs, caused by a blunt instrument used with great force.[1] Emma died of peritonitis, the following day.

The police were unaware of the assault until notified of the inquest. Inspector Reid said that Smith would have passed several officers on the way to the hospital but did not ask for assistance.[2] None of them recalled seeing her.

The next crime occurred on Tuesday 7 August 1888, also the day after a bank holiday. The victim was a 49-year-old prostitute called Martha Tabram. A fellow prostitute, Pearly Poll, said they had been with soldiers on the night of the murder until 23:45.[3]

John Reeves, a resident in George Yard Buildings Whitechapel, found Tabram's body on the first-floor landing at 04:45. Another resident Elizabeth Mahoney returned home with her husband at about 01:40 and then went back out. She did not see anything, but said she might have missed the body, as the staircase was unlit after 23:00.[4] Alfred Crow saw a body at 03:30 but, accustomed to similar sights, ignored it.

Doctor Killeen said that Tabram had been dead some three hours when he arrived around 05:30. She had 39 stab wounds. The stomach was penetrated six times, the left lung five times, the right lung, spleen, and liver twice and the heart once. All the wounds were inflicted during life, but not by the same weapon. At least one was caused by a kind of dagger.[5] The cause of death was haemorrhage.

The next victim was Mary Ann Nichols, a 43-year-old prostitute. A friend Emily Holland, also known as Jane Oram, saw her at about 02:30 on 31 August.[6] Just over an hour later, Charles Cross, a carman, found the body on a yard crossing at Bucks Row. Another carman, Robert Paul, arrived and they went to find a policeman, coming across Constable Mizen. Meanwhile Constable Neil came across the body at 03:45, having passed the spot thirty minutes earlier. There were no marks on the ground to indicate a struggle or signs of a recent vehicle on the road.

Doctor Henry Llewellyn arrived about 04:00. He felt that Nichols was killed within the previous half hour. There was a slight laceration of the tongue and bruises on the face, possibly caused by pressure from fingers or a blow. The left side of the neck had two incisions, the larger of which was about eight inches long. A jagged wound ran across the left side of the abdomen with three or four similar cuts on the right. All wounds ran from left to right and were inflicted by one long-bladed knife, moderately sharp, and used with great violence. A left-handed assailant was possible.[7]

On 8 September John Davis, a carman living at 29 Hanbury Street, found a body in the back yard of the house just before 06:00. The dead woman was Annie Chapman, a 47-year-old prostitute. She lay on her back with her left arm resting on the left breast and her

19

legs drawn up. The murderer had cut her throat in a jagged manner, from left to right. Her small intestines and a flap of the abdomen lay on the right side, above her right shoulder, and still attached by a cord. Two flaps of the skin from the lower part of the abdomen lay in a large quantity of blood above the left shoulder. The paling on the left of the body had patches and smears of blood about fourteen inches from the ground.[8]

Doctor Phillips arrived at 06:30. He believed the cause of death to be syncope, in consequence of the loss of blood caused by the severance of the body. There were signs of partial strangulation and a severed throat. The incisions of the skin indicated that they been made from the left side of the neck. It appeared that an attempt had been made to separate the bones of the neck. The killer inflicted various mutilations after death. His weapon was a very sharp knife with a thin narrow blade, at least six to eight inches long and probably longer. It was not a sword or sword bayonet. An instrument used for post-mortems could have inflicted the wounds or a slaughterman's knife well ground down. Ordinary surgical cases would not contain such an instrument and knives used in the leather trade would not have been long enough.[9]

Phillips thought that the murderer had grabbed hold of Chapman's chin, because of three scratches just below the lobe of the left ear and a bruise on the right cheek. The manner of the wounds indicated a certain amount of anatomical knowledge. The killer opened the abdomen and removed the uterus and its appendages with the upper portion of the vagina and the posterior two thirds of the bladder. The incisions were cleanly cut, avoiding the rectum and dividing the vagina low enough to avoid injury to the cervix uteri.[10] Phillips said that he could not have performed these injuries in less than fifteen minutes and, if done properly as a surgeon might, it would have taken an hour. He felt that death had taken place at least two hours before his examination but noted that it was a chilly morning and the body would have cooled rapidly.

John Richardson testified that he went through the passage to the yard door and stood on the steps between 04:40 and 04:45. He would have seen the body if it was there.[11] About 05:30, Elizabeth Long saw a man and a woman talking in Hanbury Street. She identified the body as the woman seen. Twenty minutes or so later, Albert Cadosch of 27 Hanbury Street heard two people in the yard at 29, one of whom said "No." He went indoors and returned to the yard three or four minutes later when he heard something falling against the side of the fence.[12] Coroner Wynne Baxter preferred the evidence of Richardson, Cadosch, and Long above that of Philips to decide the time of death.

At 01:00 on 30 September 1888, Louis Diemschutz, steward of the International Working Men's Educational Club on Berner Street, entered the yard of the club with his pony, and discovered the body of a 47-year old prostitute, Elizabeth Stride. Morris Eagle had passed through the Yard at 00:40 without seeing the body, although he could not be certain that it was not there.[13]

Doctor Blackwell arrived at 01:10. Stride had a packet of cachous wrapped in tissue paper in her left hand and a bunch of flowers in her jacket. She wore a cheek silk scarf with the bow turned to the left and pulled tight. A long incision in the neck corresponded with the lower border of the scarf. The lower edge of the scarf was frayed, as if by a sharp knife. The incision commenced on the left side. Blackwell felt that the murderer took hold of the scarf at the back and pulled Stride backwards. He could not say if Stride was standing when the man cut her throat. He estimated the time of death at 20-30 minutes before his arrival. [14]

William Marshall who lived at 64 Berner Street saw a man talking to a woman, about three doors away from his house at 23:45. At 00:30, Police Constable William Smith saw a couple in Berner Street. Fifteen minutes later James Brown saw a man talking to a woman in Fairclough Street. The woman had her back against the wall facing the man who had his arm against the wall. He heard the woman say, "*No, not tonight. Some other night.*"

Doctor Phillips conducted the post-mortem with Blackwell's help. He attributed the cause of death to the loss of blood from the left carotid artery and the division of the windpipe.[15] After seizing Stride by her shoulders, the murderer placed her on the ground and stood on her right side, cutting from left to right. As in the previous case, he knew where to cut the throat but there was a great dissimilarity because he had severed Chapman's neck all the way to the vertebral column, marking the vertical bone, in an evident attempt to separate the bones. There were two pressure marks on Stride's neck, caused by two hands pressing on the shoulders.[16]

On the same night someone killed Catherine Eddowes, a 46-year-old prostitute, in Mitre Square, twelve minutes from Berner Street.[17] At 20:30 the previous evening Eddowes was arrested for being drunk and disorderly and taken to Bishopsgate Police Station. She was released at 01:00. Police Constable Edward Watkins found the body forty-five minutes later. At 01:30, he passed the same spot, seeing nothing. Nobody could have been about that portion of the square without him seeing.[18]

Eddowes lay on her back, with her clothes drawn up above the exposed abdomen. The intestines were drawn out, to a large extent, and placed over the right shoulder. They were smeared with feculent matter. A piece of about two feet had been detached and placed between the body and the left arm, apparently by design. The lobe and auricle of the right ear was cut obliquely through. There were extensive facial mutilations and cuts to the abdomen.

Doctor Brown's post-mortem identified cuts through the eyelids and the tip of the nose was detached. Cuts on each side of the cheek peeled up the skin forming a triangular flap about an inch and a half. The throat was cut across about six or seven inches. The big muscle across the throat was divided on the left side; the large vessels on the left side of the neck were severed, as was the larynx below the vocal cords. A sharp, pointed instrument like a knife inflicted the injuries. The cause of death was haemorrhage from the left common carotid artery. The mutilations occurred after death. The front walls of the abdomen were open. The liver was stabbed as if by the point of a sharp instrument and cut across. One of the cuts was made by someone on the right side of the body kneeling below the middle of the body. The left kidney had been removed. The womb had been cut through and most of it taken away. Bond felt that the killer inflicted the wound on the throat first, whilst Eddowes was lying down. The knife was sharp and pointed and at least six inches long. He felt that the killer had sufficient time, or he would not have nicked the lower eyelids. The murder would have taken at least five minutes. The killer knew the position of the kidney and had a great deal of medical knowledge, although someone accustomed to cutting up animals might possess such knowledge.[19] Brown was positive that Eddowes died in the square because the clotted blood on her left side must have flowed from her at the time of the injury.[20]

Doctor Sequeira, the first medical man on the scene, did not think that the murderer was possessed of any great anatomical skill.[21] Doctor Saunders agreed about the absence of anatomical skill and felt that the murderer had no design on an organ.[22]

Joseph Lawende, a commercial traveller, was with Joseph Levy and Harry Harris when he saw a man and woman talking together at the corner of Church passage, Duke Street, leading to Mitre Square, about 01:30. He identified Eddowes' black jacket and bonnet as those worn by the woman.[23]

The next victim was Mary Jane Kelly, buried as Marie Jeannette Davies because of her claim to be the widow of a coal miner. Thomas Bowyer discovered her body in her room at Millers Court, Dorset Street just after 10:45 on Friday 9 November 1888. She was a prostitute, said to be 25 years old.[24] Kelly's landlord John McCarthy, had sent Bowyer to collect rent.

The locked door was forced open about 13:30. It knocked against a table, which was close to the left-hand side of the bedstead. The bedstead was against a wooden partition. Kelly's mutilated body lay two-thirds over, towards the edge of the bedstead, nearest the door. Doctor Phillips believed that someone moved the body after death, from the side of the bedstead nearest to the wooden partition. He felt that the severance of the right carteroid artery caused death and that this occurred whilst she lay at the right side of the bedstead with her head and neck in the top right-hand corner. [25]

Doctor Thomas Bond conducted the post-mortem. The abdominal cavity was emptied of its viscera, which were scattered around the room. The face was disfigured beyond recognition and the breasts hacked off. The whole body was terribly mutilated, with many cuts, and the heart was absent. Bond's report gave 01:00 or 02:00 as the probable time of the murder.[26]

Inspector Abberline told the inquest that there were traces of a large fire in the grate, which had melted the spout of a kettle. In the ashes were remnants of clothing, a portion of a brim of a hat and a skirt. Abberline imagined the fire was to make a light for the murderer, as there was only one small candle. He reported that the key of the room had been missing for some time and that Kelly and her former boyfriend, Joseph Barnett, put their hand through the broken window to pull back the catch.[27]

A neighbour, Mary Ann Cox, saw Kelly enter the house with a man at 23:45. Kelly was drunk and singing. Cox could still hear the singing when she went back out at 01:00. Two hours later Kelly's light was out and there was no noise.[28] Elizabeth Prater gave evidence that she was standing outside the entrance to the court from 01:00 to 01:30. In her statement to the police, she said that she spoke to Mr McCarthy.[29] After 04:00, she heard a cry of "oh murder." Such cries were common, and she took no action.

Sarah Lewis was visiting Miller's Court at 02:30. Her original statement placed the time between 02:00 and 03:00. She said that there was a man standing against the lodging house opposite in Dorset Street but was unable to describe him. About 04:00, she heard a young woman screaming "murder."[30]

Caroline Maxwell claimed to have known Kelly for four months and to have spoken to her twice. She saw Kelly standing at the corner of the court between 08:00 and 08:30 and spoke to her. When she returned about 08:45, Kelly was with a man.[31] There is no satisfactory explanation of this contradiction with the medical evidence.

The body of Catherine, also known as Rose, Mylett, a 29- year-old prostitute was discovered in Clarke's Yard between 184 and 186 Poplar High Street by Sergeant Robert Golding and Constable Thomas Costella, at 04:15 on Thursday 20 December 1888. There were no signs of a struggle or of injury. Thomas Dean worked in the yard and slept in the shop opposite. He said that the body had not been there at 22:00 the previous night and he heard no noise.[32] A friend of Mylett's, Alice Graves, saw her in the company of two men around 01:45, and noticed that she was drunk.[33]

Doctor Brownfield's post mortem revealed a slight abrasion on the right side of the face and a mark on the neck which he believed had been caused by a four-thread cord drawn tightly around the neck from the spine to the left ear. There were impressions of the thumbs and middle index fingers of some person visible on either side of the neck. Death was due to strangulation and could not have been self-inflicted.[34] His assistant, George Harris endorsed this view.[35] Two other doctors, Charles Hebbert and Alexander McKellar, the Chief Surgeon, agreed that it was a case of murder by strangulation.[36] Doctor Bond examined the body on Christmas Eve when the mark supposedly caused by the cord had disappeared. He felt that Mylett fell in a drunken state, resulting in the larynx pressing against the neck of the jacket and causing the mark.[37] Brownfield did not believe that the jacket could have produced the mark.[38] Mylett's stomach did not contain alcohol.[39]

The inquest jury returned a verdict of wilful murder by person or persons unknown but Robert Anderson, Assistant Commissioner of CID, concluded that Mylett was not a victim of homicidal violence.[40]

Police Constable Walter Andrews found the body of a 40-year-old prostitute, Alice McKenzie, in Castle Alley Whitechapel, at 00:50 on Wednesday 17 July 1889. Police Constable Joseph Allen patrolled the alley about 25 minutes earlier and stopped to eat where the body was found. A few minutes later Andrews passed through and saw nothing suspicious. The pavement beneath the body was dry, indicating that the body was in place before it started to rain at 00:45. Andrews testified that the body was still warm.[41] Under the body, the police found a broken clay pipe, with bloodstains, and a farthing with blood on it.[42] McKenzie's boyfriend, John McCormack testified that she smoked clay pipes, and another broken one was found in her clothing.[43]

The last person known to have seen Mc Kenzie alive was Margaret Franklin who saw her going into the direction of Brick Lane and Whitechapel between 23:30 and 00:00. Sarah Smith who occupied a house overlooking the alley went to bed between 00:15 and 00:30 but did not sleep. She heard nothing.[44] Doctor Phillips arrived at 01:10. He thought the murder had occurred within the previous half an hour.[45]

The body contained several cuts on the lower part. There were two wounds in the neck. The cause of death was syncope, arising from the loss of blood through the divided carotid vessels. There were five marks on the abdomen, four of them on the left, caused by fingernails and a thumbnail. The injuries to the abdomen came after death. Phillips

26

thought that the murderer was on the right side of the body when he cut the throat with a sharp instrument, which had a shortish, pointed blade. Philips believed that the killer possessed a degree of anatomical knowledge but, did not believe he was the same person who committed the other murders.[46] Doctor Bond disagreed.[47]

At 05:25 on Tuesday 10 September 1889 Police Constable Pennett found the body of a woman under a railway arch in Pinchin Street, St George's in the East. The body lacked its head and legs. Decomposition had started. Pennett passed the railway arch twenty-five minutes earlier and saw nothing there. He believed the body was carried in a sack, due to the absence of marks from dragging.[48] A carman, Jeremiah Hurley, said that he saw a man with the appearance of a tailor standing on the corner of Pinchin Street after 05:35.[49]

The body was of a stout woman with dark complexion, about five feet three inches tall and aged 30-40. She had been dead for at least a day according to Percy Clarke, assistant to Doctor Phillips, who examined the body at 06:00. There was a small amount of blood, not clotted, underneath where the neck had lain. She wore a chemise, wrapped over the back surface of the neck. It was torn down the front and cut, apparently with a knife, at the back. The body was not blood stained, except where the chemise had rested, and did not appear to have been recently washed. In addition to the wounds caused by the severance of the head and legs, there was a wound about fifteen inches long through the external coat of the abdomen. There were recent bruises on the body and two cuts on the left forearm inflicted after death.[50]

Phillips believed that death was due to a loss of blood. The mutilations were inflicted after death by someone accustomed to cutting up animals, or witnessing such, and the knife used was eight inches or longer. He had no reason for thinking that the person who cut up the body had any anatomical knowledge. The coroner asked if there was any similarity between the removal of the legs and the Dorset Street case. Phillips saw

27

similarities in the division of the neck and attempt to disarticulate the bones of the spine but the savagery in Kelly's murder was far worse. He felt that the mutilations on the torso were inflicted to help with the disposal of the body and that the killer showed greater knowledge of how to separate a joint. [51]

Police Constable Ernest Thompson discovered the body of Frances Coles, a 31-year-old prostitute, at 02:15 in Swallow Gardens, Whitechapel on Friday 13 February 1891. As he approached, Thompson heard footsteps walking towards Mansell Street.[52] Two shunters testified that there was no body in the arch a few minutes earlier. Inspector Flanagan searched the arch behind the body and found a piece of newspaper in a space between a water pipe and some brickworks. In the newspaper there were, separately wrapped, two shillings. The Inspector believed that they were deliberately placed.[53]

The killer cut Coles' throat. Doctor Phillips believed that the knife passed across the throat three times, twice from left to right and once in the opposite direction. There were no mutilations or signs of strangulation. He felt that the killer had held the knife in his right hand and held Coles' chin in his left. [54]

The police arrested James Thomas Sadler, a ship's fireman, seen with Coles on the night of the murder. A witness Ellen Callana told the inquest that she was punched by a different man, who then went off with Coles about 01:30.[55] The inquest jury returned a verdict of murder against some person or persons unknown.

The murder of Frances Coles is the last crime in the police files. All eleven victims were prostitutes, found dead in Whitechapel or neighbouring districts.[56] A knife of some description inflicted wounds on nine. Eight died in 1888. Ten bodies were found outdoors, and at least nine died there. Nine were aged over 30 and six over 40. Seven died on weekends or public holidays. Three had body organs missing. These are the similarities, but they are insufficient to conclude that the same person killed all eleven women.

On 25 February 1894 Sir Melville Macnaghten, then Assistant Chief Constable CID, of the Metropolitan Police, wrote that the Ripper had five victims, Nichols, Chapman, Stride, Eddowes, and Kelly.[57] They are referred to as the canonical five. Macnaghten believed that soldiers were responsible for Tabram's murder and dismissed the torso as a Ripper victim, connecting it to a series of offences known as the Thames Torso murders. He linked the deaths of Mc Kenzie and Coles, stating that Sadler was in London at the time of Mc Kenzie's death.

The contemporary press usually listed each murder from Tabram, and sometimes Smith, through to Coles as the work of one person with Mylett and the Pinchin Street torso often omitted. Researchers and historians have sometimes omitted Stride, Eddowes, and Kelly from the canonical five. Others have added Tabram, McKenzie, or Coles. The most respected historian of Jack the Ripper, Philip Sugden, concluded that one person killed at least four women (Nichols, Chapman, Eddowes, and Kelly), probably six (Tabram and Stride), and possibly eight (Mc Kenzie and Coles).[58]

A modern perspective based on signature analysis, follows Macnaghten in excluding McKenzie, Coles and the torso, but includes Tabram.[59] A murderer's signature analysis differs from his or her methodology by including actions unique to an offender that go beyond what is necessary to kill the victim. The report observed that Jack the Ripper's signature contained picquerism, posing, and mutilation. The conclusion of six victims cannot be regarded as a definite fact but is a reasonable assumption.

Of the other five murders, three might be linked to the series and two are not. The possibilities are Smith, McKenzie, and Coles. Smith is usually discounted as a Ripper victim because of her own statement that several men attacked her. This view has recently been challenged. Smith and Tabram were both middle-aged prostitutes, residing at neighbouring premises, who were attacked on consecutive bank holidays in the same area. Both were beaten, rendered unconscious and sexually penetrated by an object.[60] In support of the argument that Smith was not attacked at the stated spot is the lack of clarification from the local police, the absence of bloodstains at the scene of the crime, and the time that passed between the assault and her admission to hospital. McKenzie and Coles were both killed with a knife in Whitechapel. None of the three can be discounted.

In the case of Rose Mylett, only the timing of the crime, if it was a crime, links it to Jack the Ripper. No knife was used, and it occurred two miles from Whitechapel. The murders of the canonical five victims occurred in an area covering about half a square mile. It appears safe to accept the general view that the Pinchin street torso was not the work of Jack the Ripper, allowing for the coincidence of a second serial killer operating in the same area at the same time.

We can define Jack the Ripper suspects as those accused of one or more of the following murders, Emma Smith, Martha Tabram, Polly Nichols, Annie Chapman, Elizabeth Stride, Catherine Eddowes, Mary Jane Kelly, Alice McKenzie, and Frances Coles.

The Evidence

Before looking at suspects we need to examine the known facts about the murderer for clues to his identity or motivation. Excluding Emma Smith's statement there is only one other indication of theft, although it is possible that the killer stole unrecorded cash. Two brass rings were missing from Annie Chapman's body. William Stevens, a fellow lodger at Crossingham's lodging house, told the inquest that Chapman was wearing them at about 00:12 when he last saw her alive on the morning of the murder.[1]

At 02:55 on the night that Eddowes was killed, Police Constable Alfred Long found a piece of her blood-stained apron in Goulston Street below some chalked graffiti. He wrote the words in his notebook as *"The Jews are the men that will not be blamed for nothing."* A report by his inspector also used this wording but the inspector said it was spelt "Juwes."[2]

Detective Constable Halse passed through Goulston Street at about 02:20 without seeing the apron or the graffiti.[3] The direct route from Mitre Square to Goulston Street took only a few minutes but, if Halse was right, over an hour elapsed between the murder and the depositing of the apron. The police believed that the killer used the apron to clean blood from a hand or knife. Doctor Brown matched the cut piece to the corner of an apron with string attached, found on the body.[4]

A shawl said to belong to Catherine Eddowes was allegedly taken from the crime scene by Sergeant Amos Simpson and donated by his descendants to the Black Museum. Russell Edwards purchased it in 2007. He arranged for DNA testing by Doctor Jari Louhelainen, using samples from a descendant of Catherine Eddowes, Karen Miller. Louhelainen reported a match between one of the samples and Miller's DNA. He said that this alteration, global private mutation (314.1C) was uncommon in the world population, approximately 1 person in every 290,000. Four DNA experts stated that Louhelainen made an error of nomenclature and should have written the mutation as 315.1. This is shared by about 99% of people of European descent.[5] There is no contemporary record of Simpson being at the scene of Eddowes' murder and the shawl is not listed in the inventory of her belongings. It has no value as evidence, without a definite link to the victim or killer.

At the Chapman inquest, Doctor Phillips stated that the murderer had anatomical knowledge. Other doctors disagreed and there is a difference of opinion amongst researchers. In 1994 Philip Sugden asked practising surgeon and fellow Ripper author, Nick Warren, for a professional view. Warren felt that the murder of Chapman indicated anatomical knowledge and that both anatomical knowledge and surgical skill were evident in the Eddowes murder.[6] This is suggestive but not conclusive.

In his summing up at the Chapman inquest, Corner Baxter reported that, some months earlier, an American had called on the sub-curator of the Pathological museum with a request to buy organs for £20 each. The request was denied but repeated to, at least, one other institution.[7] On 6 October 1888, the British Medical Journal reported that enquiries were made early in the previous year at two London Hospitals by a foreign physician about securing body parts for scientific investigation. The physician was a highly reputable and accredited person who left the country eighteen months earlier and no money was offered.[8] The information communicated was due to an erroneous interpretation by a minor official. The article also stated that Baxter, no longer believed the theory.[9]

Doctor Brown could not think of a professional reason for removing the organs.[10]
Baxter asked Doctor Phillips if the portions of Chapman's organs could have been lost in

transit to the mortuary. Phillips replied that he had not been present at the transit but carefully closed up the clothes of the women.[11] If the murderer removed the organs, his speed suggests familiarity with the knife and, at least, rudimentary anatomical knowledge.

Doctor Bond commented that the knife used in the five murders generally attributed to Jack the Ripper was strong and straight, at least six inches long, very sharp, pointed at the top and about an inch wide. It may have been a clasp knife, a butcher's knife, or a surgeon's knife.[12] Thomas Coram testified at the Stride inquest that he had found a knife with a dagger shaped blade nine to ten inches long on the bottom step of a laundry opposite 233 Whitechapel Road at 00:30 on 1 October 1888. There was a handkerchief folded then twisted around the handle. He described it as a baker's knife.[13] Doctor Phillips believed the bloodstains on it to be human. He commented that it was a slicing knife from a chandler's shop, recently blunted. It could have used as the murder weapon, but this was improbable. Doctor Blackwell agreed. [14] Phillips also examined a knife supposedly sold by James Sadler and stated that it could have inflicted the wounds on Coles.[15] He was unaware that someone had sharpened the knife after the murder.

In 1937, Dorothy Stroud was the assistant editor on Sporting Life. The editor, Hugh Pollard, gave her a box, containing two knives, which he said were Jack the Ripper's knives. Her friend took the one and she had the other. During the war, she used it as a carving knife and later for gardening. It broke when she was cutting a privet bush. She kept the pieces and presented them to Donald Rumbelow. The knife was an amputation knife made by Weiss, a manufacturer of surgical instruments in Bond Street, in the late nineteenth century. Pollard's partner, Robert Churchill, was a gunsmith who worked as an expert for Scotland Yard. Pollard was also a former British Intelligence officer and the writer of several books including one about Irish secret societies.[16]

The Irish National Invincibles were responsible for the Phoenix Park assassinations on 6 May 1882 when the Irish Chief Secretary, Lord Frederick Cavendish, and his permanent under-Secretary, Thomas Henry Burke were murdered in Dublin. The murder weapons, knives made by Weiss, had blades twelve inches long and one-inch broad and edged to the haft along one side, tapering to a point for about three and a half inches then being double-edged. [17] Nick Warren suggested that the killer of Mary Kelly used a similar knife.[18]

What appears to be Pollard's knife is referenced in a book about Scotland Yard, published in 1956, which says that a friend of the writer owned one of two surgical knives said to have been left by the Ripper beside his victims.[19] There are no records of knives being recovered from any of the murder scenes.

The killers' modus operandi appears to have involved strangulation with his hands followed by throat cutting, and abdomen slashing. He must have moved swiftly as nobody heard a cry except, possibly in the murder of Mary Kelly. The slashing rather than stabbing suggests an awareness of animal slaughtering techniques. A degree of physical strength can be inferred, and he was able to approach and engage the victims without arising suspicion.

The alias, Jack the Ripper appears first in a letter and postcard, purporting to be from the killer.[20] Posted to the Central News Agency on 27 September 1888 and dated two days earlier the letter read:

Dear Boss, I keep on hearing how the police have caught me but they wont fix me just yet. I have laughed when they look so clever and talk about being on the right track. That joke about Leather Apron gave me real fits. I am down on whores and I shant quit ripping them till I do get buckled. Grand work the last job was. I gave the lady no time to squeal. How can they catch me now. I love my work and want to start again. You will soon hear

35

of me with my funny little games. I saved some of the proper red stuff in a ginger beer

bottle over the last job to write with but it went thick like glue and I can't use it. Red ink is

fit enough I hope ha ha. The next job I do I shall clip the ladys ears off and send to the

police officers just for jollys wouldn't you. Keep this letter back till I do a bit more work

then give it out straight. My knife's so nice and sharp I want to get to work right away if I

get a chance. Good luck.

Yours truly

Jack the Ripper.

Don't mind giving me the tradename.

wasnt good enough to post this before I got all the red ink off my hands curse it. No

luck yet. They say I'm a doctor now ha ha.

On 1 October 1888, the morning after the murders of Elizabeth Stride and Catherine

Eddowes, the Central News Agency received a postcard. It appeared to be from the same

person as the letter and read:

I was not codding dear old Boss when I gave you the tip you'll hear about saucy jacks

work tomorrow double event this time number one squealed a bit but couldn't finish

straight off. had not time to get ears for police thanks for keeping last letter back till I got

to work again.

Jack the Ripper.

The police took the Dear Boss letter and postcard seriously enough to compare the

handwriting with the Goulston Street Graffiti. Chief Inspector Swanson reported that the

officers who saw the graffiti did not see any comparison with the handwriting in the

letters.[21] As late as 1896, Swanson compared a fresh letter with the original Dear Boss

letter and supported Chief Inspector Moore's conclusion that they were not written by the

same person.[22] None of the letters contains any verifiable information about the crimes that only the killer could have known. There is no evidence that he wrote them. Any links between suspects and the letters do not constitute proof of involvement in the murders.

George Lusk was president of the Whitechapel vigilance committee, which he formed on 10 September 1888 in response to fears generated by the murders. On 27 September 1888, he sent a petition to Queen Victoria, expressing concern about the absence of a reward and the police's failures. He received several letters purporting to come from the killer. One, received on 16 October 1888, contained half a human kidney preserved in spirits of wine. The letter, believed to have a postmark of London E, read:

From hell

Mr Lusk

Sor

I send you half the kidne I took from one women prasarved it for you tother piece I fried and ate it was very nise I may send you the bloody knife that took it out if you only wate a whil longer.

Signed Catch me when you can Mister Lusk.

Doctor Openshaw, curator of the Pathology Museum at the London Hospital, examined the kidney. Initial press reports said that he identified it as belonging to a woman about 45 years old who drank heavily and that someone had removed it from the body within the last three weeks.[23] Catherine Eddowes was 45. When interviewed by the Star Openshaw gave his opinion that the kidney was half of a left human kidney but was unable to say if it belonged to a woman or when it was removed from the body as it was preserved in spirits.[24]

Chief Inspector Swanson said that it was the kidney of a human adult, not charged with a fluid as would have been the case of a body handed over for dissection. Similar kidneys were available after any post-mortem.[25] The possibility of a hoax cannot be discounted.

Several people claimed to have seen the victims with a man shortly before their deaths. The man seen by Elizabeth Long talking to Annie Chapman in Hanbury Street was over five feet, taller than Annie, with a dark complexion. Long saw him from behind and said that she would not be able to recognise him again. He wore a deerstalker hat and a dark coat and had a shabby genteel appearance. The man said, "Will you?" and Annie replied "Yes."[26] Notes in the margin of a police report on 19 October 1888 ask if this man and the one heard by Cadosch were foreigners.[27] No reply is given. Long testified eleven days after the murder and said that she did not take much notice of the couple.

The man seen by William Marshall talking to Stride was about five feet six inches tall. He was decently dressed in a small black coat, dark trousers, and a peaked sailor-like cap. He appeared to be middle aged. Given a choice of occupations, Marshall did not think he was a dock labourer, sailor, or butcher. He had more the appearance of a clerk and looked like he was in business. He had nothing in his hands. Marshall heard him say, "*You would say anything but your prayers.*"[28]

. The man seen by Police Constable Smith was about 28, five feet seven inches tall and clean-shaven. He wore dark clothes with a dark coloured, hard felt deerstalker hat and looked respectable. He carried a newspaper parcel in his hand. He had no whiskers. The parcel was about eighteen inches long and six to eight inches wide. Smith recognised the body in the mortuary as the woman he had seen. He said she was wearing a flower in her breast.[29] Marshall stated that the woman he saw had no such flower. There were flowers attached to Stride's jacket at the time of her death.

The man described by James Brown was stoutly built and about five feet seven inches tall. A long coat almost reached his heels. Brown was almost certain that the woman was Stride. He did not notice if she was wearing a flower.[30]

In a police report dated 19 October 1888, Chief Inspector Swanson referred to evidence given by Israel Schwartz, following enquiries made. Schwartz, who did not speak English, said that he was passing the gateway where the Stride murder was committed, at 00:45 when a man stopped and spoke to a woman standing there. The man tried to pull her into the street, but he turned her round and threw her on the footway. She screamed three times but not very loudly. Schwartz crossed the road and saw a man lighting his pipe. The man who had thrown the woman down called out, apparently to the other man, "Lipski", and then Schwartz walked away, running as the second man followed.[31] Schwartz was unable to say if the two men were connected.

Inspector Abberline wrote that Lipski was an anti-Semitic insult, used after the execution of a Jew.[32] On 28 June 1887, Israel Lipski killed Miriam Angel with nitric acid at 16 Batty Street, which was adjacent to Berner Street. Abberline believed that the man was insulting Schwartz. He made inquiries in the neighbourhood and could not find anyone called Lipski.[33] Angel's murderer borrowed the surname from his landlord, Phillip Lipski, when he came to live in Batty Street. Phillip Lipski had seven children, the eldest being fifteen in 1887. It is possible that they moved away after the trial or changed their name.

The first man seen by Schwartz was five feet five inches tall, aged about 30, and fair with dark hair and a small brown moustache. He wore dark jacket and trousers, and a black cap with a peak. The second man was aged 35 and five feet eleven tall with a fresh complexion and light brown hair. He wore a dark overcoat and an old black hard felt hat with a wide brim. He had a clay pipe in his hands. Swanson compared Schwartz's

39

sighting with that of Police Constable Smith, observing many differences. He noted that there was enough time for someone else to have killed Stride [34] Schwartz's story reduces the value as evidence of the sightings by Smith and Marshall as both occurred earlier in the evening. It also clashes with the evidence of James Brown, although it is possible that both Schwartz and Brown saw the same couple.

Joseph Lawende said that the man he, Joseph Levy, and Harry Harris, saw with Catherine Eddowes wore a cloth cap with a peak but provided no further description following a request from the police solicitor at the inquest. In answer to a question from a juror, he commented that the man looked rough and shabby. He also said that he did not think he would able to identify the man.[35] Swanson later expanded on the description. The man was age 30, five feet seven or eight inches tall and of a fair complexion. He was medium build and wore a pepper and salt colour loose jacket and a grey cloth cap with grey peak. A reddish handkerchief tied in a knot around his neck gave the appearance of a sailor.[36] Levy noted that the man was about three inches taller than the woman was. He commented that he did not like going home alone when he saw those characters about.[37] Swanson saw similarities between the descriptions given by Lawende and Schwartz.[38]

Mary Cox said that the man she saw accompanying Mary Kelly to her room on the night of the murder was short, stout, and shabbily dressed, He wore a long, dark coat and carried a pot of ale in his hand. He had a blotchy face, a full carroty moustache, and a black felt hat.[39]

In her statement to the police, Sarah Lewis was unable to describe the man she saw standing outside Miller's Court.[40] At the inquest, she said he was not tall, but stout, and wore a wideawake black hat.[41] The man seen by Caroline Maxwell allegedly talking to Mary Kelly about 08:45 on the morning of the murder wore dark clothes with a plaid coat. Maxwell was unable to give a description to the inquest.

After the Kelly inquest, George Hutchinson went to Commercial Street Police Station and made a statement.[42] He was walking down Commercial Street on the night of the murder, at about 02:00, when he met Kelly, who he knew. She asked to borrow sixpence. He had no money and watched as she went towards Thrawl Street. A man tapped her on the shoulder and said something. She laughed and said "alright." He said, "You will be alright for what I have told you" and put his arm on her shoulder. He carried a small parcel with a strap in his left hand. Hutchinson followed them to Dorset Street. The man gave her a handkerchief. Hutchinson waited outside the court for about 45 minutes, but they did not come out.

Hutchinson described the man as aged 34-35 and five feet six inches tall. He was pale with dark eyes and eyelashes, a slight moustache curled up at each end and dark hair. He was very surly looking and wore a long dark coat, collar and cuffs, trimmed astrakhan, and a dark jacket underneath with light waistcoat and dark trousers. He had a dark felt hat turned down in the middle, button boots, and gaiters with white buttons, a very thick gold chain, a white linen collar, and black tie with horseshoe pin. He was of respectable, Jewish appearance and walked very sharp. Inspector Abberline believed the statement to be true and said that two officers accompanied Hutchinson around the district for a few hours to look for the man.[43]

Ellen Callana described the man who assaulted her and went off with Frances Coles as very short with a dark moustache, shiny boots, and blue trousers. He had the appearance of a sailor.[44] Along with Long, Schwartz and Lawende, she is the most likely witness to have seen the killer. However, as Coles may not have been a victim of Jack the Ripper, the evidence of the others is more relevant. Schwartz was not called to the inquest, a serious procedural error if the police considered his sighting relevant to the case. There is some doubt over Long's statement because of the medical evidence suggesting an earlier

41

time of death. Lawende's sighting has limited value as he stated that he would not recognise the man again. We can make comparisons between suspects and the eyewitness descriptions but cannot categorically accept that any of these sightings were of Jack the Ripper. Suspects who do not match a description should not be eliminated.

Drawing on Kelly's post-mortem and the inquest testimony from Nichols, Chapman and Eddowes, Doctor Bond provided a profile of the killer on 10 November 1888. He concluded that the murderer's objective was mutilation and that he had no specific anatomical or medical knowledge. He possessed great physical strength and may have been subject to periodical attacks of homicidal and erotic mania. He probably was quite inoffensive looking, middle aged and respectably dressed. He could have worn an overcoat or cloak to hide the blood. He would be solitary and eccentric without a regular occupation but with some income. Others might have grounds for suspicion but be unwilling to communicate them, for fear of trouble or notoriety.[45]

Profiling has since developed as a method of identifying an offender based on an analysis of the offence and the way it was committed. John Douglas, the co-founder of psychological profiling, and Roy Hazelwood who succeeded Douglas as the head of the FBI's Criminal Identification Analysis Section, prepared a profile of the Ripper in 1988. They concluded that he was probably a local male in his late twenties, employed but free from family responsibility. He was low class with no anatomical or surgical skills. He had probably been in trouble with the police previously and interviewed during the crimes, seen as a loner. It is likely that someone abused him as a child, probably with the knowledge and/or participation of his mother. Other attacks in the Whitechapel area by this person had either gone unreported or not been connected. There would have been evidence of his violent destructive fantasies through writings or drawings of mutilated

42

women. He may have been drinking spirits in the local pubs prior to committing the crimes.[46]

Profiles are not evidence but can be of assistance in terms of defining criteria to identify and prioritise potential suspects. It is impossible to convict a criminal solely on the basis that they fit a profile or elements of it. Equally, we cannot clear a suspect just because they do not match a profile

The only known facts about the killer are that he was free to operate in Whitechapel on the relevant dates and times. We can infer that he had either a nocturnal trade or none and the freedom to roam at night without arousing suspicion. He probably had more spare time at weekends and public holidays. It is likely that he knew the area well and had somewhere close to retreat to after each crime. He was also able to blend into the surroundings. After the first two murders, people were looking for suspicious characters. The police made inquiries at common lodging houses and arrested many suspicious characters. This suggests a local man or someone who did not arouse suspicion.

At some point after the Mitre Square murder, the killer passed through Goulston Street. Earlier the same night he moved from Berner Street to Mitre Square. Apart from his presence at the murder sites, these are his only known movements.

It is possible that he had some knowledge of anatomy, such as that possessed by a slaughterman or butcher, and possibly from observation rather than experience. There may have been a specific reason for targeting prostitutes, or older women. The organs taken may have held some significance for him. The extreme violence inflicted on the victims may or may not have been on display in other areas of his life.

Possible reasons for the cessation of the murders include imprisonment, illness, death, relocation, an awareness, or perception that he was under suspicion, a voluntary decision for unknown reasons, or achievement of a specific objective.

The evidence indicates that the murderer was male, although we will consider some female suspects, able to move around the area without arising suspicion, comfortable using a knife and capable of great violence. We can now assess the suspects against these criteria.

A suspect is anyone accused of being Jack the Ripper or of being responsible for the murders of the six women identified as Ripper victims or of the three women identified as possible victims. The following exceptions apply.

- Anyone accused only in a work designated as fiction.

- Anyone accused only by paranormal methodology.

- Anyone identified only by initials or first name unless this is sufficient to attempt identification.

- Anyone who was aged less than twelve in 1888.

- People who confessed to being Jack the Ripper unless they were investigated by the police, used violence, had a criminal record or there is another reason to suspect them.

- Accusations not intended to be taken seriously.

- People who committed suicide under the delusion that they were Jack the Ripper.

The following chapters summarise the known facts about each suspect and evidence against them.

At the Scene

We begin with the people suspected because of their close proximity to the crimes. Some were witnesses. Others knew a victim. The first is Charles Cross, the carman who found the body of Mary Ann Nichols. Researcher Michael Connor first accused him on the basis that he walked through the area on a daily basis and that his inquest testimony contained timing discrepancies.[1] Cross told the inquest that he had worked for Pickfords for over two decades. About 03:20, on the day of Nichol's death he left home to go to work and passed through Bucks Row where he saw something lying on the opposite site of the road. A man approached from the direction he had just come from and they looked at the body together. Cross touched her hands, which were cold and limp, and her face, which felt warm. He believed her to be dead. The other man thought she was breathing a little. Cross suggested giving her a prop, but the other man did not want to touch her. They heard a policeman coming and left, encountering Police Constable Mizen in Baker's Row. They told him that they had seen a woman lying in Bucks Row. Cross said that she looked to be either dead or drunk, but he thought she was dead. He did not know the other man.[2]

Mizen testified that at 03:45 he was at the crossing of Hanbury Street and Baker's Row when a carman, accompanied by another man, passed and said that a policeman in Bucks Row wanted him.[3] This was Police Constable Neil who did not mention either man in his evidence.[4]

Robert Paul, referred to as Baul by the press, was called to the inquest two weeks after Cross. He said that he saw a man standing in the middle of the road and started to pass him. The man touched him on the shoulder and asked him to look at the woman who was lying across the gateway. He felt her hands and feet and they were cold. He helped pull down some of the clothes which were disarranged and detected a slight movement of breathing. The man walked with him to Montague Street where they saw a policeman. This took less than four minutes. He saw nobody running away from Bucks Row.[5]

Connor suggested that Cross killed Nichols and pretended to have just arrived on the scene when Paul approached. This was based on Connor's estimate that Bucks Row was six minutes from Cross's home at 22 Doveton Street, Cambridge Road, leaving four minutes before he encountered Paul.[6] Press reports of the inquest said that Cross found the body at 03:30 or 03:20. [7] The Times, which gave 03:20, said that Cross reached work at 04:00. Connor calculated that the workplace in Broad Street was approximately 34 minutes' walk from Bucks Row.[8] According to the Telegraph account of the inquest, which appears to be verbatim, both Cross and Paul said they were running late. [9]

Connor observed that Martha Tabram, Emma Smith, and Annie Chapman died on a route that Cross could have taken from his home to his work, although he discounted Smith as a Ripper victim. This only applies if they were killed between 03:30 and 04:00.

A second reason for suspicion is that Cross was not his real name. Living at 22 Doveton Street in the 1891 census was a carman called Charles Allen Lechmere. He was born on 5 October 1849, the son of a Whitechapel bootmaker. On 25 February 1858, his mother married a policeman called Thomas Cross.[10] Charles's surname is given as Cross in the 1861 census, when he was eleven. All other records refer to him as Lechmere, except reports of his evidence at the inquest.

At the time of the murders, Lechmere was married with eight children. Three more followed. He died on 23 December 1920. In August 2012, an amateur drama named him as the Ripper. The production raised £2,200 towards a memorial in Bethnal Green to honour 173 people crushed to death in a stampede at an air-raid shelter on 3 March 1943. Three members of the Lechmere family died in the disaster.[11]

Police Constable Neil said that the first people at the scene of Mary Ann Nichol's murder were two slaughtermen who worked at the slaughterhouse opposite. One, Henry Tomkins, gave evidence that Constable Thain had passed the slaughterhouse in Winthrop Street and stated that there had been a murder in Bucks Row. Tomkins had been working in the slaughterhouse with James Mumford and Charles Britten. None of them had left between 01:00 and the time they went to see the body. Tomkins did not see anyone pass the slaughterhouse in that time or hear a vehicle.[12]

A letter to the police, dated 3 October, blamed the murders on a slaughterman and found Tomkin's inquest testimony suspicious.[13] This was because the coroner asked if he saw any women about and Tomkins responded that he did not like them. Chief Inspector Swanson reported that the police took the statements of the slaughtermen separately, without giving them any means of communicating with each other, and they satisfactorily accounted for their time. Part of this was collaborated by the duty police.[14]

After Chapman's death, suspicion briefly fell on John Richardson, whose mother lived at 29 Hanbury Street. On the morning of the murder, he visited the premises to check that they were secure as there had been a break-in some months previously. He did not enter the yard but stood on the steps and cut a piece of leather from one of his boots with a table-knife about five inches long. Further questioning from the coroner established that he cut the leather because it was hurting him. He had removed a piece the previous day but that was not enough. His only reason for going to the house was to see that the cellar was all right and he established this by seeing the padlock was on the door. His mother confirmed an earlier theft of a saw and hammer from the cellar.[15]

Asked to produce the knife Richardson returned with a well-worn desert knife. His statement contradicted the medical opinion regarding time of death, and he did not mention the knife when he saw Inspector Chandler at the murder scene. Swanson wrote that the police specifically directed attention to Richardson. They examined his clothes and searched his house, without finding any incriminating evidence.[16]

In 2005 Stanley Dean Reid accused sixteen-year-old William Hardiman.[17] Hardiman's mother kept a cat's meat shop on the ground floor of 29 Hanbury Street. She woke about 06:00 on the day of the murder when she heard footsteps in the yard and sent William, to investigate.[18] Reid suggested that William watched Chapman with a client before killing her and used his room to clean up. As he worked at a meat shop, he would have access to cutting implements and an excuse for having blood on his clothes. The police search of the property found nothing. Eight years after his article Reid said that he would consider William not much more a likely suspect than many of the others.[19] William later became the chief modeller for metalwork for the Guild of Handicraft. Twenty-nine of his leather panels are in the Victoria and Albert museum. He committed suicide by drinking hydrochloric acid on 29 December 1905.[20]

James Hardiman was William's brother. Rob Hills claimed that he appeared twice in the 1881 census, as a resident at 29 Hanbury Street and as an inmate at Wandsworth prison.[21] The census entry for the prisoner describes him as a married meat salesman born Bermondsey in 1858. In the Hanbury Street entry, he is listed a married knacker, a dealer in horseflesh, born Mile End 1859. The 1861 census lists an Alfred James Hardiman born Bermondsey and also the James Hardiman, with mother Harriet, who grew up to live in Hanbury Street.

At the time of the murders, Hardiman lived in Heneage Street. His wife Sarah died on 15 September 1888, three months after their daughter who had contracted congenital syphilis from Sarah. Two Ripper letters, one saying "I am a horse-slaughterer" which was sent before the Dear Boss letter, and the other signed by Joe, the cats meat man, were put forward as possibly being written by him.[22] He died at 29 Hanbury Street on 22 December 1891 from tuberculosis.

Timothy Donovan was the deputy of a lodging house at 35 Dorset Street, which was listed as Mary Nichol's address on her death certificate. Donovan testified that Annie Chapman had been living at the house for about four months. She left at 02:00 on the morning of her death, telling him she had no money and that she would be back soon.[23] Donald Rumbelow suggested Donovan as a suspect in his book, The Complete Jack the Ripper.[24] Although omitted from the most recent edition in 2013, Rumbelow stated that he still believed it although there was no proof.[25] He described Donovan as a 28-year-old labourer who died from cirrhosis of the liver on 1 November 1888, suggesting that Catherine Eddowes and Mary Kelly knew he was the Ripper and wanted to extract money from him. On 13 October 1888, the East London Observer reported that Eddowes had told the Casual Ward Superintendent of Mile End that she had returned to claim the reward for the apprehension of the Whitechapel Murderer as she thought she knew him.[26] There is no record of Kelly making a similar claim.

Margaret Donovan of 35 Dorset Street gave birth to a son Timothy on 13 December 1887. His father, Timothy Donovan, senior, died on 24 April 1896 so could not have been the man identified by Rumbelow.[27]

Donovan told the inquest that Chapman was in the habit of spending Saturday nights at the lodging house with a man of military appearance whom he had heard was a pensioner. John Evans, a night watchman at the house, testified that the man called about 14:30 on the day of the murder to make inquiries about the deceased, saying he had heard of her death. Having been told the details he turned and left without a word.[28]

49

On 14 September 1888, Edward Stanley called at Commercial Street Police Station and gave a satisfactory account of himself. On the night of Nichol's murder, he was on duty with the second Brigade, Southern Division, Hants Militia at Fort Elson, Gosport and on the night of Chapman's murder he was in bed at his lodgings.[29] He denied that he was in the habit of spending weekends with the deceased, despite Donovan identifying him as the man known as the Pensioner who regularly spent time with Chapman. Recalled to the inquest to confront Stanley, Donovan stuck to his story that Stanley was at the lodging house on the Saturday before Chapman's murder. Stanley insisted that he went to Gosport on 6 August and stayed there until 1 September. The coroner felt that Donovan had made a mistake.

Stanley said that he last saw Chapman on 2 September, noting that she had a black eye. Eliza Cooper, a fellow resident at the house, testified that she gave Chapman the black eye on the Wednesday evening, 5 September, following a row over a bar of soap given by Chapman to Stanley.[30] Inspector Abberline noted Stanley's alibi and the absence of any reasons to suspect him.[31]

Researcher Simon D Wood noted that Stanley was both too old and living in the wrong locality to be a member of the Hants Militia. He suggested that Stanley was an alias used by Chapman's murderer, Colonel Francis Charles Hughes-Hallett, the Conservative MP for Rochester.[32] His motive was to conceal the scandal of his association with a prostitute.

Hughes-Hallet was in charge of the Second Brigade, Southern Division, Hants Militia. Born in 1838 he married the widow of Lord Justice Selwyn in 1871. After her death he remarried to an American heiress. In 1887 the press reported that he had impregnated his stepdaughter.[33] The scandal led to his resignation from politics. In September 1888 he went to Mexico on a commercial mission, giving him an alibi for the later murders which

Wood did not accuse him of. On 6 October he told the press that he had searched for the Whitechapel killer after Martha Tabram's murder.[34] He died in 1903.

Investigations into the Stride murder identified a man who unwittingly helped create the famous image of the Ripper carrying a black bag. Fanny Mortimer, who lived at 36 Berner Street, told the Press that she was standing at the door of her house on the night of the murder between 00:30 and 01:00. She did not observe anyone entering the gates of the club. The only person who passed down the street was a young man carrying a black bag who walked very fast.[35] Leon Goldstein visited Leman St Police Station on the day after the murder to say that he went down Berner Street at 01:00 on the morning of the murder, carrying a black bag full of cigarette boxes. He had left a coffee house in Spectacle Alley shortly before. A note in the margin to a police report of this asked, *"Who saw this man go down Berner St, or did he come forward to clear himself in case any questions might be asked?"*[36] No reply is noted. Walter Dew, a police constable at the time of the murders, suggested in 1938 that Mortimer was the only person to see the Ripper at the scene of one of his crimes.[37]

Morris Eagle, who passed through Duffield's Yard shortly before the discovery of Stride's body, briefly became a suspect on an internet forum.[38] The poster who started the thread believed that researcher Tom Westcott had accused Eagle. Westcott responded by saying that he suggested Eagle moved Stride from the doorway of the club and that this was the altercation witnessed by Israel Schwartz. Eagle had been in the club most of the day and left at 23:45 to take his girlfriend home, returning about 00:35. He was a commercial traveller, born in Russia in 1864.

In 2016 a team of researchers led by Randy Williams suggested that the murders were committed by three men, and funded by another, on specific dates to attack Christianity. The three men were Louis Diemschutz, Isaac Kozebrodski, a 17-year-old member of the club and Samuel Freidman, also a club member. The funder and organiser was Prince Pyotr Kropotkin, who made two references to Jack the Ripper in later essays. The evidence put forward is that, between them, the three men match the eyewitness descriptions, they all used violence on at least one occasion, Diemschutz traded in costume jewellery, and the crimes were local.[39] Williams acknowledged that no reliable physical descriptions of Kozebrodski and Freidman exist. He suggested that Diemschutz was the man seen by George Hutchinson, based on the suspect wearing costume jewellery because real jewellery could not have been worn in a poor area of London.

The violence occurred following a demonstration by the Jewish unemployed on 16 September 1889. A crowd gathered outside the International Working Man's club, where Stride's body was found, and a fight broke out. Diemschutz made a counter claim that a Police Constable Joseph Frost, assaulted him. This was dismissed through lack of evidence.[40] Louis Diemschutz and Isaac Kozebrodski appeared in court on 25 April charged with making a riot and assaulting various people, including Frost. Samuel Friedman failed to surrender to his bail. The defence argued that the occupants of the club were defending themselves against the mob and the police. The jury found the prisoners guilty of the assault on the police.[41]

Diemschutz has an alibi for the murder of Catherine Eddowes, as he was being interviewed by the police as a witness to the Stride murder. The comments of Isaac Kozebrodski to the press indicate that he was still in Berner Street when Eddowes was being killed. Williams suggested that Eddowes was killed by Kozebrodski and Friedman.

Israel Schwartz was proposed as a possible suspect by Gavin Bromley in 2007, with the caveat that there was not a clear case against him.[42] Four years earlier a poster on an internet forum suggested that Schwartz killed Stride but realised that he had been seen and came forward with a story that he was a witness.[43] He lived at 22 Ellen Street and was said by Inspector Abberline to have a strong Jewish appearance.[44] The Star reported that he was a Hungarian who could not speak English. On the day of the murder he was moving with his wife from their lodgings in Berner Street to others in Backchurch Lane, Ellen Street was off Backchurch Lane.[45] Chief Inspector Swanson believed the police report containing Schwartz's statement.[46]

He may be the Israel Schwartz, born Poland, living at 22 Samuel Street at the time of the 1891 census with two children and employed as a tailor's presser. The 1901 census lists a 35-year-old Russian of the same name, employed as a cigar maker, and living at 8 Little Alie Street Whitechapel. but his first child was born in Glasgow. A third Israel Schwartz was living at 21 Jubilee Street in 1901, described as a provisions seller from Russia. None of these can be the correct man if he was Hungarian.

In 1993, AP Wolf argued that Michael Kidney killed Elizabeth Stride. Kidney described himself as a waterside labourer and said he had been in the army. He had known Stride for about three years and lived with her for most of that time. On 6 April 1887, Stride charged him with assault but did not appear in court to prosecute.[47] Kidney went to jail in July 1888, for being drunk and disorderly, and using abusive language.[48] His relationship with Stride survived both incidents.

He visited Leman Street Police Station on 1 October 1888, asking to see a detective. At the inquest, he claimed that he had information and had tried to interest the police without success. He was unable to give that information to the coroner. He testified that he last saw Stride on the previous Tuesday, 25 September 1888, and that she would occasionally go away from him, usually because of drink. The inquest heard from Catherine Lane who resided at the same lodging house and had known Stride for six or seven years. She said that Stride told her on that Thursday that she had a few words with the man she was living with and had left him. On the following day, she called during his absence and took away some things. Kidney denied having the argument. In response to a direct question the deputy of the lodging house, Elizabeth Tanner, who had known Stride for six years, stated that Stride was not afraid of anyone.[49]

Wolf was convinced of Kidney's guilt because of a belief that the visit to the police station took place before the identification of the body. At that time, several people, including Kidney, had seen the body at the mortuary. On the first day of the inquest, 1 October 1888, the foreman expressed surprise at the lack of identification, as everyone knew the victim's name.[50] The delay in a formal identification was caused a witness called Mary Malcolm who erroneously claimed that the body was that of her sister.[51]

In June 1889, Kidney spent 13 days in the Whitechapel infirmary, receiving treatment for syphilis. He returned there with lumbago from 17 August to 30 September. On 11 October, he was back again with dyspepsia and discharged four days later.[52] Chief Inspector Swanson stated that the enquiry into Stride's history did not disclose the slightest pretext for a motive on behalf of friends or associates or anyone who had known her. He also said that, *"the numerous statements made to the police were inquired into and the persons (of whom there were many) were required to account for their presence at the time of the murders & every care taken as far as possible to verify the statements."* [53]

An anonymous letter, posted from Trowbridge on 13 October 1888, accused Police Constable Edward Watkins, who discovered the body of Catherine Eddowes.[54] Watkins served in the City Police Force from 1871 to 1896. At the inquest, he testified that he had been patrolling his beat from 22:00 until about 01:30. The beat took twelve to fourteen minutes to complete. At 01:30, he looked into the different passages in Mitre Square and saw nobody about. At 01:44, he found the body and rushed to the opposite warehouse of

Messrs. Kearley and Tongue, where he called the night watchman. Sixteen years earlier, he was caught having sex with a woman, possibly a prostitute, whilst on duty.[55]

The night watchman George Morris was a former policeman, employed by a wholesale grocers store in Mitre Square. His duty on the night of the murder began at 19:00. He told the inquest that he spent his time cleaning the offices and looking after the warehouse. Watkins alerted him to the crime at about 01:45. He heard no noise before then.

A letter sent to the City of London Police on 2 October 1888 by E. C. asked if the Police were sure the watchman was of good character.[56] A separate letter, dated 19 October 1888, accused a policeman dismissed from the force because of his connection with a prostitute. It was signed, "An Accessory."[57] Rob Hills suggested that the person referred to in this letter was George Morris and that the prostitute was Elizabeth Stride who sometimes used the alias Ann Morris. Some press reports on 1 October carried a story that a woman known as One-Armed-Liz who lived in a common lodging house in Flower and Dean Street identified Stride's body as Annie Morris a prostitute who lived in the same street.[58]

Michael Kidney said that Stride told him she had seen a policeman in Hyde Park before her marriage. Morris left the police force in 1882 because of ill health, having served since 1864 and previously from 1856-63. Hills speculated that Morris's brother, Thomas, married Ann Tabram and thus Morris became Martha Tabram's sister in law. There was a marriage between Ann Hannah Tabram and Thomas Morris on 13 August 1854 in Lambeth.[59] The groom's father was called Thomas, but George Morris's father was called John. They were not connected.

Hills suggested that Morris resembled a man seen stalking George Lusk and thought that Morris might bear a grudge against Alderman Sir Andrew Lusk, unrelated to George, who had recently dismissed a case of theft brought by Morris. Finally, Hills speculated that Morris was an accomplice of James Hardiman.[60]

Major General Wilcox wrote to the City Police suggesting that a man was impersonating Thomas Conway, the previous lover of Catherine Eddowes, and killed her to prevent the exposure of his secret.[61] Annie, the daughter of Conway and Eddowes, was 23. She said that she had not seen her father for the last fifteen to eighteen years. He was a hawker and a pensioner since she was eight years old. Annie also said that she had two brothers living in London and Conway was with them, but she had not seen or heard from them in eighteen months.[62] Eddowes told her that Conway was in the Royal Irish and the police found a pensioner called Conway in the regiment but two of Eddowes' sisters failed to identify him. This raised Wilcox's suspicions of an imposter. Conway was eventually discovered, under the name Thomas Quinn.[63] An anonymous letter accused Conway's son, of the same name, saying he was in a criminal gang.[64] No evidence was provided.

The last lover of Catherine Eddowes is cleared by his alibi. At the inquest Frederick Wilkinson, deputy of the lodging house at 55 Flower and Dean Street said that John Kelly was sleeping at Number 52 on the Friday and Saturday night. [65]

A 1977 novel by Mark Andrews suggested that Joseph Barnett was the Ripper. Bruce Paley independently developed this theory, writing a book in 1995.[66] In 1991, Paul Harrison had also accused Barnett but confused him with another man of the same name.[67]

Paley argued that Barnett fitted a profile of the killer and was motivated by a desire to keep Kelly off the streets. The profile involved a white male, age 28-36, who lived or worked locally. He was weak and passive with an absent father and some kind of physical ailment or disability such as speech impediment. Employed below his intellectual ability, his stress triggered the killings.

Barnett was 30 in 1888. His father died when he was three. The fate of his mother is unknown. The suggestion that he had a speech impediment is based on accounts of his testimony at the inquest. Shortly before the murders, he lost his job as a porter at the Billingsgate fish market. Paley suggested that the loss of employment pushed him over the edge, leading to the breakdown of his relationship with Kelly who he left a few days before the murder but remained on good terms with. He was literate, and Paley linked the presence of ginger beer bottles in Kelly's room to the mention of ginger beer in the Dear Boss letter.

Paley believed that Barnett fitted Lawende's description and cited the memoirs of Major Henry Smith who was acting commissioner of the City of London Police in September 1888. Writing in 1910, Smith claimed to have seen bloodstained water in a sink in Dorset Street where the murderer of Catherine Eddowes washed his hands. He later stated that Eddowes' killer used the apron to clean his bloodstained hands and Kelly's killer used the sink.[68]

A witness, Julia Venturney, told the police that she had heard Barnett say he did not like Kelly going on the streets and would not live with her whilst she lived that kind of life. Venturney also said that Kelly was fond of another man called Joe who ill-used her because she cohabited with Barnett.[69]

Barnett told the press that he last saw Mary alive at 19:30 on the day of her death. The following day he heard about a murder in Miller's Court and, on his way there, met his sister's brother in law who told him who the victim was. He went to the police station and told the inspector where he had been on the previous night. The police detained him for about four hours, examined his clothes for bloodstains and collaborated his movements.[70]

57

In other press reports, he said that he was playing whist at his lodging house until 00:30 when he went to bed.[71]

Joseph's brother, Daniel who was 36, sometimes appears as a suspect. Joseph told the Star that his brother met Mary on the night of her murder.[72] Maurice (Morris) Lewis, a tailor, was reported in the press as saying that he saw Kelly that night in the Horn of Plenty, with some women and a man named Danny or Dan who sold oranges in Billingsgate market and whom she had lived with until recently.[73] Lewis claimed to have known Kelly for five years and to have seen her on the morning of the murder.

At the inquest, Julia Venturney said that the other man that Kelly liked came to see her and gave her money. She did not repeat her previous statement that this man ill-used Kelly, but researchers have suspected him because of this allegation. Barnett testified that Kelly at one time lived with a man called Joseph Flemming, a mason's plasterer, who lived in Bethnal Green Road and used to visit her.

A Joseph Fleming, born around 1859 in Bethnal Green and described as a plasterer in the 1881 census, lodged then at 61 Crozier Street, Homerton, in Hackney. A Joseph Flemming born 1859 was in the Bethnal Green workhouse between 15 October 1888 and 9 January 1889, which, if it is the right person provides an alibi.[74] He could be the son of a plasterer called Richard and Henrietta nee Mason, discovered wandering the streets on 4 July 1892. The authorities sent him to the City of London Lunatic Asylum at Stone. Asylum records note his name as James Evans and give Henrietta Fleming's details as the address of friends. He was 37 at the time of the admission.[75] He died at Claybury Mental Hospital on 28 August 1920 when his death certificate confirmed the use of both names. A 28- year-old railway porter named James Evans was admitted to the Whitechapel Union infirmary, as insane, in both June and July 1888.[76]

A 2013 book by Robert Harris accused Thomas Bowyer. He lived at 37 Dorset Street and worked in John McCarthy's shop. He told the inquest that he last saw Kelly on the Wednesday morning before she was murdered.[77] The press reported that he claimed to have seen her with a suspicious character on Wednesday night.[78]

Bowyer said that McCarthy sent him to collect rent at 10:45. On seeing the body through the window, he fetched McCarthy who, after viewing the body, sent him to the police station and followed. There is a slight discrepancy between their original statements and the inquest testimony when they both said that they went to the police station together.[79] Don Souden suggested that they were slow in reporting the crime because McCarthy wished to remove evidence that incriminated him as Kelly's pimp.[80] An article in The Echo on 14 November 1888 said that Bowyer went to the water tap outside Kelly's room at 03:00 on the morning of the murder. [81]

Bowyer has not been traced. The Echo called him Indian Harry and described him as a young man but also said that he had travelled and formerly lived in India.[82] Some press reports of the inquest quote him as saying that McCarthy said "Good God, Harry," when hearing of the murder.[83] The Daily Telegraph referred to him as a pensioned soldier.[84] There was a sailor called Thomas Bowyer who received a naval medal in India thirty years earlier.[85] Walter Dew described a young man running into the Police Station to report the murder.[86] Dew said that he then went to Millers court but this is not supported by contemporary accounts.

A letter sent to the police six days after the murder accused John McCarthy.[87] It asked why he sent Bowyer round on that morning and why he did not know to open the door through the window. Barnett told Abberline that the key had been missing for some time and that they used to open the door by reaching through the window. At the inquest,

McCarthy testified that the weekly rent was 4/6d. Kelly was 29 shillings in arrears.[88] He was quoted as saying that rent was got "best you can".[89]

In 1882, McCarthy was fined for being involved in an illegal fistfight.[90] He may have been the John McCarthy from Dorset Street who was given six months hard labour after a violent attack on a lodging house deputy and policeman in November 1890.[91] However, two different men called John McCarthy are listed at 27 Dorset Street in the 1891 census.[92]

A separate allegation may connect McCarthy to the murder of Mary Ann Austin, a prostitute who entered a London lodging house with a man on 25 May 1901. At 08:30 the following day, she was found naked in bed with ten stab wounds. She died in hospital after telling a doctor that her attacker was short with dark hair, a moustache, and Jewish appearance.[93] Her ex-husband, William, was arrested and discharged. A stonemason, James Schulty, said that he heard three men talking in the Princess Alice and one said that he knew McCarthy was with the victim before her husband.[94] Schulty had been drinking and the police dismissed his statement.

On 25 August 1901, the Cardiff Police wrote to Scotland Yard.[95] A woman called Mrs Clark had contacted them about a couple who lived in apartments with her. The man, George Neating, beat the woman who told Clark that Neating was in the Metropolitan Police at the time of the Whitechapel Murders and would hide in Stepney Churchyard when things went wrong. He lost his job because of drunkenness. The woman's father told Clark that Neating was in London at the time of Austin's murder and threatened his wife after reading reports about it. Clark described him as about 40 with dark hair and a Jewish appearance. He had a cataract growing over one of his eyes.[96] Nobody called George Neating, or derivatives, worked for the Metropolitan Police. In 2002, Derek Osborne noted that the description given by Clark fitted that of a suspicious character reportedly seen by Thomas Bowyer in Dorset Street on the Wednesday prior to Kelly's murder.[97]

In his 1998 book, From Hell, Bob Hinton accused George Hutchinson on the basis that his statement was too precise in describing a man seen at a distance with very poor visibility. Hutchinson came forward after it was reported that Sarah Lewis had seen a man waiting outside the entrance to Miller's Court. He did not say why he decided to follow Kelly and her client. Inspector Abberline, who regarded the statement as true, wrote that Hutchinson was surprised to see a man so well dressed in her company.[98] Hutchinson claimed to have known Kelly for about three years and sometimes gave her a few shillings.

Melvyn Fairclough claimed that he and Joseph Sickert interviewed Hutchinson's son, Reginald in May 1992. George William Topping Hutchinson was born on 1 October 1866. He became a plumber as well as being an accomplished violinist and ice-skater.[99] He allegedly told Reginald that he knew one of the Ripper victims and that the police interviewed him. This identification is unconfirmed.

Stephen Senise suggested that Hutchinson moved to Australia and indecently assaulted two young boys in 1896.[100] Convicted, he was sentenced to two years imprisonment in Bathurst Gaol. There it was noted that he was born in England and arrived on the *Ormuz* in 1889. This left England just after the murder of Alice McKenzie. The Sydney port authority noted Geo Hutchinson as one of the crew. Prison records listed his occupation as tinsmith and press reports of the trial described him as a labourer. This was the occupation of the 1888 witness.

The police arrested James Thomas Sadler at the Phoenix public house in Smithfield on 14 February 1891. He was a ship's fireman, discharged from his ship three days earlier. Born in 1838 he married Sarah Chapman in 1876 and had three children by her. Before becoming a merchant seaman, he worked as a hackney carriage driver, an omnibus conductor, and a greengrocer. His former landlady, Rose Moriarty, alleged that he had threatened his wife with a knife thirteen or fourteen years earlier.[101]

Sadler made a statement saying that he had known Frances Coles previously and spent two nights with her. Some men and a woman attacked him, stealing money and a watch. He had a row with Coles, believing that she should have helped him, and left her. He tried to go back to his ship and got into a fight with some labourers. Refused entry to a lodging house, he returned to the one where he had spent the previous night with Coles and found her in the kitchen. Without money, they could not procure a bed. Sadler left first. A policeman stopped and searched him, not finding a knife, then escorted him to the hospital. He managed to get some money from the shipping office and spent the rest of the time in the Victoria lodging house and a pub called the Phoenix. He gave discharge dates to prove that he was working at sea between 17 August 1888 and 2 October 1888.[102] A crew agreement covering the period 27 July 1888 to 1 October 1888 remains extant.[103] This gives him an alibi for some of the earlier murders.

The police believed that he was lodging at the Victoria lodging house on the night of McKenzie's murder.[104] According to the Daily Telegraph of 18 February 1891, they used a witness from the Mitre Square murder who was unable to identify Sadler.[105] Sadler's statement about the Coles murder was collaborated in part. Police Constable Bogan confirmed that he found him drunk at the London docks at 01:15. He had a wound to his left eye and walked away about fifteen minutes later. At 02:00, Bogan, in company with Sergeant Edwards, saw Sadler outside the Mint, with fresh injuries. Ten or twelve minutes later Sadler walked off again. It was about five minutes' walk to Swallow gardens for a sober man. Edwards said that he left Sadler at not more than two or three minutes past two and the walk to Swallow gardens was two to three minutes.[106]

According to the testimony of Duncan Campbell, supported by Thomas Johnson, Sadler came to the Sailors Home and sold him a clasp knife.[107] The police tried to connect this with a weapon used in the alleged assault by Sadler on his wife a decade earlier, but Mrs Moriarty was unable to identify it.[108] Campbell subsequently sold the knife to Mr Robinson who testified that the knife was blunt when he acquired it. A blunt knife had inflicted the injuries on Coles. Sadler denied having sold the knife.

Doctor Oxley testified that a drunken man could not have inflicted the wounds.[109] The inquest heard Ellen Callana testify that the other man, who she was certain was not Sadler, had gone off with Coles at about 01:30. Sadler was discharged. In December 1891, he was again accused of assaulting his wife and, following a further allegation of the same offence, was bound over to keep the peace for six months on 16 May 1892.[110]

Arrested on Suspicion

In this chapter, we consider some of the suspects known to have been questioned by the authorities. On the morning of Martha Tabram's murder, Police Constable Thomas Barrett saw a soldier loitering near the entrance of George Yard at about 02:00. The man was a private in the Grenadier Guards, aged 22-26, and five feet nine or ten inches tall with a fair complexion, dark hair and a small brown moustache turned up at the ends. He wore a good conduct badge without any medals.[1] The police arranged a parade at the Tower of London of all the privates and corporals who were on leave at the time of the murder. Barrett picked out a private who was wearing medals. Inspector Reid told him to be certain by having another look. He then picked out another man. Reid asked why he had selected two. Barrett said that the man he saw in George Yard had no medals. He acknowledged that he had made a mistake in identifying the first man.

The second man gave his name as John Leary. He said that on 6 September he had been drinking in Brixton with a colleague, Private Law. When the pubs closed, they lost each other. Leary looked for Law but did not find him again until about 04:30 in the Strand. They had another drink in Billingsgate and returned to barracks at 06:00. Law's statement confirmed this. Reid felt certain that Barrett had made a mistake. [2] He added that Leary gave an account of himself, and his time, which inquiries found to be correct.[3]

On 9 September 1888, Corporal Benjamin returned to the Tower. He had been absent without leave on 6 September. Reid took charge of his clothing and bayonet and asked him to account for his time. The police confirmed his alibi and there were no marks of blood on the clothing or bayonet.[4]

Mary Ann Connelly, known as Pearly Poll, testified that she had been in the company of Tabram and two soldiers on the night of the murder. They separated on the corner of George Yard about 23:45. Tabram went off with one of the soldiers, a private and Poll took the corporal. She missed an identity parade on 10 September but attended one two days later. There she revealed that the men had white bands around their caps. This suggested that they belonged to the Coldstream Guards.

On 15 September, Wellington Barracks hosted a parade, including all the corporals and privates who had been on leave on the night of 6 September. Pearly Poll picked out two privates. One named George she called the Corporal. The other, the one who went with Tabram, she called Skipper. He stated that he was in barracks at 22:00 on 6 September and records proved this. The police verified that George was at home with his wife between 20:00 on 6 September and 06:00 the next day. Nobody else reported seeing Tabram and Poll with the privates on the night of the murder. Tabram's sister-in-law, Ann Morris, saw Tabram entering a public house about 23:00 on the night of the murder but did not mention any soldiers.[5]

On 4 September 1888, The Star introduced a suspect called Leather Apron, stating that he had not been seen in the last few days and was well known in the West End.[6] In subsequent days, the newspaper reported that he had terrorised Whitechapel prostitutes for several years, using violence and verbal threats. He carried a razor-like knife, which he had drawn on a woman called Widow Annie near the London Hospital, threatening at the same time to "rip her up." He was five feet four or five inches in height and wore a dark close-fitting cap. He was thickset with an unusually thick neck. Aged 38-40, he had black closely clipped hair and a small black moustache. He always wore a leather apron. By trade, he was a slipper maker but no longer worked, concentrating instead on

65

blackmailing women. Despite always carrying a leather knife, he had never cut anyone. Nobody knew his name, but all believed him to be a Jew.

He never attacked men. One woman prosecuted him, and he was sent to jail for several days. He had no fixed abode but slept in a lodging house at Brick-Lane. The proprietors denied this, although Apron's pal Mickeldy Joe was present at the time. Leather Apron ranged all over London and peeped through the windows of public houses and coffee rooms to find women. One lodging house allegedly turned him out several months earlier.[7]

A police report dated 7 September 1888 stated that a man named Pizer alias Leather Apron had been in the habit of ill-using prostitutes in various parts of the Metropolis for some time.[8] Pizer's first name was given as Jack by Inspector Helson.[9] He may have been the John Pozer who was convicted on 7 July 1887 of stabbing a boot finisher and sent to prison for six months with hard labour.[10] On 4 August 1888, a charge of indecent assault against Pizer did not proceed.[11] Inspector Abberline reported that a man called Leather Apron had been levying blackmail and ill-using the women if they did not meet his demands. There was no evidence linking him to the murder.[12]

Pizer was arrested on 10 September 1888. At the inquest into the death of Annie Chapman, he admitted being known as Leather Apron and provided an alibi. He stated that he had spent the night of 31 August in a common lodging house in Holloway. Coroner Baxter noted that this was collaborated.[13] On 6 September Pizer arrived at 22 Mulberry Street, the home of his brother and stepmother, and this was confirmed by several people presumably those relations. He was afraid to come out in view of the suspicions about him published in the press. The arresting officer, Sergeant Thick, stated that he had known Pizer by the name of Leather Apron for many years and when people in the neighbourhood spoke of Leather Apron, they meant Pizer.

Pizer's demonstration of innocence did not save him from public attention. On 27 September 1888, he was assaulted and called "Leather Apron" by Emily Patswold. A magistrate fined her ten shillings and another two for costs.[14] Pizer went on to claim compensation from the Star. He died in 1897.

There is a possibility that Pizer was not Leather Apron. In his memoirs, former policeman Benjamin Leeson described a slaughterhouse butcher called Jacobs who wore a leather apron and frequently had to run away when people pointed him out.[15] In October 1900, some newspapers reported the death of a man called Julius Lipman, commenting that he was a cobbler known as Leather Apron.[16] Although he proved himself innocent of the Whitechapel murders the stigma stuck and he lost his business, dying of starvation. A Julius Lippman lived in the North-East, marrying in 1887. [17] Another, perhaps the same, died in London but not until 1919.

William Piggott was the son of an insurance agent in Gravesend. He was seen there with a bad hand and carrying a black bag on the Sunday after Annie Chapman's murder. He left a paper parcel at a fish shop, saying he was going to Tilbury. Instead, he went to a public house where his comments about hating women attracted attention. The parcel contained two shirts and a pair of stockings. One of the shirts was torn and blood stained. Inspector Abberline arranged for Piggott to be confronted with Mrs Fiddymont, landlady of the Prince Albert. A man entered her pub at 07:00 on the morning of the Chapman murder with spots of blood to the back of his right hand, dried blood between his fingers and more blood behind his right ear.[18] He quickly drank half a pint of beer and left. Fiddlymont did not identify Piggott but he remained in custody because of concerns about his mental state.[19] He said he knocked down a woman who bit his hand in the yard at the back of a lodging house in Whitechapel but later said it had occurred in Brick Lane.[20]

Whitechapel infirmary records show that he entered on 10 September 1888, and left on 9 October 1888.[21] This gives him an alibi for the double event.

On 11 September 1888, Doctors Crabb and Cowan visited the police to voice suspicions about a lunatic called Jacob (sometimes called Joseph) Isenschmid. Inspector Styles, accompanied by two other officers, went to Isenschmid's lodgings at 60 Milford Road and interviewed the landlord, George Tyler. Isenschmid began lodging with him on 5 September but had been out of the house for long periods, including some nights. Arrested, and certified as a dangerous lunatic, Isenschmid was sent to Bow Infirmary. No traces of blood were found on his clothing and his whereabouts on the night of Chapman's murder were unknown.[22]

Isenschmid's wife said that she had not seen her husband in the last two months, but he visited the house during her absence on 9 September and took away some clothing. He was in the habit of carrying large butcher's knives and she did not know how he obtained his livelihood.[23] He was a Swiss who set up a business as a pork butcher at 59 Elthorne road. When this failed, he became depressed, was frequently out at night, and stayed away for several days. After spending ten weeks in Colney Hatch asylum, he was discharged in December 1887. He found employment as a butcher at Mr Marlett's High Street, Marylebone and stayed there until Whitsuntide. Since then he had not worked to her knowledge. He had not slept at home for two months. She did not think her husband would injure anyone other than her. He was known as the mad butcher.[24] The police noted that he was reported to be very violent at times.[25] Asylum records for his admission to Colney Hatch in October 1887 indicate that he had threatened violence to his wife and children and neighbours as well as saying he would blow up the queen.[26]

The superintendent at the infirmary told Sergeant Thick that the girls at Holloway had called Isenschmid Leather Apron and Isenschmid jokingly had confirmed this.

Isenschmid had left his wife and made his living by going to the market early and buying sheep's heads, kidneys, and sheep's feet which he dressed then sold to restaurants and coffee houses in the West End.[27]

Inspector Abberline believed that he was identical with the man seen in the Prince Albert. The police tried to arrange an identification parade for Mrs Fiddymont, and other witnesses but Doctor Mickle, the Resident Medical Officer at the asylum, refused as it could prove injurious to the patient.[28] Despite the lack of a formal identification, Abberline stuck to his belief.[29] Isenschmid was 45 at the time of the Ripper murders and was in the asylum when the next killings took place. He died in Colney Hatch in 1910.

In response to a parliamentary question, the Home Secretary said that on 13 September 1888, Freidrich Schumacher was arrested as a suspicious person at Leman Street Police Station. He was released, after satisfactorily explaining his reasons for being on the premises. The charge was recorded but not submitted to a magistrate. Because of this failing, an inspector was reprimanded, and a sergeant reduced in rank.[30]

Edward McKenna was detained at Commercial Street Police Station on 14 September 1888 for identification as he matched a description published in the evening papers. He had been seen at Heath Street and other places with a knife.[31] He proved that he had been sleeping at a common lodging house in Brick Lane at the time of Chapman's murder.

Charles Ludwig was a 40-year-old German hairdresser also known as Ludwig Weitzel or Wetzel. He tried to stab Alexander Freinberg, whilst drunk at a coffee stall in the early hours of 18 September 1888. Fifteen minutes earlier Freinberg had seen Ludwig with a woman. She ran away, and Ludwig returned, requesting a coffee. Freinberg refused so Ludwig produced a long-bladed knife and chased him round the stall. On his way to the police station, Ludwig dropped an open long-bladed knife. The police found a razor and pair of scissors in his possession. Police Constable Johnson gave evidence that earlier that morning he had been on duty in the Minories when he heard shouts of *"murder"* from an unlit court. Inside he found Ludwig with a woman who asked to be taken out of there. He walked with her to the end of his beat when she said that the man had pulled a big knife.[32]

The magistrate remanded Ludwig for a week. Detective Inspector Helson tried to interview Ludwig after the hearing but the prisoner professed not to speak English.[33] Feinberg told the press that Ludwig had spoken broken, but plain, English to him.[34]

The Central News Agency reported that Ludwig arrived from Hamburg about fifteen months earlier and began working for Mr Partridge in the Minories on 1 September. He asked to sleep in the house saying that there was a dead man in his previous house. On the previous Sunday he moved to stay with a German tailor called Johannes but was asked to leave because of his dirty habits. This, and being turned out of the German club, accounted for him wandering the streets. There was no trace of blood on his shirts or aprons left at his employers. The knife that he dropped was described as a penknife by Freinberg but a clasp knife by the Central News.

On the Monday before his arrest, Ludwig allegedly produced some razors at a hotel in Finsbury. The landlord told the press that Ludwig called in about 09:00 on the day of the murder in a dirty state and asked to be allowed to wash. He said he had been out all night and talked about the murder, then offered to shave the landlord who refused. He was believed to have some knowledge of anatomy, gained as a surgical assistant in the German army and always carried a razor and scissors.[35] Some newspapers said that Ludwig washed blood off his hands during the visit.

On 2 October 1888, the police released Ludwig after he had been in custody for a fortnight. This included the night when Elizabeth Stride and Catherine Eddowes died. Inspector Prinley of H division said that Ludwig had accounted for his movements on the nights of the earlier murders. Elizabeth Burns, the prostitute he attacked, gave evidence but her statement that she screamed on seeing the knife and two policemen appeared, contradicts the evidence of Police Constable Johnson. [36] On 17 October 1888, the Star reported that the police were still watching Ludwig as he had been behaving suspiciously with a knife. In March 1897, a Charles George Ludwig was arrested as a lunatic in Whitechapel. [37]

Edward Quinn was a 35-year-old labourer who appeared at the Woolwich Police Court on 17 September 1888 charged with being drunk. His face and hands were bruised and, at the time of the arrest, had bloodstains. He complained that he had been having a drink at a bar on Saturday, 15 September, having previously fallen over. A tall man gave him beer and tobacco and said that he wanted to charge him with being the Whitechapel murderer. Quinn thought it was a joke until the man walked him to the police Station. [38]

On the night of the double event, Frank Raper was arrested at a public house called "Dirty Dicks" near Liverpool Street. He was standing at the bar, drunk, and made many comments about the murders of Chapman and Nichols. When the police arrived, he was boasting about being the murderer and complimenting himself on how he had concealed his identity. He told the police that he had no fixed address and they were satisfied that he was not the killer. [39]

On 10 October 1888, John Langan was arrested at Boulogne. He was a vagrant, born in the United States, who fitted a description of the murderer. His manner was unsatisfactory. He produced a discharge from a British ship at Glasgow on 10 April 1888 and said that he had been lodging with a Mrs Davies at 30 Dufferin, village two miles from Merthyr then stayed with John Richmond, 47 Castle Street, Hamilton near Glasgow. [40] He was released after the address was verified.

George Richard Henderson was arrested on the same day as Langan, following rumours that Jack the Ripper was in Covent Garden Market. At 03:30, a policeman found

Henderson wandering around with a black bag. He also had 51 pawn tickets and a draft letter to the Home Secretary saying that people who harboured the Whitechapel murder felt equally guilty and could not come forward until a free pardon was offered.[41] He was discharged, after witnesses confirmed that he was a respectable man.

On 11 October 1888, William John Foster, sometimes referred to as John Foster, was arrested at 11 Memel Street, Belfast, on suspicion of being the Whitechapel murderer. Foster said that he had arrived from Glasgow on 6 October 1888, having previously been in Edinburgh. He was unable to say how long he had stayed in either city. He was a jobbing watchmaker and claimed that his father was a brewer but could not give an address. He had £19 in gold, 4s-4d in silver and some valuable jewellery. A black bag in his lodgings contained three razors and several knives.[42]

James O'Hagan from the Victoria Temperance Hotel identified Foster as a man who had come off the Glasgow boat. He took a bed for the night and left a small paper parcel in the room. This contained soiled collars and cuffs wrapped in a copy of the Glasgow Evening Citizen from 1 October 1888. The article described the Whitechapel murders. Goods from a burglary in Bootle were found in the lodgings.[43] Foster appeared before Liverpool magistrates on 22 October, described as a 23-year-old jobbing watchmaker. He was charged with breaking into the house of Arthur Cross in College Road Crosby between 13 and 14 September and stealing money and jewellery.[44]

The Star of 12 October 1888 reported the arrest of a man known in Spitalfields by the name of Parnell. He lodged at the Beehive Chambers but was absent on the night of the murder and the one following. The landlord reported this to the police. At Commercial Street Police Station, the man said his name was Andrews and that he was a book hawker. He had slept at another house on the night in question and gave a fair account of himself. The police apparently believed him to be innocent.[45]

On 11 November 1888, a man named Brown, who lived at 9 Dorset Street, spotted stains on the coat and shirt of another man who was drinking in a pub in Fish Street Hill. The man first claimed they were paint before admitting they were blood and leaving. Brown followed and gave him into custody at Bishopsgate Police Street. He had been arrested at Shadwell the previous day and discharged. He gave the name George Compton.[46] The police found his statements to be true.[47] Brown said that Compton made contradictory statements about his residence and place of work.

Around the same time Sir George Compton Archibald Arthur, a 28-year-old soldier and baronet was arrested. Every night young men were touring the area where the murders were committed. Arthur was watched because he fitted the description of the killer. He was quickly able to prove his innocence and the affair was kept out of the newspapers until friends leaked it to the American press.[48] The absence of reports in the British media, and the timing of the arrest, suggests that he gave his middle names of George Compton to the police.

Sir George served as private secretary to the secretary of state for war, Lord Kitchener, between 1914 and 1916. He wrote a biography of Kitchener and several other military books, becoming a fellow of the Royal Society of Literature. He died on 14 January 1946.

On 12 November 1888, Thomas Murphy was arrested at the Holborn Casual Ward following reports of suspicious behaviour. He was taken to Frederick Street police station on Kings Cross Road where he was found to have a knife with a ten-inch blade. He was described as a native of Massachusetts, age 24, and five feet six inches tall, with fair hair and complexion.[49] He was cleared after a telegram was sent to Inspector Abberline for enquires to be made and these proved satisfactory.[50]

On 16 November 1888, two men drinking in the White Hart Public House in Hampton Wick observed a man listening to their conversation about Jack the Ripper and believed that he matched a description of the killer. At the police station, he gave his name as Arthur Henry Mason of 12 Portland Road, Spring Grove, Kingston, and stated that he was a compositor working for Kelly and Co. Kingston. The police verified this and released him.[51]

Nikaner Benelius was a 27-year-old Swedish traveller arrested on 17 November 1888 after walking into the house of Harriet Rowe in Buxton Street, Mile End. When she asked what he wanted, he grinned and went outside. She followed to fetch a policeman and found Benelius asking Police Constable Imhoff for directions to Fenchurch Street. Benelius told Imhoff that he expected some letters at the post office and had entered Rowe's house to ask directions. He was not carrying a weapon. Two men, one of whom was said to be his landlord, told the police that he had been preaching in the street and acting very strangely. His address was given as a German lodging house in Great Eastern Street Shoreditch, where he owed 25 shillings to the landlord. Detective Sergeant Dew told the court that the police arrested Benelius in connection with the murder of Elizabeth Stride and released him.[52]

Benelius wrote two letters to the Lord Mayor of London on 4 October 1888 and 18 October 1888. In the first, he asked for Miss Wilkinson to be in the city on the following evening or another young lady to be at the same cathedral.[53] In the second, he expressed a desire to meet the Mayor. The Star of 19 November 1888 reported that he was discharged, and that the Charity Organisation Society was going to send him back to America.

On 17 November 1888, Oliver Matthews of 14 Wharton Road was arrested after he aroused the suspicions of a lawyer sitting next to him at the Trevor Music Hall in Knightsbridge. This was due to a black bag carried by Matthews. He was released when his identity and address were verified.[54]

The Star of 19 November 1888 reported that a man who gave the name Charles Akehurst entered a lodging house with a female and made certain remarks, which resulted in her running to a policeman. He lived at 27 Canterbury Road, Balls Pond Road North and his answers satisfied the detective.[55]

A police report of 18 January 1889 refers to an incident on 21 November 1888. Mrs Fanny Drake came to Rochester Row Police Station and said that she was walking over Westminster Bridge when a man resembling the description of the murderer grinned at her. She followed him to Westminster Abbey where she told a policeman. Inspector Walsh followed the man to the Army and Navy stores and escorted him to the station. He carried identification in the name of Mr Douglas Cow of Cow & Co, India-Rubber merchants, 70 Cheapside and 8 Kempshoot Road, Streatham. When informed of this Mrs Drake was satisfied.[56]

The firm was P.B. Cow and Co, with brothers Douglas and Peter being directors. Douglas was born in 1850. He married Florence Amy Cox on 11 March 1879 in Streatham Common and they had one child, Douglas Vernon (1881-1921).[57] Douglas senior died on 25 March 1933.

An Irishman called James Connell of 408 New Cross Road was detained on 22 November 1888 after alarming a married woman called Martha Spencer. He spoke to her near Marble Arch then, as they walked in the park, began to talk about Jack the Ripper. He expressed an opinion that the culprit was a lunatic. A telegram to Greenwich Police Station, asked if the address was valid and about his respectability. A satisfactory reply led to his release.[58]

Described as a clothier and draper, he was the poet Jim Connell who was active in the Irish Land League and served as secretary of the Deptford Radical Association. The following year, whilst on a train, he wrote the Red Flag, which became the anthem of the Labour Party and the socialist movement. He died in Lewisham Hospital in 1929.

On 25 November 1888, Police Constable King took a Dutchman called W. Van Burst into custody. Four men had seen him accost three women outside King's Cross railway station. They followed him for about an hour and saw him accost two other women then board a train to Farringdon Street followed by an omnibus. They summoned the police who made satisfactory enquiries. He gave the Bacons Hotel, Fitzroy Square as his address.[59]

On the same night the Bacons hotel, Finsbury Square, was given as the address of another suspect, Alfred Parent who also had two addresses in France. A prostitute called Annie Cook accused him. Due to the size of his offering, a sovereign, she feared that he intended to murder her. He was 54, five feet six inches tall with white hair and whiskers and a grey moustache.[60]

A man calling himself James Shaw was arrested in New York in late November 1888, after arriving on the Wyoming from Liverpool. He matched the description of a labourer, James Pennock, suspected of killing his wife near Pickering on 7 November 1888. The American authorities felt that he also matched the description of Jack the Ripper and he carried a newspaper report about the Whitechapel murders.[61] Shaw said that he was a farm labourer seeking a better life. He had left his wife, Alice, and three children in Leeds under the care of a widow named Chapman.[62] He was soon released. One newspaper said that his real name was Heddington.[63] He was not James Pennock, whose body was found in the river near Pickering on 6 April 1889.[64]

It is possible that he was the Henry Shaw arrested for attempting to murder his half-sister Edith Tyson in Los Angeles on 2 December 1910. This man told the deputy sheriffs that the face of his dead brother, Fred Shaw, haunted him. Fred was crushed to death under an elevator while working as a night watchman at the Citizen's National Bank. Earlier that year Fred had shot and wounded Henry.[65]

Fred's wife, Edith, was really his sister. She came from a respectable middle-class family in England. Henry, real name John James Moynihan, was the son of her mother's first husband. About 1898 John and his half-brother, Fred left home together and travelled around the world. Edith believed that John was guilty of some serious crime, which Fred knew nothing about. She said he was arrested whilst working in a mine in Australia, but the real crime had been committed in London as he was always nervous when he returned there.

The brothers sent money for Edith to join them in San Francisco in October 1909. Two days before the accident, Fred and John quarrelled. John returned late on the night of the murder and Edith suspected that he had killed Fred, due to previous threats that he had made.[66]

Henry Shaw told the deputy sheriffs that he fled England fifteen years earlier to escape arrest on suspicion of being the notorious Whitechapel criminal. He claimed to have lived in Whitechapel between 1884 and 1890, and then wandered through Canada and Brazil. In Canada, he got into trouble and served some time.[67] Deputy Sheriff Wood asked the British authorities for advice. He was quoted as saying: *"Statements he made during his rational moments lead me to believe that we have affected a capture that is not only important to us in connection with young Fred Tyson's death, but developments may show, as I think, more than likely that he is the man who has committed the Whitechapel crimes."*[68]

This optimism proved unfounded. Henry faced no criminal charges, except one of felony brought by his sister and this failed because the alleged offence was committed outside the county. Freed by the lunacy commission he was immediately rearrested on a

77

charge of battery on 13-year-old Marian Haines, who had been a guest at Edith Tyson's house.[69] On 7 July, he was arrested again, on a charge of improperly treating young girls. [70]

Later that month, he arrived in Salt Lake City. Calling himself John Moynihan, he told an incredible story to County Attorney I. E. Willey. He said he shipped hundreds of horses from Britain during the Boer War but could not land them in Africa due to quarantine requirements. Instead, he took them to Australia and went into the gold fields then moved onto Vancouver. There he learnt that a British relative had left him a legacy of $60,000. His half-sister and half-brother found him in San Francisco and, aided by a sinister man with a black moustache and a Los Angeles attorney named Martin, began a conspiracy to deprive him of the legacy. He was continually hounded and not permitted to send mail. The conspirators followed him to Salt Lake City and he sought Wiley's help to evade them.[71] Howard and Nina Brown located census records for a John Moynihan, born in Holborn in 1868.[72]

On 30 November 1888, a man was arrested at the Crystal Tavern on Mile End Road, 25 Burdett Road, after arousing the suspicions of a photographer.[73] He gave the name of Mr Stewart and an address of 305 Mile End Road but the name of Ever at Bow Street Police Station. The Press stated that he appeared to be a Polish Jew.[74]

On 7 December 1888, another Polish Jew, Joseph Isaacs, was charged with stealing a watch from Julius Levenson. Isaacs was a 30-year-old cigar maker of no fixed abode. Mary Cusins the deputy of a lodging house in Paternoster Row Spitalfields, about two minutes from Millers Court, said that he lodged with her for three or four nights before the murder of Mary Jane Kelly. On the night of the murder, she heard him walking about his room. He disappeared afterwards, leaving his violin bow behind. She gave this information to the police. Isaacs matched Hutchinson's description of a man with an astrakhan trimming to his coat. On 5 December, he returned and asked for the violin bow. Cusins followed him to Levenson's shop. Another lodger, Cornelius Oakes, had heard Isaacs threaten violence to all women over seventeen years of age.[75] Some newspapers quoted Inspector Abberline as being overheard saying *"Keep this quite; we have got the right man at last. This is a big thing."*[76]

On 12 November 1888 Isaacs appeared at Barnet Police Court charged with petty larceny and was sentenced to 21 days in prison with hard labour.[77] A later press report said that he was in prison for stealing a coat at the time of Kelly's murder.[78] On 2 January 1889, Isaacs received three months imprisonment for the violin theft. There was a Joseph Isaacs convicted of stealing a coat in October 1887 and given six months imprisonment, but he was 46.[79]

In his biography of Joseph Lis, Charles Van Onselen suggested that his subject was Jack the Ripper and Joseph Isaacs. Lis, also known as Joseph Silver, was born in Poland in 1868. On 10 October 1889, he was convicted of burglary in New York and sent to Sing Sing prison for two and a half years.[80] On 24 October 1895, he married Hannah Opticer at the Lambeth registry office in London. Opticer was a prostitute who disappeared from official records prior to 1905 when Lis married another prostitute, Hannah Vygenbaum, who also vanished.

On 8 November 1895, Lis was arrested in London, under the name Abraham Ramer, for the theft of an umbrella and sentenced to three months imprisonment. Six months later, he was jailed for another theft, this time receiving nine months. In 1898, describing himself as an American draper named James Smith, he and two associates were acquitted of unlawfully conspiring to procure Rachel Laskin to be a common prostitute. Alone, he was acquitted of a related charge. In subsequent years, he operated as a thief, pimp, and police informer in South Africa, France, the Low Countries, Scandinavia, and South America. It is believed that the Austrian army executed him in 1918.

Lis's whereabouts in the autumn of 1888 are unknown although his acknowledged daughter, Bertha, may have been born in London in April that year.[81] Haskel Brietstein alias Adolph Goldberg stated in a New York courtroom that he had known Lis in London in 1889.

In 1887, Goldberg lived at 3 Vine Court, Whitechapel. A man called Lewis Lis lived at 35 Plumbers Row, in the centre of the murder area. Brietstein was involved in a burglary directly opposite Lewis Lis's shop in 1887.[82] He was sent to jail for fifteen months in January 1888 and, on his release, went to America. Lis arrived in America around the same time.

Due to later attempts from Lis and his associates to conceal his whereabouts prior to arriving in America in 1889 and displays of psychopathic behaviour, Van Onselen concluded that the then-teenager was the Whitechapel murderer. He believed that marks recorded on Lis's face in prison records indicate that he contracted syphilis around 1888. He argued that Lis was the Joe known to Mary Jane Kelly, although most researchers believe this was Joseph Fleming.

On 8 December 1888 Edwin Burrows of a common lodging house, Victoria Chambers in Westminster, was detained by Police Constables Bradshaw and Godley. The police knew him as a man who slept rough. He lived on a weekly allowance of £1 from his brother who lived in Sutton and verified this. He was 45 and five feet five inches tall with a dark complexion. He wore a light brown tweed jacket suit and a sailor's peak cap.[83]

On 28 December 1888, Thomas and John Hardy observed Joseph Denny accosting two women in Houndsditch. They followed him to Finsbury where he approached another woman. PC Wright took Denny to Old Street Police Station. He was released following satisfactory enquiries.[84] His address was 64 Myddelton Square, Clerkenwell.

A police report dated 14 January 1889 stated that Richard Wingate, a baker from 10 Church Street, Edgware Road believed his business partner, Pierce John Robinson, to be the Ripper. His evidence was that Robinson became reticent during a talk about the murders and sent a letter to his girlfriend expressing fear of capture. He also asked if he could sell his share in the business to go to America. The police ascertained that Robinson was a religious fanatic who left his address in Mile End Road on 1 November 1888 and had a conviction for bigamy.[85] They established that he was sleeping with his girlfriend in Portslade, East Sussex, on the night of Mary Kelly's murder.[86]

Three suspects were arrested in the aftermath of Alice McKenzie's murder. John Larkin Mills was taken into custody at 02:35 and released at 04:30.[87] Born in December 1848 he married Esther Emma Taylor Cranmore on 6 July 1871 in South Hackney. They had two children, John born 1873 and Stanley 1877. John senior was a clerk who died in 1898.

John Sullivan was arrested about four hours after McKenzie's death. He carried a butcher's knife but was identified by the keeper of the Victoria lodging house and released.[88] The Pall Mall Gazette revealed that another suspect had accosted two or three women in the area before his arrest shortly before midnight in Commercial Street on 17 July 1889. He was married and lived at Ballspond. The previous day he had taken out life insurance and there were no doubts about his respectability.[89] Another newspaper gave his name as Charles Evison.[90] Others added the middle name of Henry. He may have been the lithographer, Charles Henry Evison, born 1859, who married at least three times. The first was to Mary Ann Mills in Islington on Boxing Day 1881. The second was to Emma

Berridge in Finsbury on 15 March 1885 and the third to Esther McNeil on 27 March 1898. With Esther he lived at 7 Spital Yard, Spitalfields.[91]

The Yorkshire Herald of 28 July 1890 reported that the police in America had arrested an Irishman, John Connors, on suspicion of being Jack the Ripper. He was fined $250 for throwing ink at strangers and sentenced to six months in jail.[92]

On 24 April 1891 Carrie Brown a 60-year-old prostitute, originally from Liverpool, was murdered in New York after checking into the East River hotel with a man. Mary Miniter, who escorted the couple to their room, described the man as being about five feet eight inches tall, about 30 years old, with brown hair, a brown moustache, and sharp nose. She thought he was a foreigner. When the body was discovered, the lower part was naked and what appeared to be clothing was knotted about Brown's neck. There were several cuts to her abdomen, and she had been disembowelled. The murder weapon was a wooden handled table knife, left on the floor. The end had been broken off, leaving a four-inch long blade, which was ground down. Death was due to asphyxiation.[93]

On 29 April 1891, the police arrested a cattleman at the public abattoir in New Jersey. Arbie La Bruckman was also known as John Frenchy or Francis. He said that he had arrived in the States from Spain on 10 April 1891. He told police that he was in a lodging house at 81 James Street at the time of the murder and that others could vouch for him. He had dark hair and a dark moustache. He said that he had been arrested on suspicion of nine murders in Whitechapel eighteen months earlier, being locked up for a month then released.[94]

A comparison of Lloyd's Ship Registry for La Bruckman's firm, the National Line, with the arrivals and departures schedules published in the New York shipping records disclosed that National Line cattle boats were docked in London during all the murders.[95] There was a man named Henry Bruckman on the electoral register in 1885 at 40 Great

Allie Street, Whitechapel and the 1891 census lists a family with that surname in Mile End.

The inquest into Brown's death heard that there were blood trails leading from her room, number 31, to number 33. The bellboy identified Amer Ben Ali as the man who had rented room 33 on the night of the murder and left about 05:00 in the morning. Ali was convicted on 10 July 1891. He was later cleared after the New York Governor received two sworn affidavits. One was from a journalist who arrived on the scene just after the murder. He was certain that there had been no blood trail to Ali's room. The other was from George Damon, who said that shortly after the murder a Danish farmhand disappeared. Bloodstained clothing and a key from the East River hotel were found in his room.[96] The murder of Carrie Brown was never solved

Accused during the Terror

The next group of suspects were accused by members of the public. At the Nichols inquest, a signalman, Thomas Ede, said that he saw a suspicious man on the day of Annie Chapman's murder. He was walking down Cambridge Heath Road at noon and the man was on the opposite side, with a blade sticking out of his pocket. Ede followed him and lost him under some railway arches. The man was five feet, eight inches tall and about 35 years old with a dark moustache and whiskers. He wore a double peak cap, dark brown jacket, and a pair of overalls over dark trousers. He walked as if he had a stiff knee and appeared to have a wooden arm.[1] Recalled to the inquest Ede stated that he had seen the man since and ascertained that his name was John James, Henry James according to some reports. The coroner said that the man James had been seen and was a well-known harmless lunatic.[2] He was said to be from Hackney.

George Cullen was a criminal, also known as Squibby, who threw a stone at a policeman but hit a girl, Betsy Goldstein, instead. On 8 September 1888, Police Constable Dew saw him and gave pursuit. Assuming he was the killer, a mob followed. He received three months hard labour for the assault.[3] This gives him an alibi.

On Thursday 20 September 1888, Thomas Mills, a 59-year-old cabinetmaker, appeared at Worship Street Court charged with being intoxicated in Wellington Row, Shoreditch, on the previous night. A Police Constable said that he found Mills with a crowd of people calling him "Leather Apron" and threatening to lynch him. Mills complained that he resembled a picture of Leather Apron published in the Police News and had been unable to get work as a result. He had appeared in the court a hundred times, charged with the same offence, most recently on the previous Tuesday. The magistrate issued a fine.[4]

On 3 October 1888, a crowed followed a 32-year-old sailor called John Lock. Bloodstains on his coat turned out to be paint.[5] The same day the Daily Telegraph published a letter from X of St Albans who reported that a lunatic, considered dangerous to women, had escaped from Leavesden asylum the previous year. The inmate's name was MacDonald. He was said to have been a doctor who practised in India and returned to England when his money ran out. He was six feet two inches tall and had a habit of shouting incessantly. He had been sleeping in the woods.[6] The chairman of the Leavesden Asylum committee responded with a statement from the asylum's medical superintendent that the escaped patient was quiet and harmless and had not shown any homicidal tendency.[7] On 4 October 1888, Mary Heard wrote to the City Police, saying that the killer was this escaped lunatic.[8]

Donald John MacDonald was born in Madras on 3 April 1850. He received a decree in medicine and surgery from the University of Aberdeen in 1874.[9] On 31 March 1876, he was appointed surgeon to her Majesty's Indian Service in Bengal.[10] He was admitted to Leavesden Hospital on 12 April 1886 and escaped on 16 September 1887, whilst out walking.[11] His case papers at Leavesden indicate that he talked to himself, shouted a lot, and used foul language. He also believed that he was going to marry a great lady and thought that everyone was against him.[12]

A letter from J Trustram of Harpenden, Hertfordshire, noting that MacDonald was a doctor who came from India and claimed to be robbed, connected him to a man who went to the cabman's reading room at 43 Pickering Place, Westbourne Grove for a meal on 30 September. There he told Thomas Ryan that he had committed the Whitechapel murders.[13] He said he had returned from India and got into trouble, losing his watch,

85

chain, and £10. He had been in Newcastle before going to India and had no fixed abode. Ryan, the secretary of the cabmen's branch of the Church of England Temperance society, asked him to sign pledges to be teetotal. He signed J. Duncan, doctor. Despite promising to return in an hour, he never did.

The Berkshire Chief Constable reported the suspicions of Captain Rathbone, who claimed to have known Doctor Duncan in the army in Bombay.[14] A solicitor's clerk read about the incident in the Newcastle Courant and informed Lieutenant William Wookey, governor of Newcastle prison and former Deputy Chief Constable of Northumberland Police. Wookey wrote to the Home Office saying that he believed the man in the cabman's shelter was one of his former charges.[15]

The convict's name was John Donkin. On the date of his second conviction for assault on 22 December 1881, he was 28. His previous conviction, also for assault, was on 6 January 1881. Both attacks were on women. Wookey wrote that Donkin was educated at college for the medical profession but turned out wild. He divorced and then spent time in the low parts of London. His manners and address were those of a gentleman, and he had considerable anatomical knowledge. The description of Donkin and criminal history enclosed by Wookey had the name Duncan crossed out and Donkin substituted.

John George Donkin was born in Morpeth on 7 June 1853, the son of a doctor who later moved to London. John allegedly served as a locum in the North of England and as a journalist before joining the 17th Lancers. One source states that he also fought in the third Carlist War, which occurred in Northern and Eastern Spain between 1872 and 1876.[16] In 1874, he married Margaret Mason. The couple had two children. John was declared bankrupt in 1876.[17] In 1881, the family lived with Margaret's mother. John had no occupation but received income from property.

In 1884, he moved to Canada and briefly tried his hand at farming before joining the Mounted Police, remaining with them until March 1888. He acted as a hospital steward at Prince Albert in the North-West rebellion and served at the border post of Wood Mountain. On his return to England Donkin wrote a book about his experiences. He thanked the Canadian High Commission in London for the loan of reference material, so it is safe to assume that he spent some time in London between March 1888 and the publication of the book in 1889. He is said to have worked again as a journalist for the Newcastle Chronicle.[18] He died in the Alnwick workhouse on 3 January 1890 from inflammation of the lungs caused by excessive drinking.[19]

Inspector Abberline reported on 10 October 1888 that the man who made the statement in the cabman's shelter satisfactorily accounted for his movements on the dates of the murders. He gave the name John Davidson.[20]

On 3 October 1888, John S. Gordon from Aberdeen wrote to the police about a Doctor Hartley who sold patent medicine named Sequah or Indian medicine. He believed there was a connection with the Whitechapel murderer.[21] On 31 August 1888, Hartley took out a full-page advertisement in the Aberdeen Journal, filling it with testimonials from across Britain and Ireland. It stated that he was on the reclaimed ground in the city at three and eight every day. In October, a similar advert appeared in the Dundee Courier and Argus.

A day after his first letter Gordon wrote again, urging the police to look for a bigamist named James Malcolm who was a butcher and may have taken a hatred to women.[22] In 1885, Malcom worked for a meat salesman at Smithfield market. He met a woman in Brighton and married her, claiming to be Captain MacDonald. He disappeared after the wedding but was discovered at the meat market and tried for bigamy, due to a previous marriage to Elizabeth Williamson in Aberdeen. The jury were unable to reach a verdict and the case was postponed to the next sessions, with the added evidence that he tricked a lady from St Albans in the same way.[23] Jailed for seven years he was released due to ill health, in January 1888.[24] In 1893, he lived in Ladismith, South Africa, and was arrested after being in a fight with a man whose house his wife had visited.[25]

A sailor called George M Dodge said that he arrived in London from China on 13 August 1888. At the Queens Musical Hall in Poplar he met a Malay cook called Alaska who claimed to have been robbed by a prostitute and threatened to kill and mutilate them all until he found her. He showed Dodge a double-edged knife that he always carried. He was about 35, five feet seven inches and weighed ten to eleven stone. [26] A representative of the Central News Agency visited a home for Asiatics in the East End and spoke to the superintendent, Mr Freeman, who said that he had never heard of a Malay called Alaska but added that Lascar was the Mohammedan name for seaman. He also stated that the residents of the home rarely went far from the docks.[27] Dodge said Alaska lived near the East India Dock Road but would not divulge an address until he had checked if a reward was offered. A seaman thought the Malay was on a vessel in the North Sea.[28] The Times commented that the ship carrying Dodge from China, the Glenorchy returned to London on 14 August, a day after Dodge said he arrived.[29]

Another Malay suspect was a cook called Maurice, allegedly suspected of the Austin axe murders, and thought to have moved to London. A journalist ascertained that he left the Pearl House hotel in Austin, close to the murder scenes, in January 1886 and was said to work on ships.[30] The axe murders occurred in the Texan town between 31 December 1884 and 24 December 1885. The early victims were black female servants, attacked in their homes, sometimes in front of children and other family members, and raped. In the last instance, two white women were hacked to death. One was Eula Phillips. Her husband, James, injured in the attack, was convicted of her murder, and sentenced to seven years.[31] The Texan Court of Appeal overturned the conviction. Moses Hancock,

88

husband of the other white victim, also faced a murder charge but the jury were unable to reach a verdict.[32]

The Austin Statesman dismissed similarities with the Ripper murders as coincidence. It also commented that the suspect in Austin seen once was a short, heavy-set personage like Leather Apron.[33] Most witnesses described the killer as black.

The inhabitants of Eltham in South-East London reported a man sleeping rough and occasionally begging. On 5 October 1888, a 23-year old Norwegian solider, Bertram Knutson, was arrested and charged with wandering abroad and sleeping in the open air without visible means of subsistence. The court sent him to the Workhouse.[34]

Mrs Luckett wrote to the police, asking who wrote Jekyll and Hyde and, if he was a likely suspect.[35] The play of Jekyll and Hyde was running at the Lyceum Theatre in London. The author, Robert Louis Stevenson, was born in Edinburgh on 13 November 1850. Most of his life after his marriage in May 1880, in San Francisco, was spent as an invalid, suffering from lung diseases, coughs, and fevers. His most famous book Treasure Island appeared in 1883 although it had been serialised the previous year. Jekyll and Hyde first saw publication in 1886. At the time of the Ripper murders Stevenson was on a cruise in the South Seas.[36] He settled in Samoa and died there on 3 December 1894.

The actor portraying Jekyll and Hyde, from 4 August 1888, was Richard Mansfield. Born in 1857, he had previous played the role on Broadway. An anonymous letter to the City Police accused him of being the Ripper due to his acting performance and ability to change quickly. The writer suggested that he might carry false whiskers in a bag.[37]

A letter dated 3 October 1888 from C. J. Denny, a medical officer in Farnborough, to the City Police accused Doctor Forbes-Winslow because his letter to the Globe showed signs of incipient insanity.[38] Lyttelton Stewart Forbes-Winslow was a psychiatrist who developed several theories about the Ripper's identity. Researcher Donald McCormick said that Winslow's ubiquity at the scene of the crimes caused detectives to check on his movements.[39]

A letter from the Rotherham Police dated 5 October 1888 claimed that a discharged soldier, James Oliver, had named a former colleague Dick Austin as the Ripper. They had served together in R. Troop in the fifth Lancers. Austin had been a sailor prior to joining the army. He would have been around 40 in 1888, five feet eight inches tall, powerfully built with light hair and eyes. A small piece had been bitten off the end of his nose. Oliver described him as a woman hater who had threatened to kill every whore and cut them inside out.[40] A further letter suggested that an application to the army would identify his place of discharge.[41]

Attestation records for the 5th Lancers, an Irish regiment, indicate that an R. Austin signed up in 1886.[42] However a James Oliver left the regiment on 19 May 1884.[43] Another Richard Austin who said that he was born St Giles, London, 1846, joined the Oxfordshire Light Infantry on 28 March 1864.[44] Naval records show a Richard Austin, born 20 September 1850 in Cushendall, Country Antrim, who signed up on 21 March 1865.[45] He was listed as a deserter in 1876.[46] Another Richard Austin appears in the 1881 census, as a prisoner in a Royal Military Hospital at Hougham, Kent. His birthplace is given as Tilbrook, Bedfordshire. Oliver stated that Austin had received twelve months for breaking into the orderly's room and tearing up his defaulters' sheets.

On 6 October 1888, W R Collett wrote to the police to accuse a man named Willie Boult who he had encountered at a boarding house in Hastings in July. Boult appeared deranged and carried a Gladstone bag containing a knife.[47] Aged about 30, he had left his employment with a firm of solicitors in London. His friends took him to live with his mother in Fulham.

Another letter of 6 October 1888 accused a Doctor Sass or Sassy who used to have a surgery in Abingdon Road, Kensington. He allegedly matched the description of a man seen by Alfred Bachert in the Three Tuns Hotel Aldgate on the night of the double event, about 23:53. Bachert, who later become chair of a Whitechapel Vigilance Committee, was in the public house when an elderly woman asked him to buy matches. He refused, and she left. A man standing nearby commented that those women were a nuisance. He then asked Bachert how old some of the women soliciting outside were. Bachert said that those who looked 25 were over 35. The man asked if a woman would go down an alley with him. Bachert thought she might so the man went outside and spoke to the woman selling matches. He gave her something and returned. Bachert left him at 00:10 and thought the woman was waiting. The man was dark, age 38, and five feet six to seven inches tall. He wore a black felt hat, a dark morning coat, and black tie. He carried a black bag.[48] In a different version, Bachert said he went with the man to Aldgate train station and parted there.[49]

The letter writer said that, of late, Doctor Sass had been loafing around like a tramp. He always carried a black bag and wore black gloves.[50] He was probably Dr Edwin Etty Sass, son of the artist, Henry Sass (1788-1844). He received his license for midwifery on 2 August 1858 and his address then was Henrietta Street, Brunswick Square.[51] In 1860, he assisted in the arrest of a pickpocket.[52] He married in Liverpool on 25 May 1867. An 1884 press account of a court case described Sass as a surgeon who said he had experience of dealing with insanity.[53] The medical directories for 1887 and 1895, give his address as 69 Gloucester Place, Marylebone. He does not appear in the directory for the years between these dates but gives his occupation as general practitioner in the 1891 census. There is no record of him at a surgery in Kensington. Sometime around 1894 he became bankrupt.[54] He died in 1902. The year prior to that he was living with his family in Wimbledon, still described as a surgeon.

In 1941, an article in a Canadian newspaper referred to a theory that Jack the Ripper was an eminent surgeon, Doctor Strauss, who disappeared just before the murders and roamed around with his scalpel.[55]

Henry Taylor, an Army Reserve Man appeared in court at Bow Street on 3 October 1888 charged with assaulting Mary Ann Perry and threatening to stab her. He then knocked her down and ran away, chased by a crowd calling him "Leather Apron." The magistrate sentenced him to two months imprisonment, giving him an alibi for the murder of Mary Kelly.

On 8 October 1888, Hans Bure, a well-dressed German, appeared at the Thames Police Court charged with assaulting Elizabeth Jennings of Duckett Street, Stepney. She refused to go with him, and he chased her. A mob gathered, calling him Jack the Ripper. He said he was drunk and took the woman to be a prostitute. The court fined him 40 shillings or a month's hard labour in default.[56]

A letter dated 9 October from W.J. Smith of 13 Red Lion Passage, Holborn, cast suspicion on an unnamed Hungarian anarchist and various people associated with him, and a man called Mac Sweeney who cost his father £600 for his education, some of it at University College Hospital. Four years earlier, he was in America.[57]

On 10 October 1888, the City Police received a letter from Mr J. Beckett, a barge owner and contractor who had studied a copy of the letter said to be from the Ripper and found the language and writing familiar. He identified James David Lampard as the person responsible. Lampard had been a frequent customer of his when he owned the Ram and Magpie public house in Shoreditch. Lampard spent time in America and had a good knowledge of anatomy. Beckett established that he was sent to a hospital as being

92

out of his mind and knew Whitechapel well.[58] His little finger was deformed, after he cut it with a knife. He was about five feet eight inches with the appearance of a military man, a red face, pointed moustache without whiskers and dark hair. He was last seen going through Fleet Street, Shoreditch, drunk on the previous Thursday night. He lived somewhere in that neighbourhood.

He was probably the James David Lampard born in 1850 in Stepney, the son of James Leonard Lampard and Elizabeth. At the time of the 1871 census, he was living as a student in Ramsgate. He travelled to America on the SS Egypt in 1872, returning some time before 1881 when he appears in the census in Hackney as a brick mould maker.[59] On 8 August 1888, he was admitted to the London Hospital suffering from Nervous Disease and released seventeen days later. His occupation at that time was commission agent and he lived at 28 Thorold Street, Bethnal Green.[60]

On 10 October 1888, the British ambassador in Vienna, Sir Augustus Paget, interviewed a man who said that he could find the Ripper.[61] Jonas claimed to be one of the chiefs of the Internationalist society and said that the killer was a former member of the society who had killed his mistress and child in New York. The published descriptions did not match the killer and Jonas did not think the man could write although he had an accomplice. Jonas wanted to go to London with a colleague and requested 2000 florins for the journey and expenses.

The ambassador advanced some money out of his own pocket, being told that the killer had worked as a butcher in San Francisco using the name Johann Stammer. John Kelly was his name in London. Aged 35-38 he was medium height with broad shoulders, strongly marked features, brilliant large white teeth, and a scar due to a stab under his left eye. He walked like a sailor having been a ship's cook for three years and was thought to be in Liverpool.[62] In further correspondence, Mr Paget reported a tale of fifteen to twenty terrorists expected in London. Jonas could only give information personally to detectives.[63] James Monro, Commissioner of the Metropolitan Police, replied on 2 January 1889 saying that he did not recommend any further expenditure.[64] The home office decided that the incident was a hoax and recommended reimbursing Paget.

In their book on Hertfordshire, murders Nicholas Connell and Ruth Stratton referred to a man who arrived in Harpenden in October 1888. He claimed to be a government surveyor called William Arthur Wills but also said that his name was Williams. He allegedly carried a selection of knives, was well versed in anatomy, and knew a lot about the murders. His landlord's daughter became convinced that he was the Ripper. He left without paying his bills.[65]

On 26 October 1888, a man called Crossley went to Mr Hallott's hairdressers in Hillsborough, Sheffield and purchased a walking stick. He said that his wife had travelled from Halifax three days earlier to see a daughter who was in the asylum. He then received a telegram saying that both were dead but had arrived too late to obtain a death certificate and needed somewhere to spend the night. Hallot offered him a bed. Mrs Hallot looked in the lining of his hat and found a letter signed by Jack the Ripper. Police Sergeant Hobson woke the man who asked, "Do you take me for Jack the Ripper?" He then admitted to having made up the story about his wife but said he needed to identify the body of his daughter and that he knew Ford who kept the Queen's Hotel. Ford subsequently identified him as an old acquaintance from Halifax. The police had no grounds to detain him and he spent the remainder of the night at the Queen's Hotel.[66]

W Cunliffe wrote to the City Police accusing H C Kromschroeder, a German of St Johns Wood who was a draughtsman and carried a knife.[67] He worked for Woodhouse and Rawsons, an electrical engineer, until midsummer 1888. Prior to leaving, he displayed a large knife to colleagues and said that he associated with prostitutes. He spoke of ripping up Frenchmen and loose women. His mother was English. He was born Christian Henry Kromschroeder in St. Georges, in 1859 and died in Bristol in 1923. In the 1891 census he is listed as an engineer, living with his wife, Harriet, and one-year-old daughter in Charlton.

A woman accused General Brown on the basis that he operated on horses for racing. Horrified she reached the conclusion that he was capable of anything. The police cleared him.[68] Another letter came from Sarah Franklin who wrote to the Lord Mayor, accusing John Davis, also known as Jack or Jacky and aged 60. He was staying with an old doctor in a village where she had previously lived. He once asked if she would look after his three children and housekeeper for a few weeks, which she did. His address was Oxford Street, Whitechapel. Subsequently it became clear that the man's wife had left him. Following the death of the doctor the man arranged the funeral then left. Franklin sent a second letter, giving the man's name as John Davies and enclosing a press cutting, which described an agricultural worker called John Davies, charged with begging in the Fulham Road. [69]

In 1911 a book by the wife of the editor of The Star, reported a suggestion that Charles Stuart Parnell was Jack the Ripper. One night Parnell visited fellow MP and journalist, Henry Labouchere, carrying a black bag and wearing a long rough overcoat and slouch hat. Labouchere joked that he was the Ripper.[70] In 1906, Labouchere said that he had advised Parnell to stay clear of the scenes of Jack the Ripper's exploits or he might be arrested on suspicion.[71] This was in a review of a book by Robert Anderson, the Assistant Commissioner of the Metropolitan Police CID at the time of the Ripper murder. He described Parnell as behaving suspiciously in prowling around at night and renting houses under assumed names. Anderson noted that the suspicions proved baseless and that

Parnell was just eccentric.[72] The first suggestion that Parnell was a suspect appeared in an anonymous letter sent to Colonel Fraser of the City Police in November 1888.[73]

Parnell was the founder and leader of the Irish Parliamentary Party. He was born on 27 June 1846 in County Wicklow, educated in England, and elected to the House of Commons on 21 April 1875. In 1877, he joined other Irish MP's in the policy of obstructionism, which involved making deliberately long irrelevant speeches to delay parliament. Two years later, he became president of the newly founded Irish National Land League. The principle was to enable tenant farmers to own the land they worked on. He was arrested in October 1881 after voicing opposition to the Land Act, introduced in April to provide a tribunal for the fixing of land rents, and not released until the following May.

On 18 April 1887, The Times concluded a series of articles on Parnellism and crime with a letter, supposedly from him on 15 May 1882, which condoned the Phoenix Park murders. Robert Anderson had contributed to the series of articles, although he made no allegations about the murders. On 8 July 1888, Parnell asked for an investigation. The parliamentary commission met 128 times, concluding in November 1889. The letter was shown to be false and Parnell accepted damages outside of court.

Henry Labouchere commented in his journal on 11 October 1888 that the handwriting of the Jack the Ripper letters resembled that of the Parnell forgeries, although he did not suggest that the forger was the murderer.[74] Parnell died in Brighton on 6 October 1891.

Officers from Woking Prison wrote to the Home Office in November 1888 suggesting that Louis Solomon was the Whitechapel killer.[75] An official noted that Solomon's was a normal criminal case. Louis Solomon was convicted on 15 September 1879 of raping a child and jailed for seven years.[76] He was 30 at the time of his conviction. In the 1881 census his occupation was given at iron riveter, and his place of birth as Poland.

On 13 November 1888, the City Police received a letter accusing William Onion.[77] The anonymous writer said that Onion had been in asylums at Colney Hatch and Wakefield twice. On release from Wakefield, he went to friends in Leicester then smashed a plate glass window in London and got twelve months. He had been out of prison long enough to do the last three murders.

William John Onion was born in Whitechapel on 24 December 1834. His father, William, died when he was very young. Between 1858 and 1896 he was said to have accumulated a thousand convictions. The most significant are summarised below.

On 22 June 1866, Onion assaulted a Police Officer, whilst drunk at the docks. Constable Brown warned him about the dangers of falling in and he responded by attempting to drown the officer, being hit with a truncheon. Inspector Ellis of the Dock Police said that Onion was frequently turned out of the dock and was violent when drunk.[78] It usually took five men to subdue him. Onion said that some time ago he suffered a fracture to his head and that, if he took a glass of rum, he was unconscious of what he was doing. The assistant judge, Mr Bodkin, sentenced him to nine months hard labour.[79]

In June 1870, he was sentenced to six months hard labour for attempting to commit suicide by strangulation. He had nearly succeeded in committing suicide on three or four previous occasions, each time being found black in the face.[80]

On 12 June 1874, he killed 52-year-old John Connor in a fight outside the Old Rose public house at 50 St George Street.[81] They were quarrelling in the house and the landlord, James Holmes, sent them outside. Connors struck Onion two or three times. Onion hit back, knocking Connors to the ground where his head collided with the kerb. When arrested Onion kissed the body and said he would be remanded for a week or two. Dr. Shapney, house surgeon at the London Hospital, found a bruise on the body that might have been caused by a fall on a kerbstone. There was a small fracture of the skull. Onion was convicted of manslaughter and sentenced to a month's imprisonment.[82]

The last of three arrests in June 1875 was for an assault on a park keeper. He had ventured into a restricted area at Victoria Park and ignored requests to leave. Eventually he was overpowered and strapped to a hand barrow. He was so violent that his boots were removed at the station. The police reported 30 previous convictions, including drunken and violent conduct, assaults, and wounding. He received two months hard labour.[83]

On 2 October 1877, he was charged with being drunk and disorderly, but proceedings took an unusual turn when a woman stood up in court and accused him of assault. Elizabeth Gawan married Onion on the morning of the arrest, 29 September. She said that he began to abuse her the moment they left the church and took up a knife saying that he would take the dross and deceit out of her. She fled, and Onion proceeded to smash her furniture. Her thirteen-year-old daughter said that he had pulled out one of her teeth and threatened to do the same to another sister. Another witness supported the story.

The couple met the previous July when Onion said that he had been a bad man but was converted by Ned Wright's mission. Wright was a reformed burglar turned preacher.[84] Onion, described as a 42-year-old traveller, said that the dispute arose because Gawan was receiving money from a gentleman, and complained that she had drunk brandy before the ceremony. She admitted receiving a pound a week.[85] He was ordered to pay a surety and keep the peace for three months.

On 30 December 1878 at the Thames Police Court he was charged with assaulting Agnes Pearson, whose father, William had taken him in out of charity.[86] They lived at 65 Silver Street, Stepney. Onion returned drunk, seized Agnes by the hair, and dragged her around the room. He also knocked several glasses off the table. The magistrate, Mr Saunders, sentenced him to fourteen days hard labour.

On 26 March 1879, he sought advice from the magistrate, claiming police harassment. He cited a letter from convicted killer, Charles Peace, describing him as a good friend. On 20 February 1879, five days before his execution Peace replied to a letter from Onion. It was addressed to 107 Jubilee Street. Inspector Woodley said that Onion always complained about the constable who arrested him and that his fears were groundless. Mr Saunders advised him to stay away from drink.[87] On 9 April, he was back before the same magistrate, charged with being drunk and incapable of taking care of himself. He complained that he had received the cold shoulder from his friends who thought that he had been on intimate terms with Peace and surrendered himself to the police station. Saunders fined him.[88]

Onion assaulted Police Constable George Carpenter in Cable Street on 7 December 1879, two days after he completed a month's imprisonment. It took four men to restrain him. He was returned to jail for a further fourteen days.[89]

On 8 August 1881, he assaulted Inspector James McCarthy of H Division. He had been arrested for striking a barber who refused to give him tobacco. He then damaged his cell at Shadwell Police Station. Mr Saunders sentenced him to two months hard labour.[90]

On 10 November 1881, he was charged with wilfully breaking one of the lamps outside Mansion House.[91] He threw his boots at the glass and was violent when arrested.[92] He was sent to the City asylum at Dartford and discharged on 16 May 1882.[93] The following day he appeared at the West Ham Police Court, charged with being drunk and riotous in Canning Town. It was reported that following his previous conviction an attempt had been made to send him to New York, with an unnamed doctor paying for his passage. On his way, he said that nobody could be redeemed without shedding of blood and that he intended to shed some.[94]

On 22 August, a day after leaving Homerton workhouse, he assaulted two police officers whilst drunk in Dock Street St Georges. Mr Saunders said that Onion had been brought before him several times. He recalled that, after a spell in the City of London infirmary, a subscription was raised to send Onion to Canada with an additional sum of money for him to spend there. Onion assaulted a policeman on the way to the boat and was returned to gaol. Saunders wished he could remand him for life, describing him as a disgrace to humanity.[95]

He was in Colney Hatch asylum from 22 December 1882 to 2 March 1883.[96] In September 1883, Onion received a month's hard labour for being drunk and using bad language in St Georges Street East.[97] He was again drunk and disorderly at Christmas that year, assaulting Police Constable Bickens in St Georges' Street. It took six constables to restrain him. Mr Saunders gave him two months hard labour.[98] Another conviction followed at the Thames Police Court in March 1884, following an assault on Police Constable George Cooper. Again, Mr Saunders punished him with hard labour.[99]

On 21 March 1887, described as aged 60, he was charged with being drunk and disorderly and assaulting Constable Mattie. Two days earlier, he was arrested for causing a disturbance outside a tobacconist's in Stepney. He attacked Mattie in his cell. The magistrate, Mr Saunders again, asked for an explanation and was not happy when Onion replied in verse. Two months hard labour was the sentence. In response, Onion said *"All right sir. The sun crosses the line today and it will be a bad omen for England. You will see a bad omen for England."*[100]

On 7 November 1887, he was indicted at the Middlesex sessions for maliciously breaking two windows worth seven pounds, the goods of Mr John, a licensed victualler. Onion said he had had nothing to eat for several days and deliberately broke the windows then gave himself up. On hearing that over two hundred previous convictions were proved against him the Assistant Judge sentenced him to twelve months with hard labour.[101]

His release date is unconfirmed as the discharge records for Pentonville prison in 1888 are no longer extant. We know he was in Pentonville because one of his fellow inmates was John Burns, a future MP, jailed for resisting police attempts to break up an unlicensed meeting in Trafalgar Square, the so-called Bloody Sunday.[102] Burns began a six-week sentence on 8 January 1888. According to Tom Cullen, Burns was himself stopped by the police one night and questioned about Jack the Ripper.[103]

On 19 November 1888, ten days after the murder of Mary Jane Kelly, William Onion was released from a charge of drunkenness by the Thames Police Court, He immediately proceeded to break the window of Shadwell Police Station and received a month's imprisonment.[104] The magistrate commented that the police knew him to be a dangerous man. A day after his discharge he was drunk and disorderly in Trinity Square, assaulting Police Constable Johnson. Described as a 60-year-old homeless labourer he said that he had been teetotal for the last five or six weeks. Hearing of sixty previous convictions the alderman sentenced him to 21 days hard labour.[105]

A further six months imprisonment followed after he assaulted a Police Officer on London Bridge on 10 August 1891.[106] The chief clerk commented that everything had been done to help Onion, including setting him up in business. On 29 October 1895, he was arrested by three constables in Shadwell. He said that when last arrested at that police station he was kept in a pool of blood for four hours and a policeman poked a lighted splint in his eye. The Reverend Hobbins, vicar of Christ Church, Stepney said he had encouraged Onion to go to Selby and hoped that he would end his days there, sending him money to help this happen. Convicted hundreds of times Onion had lost control of himself and was very dangerous. Hobbins would not be surprised if he ended up killing a constable.[107]

In January 1896, Onion received another month's imprisonment for drunkenness.[108]He claimed that, whilst in Selby workhouse, a nurse persuaded him to euthanize a patient and that this had been on his conscience ever since. The workhouse staff denied this and said that other inmates were afraid of him. They took in turns to stay awake and keep watch when he was in the house.[109]

On 4 April 1898, he was mentioned in a parliamentary debate about prison reform, with the question being asked what prison had done for William Onion, sent to gaol 175 times for drunkenness and assaulting police officers. He wrote to Mr John Burns, complaining that the injustice was shortening his life. Burns said that if Onion was maddened and brutalised much more by the prison authorities, he would become more dangerous. [110]

His last conviction was on 16 November 1898 back at the Thames Police Court, he received another month's hard labour for being drunk and disorderly.[111] The magistrate warned that from 1 January 1898, he would receive a year's imprisonment for these offences due to new legislation. [112]After his release, he reformed and became a temperance advocate, never drinking alcohol again. As well as receiving fame for his poetry, recited in the streets, he became a minor celebrity, with the press reporting his frequent visits to the Thames Police Court to report his progress. He died in 1916, with a brief obituary appearing in The Times.[113]

Accused after the Terror

Accusations from the public continued to come in after the death of Mary Kelly. Edward Knight Larkins, a customs clerk, had a theory that the murderer worked on a Portuguese cattle boat. He said the man arrived in London on the City of Porto on 30 August 1888, then City of Cork on 7 September and 27 September and 8 November. Larkins gave this information to Inspector Moore at Leman Street police station on 10 November 1888 and again two days later. He visited the CID, and Inspector Swanson took his statement on 13 November. The police noted that the Consul of Oporto said that no transfer between boats had occurred.[1]

In a letter dated 9 March 1889, Larkins named the cattlemen as Manuel Cruz Xavier and Jose Laurenco. In February 1892, he claimed that Xavier, age 37, killed Nichols and currently worked as a lighter man at Oporto. A third man, Joao de Souza Machado, age 41, arrived on the City of Cork with Laurenco, age 26. When the ship arrived again on 19 October 1888 Machado was no longer a cattleman and Laurenco had deserted. Two boats were in dock on the day of McKenzie's murder. Joachim da Rocha, age 23, was on board the Grebe, and was formerly a seaman with Xavier and Laurenco on the City of Oporto. Rocha was, at the time of the letter, a stevedore in Oporto.

Larkins sent descriptions of all the men, claimed to have identified the man who wrote the Ripper letters and spoke to the press.[2] He also met with the magistrate Montague Williams, who referred to the theory in his memoirs.[3] On 26 January 1893 Larkins claimed that the head of Criminal Investigation had deliberately connived at the escape of the men. Robert Anderson noted on 6 February 1893 that Larkins was a troublesome busybody whose theories had been tested and proved untenable and worthless.[4]

On 13 November 1888, Larkins accused Antoni Pricha of 11 Back Hill, Hatton Garden, because he answered the description of the murderer circulated in a newspaper.[5] Pricha, believed to be an Albanian national, worked as a model at the Royal Academy Piccadilly, and was at home on the night of Mary Kelly's murder.

Joseph Turner Ward appeared at Wakefield City Police Court on 16 November 1888. Formerly a clerk at Wakefield Borough Police Station, he had been acting as an insurance agent in Toronto. He faced a charge of running away and leaving his wife charged to the Wakefield Union. The Chief Constable made a statement about the rumour that Ward was the Ripper. Ward had arrived in Wakefield from America the previous Saturday, 10 November. This gives him an alibi. On the following Thursday, he made remarks about the Whitechapel murders whilst in Mrs Scowby's vaults. Some tradesmen believed that he was Jack the Ripper and reported their suspicions. Before this Clarkson received correspondence from 58 Kirkgate, which claimed to be from the Ripper. He sent Inspector Curtis and another officer to make enquiries and they found that a warrant had been out for Ward's arrest on the neglect charge since April 1885.[6]

On 15 November 1888 a prostitute, Mary Ann Johnson accosted Wolf Levisohn in Whitechapel. When he refused her advances, she and another woman, Christine de Grasse, began calling him "Jack the Ripper." Afraid of the crowd that assembled he went to Commercial Street Police Station. The women said that he looked like Jack the Ripper because he carried a shiny bag. The court fined them for the false allegation.[7] In 1903 a Wolf Levisohn gave evidence at the trial of George Chapman, a poisoner accused of being Jack the Ripper. In one of his books about Chapman R Michael Gordon speculated that Levisohn might have helped the Ripper.[8] This is based on a comment that some authors believe the Ripper had assistance and on Levisohn being present at important times in Chapman's life.[9]

On 19 November 1888 William Avenell and Frederick Moore appeared at the Marlborough Police Court, charged with assaulting Henry Edward Leake, an oil man from Gilbert Street. Leeke was drinking alone in a pub when someone accused him of being Jack the Ripper. Avenell and Moore followed him out and seized him. They dragged him back to the house of Madame Munz at 62 Berners Street, where he had recently delivered oil, to prove his identity. Avenell was acquitted of impersonating a police office. Both men were fined, with half the money going to Leeke.[10]

At Marylebone police Court on the same day James Bunyan, age 45, of Kensal Road was charged with being drunk and disorderly and with assaulting Gersie Somo. The crowd that saw him follow and attack Somo cried out that he was Jack the Ripper.[11] He was sentenced to fourteen days in jail. The magistrate remarked that there were so many similar instances that it was scarcely safe to walk the streets.

Another case heard on the same day illustrates this. Samuel Graham appeared at the Thames Police Court, charged with being a wandering lunatic. He had rushed at some people in the East India Road and behaved strangely. Inspector King stated that Graham had been wandering around for the last few days and had complained that people were following him. He had previously been charged on suspicion of being the Whitechapel murderer. He was sent to the workhouse and then on to Colney Hatch Asylum.[12] His age was given as 52 by the press report of the court appearance, and 50 by the note of his removal to the asylum, which states his profession as surveyor.

On Christmas Eve 1888, George Marsh visited the police to allege that a man named Stephenson was involved in the murders. He told Inspector Roots that they met a month earlier in the Prince Albert and had since encountered each other two or three times a week. Stephenson told Marsh that the murderer was a woman-hater who would induce a woman to go up a back street, or into a room, and would bugger her and cut her throat at the same time. His demonstration of the action convinced Marsh that he was the murderer in the first six cases, if not the last one. Stephenson then drew up an agreement to share any reward for giving information about Doctor Davies. Marsh felt that this secured a sample of Stephenson's handwriting. Stephenson sent him to see Doctor Davies and W T Stead, editor of the Pall Mall Gazette, with an article for which Stephenson expected £2. Stephenson had been paid £4 for an article about the Jews although Stead had refused to give him money to catch the murderer. [13]

Stephenson called on Roots on Boxing Day and made a statement about his suspicions of Doctor Davies. Roots had known Stephenson for 20 years and described him as a travelled man of education and ability, noting that he had been a candidate for the orphanage secretaryship at the last election.[14]

In his statement, Stephenson said that three weeks earlier he was a hospital patient in a private ward with a Doctor Evans, suffering from typhoid. Every night, Davies visited Evans and discussed the murders. Davies said that the murderer was a man of sexual powers, which could only be brought on by some strong stimulus, such as sodomy. At that time, Davies could not have known that semen was found up the woman's rectum, mixed with her faeces. Davies was a powerful man, and a woman-hater. One night, in front of five medicos, he took a knife, buggered an imaginary woman, cut her throat, ripped, and slashed in all directions in a frenzy. The editor of the Pall Mall Gazette, W. T. Stead, told Stephenson that the last murdered woman had been sodomized. Davies recently moved to Castle Street, Houndsditch and intended moving to Australia.[15] The statement was signed Roslyn D'O: Stephenson, with a postscript noting that he had shared this information with a pseudo-detective called George Marsh and agreed to share any reward.

Robert D'Onston Stephenson was born on 20 April 1841 in Sculcoates near Hull. He claimed to have studied Chemistry in Munich and to have served in Africa with Garibaldi's Italian army.[16] He was listed on the British Legion muster roll for that army in 1863 and in the 1861 census referred to himself as Lieutenant. He worked for Customs in Hull from April 1863 to 31 December 1868.[17]

On 14 January 1876, Stephenson married Anne Dreary, listed as his brother's servant in the 1871 census. At the time of the 1881 census, they lived in Islington. Stephenson described himself as Author, MD not practising and scientific writer on London Press.

From 26 July 1888 to 8 December 1888, he was a patient at the London Hospital, Whitechapel, suffering from neurasthenia.[18] On 16 October, he wrote to the City Police saying that the word Juwes in the Goulston Street Graffiti was actually Juives, the French word for Jews. He suggested that the killer was a Frenchman who had lived in the East End for years. The letter gave Stephenson's address as 50 Currie Wards, The London Hospital.[19]

On 1 December 1888, Stephenson wrote an article in the Pall Mall Gazette suggesting a satanic plan behind the killings and that the bodies lay alongside the lines of the cross.[20] He also said that there would be no further murders and repeated his suggestion that the killer was French because of the word "juives." This was challenged as being grammatically incorrect in a letter, signed by A Frenchman, published in the same newspaper on 6 December 1888. Stephenson also drew attention to a book on necromancy, recently translated into English, which listed body parts of a harlot as ingredients for spells. This reference is incorrect.[21] He claimed that nobody else had hit on the necromantic motive. Arthur Diosy subsequently contacted the Pall Mall Gazette to say that he had told the police of his belief in this theory on 14 October.[22]

Stephenson returned to the hospital in 1889, to receive treatment for chloralism. He was released eight days before the death of Alice McKenzie.[23] In the 1890s, he wrote several articles about black magic. They included claims to have visited the Cameroons, fifteen years before Western Explorers.[24] He wrote the Patristic Gospels in 1904, an English version of the gospels, as they existed from the second century AD. He died in Islington infirmary on 19 October 1916.

W T Stead stated in an introduction to one of Stephenson's works in 1896 that he had once regarded the writer as being Jack the Ripper and that the police had at least once arrested him for the crimes.[25] A later lover of Stephenson's, Mabel Collins, who also wrote about black magic, allegedly believed that he was the Ripper. She claimed to have lived with Stephenson and Baroness Vittoria Cremers in London and that the trio formed a cosmetic company. She died in 1927. Cremers told journalist Bernard O'Donnell in 1930 that Collins had suspected Stephenson of being the Ripper. Collins never revealed her reasons simply saying that it was *"Something he said to me,"* and *"Something he showed me."*[26]

Cremers found a small box containing blood stained ties in Stephenson's room. They were a few of the popular black ties. She did not remember how many.[27] In 1925, O'Donnell wrote articles for World Pictorial News about Betty May who had been influenced by the magician, Alastair Crowley. May said that, in Crowley's room, she saw a small black-enamelled tin box containing several old-fashioned ties. She asked Crowley, who never wore ties, about them and he told her that they belonged to Jack the Ripper.[28] May made the claim in her 1929 book Tiger Woman. Crowley noted in the margin of his copy of the book that it was Vittoria Cremer's story.[29]

Crowley told O'Donnell that he had destroyed the ties and that they came from a black magician who was Jack the Ripper and died around 1912-13.[30] Crowley also wrote about

Cremers, stating that she was an intimate friend of Collins. She professed devotion to Crowley, and he paid for her passage to England and installed her as a manageress. She divided her favours with a strange man who had been an officer in a cavalry regiment and a doctor but became dependant on her. This man claimed to be an advanced magician. This was at the time of the Ripper murders and there was a theory that the killer was performing an operation to obtain the Supreme Black Magical Power. Seven women had to be killed so that their bodies formed a Calvary cross of seven points with its head to the west. After killing the third or fourth victim, the killer obtained invisibility, a theory that Crowley believed because in one case a policeman heard the shrieks of the dying woman and found her alone in a cul-de-sac.[31]

According to Crowley, Collins' friend discussed the murder with her and Cremers, demonstrating how they might have been committed and saying that bloodstains could be hidden. Wanting to steal letters belonging to Collins, Cremers went into the man's room and found seven white evening dress ties, all stiff and black with clotted blood.[32]

O'Donnell said that Cremers found the letters and returned them to Collins who was too scared to approach Stephenson herself. When he discovered this Stephenson brought out a court case to recover them and lost.[33] Crowley said that, in 1913, he found evidence that Cremers had been embezzling money from him. [34] In a later essay, Crowley named Captain Donston as the friend of Collins, dismissed the idea of the pentagon, and reduced the number of ties found from seven to five.[35]

Cremers became convinced that Stephenson was Jack the Ripper. She told O'Donnell that she did not go to the police because of her religious beliefs and because Stephenson said there would be no more murders. Melvyn Harris outlined the case against Stephenson in three books.[36] Ivor Edwards also wrote a book accusing Stephenson, arguing that he selected the murder sites because of their geometrical alignment.[37]

In 2007 researcher Mike Covell obtained information from Jonathon Evans, curator of the London Museum hospital, which confirmed that Stephenson was in the Currie Ward of the London hospital at the time of the murders, although this had been deleted on the discharge papers and Davis substituted. Both wards were on the third floor and the seven feet high gates were locked at night.[38] Moreover, the hospital routine, involving breakfast at 06:00 would not have allowed D'Onston to kill Chapman and return in time.[39]

Stephenson told his story about Morgan Davies to Marsh, the police, and Vittoria Cremers. One night in July 1890, according to Cremers, Stephenson said that he knew Jack the Ripper. When he was in hospital for treatment due to the Chinese slug, he became friendly with a surgeon. This surgeon claimed to have killed the women from behind.

Morgan Davies was born in Whitechapel in 1853. His mother died when he was young, and he was brought up by his grandparents in Cardiganshire. He returned to his father's house to study medicine and, after a spell in Scotland, worked as a house surgeon at the London Hospital. He later practised medicine from 10 Goring Street, Houndsditch. In January 1885, he was elected president of the Cambrian Union of London.

He married a divorcee, Margaret Julian on 18 June 1890. His stepdaughter, Jano, married the Liberal Party Leader Clement Davies who allegedly compared Morgan's manner of conversation to Winston Churchill.[40] Morgan Davies died in Aberystwyth in 1920.[41]

A letter from the British Consul in Dresden, dated 11 December 1888, reported a statement from an American German, Julius I Lowenheim. Before the first murder, he became acquainted in a Christian home in Finsbury Square with a Polish Jew called Julius Wirtkofsky who consulted him on a pathological condition and said that he was determined to kill the person concerned and all her class.[42] Lowenheim claimed to have

110

contacted the police before, without receiving a response. Although there was a suspicion that he sought a journey to London the overall impression he made was not unfavourable.

A Julius Witkosky is listed in the 1900 Manhattan census as born Poland, Russia. He claimed to have moved to the United States in 1888 but gave New York as the birthplace of all his children, with the oldest being 15. Charles Van Onselen said that Joseph Lis had an accomplice called Wilf or Wulf Witkofsky.[43] The two worked together in South Africa in the 1890s.

On New Year's Eve 1888, Harriet Sinfield was charged at the Worship Street Police court with robbing a seaman named William Barrett at 19 George Street, Spitalfields. She claimed to have run away after Barrett told he was Jack the Ripper and meant to cut her up.[44] The magistrate, Montague Williams, ordered that she be remanded for enquiries, as she did not look sixteen but claimed to be 21.

On 5 January 1889, Police Constable James Farrow appeared at the Greenwich Police Court on a charge of assaulting Margaret Warren by kissing her on Christmas night. Warren had been walking home with a friend when she saw a man crouched in a dark corner. He jumped out and kissed her. He was then assaulted by Edward Isaac Smith, Warren's brother. Warren referred to Farrow as Jack the Ripper.

Home office files dated 12 March 1889 refer to a letter from A. H. Skirving of the Canadian Police saying that a man called Jack Irwin imprisoned in Chatham, Ontario, was the Ripper. He was not in England at the time of the murders.[45]

Robert Hiron was a shoemaker who committed suicide on 22 April 1889, by slashing his throat in the street. He had been an inmate of Edmonton workhouse where he earned the nickname "Mad Jack."[46] His sister testified at the inquest that the Ripper crimes had preyed on his mind.[47]

A hatmaker named Antonio Brisighkali or Busighkali, age 44, was acquitted of maliciously wounding on 12 June 1889. The wound was superficial. Busighkali claimed that he thought his victim was Jack the Ripper or a maniac and likely to do some serious mischief.[48] The victim was William M'Kellick, landlord of a public house in George Street, Borough, who refused to serve Brisighkali. Later Brisighkali returned to the house and was said to be carrying a revolver. M'Kellick and another man followed him. The revolver turned out to be a knife and M'Kellick was stabbed in the struggle.[49] Brisighkali or Busighkali was an Italian, who required an interpreter in court.

On 19 September 1889, Doctor Forbes Winslow was quoted in the New York Herald, and subsequently copied in British newspapers, with a theory about a lodger who had committed the crimes. On 30 August 1889, a man approached a woman in Worship Street Finsbury and offered to pay her to go down a court. She refused. Previously, on the morning of Alice McKenzie's murder, she saw him washing his hands at four o'clock. The man lived with a friend of Forbes Winslow 's who observed his strange behaviour. Winslow showed the reporter a pair of boots that had belonged to the lodger.

The suspect was G Wentworth Bell-Smith, a Canadian working for the Toronto Trust Society.[50] He lodged with a Mr and Mrs Callaghan at 27 Sun Street, Finsbury Square. Mr Callaghan described him as a religious fanatic who talked to himself, kept three loaded revolvers, stayed out late, and said that prostitutes should be drowned. On the morning after the Tabram murder, the maid found a bloodstain on Smith's bed and recently washed shirt cuffs. Callaghan told Forbes Winslow.[51]

On 23 September 1889, Chief Inspector Swanson visited Forbes Winslow in response to the press reports. Forbes Winslow said that the reporter had misrepresented his comments. He produced a pair of felt galoshed boots, common to Canada, and an old coat. The boots were moth-eaten. He had a statement from Mr Callaghan, dated 8 August

1889, which relayed the allegation against Wentworth Bell-Smith. Swanson noted that someone had changed the statement, specifically the date of a night when Wentworth Bell-Smith returned late from 9 or 7 August to make it fit with the night of Martha Tabram's murder.

Shortly after the murder, Wentworth Bell-Smith left the house. Callaghan claimed to have visited the police with his allegation in August. He also said that detectives visited to make inquiries about the same man, at the instigation of a lady on the Surrey side of the water. Swanson noted that Inspector Abberline had no record of receiving this information.[52]

The lodger may have been Henry Bellsmith. He was born in London on 3 September 1849 and had eleven siblings. He married Susannah Anne Sturch in 1871 and moved to Canada seven years later. The couple had five children and separated in 1888. Henry returned to England, leaving on 4 November 1888, five days before Mary Kelly died.[53] For the next few years, he travelled back and forth between England and New York. In 1897, he wrote a book, Henry Cadavere: A Study of Life and Death, a semi-fictional account.

Winslow stated in an interview with the New York Times in September 1895 and in his memoirs that he still believed this unnamed suspect to have been Jack the Ripper.[54] He added that the man had attempted suicide and been taken to an asylum. Winslow also stated that he had traced the Ripper from lodgings to lodgings. After each murder, the man changed lodgings and Winslow received pieces of ribbons and feathers from his victim's hats. The police refused to cooperate when he offered to catch the Ripper on the steps of St Paul's cathedral one Sunday.[55]

Herbert Percy Edmund Freund was born in London in 1855, the son of physician, Jonas Freund. He had eight siblings. As Percy Herbert Edmund Freund, he graduated with a second-class degree in 1873. He believed that he was the prince of Israel and destined to rule over the Jews.[56] In 1882 shortly after his release from Stone asylum, he was charged with causing a disturbance and returned to the asylum, described as a medical student.[57] In March 1883, he received a month's imprisonment for preaching outside St Paul's Cathedral and refusing to go away.[58] He was charged with the same offence in June that year and, again in October, when he began brawling in the cathedral during a service.[59] He was arrested on Christmas Eve 1884 for causing a disturbance by the Royal Exchange. The magistrate decided to spare him jail.[60] The following year he received two months in jail for being disorderly in the churchyard during the funeral of the Lord Mayor.[61] On 29 September 1887, he was charged with being disorderly in the synagogue in Great Portland Street but was released after promising to behave, and with the support of the congregation.[62] On 24 October that year, he received a fine for disorderly conduct in the Strand.[63]

His whereabouts in 1888 are unknown. On 21 April 1889, he again interrupted a service in St Pauls and became violent in court, throwing a glass bottle at a window.[64] He received four months imprisonment.[65] The 1891 census lists him at an address in Primrose hill. By 1901, he had moved to at 111 Cornwall Road, Brixton Hill, selling Christian literature.

On 27 July 1889, the Spectator published an article about an unnamed journalist for the New York Herald whose investigations into Jack the Ripper led to a sailor. Albert Bachert received a letter from Jack the Ripper. It was headed The Eastern Hotel Pop with the rest of the word scratched out.[66] Assuming it meant Poplar the reporter found the Eastern Hotel, Limehouse where an inmate said that a previous inmate, Cornwall, had behaved suspiciously and dressed in disguise at the time of the murders. Armed with a replica of the letter's handwriting, from Bachert's memory as he had destroyed the

114

original, the reporter tracked down a captain of Cornwall's former ship. He ascertained that this ship was in dock at the time of the Smith and Tabram murders. The handwriting matched, and a photograph compared favourably with witness descriptions of the Ripper. Enquiries to the board of trade revealed that Cornwall was aboard the Ben Lomond, which sailed for China on 14 October 1888.[67]

On 13 October 1889, a mob accused Edward Hamblar, a 61-year-old ship's joiner, who was wearing women's clothing in Burnley Street, Ratcliffe.[68] He was bound over to keep the peace.

On 14 October 1889 H. T. Haslewood of White Cottage, High Road, Tottenham said he had information incriminating Sergeant T Thick, also known as Johnny Upright.[69] It has been suggested that Upright was a term used to describe policemen in the pay of criminals but Walter Dew, a contemporary who served with Thick, said the nickname was due to him being upright in walk and methods.[70] The Police noted that the accusation was rubbish, perhaps prompted by spite. Thick was born in Dorset in 1845 and served in the Metropolitan police between 1868 and 1893. Haslewood was a law clerk.[71]

On 19 March 1893, the press reported that a New York woman was ripped up her side. The knife was left in the wound and traced to Frank Castellano, an Italian Barber, who had been a fireman on board a trans-Atlantic steamer.[72] He was also rumoured to have been implicated in the murder of Carrie Brown.

On 28 May 1894, the steamer Paraguay arrived in Dunkirk from Buenos Aires. One of the passengers was arrested on suspicion of having murdered a woman in the Argentinian city and the Press described him as Jack the Ripper. Claims that a body was in his luggage proved false but large amounts of currency were found. His name was variously cited in the press as Jean Templier, Templier, Tremblier, and Frenther. He was said to be 29 and from Bordeaux.[73]

Some contemporary police documents were kept in the archive of the Metropolitan Police Special Branch, listed as the Chief Constables CID Register "Special Branch" (1888-1892) and the Metropolitan Police Ledgers "Special Account" in three volumes (1888-1912). The register functioned firstly as a register of correspondence sent to Special Branch by the rest of the Metropolitan Police, other Police Forces, the Home Office, other government departments, and members of the public.[74] The Special Accounts listed, amongst other things, cash payments to individual informers.[75]

Two entries from the police information in the Chief Constable's register, referred to a William McGrath. The first reads Mc Grath, William, suspicious Irishman at 57 Bedford Gardens. Underneath it says Mc Grath, William, said to be connected to Whitechapel murders."[76] The Post Office Directory for 1889 lists a painter named William Magrath, and several artists at that address.[77]

Magrath was born in Cork on 20 March 1838 and moved to America in 1855, becoming a sign painter in New York. He opened a studio in 1868, painting scenes of Irish rural life. In 1874, he was elected an associate of the National Academy. Between 1879 and 1883, he lived in England. He was also there at the time of the Whitechapel murders, leaving on the Egypt, which arrived in New York on 22 December 1888.[78] He died on 13 February 1918, in London.

Another entry from Chief Inspector Littlechild, who oversaw Special Irish Branch, read Suspect O' Brien and the Whitechapel Murders. Trevor Marriott connected this to William O'Brien, the Member of Parliament who was involved in the Fenian movement.[79] O'Brien was a journalist, born in Mallow, County Cork on 2 October 1852. He edited the land league newsletter, United Ireland, from 1881. In that year, he was jailed with Charles Stuart Parnell. He was elected as MP for Mallow in an 1883 by-election, and later represented Tyrone South, North East Cork, and Cork City. He withdrew from politics following the 1918 general election and died at the Belgravia Hotel, in London on 25 February 1928.

Another entry in the Chief Constables Register read, "Jack the Ripper, the name given to Wilson at Bushmills." Bushmills is a small village in Northern Ireland with a large whisky distillery. Trevor Marriott connected this suspect to one called James Wilson, arrested for indecent behaviour in Belfast on 26 November 1888.[80] This Wilson was a travelling singer from Wicklow, who allegedly threatened to cut the throats of two children, claiming that he was the Ripper. James Wilson was an alias of John Alexander Fitzmaurice. On 16 March 1889, Fitzmaurice was remanded in Wicklow for enquiries. Claiming to be a native of Cardiff, he told police that he was Jack the Ripper and gave them a list of murders he had committed in London and elsewhere. Later he revised this to say that he only killed once, Mary Jane Wheeler in 1886 or 1888. Information from Cardiff Police that Fitzmaurice could not have been involved in the Ripper murders led to his discharge.[81] .

The final entry of note in the Chief Constable's register regarded a Mr Churchill, or possibly R. Churchill, described as Perpetrator of the Whitechapel Murders. Lord Randolph Churchill, father of Winston, was linked to the crimes by researchers as part of a wider conspiracy theory discussed later in this book but we cannot say if this is the same person.

Mad Confessions

A surprisingly high number of men accused themselves of being the Whitechapel murderer or used the name Jack the Ripper to intimidate potential victims. Eighteen-year-old Joseph Woods faced charges of assaulting a woman named Eleanor Candey. She testified that he, and another man, had seized her in the street shortly after midnight on 11 September 1888 and produced a knife. She asked if he was one of the Whitechapel men and he confirmed this. She then blew a whistle and the police came to her assistance. The arresting officer said that Woods admitted telling Candey he was the Whitechapel murderer but denied assaulting her. The charge was dropped, but Woods was bound over to keep the peace.[1]

Shortly before midnight on 24 September 1888, John Fitzgerald entered the charge room at Wandsworth Police Station and confessed to Inspector Blakemore that he had murdered Annie Chapman. He was a stranger to the area and unknown to the police. Earlier that evening he had been drinking in public houses. The press claimed that he had first confessed to a private individual who informed the police and they discovered him in a common lodging house in Wandsworth. He had previously lived at Hammersmith. [2] Another newspaper reported that Chapman was seen in Wandsworth the night before her body was found and Fitzgerald's statement was investigated.[3]. It was claimed in a Swedish pamphlet that John Fitzgerald had visited a pathological museum and medical conventions, saying that he needed to procure uteri for research.[4] The police cleared him.

In the early hours of 2 October 1888, a 52-year-old tailor called Augustus Nochild of 86 Christian Street met a prostitute, named in some papers as Sarah Mc Farley, in Holborn and asked her to go to his house. She refused. He then seized her by the throat and said he would kill her and that he had killed others in Whitechapel. She screamed, attracting the attention of a Police Sergeant. Hearing that both were under the influence of alcohol, the magistrate dismissed the case.[5] The Star described him as a portly German.[6] He was not carrying a knife.

A 27-year-old man called William Bull entered Bishopsgate Police Station on 3 October 1888 and admitted killing Catherine Eddowes. He claimed to be a medical student at the London hospital, but the police found no trace of him there. In the 1881 census his occupation was given as cellar warehouseman. His father, William Bull, said that he had been asleep at their home in Dalton at the time of the murder.[7] He received a severe caution.[8]

Alfred Napier Blanchard appeared before the Birmingham Police Court on 6 October 1888, charged on his own confession with committing the Whitechapel murders. He was a 34-year-old canvasser, residing in the Handsworth district of the city. He entered the Fox and Goose public house in Newtown Row at 11:00 the previous day and stayed there for nine hours, drinking about five half-pints of ale. He asked the landlord about the capabilities of the Birmingham detectives and was told that they were very smart. He then remarked that it would be funny if a murder was committed in Birmingham and told another customer that there was a murderer in the house. This led to a discussion in which he said that he had committed six murders in London and invited his fellow drinkers to claim the reward for his apprehension. He told the court that he was working for a London firm and had been in the North of England. He had been under great excitement at the time of the confession. When pressed he admitted that he had been drinking for three days. Anxious to keep the matter out of the press he offered to provide character references.[9] The police received a telegram from their Manchester colleagues which said that Blanchard had been living there for the last two months and was addicted to drink and very excitable. He was released, after a weekend in custody.[10] Census records indicate that he was born in the Manchester suburb of Chorlton, circa 1855. An Alfred Blanchard, age 37, died in Camberwell in 1892.

On 8 October 1888, William Stanley appeared at the Oldbury court, charged with assaulting Mary Ann Hill, two days earlier. He caught hold of her, pulled her about, and said he was Jack the Ripper. Stanley, described as a 35-year-old furnace man, said that she had approached him and made indecent proposals. The magistrate accepted his argument and dismissed the case.[11]

On 10 October 1888, a 42-year-old commission agent, Frederick White, approached Mary Ann Galling at Moorgate Railway Station and said, "*I will rip you up. I am Jack the Ripper. If I don't do it now I will know you again.*" She ran to Police Constable Stringer who apprehended White. He was fined ten shillings.[12]

On 15 October 1888, John Williams appeared before Chorley magistrates. He had produced a knife in The Kings Arm's public house on the previous Saturday night, boosting that he was the Whitechapel murderer and had killed four women. An itinerary found on him showed that he had recently travelled in London and the Eastern counties.[13] The outcome of his case is unknown.

John Murray said he was Jack the Ripper during an argument with a ticket collector at Bowes Park Station. He also assaulted the collector, George Croxford. In his defence, he said he had been searching for his lost boy, had drunk too much, and fallen asleep which made him miss his stop at Kings Cross. He was fined, with fourteen days imprisonment in default.[14]

On 21 October 1888 Henry Skinnerton, described as a 50-year-old labourer from High Street Chingford, seized Henry Corney by the throat, saying that he was Jack the Ripper and had also killed a woman in Hatton Gardens. Pursued by Corney and a friend to a house owned by John Cricks, he broke some glass. Previously of good character, he was fined and ordered to pay damages with the court costs or go to prison for fourteen days with hard labour.[15]

On the same day, John Foy walked around Tilston village in Cheshire throwing stones at people. He stopped several women, saying he was Jack the Ripper, and carried a clasp knife.[16] He was an Irish labourer who said that he had been involved in various military campaigns. The magistrate ordered him to pay costs and censured him for disgracing his uniform.[17]

On 25 October 1888, 42-year-old Benjamin Graham was charged at the Guildhall on his confession of being the Whitechapel murder. He was described as a glass blower of 14 Fletchers Row, Clerkenwell. On 17 October, he was taken to Snow Hill Police Station by a man who said that he had confessed. Detective Constable Rackley asked if he had anything to say. He replied that he did kill the women and would have to suffer with a bit of rope.[18] The Alderman remanded him, for further inquiries. A week later, he was found to have no traces of insanity but drank heavily.[19] The Alderman regretted that he did not have the power to send him, and other such persons, to jail.

On 11 November 1888, the police arrested a man on the corner of Wentworth Street and Commercial Street in Whitechapel. His face was blacked, and he allegedly proclaimed himself the Ripper. In custody, he said that he worked at St George's hospital and gave the name of a physician there. Aged 35, he was five feet seven inches tall with a dark complexion and moustache and wore glasses. He had a double peaked light check cap in his pocket. His name was Holt and he had a residence at Willesden.[20] He wore a disguise to catch the Ripper. Telegrams from friends confirmed his identity and ensured his release. He may have been the William Holt who qualified as a doctor in 1881 and is listed at St George's Hospital in the 1887 medical directory.[21]

In 1935 Edwin T Woodhall, described a man with a blackened face who was an amateur detective chased by a mob and arrested in November 1888. Woodhall claimed the man's body was found in the Thames near Waterloo pier and that a retired police sergeant from H Division showed him a photo of the corpse.[22] Waterloo Pier was a popular place for suicides with an average of 30 each year in the mid nineteenth century.[23]

On 12 November 1888, at midnight, John Avery was taken into custody at Kings Cross Road Police Station. Two witnesses said that Avery confessed to the murders. His statement proved satisfactory, but he received fourteen days hard labour for being drunk and disorderly.[24]

On 14 November 1888, John Benjamin Perryman, a 40-year-old hairdresser known as the mad barber of Peckham was arrested in the Old Kent Road for being drunk and disorderly. He declared himself Jack the Ripper, accosted several women, and exhibited a black bag. The bag contained two pairs of scissors, a dagger, a sheath, and a life preserver. When asked to account for these he said he was going to have then ground. His sister testified that he had been intoxicated for some time and carried a dagger. He lived in Pennethorne Road, Peckham. He was remanded, with a warning that he might be sent to an asylum.[25]

He may be the man reported in other newspapers as leaving a shiny black bag in the Thomas a Beckett pub in Old Kent Road on 14 November 1888. The bag contained a sharp dagger, a clasp knife, two pairs of long and curious looking scissors, and two life preservers. The man was arrested leaving a pawnbroker's shop.[26]

Perryman was born in Rotherhithe in 1848, the son of John and Eliza. He married Sarah Ann Golding on 3 March 1872. The couple appear in the 1881 census at 4 Middle Street, Peckham. No children of the Perrymans' were listed, but a James Benjamin Perriman was baptised on 19 August 1877 with parents John and Sarah.[27] Perryman

122

unsuccessfully filed for divorce on 18 July 1884.[28] The death of a John Benjamin Perryman was registered in Croydon in the September quarter of 1889.

On 19 November 1888, John McCarthy appeared in court charged with robbery and violence. He and four other unknown men were accused of stealing five shillings from Michael Hertzberg, named as Ladsburgh in some press reports. Hertzberg, whose address was 3 Well Street, had been drinking in the Golden Lion public house when McCarthy asked if he was Jack the Ripper. He said he was then the men attacked him and stole the money. A barmaid named Florence Murphy said Hertzberg had entered the pub saying that he was Jack the Ripper and could prove it. She did not believe him. McCarthy was acquitted.[29]

In Wrington, Somerset, a 33-year old-painter, John Lewis, was indicted for assaulting two policemen, and a labourer. On 19 November 1888, he had been wandering the streets, calling himself Jack the Ripper. Acting Sergeant Cook spoke to him. The following day Cook went to Lewis's house after he threatened to stab his wife. Cook chased Lewis upstairs and Lewis slashed at his throat. Cook recalled prosecuting him on previous occasions, mostly recently for attempted suicide that July when he was sentenced to six months imprisonment. This was reduced to three, but still means that he was in prison when some of the Whitechapel murders occurred. Lewis received twelve months hard labour for the assault on Cook.[30]

The City Press reported, on 24 November 1888, the arrest of a 40-year-old man, Benjamin Isaacs, who said he was the Whitechapel murderer and threatened to rip up a woman on an omnibus. He boarded the bus two days earlier at Highgate and made the comment at London Bridge. When arrested he told Police Constable Coots that he was Jack the Ripper and became disorderly.[31]

George Pierilli, a 20-year-old Italian of 8 Fleet Row Holborn, was convicted of being drunk and disorderly in Farringdon Road on 7 December 1888. He stripped to the waist shouting, "I'm Jack the Ripper and will do for some of them." He had a previous conviction for assault and was jailed for a fortnight.[32] He is probably the George Pierelli who, at the age of 18, was acquitted on 12 September 1887 of raping Florence Louisa Platt.[33]

On 7 December 1888, John Tyson was indicted for stealing a pair of boots from outside a shop in High Street Tooting. When arrested he said he was Jack the Ripper and threatened to kill the constable. He claimed to be the champion fighter of the world and received seven days hard labour.[34]

On the same day William James assaulted and killed a man called William Hall. The victim was walking with a colleague at 00:25 when they found a young woman crying in Marshalsea Road. She complained that a man had insulted her. James came up and hit Hall then ran off. Several people chased him, and the police were informed. He returned and struck Hall again, knocking him onto the kerb. He was quickly arrested and considered sober. Inspector Marriott said that the police knew the accused who claimed to be a costermonger. The arresting officer, Police Constable Sutherland, said that James said he was Jack the Ripper, but he took no notice of this. James was charged with wilful murder.[35] Described as a 32-year-old leather worker he was committed for charge at the Old Bailey.[36] The charge was reduced to manslaughter and James changed his plea to guilty after hearing the evidence. He received a year's hard labour. A previous conviction for assaulting the police was noted.[37]

At Dalston Police Court on 22 December 1888 Theophil Hanhart, age 24, was charged with wandering whilst of unsound mind at Haggerston the previous day. He told Police Constable Whitfield that he had committed the Whitechapel murders. Reverend Mathias said that the prisoner had been in his employment as a language master since September 16 that year at a school near Bath. Suffering from delusions, he was brought to London on 20 December 1888 for a change. He was remanded to Shoreditch infirmary.[38] Inspector Reid was said to be satisfied of his innocence.[39] The 1891 census lists him as Theophile Hanhart, a Swiss national and patient at Bethnal House lunatic asylum. He died in Uxbridge in 1900.

On 2 January 1889 William Petitt, a builder, had to choose between a fine of fourteen shillings or a fortnight's jail, for chasing some boys and saying he was Jack the Ripper.[40] In June that year eighteen-year-old, John Davies, marked his arrival in Alfreton from Wales with a charge of being drunk and disorderly. He had brandished a knife in front of several women, said he was Jack the Ripper, and acted violently. He was jailed for fourteen days.[41]

William Wallace Brodie confessed to killing Alice McKenzie. On 7 May 1877, he was sentenced to fourteen years for theft under the name Broder, which seems to be a spelling mistake.[42] His age was given as 20 and he was recently discharged from the army. Released from prison early, he sailed on the SS Athenian on 6 September 1888 to Kimberley via Southampton and returned on 15 July 1889.[43] This gives him an alibi for the earlier murders. Evidence accumulated by the police suggested that he was addicted to drink. He slept at 2 Harvey Buildings Strand on the night of McKenzie's murder but denied this.[44] On 27 July 1889, he appeared at the Thames Police Court when he was released and immediately rearrested on a charge of obtaining a gold watch with intention to defraud. Back in court, he said that he was there for the murder of Alice McKenzie.[45]

On 17 October 1889, William Sheals approached four women in the Thames Police Court district and told them he was Jack the Ripper. He then kicked a constable who tried to remonstrate with him.[46] The same month in Beverley William Jones, a repulsive looking man who said he came from Wrexham was charged with being drunk and disorderly and assaulting a girl called Annie Park, and stealing a brass table bell from the Rose and Crown Inn. He had gone to a shop owned by the girl's father, said he was Jack the Ripper, used bad language and threatened to rip her up. Superintendent Knight said several young people had been alarmed in a similar fashion. Jones was sent to prison for six weeks.[47]

William Gilbert was charged with being drunk and disorderly in Piccadilly on the morning of 3 August 1889. Several women said that he called himself Jack the Ripper. He also carried a knife. The case was adjourned, due to Gilbert's insistence that he was not drunk at the time of the offence. The magistrate wanted the arresting inspector to testify.[48] The outcome is unknown.

James Glen, charged with killing his wife, in Glasgow kept shouting that he was "Jack the Ripper" whilst being taken from his cell to the Sherriff's room.[49] On 27 December 1889, he was found not guilty of murder on the grounds of insanity and sentenced to be detained at her majesty's pleasure.[50] Glen was a 29-year-old cabinetmaker who lived with his wife, Elizabeth, at 245 High Street, Glasgow. Just before the murder, he was treated in the infirmary for an illness brought on by dissipation. On 10 November 1889, he stabbed Elizabeth more than 40 times whilst their eight-month old son was in the room.

At the Thames Police Court on Saturday 28 December 1889 Henry Denker, age 34, was charged with assaulting a police officer and Thomas Taylor. When the constable asked him his name Denker replied, "Jack the Ripper" and became violent. He received seven days hard labour.[51] He is probably the Henry Denker who appears in the 1871 census as the twelve-year-old son of 67-year-old Rebecca Vas, living in Whitechapel.

In March 1890, John Henry Thompson alias John Henry Jones, a 36-year-old painter was indicted on two counts of sacrilege. He confessed to murdering a soldier by pushing

126

him in the lake and to various thefts from churches in Tottenham, Kentish Town, and elsewhere. He wanted to sign his confession Jack the Ripper, but Superintendent Walker would not allow this.[52]

In April 1890, Charles Corbett appeared at Marlborough Street Police Court accused of threatening a postman, Albert Hearn, with a knife. He apparently said, "*I am Jack the Ripper and mean to have blood tonight.*" Corbett was a French polisher, with a history of drunkenness, and delusions. He had twice abandoned his wife and five children.[53] He was living at 163 Wardour St, St James at the time of the 1881 census, aged 26. He may have been the Charles Corbett who married Mary Ann Shaw in Willenhall on 5 June 1876.

On 11 April 1890, the Fresno Republican Weekly reported allegations by Jennie Sweet, owner of a boarding house in the city. She said that a man named Charles Bond called to visit her cook and they had an argument. When Mrs Sweet intervened, Bond assaulted her and said he was Jack the Ripper.[54]

In August 1890, a labourer named Samuel Scar was sent to jail for fourteen days for being drunk and disorderly. He had approached a woman, Mrs Yates, in Whitehall with an open knife in his hand and said, "I'm Jack the Ripper and will rip you up."[55]

In September 1890 a discharged soldier, Charles McClintock was committed to trial for stabbing a prostitute, Amelia Lewis, with a penknife in Falmouth. They had drunk beer together, but he then accused her of stealing fifteen shillings, hit her and stabbed her in the lip whilst stating that he was Jack the Ripper.[56]

On 10 March 1891, John Hill, a 31-year-old ship's fireman, attacked a laundress named Elizabeth Tilley in Bromley. She was walking home along the Old Brunswick Road when Hill ran out from a dark passage. He threw her to the ground and stuck a handkerchief in her throat. He said "Jack," and threatened to use his knife. A man witnessed part of the assault but did not intervene. Hill was found by a constable, in possession of a parcel that Tilley had dropped. He resisted arrest.[57] Convicted of assault with intent to ravish he was sentenced to a year in jail with hard labour.[58]

On 14 September 1891, James Malone appeared at St Helens Police Court after a policeman discovered him wandering in a strange manner at 03:00. He had a sister, living in Tontine Street, who was afraid of him because he had a habit of throwing knives around and calling himself Jack the Ripper. He was a sailor, who had been in an asylum and suffered from sunstroke whilst in India. He was sent to the workhouse for two weeks.[59]

On 3 June 1892, a man named Gee, described as powerful looking, tried to stab women with a clasp knife in Gloucester whilst saying he was Jack the Ripper.[60] This may have been the last such incident in Britain. The last globally was in 1905 when Charles Y Hermann told the Tombs Police Court in New York that he wished to unburden himself of the murders. He claimed to have been born in Cairo, with an Egyptian mother and a father who was a non-commissioned officer in the British Army. Fifteen years earlier, he was living in Whitechapel and possessed by an evil spirit. The police believed him to be suffering from hallucinations.[61] Doctor Forbes Winslow told the Press that Hermann could be his lodger suspect.[62]

False Confessions

We now move away from those accused at the time of the murders to consider alleged confessions made later. In August 1896, James Everard Brame, the son of a surgeon at Lowestoft said that in October 1894 he was steward on a coal and saltpetre boat, the Annie Spear, between South Shields and Iquique. A man called Anderson was also on board. Both were ill in hospital in Iquique and there, Anderson confessed to the Whitechapel murders. He was a cook on a weekly boat between London and Rotterdam, committing the crimes on the days between sailings. He wore a butcher's smock to escape to lodgings in Bromley and was motivated by revenge after a woman robbed him. He died in Iquique. [1]

Two months later Brame gave more details to the press, describing Anderson as about 38, fair with red-hair and smallpox marks on his face. He said that Anderson's illness grew progressively worse, until he was diagnosed as being in the last stages of consumption. Brame suffered from diabetes. They were patients together, sometime after April 1895. Anderson said that he had obtained a knowledge of surgery when working as a hospital assistant in the US navy. He gave up his shipping job to commit the murders and had an accomplice who helped him change his clothes. [2] Interviewed by the Canberra Times in 1927, Brame accepted the possibility that the man had been recounting stories from the press. [3]

On 6 December 1897, the Galveston Daily News printed a variant. A sea cook, John Long, claimed that he and John Sanderson were on the crew of the Annie Laurie sailing from Shields to Iquique. Sanderson was hospitalised in Iquique and put in the bed next to Long. He confessed to both Long and a priest, saying that he was the son of a surgeon and knew how to handle a knife. One night he killed a woman in Whitechapel and developed

a taste for these murders. He had an accomplice, and both wore smocks. Subsequently he

worked on a country farm before returning to the sea and sailing again on the Annie

Laurie. The reporter doubted the truth of this story, due to Long's request for money.[4]

Leonard Matters developed the revenge theory in an article in The People on Boxing

Day 1926, followed by a book in 1929.[5] His suspect, referred to as Doctor Stanley, was a

Harley street surgeon whose son contracted syphilis from Mary Kelly and died. Stanley

attacked prostitutes, collecting the organs for his private collection, and trying to locate

Kelly. When Catherine Eddowes told him Kelly's address, he was able to claim his

revenge. He died in a Buenos Aires hospital of cancer in the 1920s. Matters worked as the

editor of a newspaper in Buenos Aires and claimed to have found the confession of

Doctor Stanley published in a local Spanish paper. A surgeon living in the city received a

letter from Jose Riche, senior house surgeon, summoning him to the deathbed of Stanley,

his former teacher. Stanley then confessed. According to Matters, he also confessed to a

seventeen-year-old girl who contacted Matters after the publication of his article and said

that she met a man at the Café Monico in Shaftesbury Avenue on several occasions

during 1888. He once teased that he was Jack the Ripper. Matters referred to her as Mrs

North.

In 1989, a priest Alfred MacConastair told Juan Jose Delaney that a former chaplain of

the British Hospital in Buenos Aires heard the confession of a man of another faith, on his

deathbed, in the 1920s.[6] John Taylor Sullivan, an actor and theatrical manager, who

played alongside Richard Mansfield in the Broadway and London productions of Dr

Jekyll and Mr Hyde, said that the murderer was a physician who developed a homicide

mania. He was confined in a private sanatorium in London then escaped to Buenos Aires,

where he was safe because no extradition treaty existed.[7] Dr E, as Sullivan named him, was under close supervision in Argentina. Britain signed an extradition treaty with Argentina on 22 May 1889.

There is a report that Jack the Ripper owned Sally's Bar in Buenos Aires. Mr Barca of Streatham wrote to Dan Farson in the 1970s saying that he lived in Buenos Aires between 1910 and 1920. He was told that the bar was named after Sally, a young girl brought over by Jack in 1889. She eventually settled in Paris, but the inference was that Jack was alive in 1919.[8] This bar was near the port and frequented by sailors and people of ill repute. Historian Enrique Mayochi has confirmed that there was a Sally's bar near the port.[9] A bar or cafe called Jack the Ripper is still in the city, at Libertad 1275.

The story of Stanley's confession appeared in some Australian newspapers in 1925, with claims that it was recently published in a Buenos Aires newspaper. In these accounts, the surgeon who heard the confession was named as H. Maris.[10] He kept his secret for many years, implying that the date of Stanley's death was some years earlier. There was a doctor called William Marris who studied in London and qualified in 1889.[11]

In 1972, following a television interview where Colin Wilson asked two authors their views on the Ripper, Mr A. L. Lee wrote from Torquay to Wilson, saying that he believed he knew the Ripper's identity and that his father had worked at the City of London mortuary at the time of the murders. When Wilson replied a second letter from Lee said that his father's immediate superior was the City of London coroner, Dr Cedric Saunders. Saunders had a special friend called Doctor Stanley who visited the mortuary once a week. One day Stanley told Saunders that the cows had got his son and that he would get even. Soon afterwards the murders started. Stanley continued to visit the mortuary until the murders ceased. Mr Lee senior asked Saunders if Stanley would visit again. Saunders said "no" and, when pressed, said he believed that Stanley was the Ripper. Mr Lee junior recalled reading in "The People" in 1920 that a Dr Stanley believed to be Jack the Ripper

131

had died in South America.[12] Matters made it clear Stanley was not the doctor's real name. He also said that Kelly and Stanley's son met after the 1886 boat race. None of the victorious Cambridge team are known to have died in the following two years.

James Maybrick was a cotton merchant resident in Liverpool, in his fiftieth year at the time of the Ripper murders. He lived with his wife Florence, 24 years his junior, and their two children. His mistress Sarah Ann Robertson once lived in Whitechapel and bore five children by him. Maybrick died on 11 May 1889 of arsenic poisoning. Florence received a death sentence for murder. Reprieved, she remained in prison until 1904, maintaining her innocence.

In 1992, a diary appeared, purporting to be by Jack the Ripper. It was originally a photograph album or scrapbook. The first 48 pages were missing. It contained 63 handwritten pages with seventeen blank pages at the end. There were no dates, just a narrative ending with, "Yours truly, Jack the Ripper."[13]

The information in the text identifies the narrator as James Maybrick. Michael Barrett, a Liverpool man, said that he was given the diary by a friend, Tony Devereux, who died in August 1991.[14] Barrett later claimed to have written it himself.[15] He retracted the confession, then confessed again and made other conflicting statements.[16] In 1994, Barrett's ex-wife, Anne said that her father, Billy Graham, inherited the diary with a pile of books on Christmas Day 1950 from his stepmother Edith. She first saw it when he moved to a new house in 1968 or 69. She claimed that Edith's mother had been a good friend of Alice Yapp, a nurse at the Maybrick's house who gave evidence at the trial. In 1989, Anne's father moved again, this time to sheltered accommodation and gave Anne the diary. She gave it to Devereux to present to her husband.[17]

James Rendell, a document examiner conducted tests with the help of experts in various fields and reported that the Maybrick diary contained too many anomalies and inconsistencies to be genuine.[18] The handwriting did not match Maybrick's or that of the Dear Boss letter, which the diarist claimed to have written.[19] Some phrases from the letter appear in the diary. Rendell considered the style of handwriting to be from the early to mid-twentieth century at the earliest and a test to determine how long the ink had been on the paper dated it to 1921, plus or minus twelve years either side.[20] The Sunday Times, which had been offered serialisation rights, concluded that the diary was a forgery.[21]

There are errors in the description of the crimes, such an attempt to sever the head of Polly Nichols and a statement that Mary Kelly's breasts were left on the table when one was found under the head and the other by the right foot.[22] Another discrepancy is the diarist's comment that he took refreshment at the Post House and there decided, "*London it would be.*"[23] The Liverpool Post House did not exist in 1888. The public house on its site was known as the Muck Midden.[24]

In 1993, James Maybrick was further linked to the Ripper crimes by a watch, which had the initials of the five canonical Ripper victims scratched around the edge. In the middle were the words "I am Jack" and, at the bottom, the signature of J Maybrick. The owner of the watch, Albert Johnson, had a receipt from a jeweller's shop in Merseyside, dated 14 July 1992. The hallmark dated the watch to 1846.[25]

Preliminary analysis of the watch by two independent experts concluded that the markings were several tens of years old.[26] A more detailed and expensive examination never happened. Timothy Dundas, who serviced the watch in 1992, swore an affidavit in 1996 that the marks relating to Jack the Ripper were added to the watch after the repair. Two years earlier, in a phone conversation with Paul Feldman, he described a different watch.[27] Feldman felt that there were two watches in the possession of Albert Johnson and that Johnson was part of the Maybrick family.[28]

In 2009 James Stettler proposed Michael Maybrick, James's brother, as the forger of the diary, Jack the Ripper and the murderer of James Maybrick.[29] Bruce Robinson suggested that Michael Maybrick's crimes were covered up by the establishment to protect freemasonry.[30] Paul Feldman also suggested that Michael killed James.[31] Michael Maybrick (1841-1913), was a singer with a secondary career as the composer Stephen Adams. His work included *Nancy Lee, The Holy City, and The Star of Bethlehem.* In 1889, he became organist to the Grand Lodge of Freemasons.[32] From 1900 to 1911, he served as mayor of Ryde, on the Isle of Wight. In 1888, he lived in London at Wellington Mansions, Northbanks.[33]

There was a suggestion that Inspector Abberline wrote the diary and was Jack the Ripper.[34] In a book published in Spain, Jose Luis Abad claimed to have compared the handwriting in the diary with the signature at the end of Abberline's memoirs and a handwritten police report. He also said that Abberline was illegitimate and believed that he was murdering his mother. Abberline's parents were legally married.

A writer using the pseudonym Frank Pearse claimed that he was made to learn a complex story about the Ripper murders. He was bequeathed a brown attaché case by his father. Inside was a brown manila envelope, containing six sheets of closely written paper signed by John Pavitt Sawyer, a single larger rolled printed sheet of thicker paper, three photographs of family members, a Masonic apron and collar, and a document relating to a property in East London. Sawyer was Frank's grandfather in law. The document was a confession to the Whitechapel murders, which he claimed to have committed in conjunction with three others. It was dated 1919 and written on headed notepaper from West Ham Workhouse Hospital.

Pearse published a short book, including his transcript of the confession. [35] Sawyer was a freemason interested in the occult. Amongst the members of his lodge were three British

Army Officers, Lister, Hotham, and Duberly. Sawyer's initiation into the Triptolemus Lodge was in a public house called the White Swan. Lister said that he met a fakir, Abou Ali, whilst serving with the 35th Foot Royal Sussex Regiment in Egypt. Ali learnt some mutilation rituals from a gang of thieves and adapted them for his own methods.

The three officers instructed Sawyer, as part of his initiation, to kill an unclean woman on three specific dates and bring part of her anatomy to the temple. Sawyer did a trial run by killing Mary Nichols. He then killed Chapman but was disturbed before he could remove any of Stride's organs and went on to kill Eddowes and Kelly. The murders ceased when he was diagnosed with melancholy.

Census records confirm that Sawyer lived in Whitechapel and was first a hairdresser then a perfumer. Pearse cited evidence that all four men were part of the stated lodge and that the named regiment was in Egypt at the stated time with Hotham and Duberly as officers but not Lister. The author of the confession claims to have spent the period between the double murder and that of Kelly in solitude. The real Sawyer signed a petition in October 1888 asking the home secretary for additional police to deal with the problem of the Ripper. [36]

The 1911 census lists a John Sawyer, born 1839, living in the West Ham Union Workhouse. He was a retired merchant seaman. John Sawyer, the retired perfumer from Whitechapel lived in Leyton at that time. He died in 1912, seven years before the confession. The John Sawyer who died in the workhouse left money to a wife of a different name to the one who married the perfumer. They were not the same person.

In 2012, the autobiography of Jack the Ripper was published. [37] Found in a collection of artefacts belonging to Sydney Hulme Beaman (1887-1932), it was sold by his descendants to Alan Hicken in 2007. The manuscript appears to date from the late 1920s and tells the life story of James Willoughby Carnac. His father was a doctor in Tottenham

135

who committed suicide. The younger Carnac studied medicine for a while then dropped out and was living in lodgings in 1888 when he killed Martha Tabron (his spelling), Polly Nichols, Annie Chapman, Elizabeth Stride, Catherine Eddowes, and Mary Kelly. Run over by a cart he lost the use of a leg. He then lodged with the sister of a Ripper victim, not one of his, and she found the manuscript. A coroner's report relating his death in a fire at the house concludes the book.

Contemporary Killers

The next three chapters consider suspects linked to different offences, beginning with murderers accused prior to 1892. Broadmoor archivist Mark Stevens stated that the police asked in 1891 if William Bisgrove could be James Sadler.[1] Bisgrove was sentenced to death, with Robert Sweet, for the murder of George Cornish at Wells on 3 August 1868. He confessed that he had dropped a stone on Cornish, whilst under the influence of drink.[2] Declared insane he went to Broadmoor hospital, escaping on 12 July 1873. He is the only escapee from Broadmoor not to be recaptured. The Press reported a sighting in Staines at the time of the Thames murder later in 1873.[3] The 1881 census lists a William Bisgrove in Plymouth, working in the Navy and born about the same time as the Wells murderer. It is unclear why the police confused Bisgrove with Sadler, but they were wrong to do so because the birth date of the real Sadler is known.[4]

James Kelly also escaped from Broadmoor. He was born in Liverpool on 24 April 1860, the illegitimate son of Sarah Kelly, and raised by his grandparents. Sarah married John Allen. Both died in 1874 with Sarah's estate, including John's effects, left to James.

He moved to London in 1878 and married Sarah Brider five years later. Seventeen days after the wedding he stabbed her twice in the neck, after she refused to forgive him for calling her a whore. One of the wounds was three inches deep and severed the spinal cord. The blade of the knife was broken.[5] Convicted of murder on 1 August 1883, he was sentenced to death, reprieved, and sent to Broadmoor. He escaped on 23 January 1888, returning voluntarily on 11 February 1927. He died there on 17 September 1929.

Kelly gave an account of his movements during the 39 years between his escape and return.[6] He went first to a lodging house in the East London docks then tramped to a port, probably Harwich, where he was disturbed by a constable and returned to London. Later he travelled from Dover to Dieppe. In 1892, he returned to England and sailed, via Rotterdam, to New York. He left America the following year, finally arriving back in Deptford. Soon afterwards, he went back to the States and on 27 January 1896 surrendered himself to the British Consulate in New Orleans. As there was no extradition treaty, or process, for escaped lunatics Kelly agreed to work his passage home. This was on the SS Capella under the name John Miller. The ship arrived a day early and Kelly did not wait for the police. He went from Liverpool to London then Guildford where he worked as a coach trimmer. About three years later, he sailed on the Beechdale to Canada.

Shortly after the visit of the Prince of Wales, the future George V, to Vancouver Kelly gave himself up to the British Counsel. After a delay of about three months, with no response from the British authorities, he again worked his way home. In 1902, he became a coach trimmer in Godalming and obtained similar jobs in Aldershot and Luton, with the help of a trade society. As his health failed, he sought refuge back in Broadmoor.

In 1906, Kelly's solicitors brought an action in the Chancery Court of Lancashire for payment out of court of the sum of £351 in the matter of Sarah Allen deceased. The Vice-Chancellor was unable to make a presumption of Kelly's death. The solicitors referred to an anonymous letter, postmarked Liverpool 25 January 1906, which said that Kelly had been living on the Caledonian Road, London, under the name John Miller. He was still crazy and dangerous. Some Liverpool people recognised him as Jim Allen.[7]

Scotland Yard responded by issuing a circular, saying that Kelly was not to be arrested but information to be given. An undated report signed by Chief Inspector Charles Arrow and Superintendent A. Hare, confirmed Kelly's visit to the British Counsel in New Orleans and arrival back in Liverpool. It stated that he had not been seen since and that

138

there was little chance of tracing him in the neighbourhood of Caledonian Road or East Ham, but special enquiry might be called for with upholsters.[8]

He was first proposed as a suspect in 1984 by John Morrison who claimed that he deliberately targeted Mary Kelly whom he had had an affair with in 1883.[9] According to Morrison, the police covered up their knowledge of this, although Sir Charles Warren desisted and resigned as a result. The real reasons for Warren's resignation were due to an ongoing dispute with James Monro, who had a brief involvement with the James Kelly case.[10] In February 1883, Monro reported to Broadmoor that the police had traced Kelly's friend, Merritt, who stated that he had not seen Kelly since visiting him at the asylum.[11]

Morrison believed that Kelly was the suspect in a novel, The Lodger, by Marie Belloc Lowndes. This first appeared as a short story in McClure's magazine in January 1913, then became a novel serialised in the Daily Telegraph. In her autobiography, Belloc Lowndes wrote that she once sat next to a man who told her that a butler and lady's maid, previously in the service of his parents, were convinced that Jack the Ripper had stayed in their lodging house before and after the most horrible of his murders. She drew the inspiration for the Lodger from this.[12]

James Tully's case against Kelly was based on him being a convicted and insane killer who fitted profiles of serial lust murders. In addition, Kelly's victim had injuries like those inflicted on Tabram, and Kelly had a sound knowledge of the East End and used sharp knives and chisels in his trade. Sarah Kelly was stabbed in her own home three times, following an argument and in front of her mother. Martha Tabram was stabbed 39 times in the street.

On 12 November 1888, a Home Office official wrote on Kelly's file, *"Would it not be well to make inquiry as to what steps have been taken to recapture this man? It is not likely that he is the Whitechapel murder; but his offence was cutting his wife's throat and he escaped last January, it would be well to know what has become of him."*[13]

The superintendent at Broadmoor, Doctor Nicholson, wrote to Sarah's mother, asking if she had any knowledge of Kelly's whereabouts.[14] He received a letter from her solicitors, stating that there had been no contact and that Mrs Brider had been visited by detectives on the previous Saturday, 10 November. Their questioning was so severe and their treatment so rude that she was in a state of ill health. The Solicitor also said that he would complain to the Police Commissioner, if she was visited again.[15] Nicholson forwarded the correspondence to the Home Office, with his own comment that he had no reason for thinking that Kelly committed the Whitechapel murders.

Thomas Lott was charged with murdering a five-year-old boy, John Harper on 20 October 1888, by cutting his throat in Pontardawe and opening his abdomen. Press coverage of the inquest suggested attempts had made to stab the body in imitation of the Ripper.[16] Harper had previously complained that Lott had tried to undress him in the woods.[17] Lott was a butcher who borrowed a knife from the slaughterhouse. On Wednesday 19 December 1888, a jury decided that he was unfit to plead, and he was ordered to be detained at her majesty's pleasure.[18] He was not at liberty when Mary Kelly was killed.

William Waddell was executed on 18 December 1888, for the murder of his girlfriend Jane Beadmore in Birtley, County Durham, in September that year. In his confession, Waddell said that he had been reading about the Whitechapel murders and his mind must have been deranged.[19] The murder occurred on 22 September 1888 and Waddell was arrested on 2 October. He then remained in custody under his date with the gallows.

On 24 April 1889, William Henry Bury was executed for killing his wife in Dundee. At the time of the Ripper murders, he lived in Bow, near Whitechapel. His wife was a prostitute who he threatened with a knife before killing her and mutilating the body.

He was born on 25 May 1859. Less than a year later, his father, William, was killed in an accident. His mother, Mary, was admitted to Powick asylum and the couple's three children passed into the care of relatives. William was educated at the Bluecoate charity school in Old Swinford near Stourbridge.

At the time of the 1881 census, he worked as a clerk in Wolverhampton. He became a locksmith and street vendor and moved to London in 1887. There he sold cats meat before making a business deal with James Martin of 80 Quickett Street, Bow. He paid Martin for the use of a horse and cart and supplies of sawdust and silver sand to sell.

On 2 April 1888, he married Ellen Elliott, a prostitute who worked in a brothel operated by Martin. She had a modest legacy through shares. On 7 April 1888, five days after the wedding, Mrs Hayes the landlady found Bury holding a table knife to Ellen's throat. Martin also saw Bury assault Ellen at a public house in Whitechapel, and on two other occasions.

On 18 January 1889, Bury approached one of his former landlords William Smith, a builder of 3 Spanby Road, and ordered a large packing box. He said he was going to Adelaide.[20] The following day he sailed to Dundee with Ellen. After a week in lodgings, they moved into the basement at 113 Princes Street. Ellen told a neighbour that Jack the Ripper was quiet now and said that her husband had fallen into bad company in London and stopped out all night. [21]

On 10 February 1889, Bury visited a painter, David Watson, and started reading a newspaper. Watson mentioned Jack the Ripper and he put the paper down saying that he did not know anything about that. There was no article about Jack the Ripper in the paper.

[22] Later that day Bury went to the police station, claiming that he found his wife dead on the floor and, afraid of being called "Jack the Ripper," had cut her up. The police discovered Ellen's body in a wooden crate. She had been strangled and there were cuts to her lower abdomen. Her intestines stuck out and one of her legs was broken. The killer had approached from behind and hit her on the head with a stick or poker then strangled her with a rope. As she lost consciousness, she was lain on the floor and the abdomen slashed.

The Dundee Advertiser of 12 February reported that at the back of the house, on an old door, a chalk message said, "*Jack Ripper is at the back of this door.*" At the back of the door and just at the turn of the stair was another inscription, "*Jack Ripper is in this seller.*"[23] Both messages were thought to have been in the hand of a small boy and written before Ellen's death.

On the same day, the Birmingham Post reported that Inspector Abberline and other detectives involved in the Whitechapel murder investigation had instigated enquiries among Ellen Bury's relatives. [24] Bury was tried for murder on 28 March 1889, arguing through his lawyer that Ellen had committed suicide. The jury heard from Mrs Hayes and James Martin about the assaults and from Ellen's sister, who testified that Ellen found a pocketknife in Bury's bed. [25]The jury found Bury guilty but recommended mercy in view of conflicting medical evidence. The judge sent them back and the recommendation was dropped.

James Berry, who executed Bury, believed that his victim was Jack the Ripper. He later claimed that Bury had said to him "*I suppose you think you are clever because you are to hang me but because you are to hang me you will not get anything out of me.*" He described Bury, incorrectly naming him as Burey, as the owner of a cat's meat shop in the East End who started killing women after one of them stole money from him. [26]

On 25 April 1889, the Dundee Courier published an interview with Berry, which had allegedly taken place inside the prison thirty minutes before the execution. Berry was quoted as saying that he had not yet met Bury.[27] In his memoirs, serialised by Thompson's Weekly News in 1927, Berry said that two Metropolitan Police Officers who visited Bury in Dundee, were satisfied that he had had hanged Jack the Ripper.[28] He did not refer to this or mention Bury in his book, My Experiences as an Executioner, published in 1892.[29] The book includes a chapter called Incidents and Anecdotes as well as comments on many of the men and women that he executed.

On 28 March 1908, a journalist called Ernest Parr wrote to the Secretary of State for Scotland asking for information on Bury's connection with the Ripper murders. He wrote again on 4 April stating that further details had come to hand since his first letter, which pointed strongly to Bury having something to do with the Ripper. The response from the Secretary of State's office stated that Bury made no acknowledgment of participation in the Ripper murders.[30] Bury confessed to the murder of his wife, without mentioning other crimes.[31]

The mutilations on Ellen Bury's body, has led researchers to accuse William of also being Jack the Ripper. Steve Earp argued that this crime matched the signature analysis of the Ripper. This included picquerism, incapacitation, genital trauma, and posing.[32] The objections include the fact that Ellen's throat was not cut and a belief that Jack the Ripper would not voluntarily have informed the police about Ellen's murder.

Thomas Harding shot his lover, Florence Varny in 1890 at the Victory Public House in Kentish Town. His defence included two statements from doctors that, from 1886 onwards, he had been treated for syphilis and nervous disorders.[33] There was conflicting medical evidence as to his sanity. He escaped the gallows. In 2009, a poster on Jack the

Ripper Casebook suggested he might have been the Ripper, because of the medical statements.[34]

Doctor Thomas Neil Cream poisoned four prostitutes. During the inquest into one of his victims, the coroner received a letter signed Juan de Pollen, alias Jack the Ripper, which declared Cream's innocence. Cream had a habit of sending letters to the authorities, although it is not certain that he despatched this one.

Born in Glasgow on 27 May 1850 he grew up in Canada and studied medicine at McGill College, Montreal. He married Flora Brooks but went back to Britain alone on the day after the wedding, in September 1876. He qualified for a license in midwifery at Edinburgh in 1878, returning to Canada in May that year. He established a medical practice in London, Ontario but fled to Chicago after one of his patients, Kate Gardener, died from an overdose of chloroform. Sarah Long, a friend of Gardener's, said that Gardener had gone to Cream seeking an abortion. Cream claimed it was a suicide, but the coroner's jury returned a verdict of murder by a person or persons unknown.[35]

Cream was given a license to practice medicine by the Illinois State Board of Health in August 1879 and set up shop at 434 Madison Avenue, close to Chicago's West side prostitution district. A year later, the body of a woman, Mary Anne Faulkner, was found in the apartment of Hattie Mack, a midwife who had assisted Cream. Mack told the police that Cream had performed an abortion on Faulkner and suggested that she burn down the house to hide the evidence. Cream claimed that Mack had attempted the operation and that he had tried to save Faulkner. He was acquitted of murder in November 1880. [36]

The following month Ellen Stack died after taking medicine prescribed by Cream who then tried to blackmail the pharmacist who had provided the prescription. A police investigation was inconclusive.[37]

Cream poisoned Daniel Stott, the husband of his lover, in June 1881. The death was attributed to natural causes until Cream wrote to the coroner stating that the pharmacist was responsible. When an exhumation found strychnine in the stomach Cream was arrested and sentenced to life imprisonment. He was released on 31 July 1891, after the Ripper murders.

Following his return to England on 5 October 1891 Cream began selecting and killing prostitutes. Ellen Donworth collapsed in the street on 13 October 1891 and Matilda Clover followed a week later. Cream then became engaged to Laura Sabbatini and spent three months back in Canada. After his return to London, he poisoned Alice Marsh and Emma Shrivell on 11 April 1892.[38]

At his execution on 15 November 1892, Cream is alleged to have said, "*I am Jack...*" as the noose tightened around his neck. The earliest known reference to this confession is in The People on 5 January 1902, shortly after the death of the hangman James Billington who was credited with the story. Thirty years later it was claimed that Billington was convinced that Cream was the Ripper.[39]

Imprisonment is the finest alibi there is, but some have tried to break it. In 1974 an article by Donald Bell highlighted corruption in the Chicago prison service.[40] There was a suggestion in a contemporary newspaper that Cream's father gave $5000 to a local politician just after Cream's 1881 conviction.[41] Handwriting expert Derek Davis compared samples of Cream's handwriting to a Jack the Ripper letter and the letter sent to Mr Lusk, concluding that they were the same.[42] Cream wrote from prison to Pinkerton's detective agency on 10 December 1890 and 26 July 1891.[43]

Edward Marjoribanks reported that the barrister Sir Edward Marshall Hall once defended Cream in a bigamy case. Confronted by several women who claimed to have been married to him Cream maintained that it was mistaken identity and the Sydney gaol soon confirmed his alibi. Marshall Hall attended Cream's murder trial and recognised him as the bigamist. He developed a theory that Cream had an underworld double who went by the same name and that both used terms of imprisonment as alibis for the other. Marjoribanks did not accuse Cream or his double of being Jack the Ripper. He merely reported a rumour that Cream was said to be Jack the Ripper after the hangman thought he heard a confession. He makes it clear that Marshall Hall would not have believed such a confession.[44] Marshall Hall was called to the bar in 1883, when Cream was already in jail. Professor Tony Barrett highlighted this as evidence that Cream was in London not Chicago.[45]

Frederick Bailey Deeming was a bigamist who killed two of his wives, and four of his children. He went to the gallows in Melbourne on 23 May 1892. A file on him is in the police files on the Whitechapel murders. This is due to correspondence from Charles Barber who contacted the police and the Vigilance Society in 1889 after experiencing visions and dreams of the murderer. In one dream, he saw the culprit depart on the ship Alaska, which was in port on the days of the murder. He described the killer as five feet seven inches tall, rather stout, a little round-shouldered, or short necked, with not much hair on his face and aged 40 or over.[46]

In his letter dated 6 May 1892, Barber told the Home Office that Deeming was the killer. In an article in Spy magazine, he said that in his visions he had seen the man at the railway station after each murder, including that of Alice McKenzie. The man was dressed in black clothes, with a longish coat on, a kind of billycock hat and carried a black bag.[47]

Deeming was born in Ashby-de-la-Zouch on 30 July 1853. He may have been the Frederick Deeming acquitted in Chester on 6 August 1868 of throwing stones at a railway

146

carriage.[48] As an adult, he went to sea. In 1878 he was admitted to the Presidency General Hospital in Calcutta with tonsillitis and treated for epilepsy.[49]

On 28 February 1881, Deeming married Marie James in Tranmere then travelled alone to Australia. He may have been the Frederick Deeming who reported the theft of a plumber's bag from a building in Union Street, Pyrmont, New South Wales, overnight on 25 November 1891. Deeming was living at 24 Macquarie Street South and valued the stolen property at two pounds and fifteen shillings. The property of a plumber called Thomas Tuck from Oxford Street was stolen at the same time.[50]

In April 1882, he was sent to prison for six weeks for stealing eight gas burners.[51] Doctor O'Connor, visiting surgeon to Darlinghurst Gaol confirmed that Deeming was suffering from epilepsy when imprisoned there between 5 April and 16 May 1882.[52]

Marie joined him in Sydney on 1 July 1882.[53] He worked at a founder's firm in Bourke Street, Melbourne, from 10 May to 6 July 1883.[54] Later that year he was in Rockhampton, where he placed various adverts for trade and staff between August and October 1883, working for Williams Brothers, based in William Street.[55] One of his later aliases would be Albert Oliver Williams.

On 20 November 1883, he was charged at Rockhampton Police Court with discharging firearms near a public court. He pleaded not guilty and the case was dismissed.[56] Newspaper adverts suggest that he attempted to set up a rival company to Williams Brothers who responded by saying they had secured a thoroughly practical and reliable tradesman for plumbing and gas fitting and W. B. Deeming was no longer in their employment.[57]

Deeming returned to Sydney, being declared bankrupt in November 1887.[58] On 2 December, he appeared at the Insolvency court to add a further debt.[59] On 15 December at the examination hearing, the judge sent him to Darlinghurst Gaol for fourteen days for

147

prevarication and evasion.[60] The accounts and plans for the bankruptcy were confirmed on 14 June 1888.[61] Press reports do not state if Deeming was present at the hearing but a police report, written in 1892, said that he disappeared with his family shortly after his release from gaol.[62]

His movements after this, covering the period of the Whitechapel murders, are unknown. One report said that he left Australia on the Barossa with his family bound for St Helena in January 1888. The former steward of the ship claimed to recognise him, saying that he had used the name Ward.[63] Another report said Deeming arrived in the Cape on 3 April 1888, under the name Ward, and remained there until after the Ripper killings.[64] He posed as a mining engineer in Durban and continued to Johannesburg where he committed another fraud. Several reports, possibly from the same source, claim that he left Durban in the steamer Dunkeld, under the name Leary in September 1889.[65] Others say that he arrived in England on board the Jumma in that month, using the name Levey, Levy, or Leavey. In 1892, a South African detective, called Brandt, claimed that he knew Deeming, under the alias Williams at Kimberley in 1877. He connected Deeming to three murders in Johannesburg in September 1888 and stated that he was arrested for a banking fraud in September 1883.[66] In conversations with doctors, Deeming claimed to have contacted syphilis in Cape Town.[67] Researcher Mike Covell found no evidence of Deeming, under any of his known aliases, in South African archives for the relevant period.[68]

On 18 February 1890, Deeming married Miss Matheson in Beverley as Harry Lawson, a sheep-farmer. On 15 March, he obtained jewellery under false pretences and, the following day, left Southampton for South America. Arrested in Montevideo he arrived back in Southampton on 31 August 1890. He received six months imprisonment in Hull for the theft.[69]

Five days after his release on 16 July 1891, he arrived in Rainhill, calling himself Albert Oliver Williams. He signed a tenancy agreement for Dinham Villa, in the company of a local girl, Emily Mather. On 25 July, the original Mrs Deeming and the couple's four children arrived at Dinham. Deeming married Emily Mather on 23 September and moved to Melbourne. On Christmas Eve, Emily was killed and buried under the hearthstone of their rented house. Her skull was fractured, and her throat cut.

In January 1892, using the name Swanston which probably came from a major Melbourne street, Deeming applied to a marriage agency for a wife. Kate Rounsefell accepted his proposal. In February, he wrote to Miss Matheson, asking her to join him. Following his arrest in March, Emily's body was discovered. This prompted the British police to look at Dinham Villas where they found the bodies of Deeming's first wife and children, buried under the house.

The press connected Deeming with all manner of crimes in Britain, America, Australia, New Zealand, and South Africa. One tale said that Deeming was attracted to a cinema usherette named Nelly who lived near Belmont Road in Everton. He told her that he had been a ship's captain and made a lot of money in Australia, showering her with valuable presents. She rejected his advances and a proposal. Deeming often discussed the Ripper murders with her and commented on the bungling method. Some accounts have him demonstrating the murders with a stiletto. He suddenly disappeared, around the time that he appeared in Rainhill.[70]

A dressmaker identified a photo of Deeming in Sunday newspaper as being a man she knew by the name Lawson in 1888. She recalled walking with him on 29 September that year, leaving him at 23:00 at Portland Road station. The following afternoon she kept an appointment with Lawson who spoke with intimate knowledge of the murders. He purchased a newspaper and, reading that the crimes happened after midnight, said *"Look at the time, I couldn't have committed them, could I?"* Soon afterwards, he disappeared.[71]

William Taylor, of Chelsea Road, Southsea said that in November 1888 he was lodging at Williamson Street, Morice Town, Devonport where Lawson and his wife took lodgings for their honeymoon. One evening Mrs Lawson came home alone and said that her husband had received a letter at Plymouth post office calling him to London and that he left by train. Two days afterwards came the Whitechapel murder. The wife heard nothing until she was summoned by telegram to Weymouth. Very distressed she packed up, intending to return to Jersey where she had come from.[72] Another newspaper said that a brown cloak belonging to Deeming was believed to have been worn by the Ripper.[73]

A correspondent claimed that Deeming visited Halifax Nova Scotia a few years previously and showed an acquaintance a friendly letter from Catherine Eddowes.[74] In another version, the letter complained about the treatment Eddowes had received from Deeming, who went by the name Jacobs. He also talked about enticing a girl called Kelly away from her Welsh home.[75] The correspondent failed to identify Deeming's photo.

Deeming's involvement in the Ripper crimes was apparently indicated when he sold a book called "Jack's secret" on his departure from Melbourne.[76] A former London bus driver who had since moved to Melbourne said that he had a strange conversation with a man identified as Deeming, in London 1889, who showed him a knife.[77]

Deeming supposedly matched a secret description from one of the three witnesses in Mitre Square.[78] This suspect was 35, standing five feet seven to eight inches tall with rather square shoulders and clean-shaven with the exception of a heavy moustache inclining to be sandy. The Illustrated Police News on 16 April 1892 placed an image of George Hutchinson's suspect next to a recent picture of Deeming on its front page.

The Pall Mall Gazette reported on 26 March 1892 that Deeming had confessed to his solicitor that he was responsible for the murder of his family and the last two crimes in Whitechapel.[79] Deeming was in jail at the time of Frances' Coles murder. His solicitor denied the confession, which was said to have originated in gossip from a jail employee to a reporter.[80]

Deeming told his solicitor that he had been in a lunatic asylum in London in 1871 under the name Teddy Williams.[81] He stated that he was sent to a London asylum by his father at the age of 12 and then went to live with his mother. He had the nickname "Mad Fred." After throwing a girl into a canal he changed his name to Harry and was ran away to London where he entered the asylum. He fled again, ending up in a house of correction where the chaplain from the asylum recognised him and arranged for him to go to sea. He caught a contagious disease in Cape Town in 1889 and said that both his parents had died in asylums.[82] Family members denied the charges of insanity.[83]

The Times reported that Deeming owned a dissection knife.[84] Despite this the police were apparently satisfied that he could not have been the Ripper because he did not have the required knowledge of London. They had also received many communications about him.[85] A copy of Deeming's death mask in the Scotland Yard museum was reportedly said by guides, on at least one occasion, to be that of Jack the Ripper.[86]

Alois Szemeredy committed suicide in Pressburg, now Bratislava, on 27 September 1892, following his arrest for theft and the murder of a watchmaker's assistant. Born in Budapest on 7 July 1840, he deserted from the Austrian-Hungarian Army on 29 June 1863. Military records give his occupation as butcher then tanner. In October 1865, he appeared at the Argentinian consulate in Genoa and signed up for four years to fight the war of the triple alliance. He joined the Argentinian army on 17 March 1866 but was declared insane and sent to an asylum, escaping on 17 September. During the next decade, he worked as a barber, committing several acts of theft, one of which earned him six months in jail and embezzlement. He used several aliases.[87]

On the 24 July 1876, he broke in the Hotel De Roma, Buenos Aires, and robbed Lieutenant Colonel Domingo Jerez of his jewellery and money. On the following day a prostitute, Caroline Metz, was murdered at 36 Corrientes Street. Arrested for this offence Szemeredy was extradited from Rio de Janerio, arriving on 8 October 1877. On 12 September 1881, he was acquitted, on appeal.

On 30 March 1882, he was arrested for desertion and sent to a military prison. Declared insane in 1885, he went to a military asylum then a state asylum near Pest before being released into the custody of his family. In 1886, he offered to sell his memoirs to a newspaper.[88] After March 1890, he lived in Vienna with a widow called Juliane Karlovicz who employed him as an assistant in her pork butchers shop.[89]

On 25 September 1892, he was arrested in Pressburg as a suspicious character in possession of stolen jewellery. The jewellery came from the shop of Andras Schultz who was killed in a robbery. Szemerdy was linked to a series of other murders in Vienna that year. Victims included an innkeeper, a porter and a watchmaker's assistant. [90] Szemerdy cut his own throat with a razor.

The Vienna correspondent of the Standard interviewed the president of the Vienna Police, Hofrath Ritter Von Steiskal, who said that there was no connection with the Whitechapel murders. He read of Szemerdy in the newspapers and knew from police forms that he was in Vienna from 2 August to 13 August 1889 when he left for America. On both forms, Szemerdy called himself an American surgeon but on his 1892 visit, he called himself a sausage seller.[91] In 1908, he was named as a suspect in the book Hvem Var Jack the Ripper by Carl Muusmann.[92] The story came from a man called Kattrup, mayor of the Danish town of Sorrell. On 4 October 1892, he wrote about Szemerdy in a Danish newspaper.

Later Killers

Several murderers, convicted after the death of Frances Coles, were accused of being Jack the Ripper. Hendrick de Jong was born in Holland in 1861. After two brief spells in the Dutch army he drifted into petty crime and was sent to a lunatic asylum in March 1888. On 21 March 1889 he married Antje Delnema, then persuaded her mother to invest in worthless shares. He was jailed from 6 November 1889 to 13 May 1892. In November that year he sailed from Amsterdam to Middlesbrough, where the police discovered him sick with some stolen cigars and claiming to be sick with asthma. In hospital he met a nurse, Sarah Anne Juett and married her in Maidenhead on 15 July 1893. They moved to Holland, but De Jong returned to his in-laws in August, saying that Sarah had left him and taken all his money. Mr Juett went to the police.

They discovered that De Jong had married another woman, Maria Schmitz, who came to London with him then disappeared in Holland. Searches failed to find either wife. Clothes and jewellery belonging to Sarah Juett were discovered in a pawn shop. The Pall Mall Gazette reported that the Dutch police had found surgical instruments amongst De Jong's effects and were aware that he had claimed to be a surgeon. He pretended to be insane, drawing on his experiences of working in lunatic asylums. [1] According to the Huddersfield Chronicle there were rumours going around the sailor's quarters in Gibraltar, that it was a matter of common belief among the crews of vessels travelling between Rotterdam and London that Jack the Ripper was a Dutch ship's surgeon named Jung or Jong.[2]

Prior to marrying Juett, de Jong proposed to the daughter of a hotel keeper named Kramer, then pretended to be short of money as the wedding approached. Kramer gave him a loan, which he used to abscond to London.[3] For this swindle, he was sentenced to four years in jail on 26 April 1894.[4] Released on August 1897 he was arrested the following month on another charge of swindling.[5] He was acquitted on appeal.

On 18 July 1898 two women were murdered in Ghent. Philomene Wauters, a publican, and a waitress, Jeanne Pauwels, were found in their bedrooms above a café. They had been bludgeoned and the killer attempted to hide the crime by starting a fire. A man resembling de Jong had registered, under different names, at various hotels in the area and had approached women, including Pauwels with stories of wealth and promises to marry them. De Jong was identified as a man seen leaving the building with a suitcase on the night of the crime.[6] On 8 August he was staying in a hotel in Brussels under an alias, F. Jamar. However, he wrote a letter to his Dutch lawyer, from Philadelphia in early August. In November 1900 he was tried in absentia for the murder and sentenced to death.

His movements between May 1888 and January 1889 at the time of the Whitechapel murders are unconfirmed. It is known that he associated with a widow in Amsterdam, and Antwerp, from June 1888, then became resident at a seaman's home in Rotterdam in January 1889.

Carl Feigenbaum killed his landlady, in New York on 1 September 1894. Mrs Juliana Hoffman advertised for a lodger and Feigenbaum applied saying that he was out of work but would be able to pay his rent on the next Saturday from a new job as a florist. On the Friday evening, a scream woke Mrs Hoffman's son, Michael. He saw Feigenbaum standing over his mother with a carving knife in his hand. Michael tried to attack Feigenbaum but was himself threatened with the knife and fled. Feigenbaum stabbed Mrs Hoffman in the neck then drew the knife across her throat. Caught fleeing the scene, he dropped his knife in an alley.

His unsuccessful defence was that his friend, Jacob Weibel, had committed the murder. Mrs Hoffman did not approve of dual occupancy so Weibel was supposedly smuggled into the room each night. Feigenbaum died in the electric chair at Sing Sing Prison on 27 April 1896. He left money in the bank and a house in Cincinnati.[7]

After the execution, his lawyer, William Sanford Lawton, said that Feigenbaum had admitted to being in London at the time of the Ripper murders. He believed that his client had been the Ripper. When he asked Feigenbaum if he had killed Mrs Hoffman he received a cryptic reply, *"I have for years suffered from a singular disease, which induces an all absorbing passion; this passion manifests itself in a desire to kill and mutilate the woman who falls in my way. At such times, I am unable to control myself."* [8] Lawton pointed to evidence that his client had been in Wisconsin and connected him to cases of murder and mutilation there some years previously. The National Police Gazette believed that he matched the description of Carrie Brown's killer.[9]

Lawton committed suicide on 13 February 1897. His associate, Hugh Pentecost, said that he was only able to speak to Feigenbaum through an interpreter. An interpreter was provided in court.[10] The prosecutor, Vernon M. Davis, said that he would not be surprised if Feigenbaum was proved to be the Ripper.[11]

There the matter rested for over a century until researcher Trevor Marriott investigated the Whitechapel murders with a theory that the Ripper was a sailor.[12]. He ascertained that a German merchant vessel belonging to the Norddeutsche Line, the Reiher, was berthed in St Katherine's Dock on all the Whitechapel murder dates in 1888 except for the double event when another vessel from the same line, the Sperber, was there. The Reiher was also there on the night of Alice McKenzie's murder and two ships from the line were there on the date of Frances Coles' murder.[13] The crew list for the Reiher for November 1888 showed a Carl with a surname that looked like Feigenbaum.[14]

The shipping archives in Bremen contained entries for a Carl Feigenbaum born 1844. The Norddeutsche Line employed him until 1878, when the records stopped. When arrested Feigenbaum gave his age as 54, indicating a date of birth around 1840. The police found a box at a house where he had previously lodged. This contained papers and letters in the names of men who had stayed at lodging houses where he had also stayed. Some of the letters were addressed to Anton Zahn. Feigenbaum initially denied owning the box but then said that he had used the name Anton Zahn to stay at lodging houses. He claimed that Zahn was a merchant seaman, working as a fireman on a Bremen registered vessel either the Emms or the Elder. Feigenbaum had been collecting his mail to reply to Zahn's sister in Germany. Marriott ascertained that the Eider ran aground in 1892. Its crew included an A Zahn in October 1890 and a C Zahn in November 1890.[15]

Feigenbaum said he had a sister in Germany called Magdalena Strohband. The letters addressed to Zahn were from a woman called Magdelena. Feigenbaum admitted that the letters were from his sister to him, which would seem to confirm that he was Anton Zahn.

Marriott suggested that Feigenbaum was responsible for several other murders between 1889 and 1892. He later added the murders of Elizabeth Jackson and Harriett Buswell in London in 1863 and 1872, respectively.[16] Jackson died in a brothel on 9 April 1863. She entered with a man at 07:00 and her body was found in the afternoon. Her throat was cut and there were five stab wounds.[17]

Buswell was killed on Christmas Day 1872 at her lodgings in 12 Great Coram Street, Russell Square. She had returned there with a man. There were two wounds in her throat. The chaplain from a German ship, Dr Gottfried Hessel was arrested after being picked by witnesses in an identify parade for a fellow seaman, Carl Wohlebe. Hessel provided evidence that he was in his hotel at the time of the murder and this was sufficient to clear him.[18]

The deaths of Buswell and Jackson were cases of documented murder, which cannot be confirmed for all the offences that Marriott accused Feigenbaum of. On 24 January 1889, a despatch from Managua, Nicaragua, suggested that six women had been killed in a similar way to the Whitechapel murders.[19] No evidence has been found to confirm this. In October 1889, the press reported the murder of a ten-year old girl called Petersen in Flensburg.[20] Researcher Wolf Vanderlinden ascertained that she died in an accident.[21]

On the morning of 11 April 1890, the body of Laura Whittlesay also known as Lottie Morgan was discovered at the back of a saloon in Hurley, Wisconsin. The skull had been crushed, with two blows. A bloodstained axe was found in a nearby woodshed. Nobody was ever charged with the murder.[22] Marriot found evidence that a Carl Zahn was resident in Waukesha County, Wisconsin at the time of her death.[23]

Seventeen days later, according to Marriott, a woman was killed in Benthen, Germany. Vanderlinden showed that this occurred on 27 April 1891 in Beuthem, now Bytom. This was just three days after the murder of Carrie Brown, meaning that one person was not responsible for both crimes. The Beuthem victim was not a prostitute but the wife of a tailor who had been having an affair with a doctor.[24]

The next murder referred to by Marriott was of a peasant girl in Berne on 4 December 1890. This was reported in the British Press on that date, so the actual murder would have been earlier.[25]

Hedwig Nitsche, a Berlin prostitute, was murdered in her home on 24 October 1891. She had entered with a man who drew a knife, causing her to scream. The landlady of the house and another prostitute with her client entered the room but the killer escaped. Nitsche's throat was cut with a long incision running downward. The press claimed that the London Police had requested official case documents because it resembled the Ripper crimes.[26] Ernest Schulz, sometimes called Schulse, an unemployed clerk was arrested then released, due to a lack of evidence.[27] There are occasional references to him as a Ripper suspect, stemming from press reports.[28]

The following year a prostitute was killed in Berlin by Friedrich Heine, who was mentally ill, but it was believed that he could not be identical with the killer of Hedwig Nitsche.[29] Marriott connected Nitsche's murder with the death of a woman in Berlin in April 1892. The police connected that crime to a similar one in September 1892.[30] Both were prostitutes, and both were strangled. The second murder was after Feigenbaum settled in America.

A man named August Lentz was arrested for the murder of 73-year-old Elizabeth Senior on 31 January 1892 but there was insufficient evidence against him.[31] Senior was found dead in her New Jersey candy shop. She had been strangled and her throat cut. There were eleven stab wounds. Robbery was the obvious motive.[32]

Almeda Chatelle, was arrested in Ontario for the murder of 14-year-old Jessie Keith on 19 October 1894. The press compared his crime to the Ripper murders and said that he had visited London in 1888.[33] Chatelle, born in Quebec in 1847, confessed to killing Keith. He was executed in Stratford County Gaol on 31 May 1895. He had apparently spent time in a mental institution in Boston and had a tendency to steal women's underwear.[34] The detective who arrested him recalled, a decade later, that Chatelle had been unusually hairy and confessed quickly.[35]

On 25 November 1894, a 29-year-old prostitute, Augusta Dawes was found dead, with her throat cut in Holland Park Road Kensington. Twenty-one-year-old Reginald Saunderson was arrested in Ireland on 3 December 1894. His father, Llewellyn Traherne Basset Saunderson, told the Police Court that Reginald was placed in the care of a clergyman at the age of thirteen. When returned home his extraordinary conduct led Mr Saunderson to consult three doctors, and Reginald was placed under the care of Doctor

Langdon-Down. He had been in Down's home for six years and three doctors certified him in Switzerland in 1893. Mr Saunderson senior now knew that his son had committed several serious acts.[36]

The press reported that Saunderson wandered the grounds of the home without supervision. He often escaped at night and went to the railway station. As officials kept catching him, he started walking to Wimbledon instead. Seven months earlier, he had enlisted in a regiment of Dragoons at Aldershot and been drafted to Ireland. His last escape was on the day of the murder when he received permission to attend church without an attendant.[37] Another newspaper said he joined the 3rd Battalion Royal West Surrey Regiment, based in Guildford on 15 July 1892, being discharged on 20 August.[38]

He wrote a letter from Ireland, to Kensington Police Station, signed Jack the Ripper. Received on 28 November 1894 it contained a confession to the Dawes murder.[39] On Christmas Eve 1894, Saunderson told Doctor Forbes Winslow that he kept hearing voices, which had persecuted him for some time. Declared unfit to plead, he was sentenced to be detained at her majesty's pleasure.[40]

Henry Harold Holmes was born Herman Webster Muggett in Gilmanton, New Hampshire on 16 May 1861. He graduated from the University of Michigan medical school in 1884 and moved to Chicago where he began using the name by which he is known to history. In 1886, he took charge of a drugstore, persuading the widow owner to sell to him. She was allowed to stay in the upstairs apartment but disappeared shortly afterwards. Holmes told people that she was visiting relatives in California and then that she had moved there.[41] He purchased land opposite the drugstore and erected a three-storey building that became known as the castle. It opened as a hotel for the 1893 World Exposition, with many of the building bills unpaid. There he began torturing and killing people in rooms designed for the purpose. Some were asphyxiated, and others locked in a huge vault to suffocate. The bodies were stripped to skeletons and sold, cremated, or destroyed in lime pits.

Holmes left Chicago when his creditors began chasing him for payment. Along with a former employee Benjamin Pietezel, he went to Fort Worth, Texas then St Louis and finally Philadelphia. There he was accused of fraud by faking Pietezel's death. The body was burnt in a house rented by Holmes. After the insurance benefit was paid Holmes told Pietezel's widow that her husband was still alive and in hiding. He persuaded her to let him take three of their children to find Pietezel. The bodies of the two girls were discovered in a house that Holmes had rented in Toronto and the boy's in Irvington, Indianapolis. By then the Chicago police had searched Holmes' hotel and discovered the remains of several people, including a child. Holmes received a death sentence for the murder of Benjamin Pietezel and went to the gallows at Moyamensing Prison on 7 May 1896.

In 2011 Jeff Mudgett, a direct descendant of Holmes, wrote a book based on his inheritance of his ancestor's diary. He claimed that Holmes avoided execution by substituting himself for a prison guard and lived on until 1960. He said that Holmes arrived in London in August 1888 and returned just before the New Year.[42] There were seven entries in the diary that Mudgett deduced as being relevant to Jack the Ripper. They concerned Holmes' meetings with a physician in Wales and a scientist in London and his sale of skeletons. He sailed from New York to Southampton with a servant named Alan. In London, he tried to obtain fresh ovaries as part of an unsuccessful attempt to procure the elixir of life. He trained Alan to kill the prostitutes and remove organs whilst he sought them from other sources.[43] Mudgett wrote that Holmes made no mention of the Jack the Ripper letters and they were not his style. The evidence against him was his

161

presence in London, similarity to witness descriptions and attempts to sell skeletons at medical schools.

The following year Mudgett claimed that Holmes had written the Jack the Ripper letters after all. A handwriting expert, Margaret Webb, concluded that Holmes wrote the Jack the Ripper letter, presumably the Dear Boss letter, and a computer program found a 97.5% match between the two samples.[44] This program, the Cedar Fox software, was developed following a 1993 Supreme Court decision, Daubert v Merrell Dow Pharmaceuticals. It ruled that expert testimony, including handwriting analysis, was inadmissible unless generated by scientific knowledge resting on a reliable foundation.[45]

The letter was posted in London so, if Holmes wrote it, then he was in London at the time of the murders. Against this, he purchased the land for his castle in 1888, is suspected of having killed five people in Chicago during that year and conceived a daughter in the autumn.

George Robertson was executed at Newgate prison on 28 March 1899 for murdering a four-year-old girl, Mary Kenealy. The crime occurred in the rooms of Mrs Caldon at 19 Goldsmith Street, Drury Lane on 23 January. Robertson used to do odd jobs for Caldon and the Kenealy family lived above. Mrs Caldon's son found the body on a landing. There was blood leading into the Caldon's room where Robertson was. There was also blood on his boots, but he denied seeing the child. Earlier that day he had asked Mrs Caldon's ten-year old daughter to kiss him. He told a witness that he had been in a fight with a big man and had to leave to go to Bristol. Two days later, he was arrested at a lodging house in Canning Town. He was also known as Little Tich.

A post-mortem showed bruising and a knife wound on the left side of the neck. There was a slit in the anus. The surgeon, Percy Levick, thought that the anus had been dilated with a fingernail and then cut. A third wound in the rectum was caused by a knife being put inside the anus. The weapon used was a shoemaker's knife belonging to Mary's father.[46]

Robertson's mother testified that he had once filled his sister's mouth and nose with dead flies, almost suffocating her. He went to America in 1883 and worked for a slater in New Brooklyn. He was in London from 1888 to 1889. His sister in Liverpool sent him back to Brooklyn. He returned to England on a cattle ship in 1894, assisting with the cattle. He had not had a regular job since then.[47] He was suggested as a possible suspect on the forums of Casebook Jack the Ripper.[48]

Sampson Silas Salmon was also accused on the forums of Casebook Jack the Ripper. He went to the gallows on 19 February 1901 for murdering his cousin in Bow. He had a conviction for assault and four for drunkenness and assaulting police officers. Aged twenty at the time of the Whitechapel murders he was on HMS Duke of Wellington, in Plymouth, but discharged sick for some of the period.[49]

George Chapman was born Seweryn (pronounced Severin) Antonio Klosowski in Poland on 14 December 1865. At the age of fifteen, he left school and spent four and a half years as an assistant to a barber's surgeon then moved to Warsaw where he paid fees for this role until 3 March 1887.[50] In London, he worked as a hairdresser for Abraham Radin. Radin's wife testified that Chapman helped treat her sick child, Solomon, born 26 May 1887.[51] Radin's shop was at 70 West India Dock Road. About five months after Klosowski's arrival the Radins moved to Aldgate and he temporarily took over their shop before opening his own at 126 Cable Street. The 1889 Post Office Directory lists him Severyn Glosovski. The deadline for the directory was December 1888 so it is reasonable to assume that the shop was open then.

He married Lusie Baderski on 29 October 1889 and, on 20 June 1890, registered the birth of a child, giving the family address as 20 Scarborough Street Whitechapel. The child died on 3 March 1891. Severin and Lusie, who later adopted the more conventional spelling, moved to the US sometime after 5 April 1891. Lucy returned to England in February 1892 and gave birth to a daughter, Celia, on 15 May. Klosowski had left his wife and family by November 1893 to live with a woman called Annie Chapman, unrelated to the Ripper victim. He took her surname.

Following the failure of a shop in Tottenham Klosowski worked briefly for a William Wenzel in Leytonstone in 1896. He rented rooms from John Ward and met Mary Spink, the wife of a railway porter. After Ward complained about the two of them carrying on Klosowski pretended that they had got married. Around February 1897, the couple moved to Hastings where Klosowski opened a barber's shop in George Street. In September, he became license of the Prince of Wales public house in St Bartholomew Square, London. Mary died on Christmas Day, after suffering weight loss, sickness, and diarrhoea.

Klosowski moved to The Grapes public house in Bishops Stortford with a barmaid, Bessie Taylor, who posed as his wife. In March 1899, they transferred to The Monument Tavern in Southwark. Bessie consulted Dr James Stoker about exhaustion, stomach pains, vomiting and diarrhoea. Neither he, nor three other doctors whom he asked for advice, were able to diagnose her ailments. She died on 13 February 1901. Dr Stoker recorded the cause of death as intestinal obstruction, vomiting, and exhaustion.

In August 1901, Klosowski employed Maud Marsh and began calling her his wife. On 25 October, a fire broke out in The Monument. A police report for the insurance company established that Klosowski had insured the contents for £400. It concluded that the probable cause was a candle inserted in rubbish and allowed to burn down. The insurance company paid a small portion of the claim and Klosowski, who claimed to have been in Croydon when the fire started, was not arrested.[52] On 11 November, he paid to lease the

Crown public house and moved there with Maud. He soon made advances towards another barmaid, Florence Rayner.

Whilst at the Crown he prosecuted Alfred Clarke and Hilda Oxenford for false pretences. Hilda claimed that she borrowed £7 from Klosowski, secured by a share certificate. She said that Clarke had asked her to obtain these loans on behalf of his mother-in-law. Klosowski claimed that he lent her £400, followed by another £300. He took out a private prosecution and provided the serial numbers of the banknotes. Clarke was convicted and sentenced to three years imprisonment. Oxenford was acquitted.[53] After Klosowski's arrest, the police found the notes in his belongings and Clarke was released.

Maud became ill. Dr Stoker attended but her father arranged for his own doctor, Dr Grapel to visit. Grapel believed that there were symptoms of arsenic poisoning. Maud died, on 22 October 1902, before he could share his suspicions. Tests showed the presence of arsenic and antimony in Maud's organs. The bodies of Mary Spink and Bessie Taylor were exhumed. Both contained antimony. Klosowski came to trial on 16 March 1903. Convicted of murdering Maud he was executed in Wandsworth prison on 7 April 1903.

The retired Chief Inspector Abberline stated his opinion that Klosowski was the Ripper.[54] He based this on the timing of Klosowski's arrival in London and departure to America, where he believed that similar murders occurred. He noted Klosowski's surgical training, recalling Coroner Baxter's theory that there was a market for the organs taken from the victims. Klosowski's residence in George Yard was commented on, which is presumed to be a reference to a barber's shop in the basement of the White Hart public house. Wolf Levisohn claimed to have seen Klosowski at a barber's shop in Whitechapel in 1890.[55] There is no evidence that he resided in George Yard before this time. Abberline noted that Klosowski's description, based on height and a peak cap, tallied. The only discrepancy was the witnesses who said the Ripper was aged 35-40 but Abberline felt that it was difficult to judge age from a rear view.

Ex-Superintendent Arthur Neil wrote in 1932 that the police were never able to secure definite proof that Klosowski was the Ripper.[56] Donald McCormick quoted Thomas Dutton's Crime Diaries, which said that Abberline discussed his suspicions with Dutton. Klosowski was allegedly seen in George Yard with one of the victims on the night of her murder and Abberline became convinced that Lucy Balderski, who he spoke with, suspected Klosowski.[57] The extract further alleges that Abberline discovered that Klosowski had a double in London who was a Russian and a barber-surgeon who posed as Klosowski on occasions. It was the double who had been seen in George Yard.

Dutton's diaries were first mentioned in the Sunday Chronicle, after his death.[58] Miss Hermione Dudley allegedly received what she described as three volumes of handwritten comments on all the chief crimes of the last 60 years. She said that Dutton knew Jack the Ripper as a middle-aged Doctor but did not reveal his name to her or in the diaries. She has not been traced although there was a Hermoine Dudley living in the borough of Merton in 1965.[59]

Donald McCormick worked for the Sunday Chronicle and the Daily Express, which reported Dutton's death on 12 November 1935 and commented that detectives took away documents.[60] In a letter written in 1995, McCormick said that he first reported the story of Doctor Dutton nearly 60 years earlier.[61] Dutton wrote in 1929 that he believed the Ripper to be a ship's butcher, having seen such men during his time in the mercantile marines.[62]

Philip Sugden regarded Klosowski as the most plausible of the historical suspects.[63] R Michael Gordon connected him to various other murders, including that of Jane Beadmoor.[64] Then there was a murder of a prostitute in Paris in November 1886, which

Gordon described as like the Thames Torso murders.[65] Added to the list were Carrie Brown, Hannah Robinson, Elizabeth Senior, and Herta Mary Anderson in New York and New Jersey. Robinson was found strangled on a building site near Long Island on 2 August 1891.[66] Anderson was a sixteen-year-old Danish domestic servant in Perth Amboy, found dead on 8 June 1892. She was shot in the back and her throat was slit. A railman, Harry Schliff or Schlipf, was arrested on suspicion.[67] He later proved an alibi.

Emil Totterman, also known as Carl Nielson, was a seaman who murdered a prostitute called Sarah Martin in New York on 19 December 1903. At least one newspaper report referred to him as Calor.[68] He is sometimes described as Finnish but, in court, he said he was a native of Sweden and 41 years-old.[69] This age is unconfirmed with newspapers reporting it as anything over 29. He confessed to the murder saying that Martin had approached him in a bar asking to treat. They went to a hotel room signing the register as Carl Nilson and wife.[70] Totterman drank some whisky. He claimed not to have known anything else until he was choking Martin. He then took the knife from his pocket and cut her throat, saying he did not remember this. When he came to his senses, he cleaned up and went back to the bar where he had a drink. Some newspapers claimed that the body was mutilated in the manner of the Ripper murders and that the crime resembled them.[71]

His death sentence was commuted, due to his bravery in saving three men from death during the battle of Santiago of 1898.[72] He briefly escaped from jail on 20 August 1916, remaining at liberty for eight months.[73]

Other Criminals

The next suspects are those accused, or convicted, of crimes other than murder. The police were interested in a German hairdresser known as Mary who was in the habit of assaulting young women and striking them in the breasts with a sharp object. Bremen Police advised that he was in prison until 7 August 1889.[1]

James Johnson described as a pale-looking 35-year-old waiter with an American accent appeared at Dalston police court on 28 September 1888 charged with assaulting Elizabeth Hudson by throwing her on the pavement and threatening to stab her with a knife. Alice Anderson, a friend of Hudson's, said that Johnson attacked her fifteen minutes earlier. Johnson claimed that the women accosted him. The police did not find a knife on him. His landlady, Mrs Seaton, deposed that she had known him as a respectable man for some time and he worked at Spiers and Ponds. He said he had a delicate wife and did not want the police making enquiries. The police knew Hudson as a disorderly woman, with previous cautions for accosting men. Johnson was discharged.[2]

On 15 November 1888, Collingwood Hilton Fenwick was charged at Southwark Police Court with cutting and wounding a prostitute, Ellen Worsfold, with intent to do her grievous bodily harm. They met on Westminster Bridge Road and he accompanied her to her lodgings at 18 Great Ann's Place, Waterloo Road, Lambeth, where he stabbed her in the abdomen with a penknife.[3] Six days later Fenwick, his age given as 26, and address as 34 Methley Street, Kennington, was committed for trial. Information had reached the treasury that the prisoner was guilty of other offences beyond the jurisdiction of the court.[4] Convicted of unlawful wounding he was sentenced to a year's imprisonment with hard labour.[5]

He was born in West Derby on 14 May 1861, the son of Henry, a solicitor, and Sarah Fenwick. In 1871, he was living with his widowed mother and two siblings in Toxteth Park, Merseyside. In 1904 and 1905, he was at 53 Bedford Road, Clapham. In the 1911 census he is listed in West Derby with wife Annie, twenty years his junior, and received income from property. He died, aged 55, in the Bodmin asylum on 21 July 1917 with effects of over $3000.[6]

Alfred Gray was captured with a gang of robbers in Tunisia in January 1889. He gave the name of a Whitechapel resident as a character reference. He had a tattoo of a naked woman on his arms, and the initials M and P standing for girls named Mary and Polly whom he once knew. He was accompanied by an Italian woman who spoke English fluently and said that she had been living in Whitechapel. His real name was Boxall. He had deserted from the 3rd Battalion Rifle brigade, subsequently going abroad with his regiment in October 1887 before deserting again. The references from Whitechapel proved false, and he was sentenced to three months as a vagrant.[7] There was an Alfred Boxall born 1867 in Southampton who joined the Royal Artillery on 6 May 1886. He was discharged from the 2nd Field Battalion on 23 January 1889.

On 20 July 1889, John Royall, a 35-year-old labourer, assaulted and threatened to murder Norah Brown at Borough. She had agreed to walk with him when he produced a knife and told her to keep quiet or he would rip her up. Hearing someone approaching he hit her and ran off, being apprehended by Police Constable Crancy. He said he was drunk and made a mistake. Crancy regarded him as sober. [8] He was remanded for a week. A 36-year-old labourer called John Royall was living in Battersea, with his wife Mary, at the time of the 1891 census.

On 18 September 1889 Knightly Besley, age 44, a draper's commission agent was charged at Westminster Police Court with being drunk and disorderly in Kings Street Chelsea and being in possession of a large and deep knife with a nine-inch blade.[9] Chief Inspector Swanson and Inspector Marshall were present at the hearing along with many police officers from Whitechapel. Besley had flashed the knife in the faces of several women and given contradictory statements. Inspector Kemp's request to remand him was declined. He was fined ten shillings, plus the fee for the doctor who certified him as drunk. The police confiscated the knife. He was probably the Knightley Bazeley who was born in Northamptonshire in 1845 and married Mary Leaton on 13 September 1879. The couple lived in Fulham then Kensington, where he died in 1894.

On 26 October 1889, a homeless woman named Anne Ellis made an allegation at Bow Street court that a man took her down an alley, started knocking her about and pulled a knife. He threatened to harm her as he had many others. Her screams attracted attention. The man was caught but got away and entered a house. The magistrate summoned the police and Inspector Moulford from Tottenham Court Road attended. He said that the woman was drunk. The police spoke to Thomas Jones of 27 Duke Street Bloomsbury who admitted being with a woman and the magistrate granted a summons.[10] The case was dismissed on 2 November 1889, when Ellis did not attend.

A married man from Doncaster, John Batterson, was arrested on 28 January 1891 in connection with assaults on women. One of his alleged victims was Edith Bellingham, governess to Sir William Cook. She hid at the Railway Company's works where Batterson worked and identified him.[11] A newspaper alleged that he had called himself Jack the Ripper and brandished a knife. [12]

He appeared in court charged with indecent assault against Mrs Rebecca Teale on 30 June 1890, Miss Blanch Hartley on 16 December 1890, and Miss Bellingham on 17

January 1891.[13] He was committed for trial on all three counts but was discharged at the assizes because the evidence was too weak. In an article headed "The Doncaster Jack the Ripper (again)" the Yorkshire Herald of 31 August 1891 reported that he was back in court charged with attempting an outrage, meaning rape, on Priscilla Scholes of Warmsworth.[14]

Leonard Harting, age 29, who also used the name Carl Muller, was acquitted of cutting a woman called Alice Seymour with intent to do her grievous bodily harm on 21 February 1891. The press described him as a brewer, but the court record said he was a labourer. Under the influence of alcohol, he enticed Seymour to his rooms and attacked her with a dagger knife.[15] His landlady believed that he had arrived from Germany in January that year.[16] The transcript of the court case implies that Seymour, who had three previous convictions for theft, had attempted to rob him.

On 28 March 1892, the Belfast Newsletter said that Scotland Yard considered the Ripper to be serving a sentence of 20 years in Portland jail.[17] He was a Belgian, sentenced six months earlier for attempting to obtain money from ladies by threats of violence. The police were missing one link in the chain of evidence and expected soon to supply it.

This suspect appears to be Christian Briscony also known as Charles Le Grand. In 1888, he was one of two men hired by the Whitechapel vigilance committee and given responsibility for organising and overseeing the committee's patrols.[18] In conjunction with a colleague, he escorted Matthew Packer to Scotland Yard so that the grocer could make a probably false statement about selling grapes to Elizabeth Stride and a man on the night of Stride's murder.[19] Packer said nothing when interviewed by police then changed his story.[20] Doctor Philips testified at the inquest that the deceased had not swallowed the seed or skin of a grape within many hours of her death.[21] Packer was not called as an inquest witness. He made three later claims to have seen the Ripper, but Chief Inspector Swanson noted that his evidence was valueless.[22]

On 21 March 1887, Le Grand was charged at Marlborough Street Police Court with assaulting Henrietta Pasquier in Great Portland Street.[23] Previously charged with the same offence he employed others to stalk and harass Pasquier. Two days earlier, one of those men, John Tysell, received two months in jail for assaulting her.[24] Le Grand hit Pasquier twice in front of two witnesses. Detective Sergeant James investigated his background and reported to that the man known as the French Colonel was Danish. Formerly a clerk in Great Tower Street, discharged for incompetence, Le Grand had complained several times about women in the street and had allegedly offered a constable money to lock up Pasquier and others. He was supported by the woman he lived with and had no other visible source of income.[25] The magistrate called him impertinent for living off immoral earnings whilst complaining about other women walking the streets. He was fined and ordered to keep the peace for three months.[26]

On 8 June 1889, Le Grand appeared at Marlborough Police Court with Amelia Marie Pourquoi Demay charged with attempting to extort money from a surgeon, Malcolm Morris of Harley Street, by threats and menaces. This involved a claim that Morris had promised to marry Demay. Morris testified that Le Grand had stalked him and his family.[27]

Morris's solicitor knew Le Grand as a private detective who had twice approached him for work and claimed to have worked on the Parnell Commission. Detective Sergeant James told the court that he had known the prisoner for a little over three years and commented further on the 1887 conviction. He said that Demay was the woman Le Grand lived with then. She had been a prostitute since 1886. Apart from a five or six-week spell in the same year James had not known Grand to work and said that he lived off

172

prostitutes, specifically Demay. James gave evidence to Grand's character when he was accused of assaulting Bachelor in the Strand. That charge was dismissed. James also appeared when a woman named Planette was acquitted of stealing Grand's watch and chain. Grand allegedly molested women in Regent Street and charged them to clear the street for Demay. On 24 June 1889, he received a two-year prison sentence and Demay received eighteen months.[28]

On 28 September 1891, described as Charles Grande, a 38-year-old engineer from 83 Kennington Road, he was charged with feloniously and with menaces demanding £500 from Mrs Baldock of 8 Grosvenor Place. He sent her a threatening letter, signed A.M.M and written in red ink. Using the name Grant, he had lodged at Kennington Road, owned by Baldock, since June that year. Baldock's daughter, Anne Desmond, testified to seeing similar letters in his room. James Hall said that from September 1888 to June 1889 he was a clerk at Le Grande's detective agency and recognised the handwriting. Detective Sergeant Williamson submitted evidence that Grant and Grande were identical.[29]

In October 1891, Grand was sent for trial on a charge of threatening to murder Lady Jessel, Baroness Bolsover and other ladies with a view to extorting money. The letter to Lady Jessel as read out in court included the comment, *"Hell itself will not protect you from my hand, far less the English detectives, who could not even find the man who murdered seven or eight women in the open streets in Whitechapel."*[30]

On 16 November 1891, he was convicted of sending the letter to Mrs Baldock and threatening to murder her.[31] A second conviction for being in possession of a forged cheque followed. [32] The press reported that he fainted during the trial and became violent.[33] On the way to the police station he tried to push the arresting officer, his nemesis Sergeant James, under a train.

The court heard that Le Grand had a previous conviction on 9 July 1877 for felony under the name Christian Neilson, being sentenced to eight years imprisonment followed by seven years police supervision. He had not reported since 6 May 1884.[34] The jury decided that he was not the same person, but later prison records still refer to the alias Christian Neilson. On the wanted list in 1884, Neilson was described as a German who pretended to be a waiter and obtained money from young girls on pretence of marriage.[35] He may have been the Christian Nelson convicted in Hull in April 1876 of stealing two pocketknives and seven razors and sentenced to four months imprisonment.[36]

Le Grande was released from jail on 5 January 1907, his year of birth noted as 1856 and his name as Charles Grande, alias Christian Brisconey, Christian Nelson, Charles Colnette Grandy and Briscona. In March that year, he complained about his sentence, and claimed to be known as the most dangerous man in his majesty's prisons.[37] In 1908, he was convicted of forgery under the name George Jackson although he claimed that his proper name was Charles Granday. He was sentenced to four years imprisonment.[38]

According to the 1911 census, he was born at sea. Deportation followed his release in 1917.[39] Le Grand died under the name Charles Grant in Copenhagen on 6 December 1923. Danish records state that he was born at sea, near Cork, on 24 March 1853.[40] It is possible that he was the Charles John William Granday born on the Isle of Sheppey, Kent in 1856. The year of birth fits prison records and it is the name given by Le Grand in court. There was a Charles Grand in the Seaman's hospital in London 1868, age 20.[41]

He appears to have been the Charles Grande who married Elizabeth Clarke in Kensington on 20 June 1907.[42] He gave his age as 49. In the 1911 census, the only Elizabeth Grande with a similar date of birth to the bride was working as a servant. Charles' Grande's father was Peter Grande, deceased. A Peter Grande was born in Liverpool, c. 1821 and intended to marry a widower called Mary Smith in 1842.[43]

The press accused Thomas Haynes Cutbush in 1894. Inquiries made into Cutbush's antecedents by police officers were summarised by Sir Melville Macnaghten.[44] Born in Kennington in 1865, Cutbush lived there all his life. He worked as a clerk and then as a traveller in the tea trade. Around 1888, he came to believe incorrectly that he had contacted syphilis. In November that year, he developed a delusion that Dr Brooks had tried to poison him. He wrote several letters to the authorities asking them to support a bill from Lord Grimthorpe making it illegal for medical practitioners to dispense their own medicines. He was said to have studied medical books by day and rambled about at night. His movements at the time of the Whitechapel murders were unknown.

Cutbush allegedly seized a female relative by the throat and brandished a large knife. His family arranged to have him examined at St Saviour's infirmary and five attendants arrived to collect him on 05 March 1891. He escaped, breaking into a house, and stealing clothing. On the following night, he encountered a couple in Camden, apparently explaining that people thought he was Jack the Ripper.[45] The man subsequently wrote to Cutbush's aunt. This letter was published in The Sun on 15 February 1894. It said that Cutbush said he was wanted for some grave and serious charge and that the whole of London was after him. The letter-writer understood that it was a hospital inquiry, implying that Cutbush was trying to stay away from the attendants.[46]

Cutbush was back at home on Sunday 8 March 1891 but left between 04:00 and 01:00. His aunt took a knife while he was asleep and gave it to the police who connected it to two assaults on women. Grace Florence Johnson was stabbed from behind whilst walking with her parents on 5 March 1891, on Kennington Park Road. Two days Isabel Anderson was walking with a friend on the same road when she felt her dress being pulled from behind and a sound as if the dress was torn. Later she discovered a wound.

Cutbush told his aunt that he had brought the knife from a Mrs Dickinson in the Minories. A journalist found Mrs Dickinson who seemed certain that the purchase was on 7 March 1891.[47] The aunt said that there was no stain on the knife when she handed it over.

Cutbush was arrested on 9 March. According to Inspector Race, he asked, *"Is this for the Mile End job? I mean, the public house next to the syndicate (Synagogue) where I just missed her that time. They took me to be of the Jewish persuasion and I got away."*[48] The Sun reported that there was a public house next to a synagogue and in the middle of September 1888, a prostitute said that she had been speaking to Jack the Ripper in the bar.[49] Allegedly this was reported in a daily newspaper in an article headed "Another Jack the Ripper Scare." The name "Jack the Ripper", is not known to have been printed in any newspaper before October.

After Cutbush's arrest, the police discovered some torn pieces of thick paper or cardboard in one of his overcoat pockets. Put together these showed diagrams of women. One represented the trunk of a woman with the walls of the stomach thrown open and the intestines exposed. Another was drawn in red ink. Macnaghten described these as two scribble drawings of women in indecent postures, found torn up in Cutbush's room. The head and body of one had been cut from a fashion plate and legs added to show a woman's naked thighs and pink stockings.[50]

Sergeant McCarthy stated that after remand Cutbush said to his mother that the police could do nothing because they only found the sheath. His aunt then said that she had given the knife to the police and asked where he had brought it. He replied *"Oh you booby! They only found the sheath on me."*[51] Johnson identified Cutbush as her attacker. She did not testify at the trial on 14 April 1891, when Cutbush was ordered to be detained at her majesty's pleasure as insane, and unfit to plead.

176

Two days later, his solicitor wrote to the press saying that he had many witnesses ready to establish his client's innocence and that he had been advised by counsel that an acquittal was almost certain. Cutbush's aunt said that he never went out after midnight and they had witnesses to prove that he was innocent of the stabbing charges. She said he spoke to Mr Clarke, the sexton of the City Temple, at 21:05 on 05 March, and had no knife then. The stabbing was alleged to have occurred around 20:30. It was later suggested that Cutbush purchased the knife to defend himself against the asylum attendants who had taken him from his home.[52] An article in Lloyd's Newspaper on 19 April 1891 hinted that the case was linked to Jack the Ripper. The reporter spoke to a Mrs Dickinson who owned a gun shop in the Minories. She said that she sold the knife to Cutbush after the assault.

David Bullock suggested that Cutbush was involved in the unsolved murder of Louisa Smith who died from a fractured skull caused by a blow from a heavy instrument on 10 February 1889 in Lewisham.[53]

In Broadmoor, Cutbush hit another patient, Gilbert Cooper, on 20 May 1891. The same day Attendant Slater reported that Cutbush had threatened to "*stick a knife in anyone of us, if he had the chance.*" The following day another attendant, Bailey, heard Cutbush threat to rip up the attendants or anyone else who upset him.[54] His health declined with records indicating that he was violent at times and becoming an imbecile. He died on 5 July 1903 from chronic kidney disease.

In 1894, a journalist from the Sun visited Broadmoor and spoke to Dr Nicholson. The newspaper alleged that Cutbush stabbed six girls prior to the Whitechapel murders, assaulted other people including a colleague who he pushed down the stairs and a female relative who he threatened with a knife. The journalists claimed to have the knife, which was of the bowie pattern with a sharp blade tapering to a point. It was nearly six inches in length and had a kind of sword-hilt. The black handle was knotted with several points being tipped with pearl. It bore the name of a firm in the Minories.[55]

On 14 February 1894, the same day that the Sun began their series of articles about Cutbush, the Morning Leader published an interview with an unnamed Police Inspector who claimed that the Ripper had been incarcerated in Dartmoor following the last murder. He said that he had the knife used in the crimes, which was from a Chinese manufacturer.[56] The officer is believed to be Inspector Race who investigated the Cutbush case.[57] Macnaghten commented that the knife was purchased in Houndsditch in February 1891. He expressed surprise that it was retained by Chief Inspector Race, instead of going to the Prisoners Property Store.[58]

Macnaghten dismissed the allegations against Cutbush, whom he described as a nephew of the late Supt Executive. Superintendent Charles Cutbush retired in August 1891 and committed suicide five years later. There was no blood relationship between the two men. Researcher AP Wolf, the first to revive Cutbush as a suspect, thought that Macnaghten issued his rebuttal of Cutbush's guilt to avoid embarrassment to Scotland Yard.[59]

Macnaghten said that a few weeks before Cutbush's arrest there had been several cases of women being stabbed or jabbed from behind. A man called Colicott was arrested and discharged, due to faulty identification. The cuts made by Colicott were different to those made by Cutbush. Macnaghten appears to have still believed Colocitt guilty of the attacks, despite his release, and regarded Cutbush as an imitator.

John Edwin Colocott was charged under the name of Edwin Colocitt on 21 January 1891 with cutting and wounding, with intent to commit harm, on the bodies of Maud Kerton, Christina Grey, and Victoria Charter by stabbing them with some sharp implement.[60] Doctor Gilbert of Holloway Gaol, the same doctor who assessed Cutbush, considered Colocott to be deficient in intellect but not sufficiently so to justify detention in a lunatic asylum. The court agreed that Colocott' s father and uncle would each provide bail of £100 and that the father would provide a personal attendant to ensure the prisoner's safe conduct and prevent a reoccurrence.[61] Colocott, never regarded as a Jack the Ripper suspect, died on 9 May 1930.

In March 1891, Daniel Gavan was arrested in Ireland after stabbing five people on a train. Travelling from Liverpool to Castlebar, he disembarked at Castlerea and was detained at the barracks there, believed insane.[62] Police inquiries revealed that he had twice been imprisoned for stabbing people. One involved a four-year sentence for attacking a sailor in Liverpool.[63] Some American newspapers reported that he bore a resemblance to Jack the Ripper.[64]

On 22 August 1891, Percy Greathead appeared at the Worship Street Police Court for presenting a loaded revolver at Margaret Sweeney in Queen Anne Street, Whitechapel. Six cartridges and a knife were found on him. The knife was new. Greathead said that he had brought it in the Strand two days earlier. He said that he went to Whitechapel to look at the scene of the crimes and was under the influence of drink.[65] Detective Helson said that enquiries had revealed the prisoner was a rowdy fellow, given to drink and the flourishing of revolvers. His mother, a widow, lived near Sandringham. When he obtained money from her, he spent it in London. Greathead was fined and ordered to provide his own bail or spend six months in jail.[66]

William James Percy Beresford Greathead was born on 27 June 1862 in Milford, Hampshire. He was educated in Belgium and was living in St Vincent in the Caribbean in 1885 when he made a will, leaving everything to a Miss Flora Battersby, age fourteen of Honfleur, Calvados, Normandy. The 1891 census gives his address as 13 Spencer Row, St Mary, Docking, Norfolk, describing him as a widower and West Indian Planter. His mother lived next door. On 3 August 1894, the British Colonist reported that he was sentenced to four months in jail for forgery in British Columbia. On 29 January 1897, he was admitted to the Macclesfield Union workhouse, described as an interpreter, and released two days later.[67]

In August 1893, a man named James Farley in Dundee, known locally as Jack the Ripper, shot a neighbour and her daughter and stabbed a police inspector.[68] He came from Covan in Ireland and the family had lived in various towns and countries before arriving in Dundee five years earlier.[69]

In 1895, William Grainger, also known as Grant, was jailed for ten years after being convicted of wounding Alice Graham in the abdomen.[70] Graham testified that Grainger was treating prostitutes on the night of 9 February 1895. They met in Spitalfields around 22:00 and drank together then she accompanied him to various lodging houses, trying to get a bed. On the way, he got into a fight with three men. A constable approached, and the men ran away. Grainger refused to go with Graham. A constable, perhaps the same one, separated them. She saw Grainger later and went over to talk to him. They were near McCarthy's lodging house. He pulled into an entry and threw her down. She did not see the knife but felt it inside her. [71]

Police Constable Fraser heard her moaning and found Grainger standing over the body. Another Constable arrived from the rear, blocking off the exit. On the way to the police station, Grainger said that the woman had been extortionate.[72]

It was reported that Grainger had recently been in Holloway prison for a similar offence, but the woman declined to press charges.[73] The Pall Mall Gazette published an article suggesting he might have been involved in the Whitechapel murders. It included the following comment,

"There is one person whom the police believe to have actually seen the Whitechapel murderer with a woman a few minutes before that woman's dissected body was found in the street. That person is stated to have identified Grainger as the man he then saw. But obviously identification after so cursory a glance, and after the lapse of so long an interval, could not be reliable."[74]

In an article published in Weekly Dispatch 1906, Jabez Spencer Balfour said that a warder in Portland Jail pointed out the Ripper to him.[75] A prisoner, who had once been high up in the detective service, was of the same opinion. The detective knew the man and had arrested him for another offence. Balfour was not convinced. He commented that the man had lived amongst abandoned women and thrived on their sin. The killer was skilled with a knife and known to have been the perpetrator of many serious offences but only convicted of two. Grainger, along with Charles Le Grand, was in Portland at the time. Balfour's memoirs, published a year after his release, do not refer to this incident.[76]

Grainger was released in 1902 but his license was revoked and he returned to prison, finally leaving on 26 April 1907.[77] In a letter published in the Pall Mall Gazette on 16 April 1910, his solicitor, George Kebbel, said without mentioning his name that he was Jack the Ripper.[78] Kebbel, who represented Grant at the magistrates' court, described him as an Irishman who had worked as a fireman on a cattle boat. The police watched him and observed him using an unusual knife to slice an apple in a public house. Grainger always carried this knife. He had medical training.

Kebbel's remarks prompted a response from Doctor Forbes Winslow who contended that his identification of a religious homicidal monomaniac led to the end of the murders after Alice McKenzie's death.[79] Kebbel responded saying that the man referred to Winslow was out of the country at the time of the murders.[80] As the correspondence continued, he said that there was no secret and that various London newspapers had discussed his suspect as Jack the Ripper.[81]

Forbes Winslow later claimed to have received a letter from Melbourne postmarked 10 June 1910. The anonymous female writer said that Forbes Wilmslow had scared the Ripper, causing him to flee to Melbourne then to South Africa where he became a railway employee. He had gained his medical knowledge from watching post-mortems at his family doctor's surgery. The writer said she had also written to the Melbourne Police and Doctor Robert Anderson, who retired nine years earlier, but not received a reply. She wanted to exonerate the Irish student who had suffered in the Ripper's place.[82] Forbes Winslow believed the student was William Grainger and that he was innocent of the assault.

Grainger told Wilmslow that a gang of hooligans attacked him, and Alice Graham just happened to be in the area, leading to the supposition that he had assaulted her. Wilmslow stated that he applied to the magistrate to stop Kebbel from calling Grainger the Ripper and that the magistrate said this was actionable.[83] The press reported that the man accused by George Kebbel of being Jack the Ripper was told by the magistrate, Mr Marsham, at Bow Street that he could sue for slander.[84]

Grainger was born in Cork on 3 June 1860. He went to sea in 1873 and was in the Cork City Artillery from 1883-89. An eighteen-year-old William Grainger was accused of fatally stabbing John Tevana in Dublin on 19 October 1878.[85] Irish prison records indicate that he was jailed for four days for assault on 5 October 1887.[86]

Between 1887 and 1889, Grainger spent periods in Cork and Fulham workhouses. The Pall Mall Gazette gave the following dates

16 May 1888 to 7 July 1888, Cork Workhouse.

9 July 1888 to 4 August 1888, with the militia at Cork.

182

25 March 1889 to 5 April 1889, Cork Workhouse.

10 June 1889 to 6 July 1889, with militia in Cork.

30 January 1891 to 12 February 1891, Fulham workhouse.[87]

He was transferred to Banstead Asylum where he was detained until 26 March 1891. Between 1889 and 1893 workhouse registers for London contain other references to a William Grainger, born between 1860 and 1864, who was usually described as a fisherman.

He may have been the William Grainger who appeared at Bow Street Court on 26 January 1891, charged with drunkenness. A piece of paper was found on him saying that he had been in jail for three months for felony. He claimed it was three days. The Assistant Gaoler confirmed a previous conviction for drunkenness when Grainger claimed to have been robbed. He tore up his clothes and said that he came to London from New York in October 1890.[88]

Researcher Rob Clack ascertained that Graham's injury was described as a wound of the vagina wall.[89] An attack on the abdomen explains why the police regarded Grainger as a serious suspect.

A poster on Jack the Ripper casebook reported that a friend had a chest belonging to Fred Johnson, who lived in London during the 1880s. Inside was a pad of paper called "Fred Johnson's Drawing Book." One picture was of a man with the title, Mr J. McDermott, the supposed Jack the Ripper.[90] Fred Johnson migrated to America before the Whitechapel murders.

Jim McDermott was a Fenian and police informer. A picture of him has similarities to the illustration.[91] Michael Davitt, founder of the Irish Land League, obtained a biography of McDermott from another informer. He was born in Dublin and believed to be the illegitimate son of a lawyer named O'Brien. He was one of the founders of the Irish Papal

183

brigade in 1859 and became private secretary to Colonel John O'Mahoney in the Fenian Brotherhood. In the 1860s, he was assistant adjutant general of the Fenian brotherhood in Kentucky.[92] Davitt believed that he began working for the British Secret Service in 1865.

In 1880, McDermott gave evidence in the trial of Kenward Philp who was acquitted of forging a letter from President Garfield. McDermott claimed to be superintendent of the New York Life Insurance Company in Brooklyn but admitted he was just the manager. Previously he worked as a journalist for the Brooklyn Eagle. He also admitted being expelled from a Republican club for taking a bribe and to a previous conviction in New York for felonious assault. He was acquitted of libel during a previous trial.[93]

In June 1880, he was part of a convention of revolutionists who met in Philadelphia and condemned the activities of the Irish Land League as inadequate.[94] In 1883, he visited Michael Davitt and two other MPs in Richmond prison, Dublin. Posing as a Brooklyn journalist, he said he had come on a mission from the boys and proceeded to praise the Phoenix park murders. Davitt terminated the meeting.[95] The following night McDermott was arrested for being drunk but allegedly appealed to Edward Jenkinson, the under-secretary of state for Ireland, and no charges were brought. Davitt claimed to have received copies of documents on McDermott's person at the time of the arrest, which proved that he was a spy.[96]

On 16 March 1883, there were two explosions in London. Nobody was injured. McDermott told some Fenians in Cork that he was responsible and enlisted their help in planning another attack. Two men took explosives to Liverpool. They, along with two other men were arrested and convicted of treason-felony.[97] McDermott wrote a letter from London to New York on 3 April 1883, lamenting the loss of the men.[98]

In Montreal McDermott used the name of Michael Davitt to ingratiate himself into the Irish community. The proprietor of the Montreal Evening Post contacted Davitt who advised that McDermott was credited by many with being the organiser of the bogus dynamite campaigns.[99] McDermott fled to New York then to Liverpool where he was arrested.[100] The charges were dropped. Davitt regarded this as an attempt to give McDermott the credentials of a suspected revolutionist.[101] On 10 September 1883, the Home Secretary wrote that he had settled the McDermott business and that prosecutions, which were not bona fida, should not be entered into.[102]

In a newspaper interview on 26 January 1885, Davitt said that secret agents were committing the dynamite outrages and named McDermott as one of them.[103] A leaked letter to Fenian agents at Havre and Antwerp from Jeremiah O'Donovan Rossa, one of the leaders of the Irish Republican Brotherhood, said that reports of McDermott's death were invented. He offered £10,000 for his execution.[104]

The Times of 29 October 1887 reported that McDermott had died in Toulouse from a virulent attack of fever. It also alleged that McDermott was once private secretary to Father Nugent on a lecturing tour and defrauded him of a considerable sum of money.[105] The report of death was premature as, in 1889, he was interviewed in London by the New York Herald and in 1891 and 1894 wrote letters from a London hotel.[106]

On 10 March 1895, Reynolds News published a series of articles by Patrick McIntyre, a former special branch detective. He confirmed that McDermott was allowed to escape and had been the subject of a bogus arrest. McDermott was described as about five feet ten, full faced and red faced with a ginger moustache. He associated with a gentleman called O'Brien, also believed to be a government spy. They turned up in London together where O'Brien introduced McDermott to Edward Jenkinson.[107]

Macnaghten's Memorandum

In dismissing Thomas Cutbush as a serious suspect in 1894, Melville Macnaghten commented that it was unlikely the Ripper would have stopped in November 1888 and then recommenced by prodding a girl from behind two years and four months later. A more rational theory was that the Ripper committed suicide after Millers Court or, alternatively, was confined in an asylum by relatives. After stating that there was no proof against any of the suspects, Macnaghten described three men, any one of whom would have been more likely than Cutbush to have committed the murders.

(1) A Mr M. J. Druitt, said to be a doctor & of good family -- who disappeared at the time of the Miller's Court murder, & whose body (which was said to have been upwards of a month in the water) was found in the Thames on 31st December -- or about 7 weeks after that murder. He was sexually insane and from private information I have little doubt but that his own family believed him to have been the murderer.

(2) Kosminski -- a Polish Jew -- & resident in Whitechapel. This man became insane owing to many years indulgence in solitary vices. He had a great hatred of women, specially of the prostitute class, & had strong homicidal tendencies: he was removed to a lunatic asylum about March 1889. There were many circumstances connected with this man which made him a strong 'suspect'.

(3) Michael Ostrog, a Russian doctor, and a convict, who was subsequently detained in a lunatic asylum as a homicidal maniac. This man's antecedents were of the worst possible type, and his whereabouts at the time of the murders could never be ascertained. "[1]

Major Arthur Griffiths referred to the three suspects, but not by name, in his 1898 book.[2] Two years earlier, he mentioned police theories that the killer was a foreign sailor or a man with a split personality.[3]

In 1936 Basil Thompson, Commissioner of the CID from 1913 to 1921, wrote that the police believed the killer to be an insane Russian doctor who committed suicide at the end of 1888. The police had brought their investigations to suspecting one or other of three homicidal lunatics. One was a Polish Jew reported by Police Constable Thompson, the second was an insane Russian doctor reported to be in the habit of carrying surgical knives in his pockets and the third was a doctor on the borderland of insanity who was said to have committed suicide in the Thames at the end of 1888.[4]

A transcription of Macnaghten's original document, known as the Lady Aberconway version after his youngest daughter who was responsible for it, contains some variations. Of Druitt it states, *"No 1. Mr M.J.Druitt, a doctor of about 41 years of age & of fairly good family, who disappeared at the time of the Miller's Court murder, and whose body was found floating in the Thames on 31st Dec: i.e. 7 weeks after the said murder. The body was said to have been in the water for a month, or more, on it was found a season ticket between Blackheath & London. From private information I have little doubt but that his own family suspected this man of being the Whitechapel murderer; it was alleged that he was sexually insane."[5]*

Macnaghten prefaced this with *"Personally, after much careful & deliberate consideration, I am inclined to exonerate the last 2 but I have always held strong opinions regarding no 1, and the more I think the matter over, the stronger do these opinions become. The truth, however, will never be known, and did indeed, at one time lie at the bottom of the Thames if my conjections be correct."*

Montague John Druitt was a barrister and a teacher at a boarding school in Blackheath. He was born on 15 August 1857 in Wimborne, Dorset and educated at Winchester then New College, Oxford. He played cricket for the MCC, Oxford University, Winchester College, Blackheath, and Dorset. For the MCC he played alongside WG Grace and, for Oxford, with Evelyn John Ruggles-Brise who was private secretary to the Home Secretary at the time of the Whitechapel murders.[6] Druitt became treasurer and honorary secretary of the Blackheath Cricket, football, and Lawn Tennis Company. He was 31 when his body was pulled from the Thames on New Year's Eve 1888. It was thought to have been there for about a month. Four stones were in each pocket. Amongst the other possessions were £2.17s.2d in cash, two cheques totalling £66, a first-class half-season rail ticket from Blackheath to London and the second half of a return ticket from Hammersmith to Charring Cross dated 1 December 1888.[7]

The exact date of death is unknown, although it must have been on or after 1 December because of the train ticket. When probate was granted to his brother William on 24 July 1891 the record stated that he was last seen alive on 3 December and gave his address at 9 Kings Bench Walk as a barrister. His personal estate had 2600 pounds.

At the inquest, his brother, William, testified that Blackheath School dismissed Druitt from his post for reasons unknown. William produced a letter, addressed to him. This included the comment *"Since Friday I felt I was going to be like mother and the best thing was for me to die."*[8] Their mother Anne went insane, in July 1888, and was in a lunatic asylum where she died in 1890. This was Brooke House asylum in Clapham, a few miles from Whitechapel. William said that there were no other relatives, although other family members were still alive. On 2 January 1889, the jury returned a verdict of suicide whilst of unsound mind. Druitt's grandmother and aunt both committed suicide and his older sister would do so.

Druitt's cricketing fixtures in 1888 included a game on 1 September at Canford, Dorset and another on 8 September at Rectory Fields, Blackheath. If he was the killer of Polly Nichols and Anne Chapman, he recovered to participate. In the Blackheath game, he scored two runs and took three wickets.[9] He was also playing cricket at Bournemouth when Martha Tabram was killed. Druitt was present at a board meeting of the Blackheath Cricket Club on 19 November, ten days after Mary Kelly's murder.[10]

Post Office Directories for 1887, 1888, and 1889 show him as a tenant at 9 King's Bench Walk, about a mile from Whitechapel. It is unknown if he had boarding duties at the school or other residential accommodation. There is a possibility that he would have been night-master at the school, fitting that around his work as a barrister. In 1888, there were no trains from London to Blackheath between 00:25 and 05:10.

He had some legal engagements in the year of his death. In June he appeared at Hampshire County Court to represent two men who claimed that their field had been damaged by the actions of a railway company.[11] On 19 September he defended Christopher Power at the Old Bailey on 19 September.[12] On 27 November, he won an appeal, regarding the tenancy claim of two tenants called Hake who lived at St Michael's vicarage.[13] This was a small boarding school in Holdenhurst, Bournemouth.[14]

The source of Macnaghten's private information is unknown. As Macnaghten overstated Druitt's age by ten years and incorrectly referred to him as a doctor, he either repeated incorrect information or altered it himself. An initial police estimate placed the unidentified body at 41 years of age, which tallies with Macnaghten and suggests he read the report.[15]

JJ Hainsworth discovered a family connection between Druitt and Colonel Vivian Majenide (1836-98), a Home Office expert on explosives, and close friend of

Macnaghten. Hainsworth suggested that Macnaghten knew of Druitt's guilt and leaked information which was then disguised by journalists such as George Robert Sims.

In 1902 Sims stated that the police had reduced the suspect list to seven then to three and were about to match the movements of those people to the murder dates when the real Jack was found in The Thames where he had flung himself, a raving lunatic, after the last murder. Before this, his name was bracketed with two others and the police were in search of him alive.[16] Sims first stated that the Ripper had drowned in an article on 22 January 1899. He referred to this in later articles and his autobiography.[17] He also wrote of a mad doctor who lived with his people at Blackheath and committed the crimes during absences from home.[18]

A journalist writing in 1905 said that Sims was convinced that a medical man who committed suicide near the Embankment committed the murders. The man was well known in London, subject to fits of lunacy and from one of the best families. Sims had not made his knowledge public due to consideration for the man's relatives.[19]

Donald McCormick cited Thomas Dutton as saying that the police told Albert Bachert that Jack the Ripper had committed suicide.[20] In a letter published in the East London Advertiser on 14 September 1889 Bachert said he was still looking for the killer. On 14 February 1891, the Pall Mall Gazette published a letter in which Bachert claimed to have seen Francis Coles with a man shortly before her death. Called to the inquest jury and not selected he wanted to inquire into the case. He said, *"if evidence is brought forward which can prove that it was committed by the late Whitechapel fiend, I shall at once reform the vigilance committee and appeal to the public for aid."*[21] Late could mean deceased or inactive.

On 11 February 1891, a Bristol newspaper reported that a West of England MP privately declared he had solved the mystery of Jack the Ripper. He stated that a man with

190

bloodstained clothes committed suicide on the night of the last murder. The man was the son of a surgeon and suffered from homicidal mania. Other newspapers slightly altered the wording to remove son of a surgeon and imply that the father suffered from mania. The MP stuck to his story even after Frances Coles' death.[22] The Western Mail, of 26 February 1892, said that Mr Henry Farquharson MP was credited with having evolved a theory that the killer committed suicide.[23] Farquharson was the elected member for West Dorset from 1885 until his death in 1895. He went to school at Eton, at the same time as Macnaghten. His constituency included the county home of the Druitt family.

In January 1899, the press reported that a North Country vicar had written a book called The Whitechurch murders based on a confession given to a fellow clergyman. The murderer died shortly afterwards. He was a man engaged in rescue work amongst the depraved women of the East End and was at one time a surgeon. The vicar writing the book had received the information in confidence with directions to publish the facts after ten years with sufficient alterations to defeat identification. The murderer was of a good position and otherwise unblemished character.[24] Druitt's cousin, Charles, was vicar of Whitchurch Canonicorum in Dorset. He died on 20 October 1900. Lewis Fras Hake, the vicar in the appeal won by Druitt in November 1888, was at Wraysbury in Buckinghamshire in 1899. [25]

In a novel, "The Worst Man in the World" published in 1908, Frank Richardson wrote "*Doctor Bluitt whose fantastic ability was so strikingly exhibited in his admirable series of Whitechapel murders, flung himself raving into the Thames. If he had been sane he, I fondly fancy, might have opened a school.*" [26]In another novel by the same author, The Other Man's Wife, Richardson wrote "*I believe, Montague, that you would consider it a good advertisement to be tried for murder.*" [27] The main character in this book is a struggling barrister with a brother called Montague.

Richardson was born on 21 August 1870 and educated at Christ's College, Oxford. He briefly became a barrister before writing sixteen novels between 1902 and his suicide on 31 July 1917. The first of the above extracts suggests that he was aware of a rumour linking a suicide victim with the Ripper crimes, a school, and a name like Druitt.

Watkin W. Williams was quoted by Richard Whittington Egan as saying that his grandfather, Sir Charles Warren, rarely spoke about the Ripper. Williams's impression was that Warren believed the murderer to be a sex maniac who committed suicide after Millers court, possibly the young doctor whose body was found in The Thames on 31 December 1888.[28] There was no such suicide of a young Doctor in the Thames at that time. Druitt's father and brother, Lionel, were both doctors. Lionel moved to Australia in 1887.

In 1959, Dan Farson received a letter from a Mr A. Knowles who said that he had seen a document called *The East End Murderer- I Knew Him*, by a Lionel Druitt, Drewett or Dewerey and privately printed by a Mr Fell of Dandenong in 1890. [29] Farson pursued this link after receiving a separate letter from Maurice Gould who claimed that two men in Australia told him that they had seen papers identifying Jack the Ripper. The papers were owned by Mr W.G. Fell, who died in 1935.[30] In 1986, Martin Howells and Keith Skinner traced Gould. He informed them that Fell's document was two or three sheets of handwritten paper and connected these to Frederick Deeming, who had used the alias Drewen whilst in Australia. Research by Adam Went linked the story of the document to recollections of an article about Jack the Ripper in the St. Arnuad Mercury on 29 November 1890. Lionel Druitt advertised in this same newspaper.[31]

Farson established that Lionel Druitt had a surgery in the Minories in 1879. Maurice Gould told him that a former librarian recalled seeing the name M.J. Druitt in either an old directory or voting list for that area. [32] Another correspondent, Frederick Martin

Pocock, informed Farson that a relative owned a friend fish shop in the Minories, next to the Railway arch. Druitt had an attic room on the third floor and used to burn rubbish in the cellar. Pocock said that a man accosted his mother at the Aldgate East End of the Minories, and she suspected him of being the Ripper. His description was like that of the lodgers.[33] Pocock was born in 1892. The 1891 census lists a 69-year-old widow, Eliza Pocock, at 1 Peacock Court, The Minories. Her late husband Maurice (c. 1837-76) gave his occupation as Metropolitan Police officer in the 1871 census.

In a 1956 book on Scotland Yard Douglas Brown commented that Macnaghten appeared to identify the Ripper with the head of a plot to assassinate Mr Balfour at the home office.[34] A diary entry from Queen Victoria on 11 August 1888 noted that the government had notice from America of a plot to kill Mr Balfour.[35] Earlier press reports also referred to Fenian plots to assassinate Balfour.[36] In his 1914 memoirs Macnaghten stated, in a section on Jack the Ripper, that *"certain facts were not in possession of the police until some years after I became a detective officer."*[37] He joined the force in 1889.

Kosminski was the second man named by the Macnaghten memorandum. The Lady Aberconway version states:

"Kosminski, a polish jew, who lived in the very heart of the district where the murders were committed. He had become insane owing to many years indulgence in solitary vices. He had a great hatred of women, with strong homicidal tendencies. He was, (and I believe still is), detained in a lunatic asylum about March 1889. This man in appearance strongly resembled the individual seen by the City PC near Mitre Square."[38]

Philip Loftus said that Macnaghten's grandson showed him a version of the memorandum in the early 1950s.[39] One of the three suspects was a Polish tanner or cobbler whom Loftus recalled 20 years later as being nicknamed "Leather Apron."

In his memoirs, Macnaghten elaborated on the PC who saw the Ripper near Mitre Square, saying it was probable that the officer on duty saw the murderer with his victims a few minutes before the crime but no satisfactory description was forthcoming.[40] The only known record of a Police Officer seeing a man with the victim just before the crime was the sighting of Police Constable Smith, which did not relate to Mitre Square although it was the same night.

In an article in the People's Journal on 26 September 1919, Sergeant Stephen White said that the police had been watching an alley just behind the Whitechapel Road at the time of the murders. White arrived one night to take the report of those watching when he saw a man coming out of the alley. The man seemed to be wearing rubber shoes, which was unusual then. White stood aside to let him pass and got a good look at him under the wall lamp. He was about five feet ten inches tall and was dressed shabbily but the material of his clothes was good. His face was long and thin and his hair jet black. He had a sallow complexion and seemed to be a foreigner. His shoulders were slightly bent. His eyes shone. He was about 33 and gave the idea of having been a student or professional man. White had an intuition that there was something wrong but saw no grounds to detain him. The man stumbled, and White used that as an excuse to initiate a conversation. The man said good night and agreed that it was cold. His voice was soft and musical, with a touch of culture. As he walked away one of the police officers walked out of a house and into the alley. There he found the body. White chased after the man but could not find him.[41]

White did not give evidence at any inquest. He stated that the alley could only be entered from the place where two policemen hid. Neither saw the victim and the killer enter or commented upon the murder. Donald Rumbelow suggested that they had left their posts.[42] Martin Fido pointed out that Mitre Square was not off the Whitechapel road

194

and had three exits.[43] None of the other locations, except perhaps Castle Alley, fit White's story.

On 22 September 1907, George Sims wrote in The Referee that the first suspect was a Polish Jew of curious habits and strange disposition who was the sole occupant of certain premises in Whitechapel after nightfall. He resided in Whitechapel during the murders and soon after they ceased certain facts came to light, which showed it was possible that he may have been the Ripper. He had once been employed in a Polish hospital. He was a known lunatic and, sometime afterwards, displayed signs of homicidal mania that led to him being incarcerated in an asylum. Sims said that the policeman who glimpsed the Ripper in Mitre Court declared, when he saw the suspect some time later, that he was the height and build of the man seen on the night of the murder.[44] The Police Gazette carried a description of a man seen with Catherine Eddowes, which appears to be the man seen by Lawende. Researcher Jean Overton Fuller wrote to the curator of the Black Museum asking for the name of the witness and was told that it was Sergeant White.[45]

Dr Robert Anderson's book, The Lighter Side of My Official Life, published in 1910, stated that the Ripper was a Polish Jew. Anderson continued that "*the only person who ever had a good view of the murderer unhesitatingly identified the suspect the instant he was confronted with him but refused to give evidence against him.*" In a 1901 article, Anderson stated that the Ripper had been caged in an asylum.[46] He repeated this in 1904 and 1907.[47]

In May 1895, Major Griffiths, under the pen name Alfred Aylmer, wrote that Anderson had a perfectly plausible theory that Jack the Ripper was a homicidal maniac, temporarily at large, whose hideous career was cut short by committal to an asylum.[48] It is reasonable to assume that Anderson's theory developed into certainty between 1895 and 1901.

In his copy of Anderson's book Detective Chief Inspector Swanson wrote in pencil, "*because the suspect was also a Jew and also because his evidence would convict the suspect and witness would be the means of murderer being hanged which he did not want to be left on his mind.*" He continued, "*and after this identification which suspect knew, no other murder of this kind took place in London.*" At the end of the book, Swanson further noted, "*After the suspect had been identified by us, at the seaside home where he had been sent by us with difficulty, in order to subject him to identification and he knew he was identified. On suspect's return to his brother's house in Whitechapel, he was watched by police (City CID) by day and night. In a very short time, the suspect with his hands tied behind his bank he was sent to Stepney Workhouse and then to Colney Hatch and died shortly afterwards. Kosminski was the suspect.*"[49]

A newspaper article on 7 May 1895 commented that Swanson believed the Ripper to be dead.[50] Martin Fido located a man called Kosminski, who was admitted to a lunatic asylum in the relevant period.[51] Aaron Modke Kosminski was born in Poland on 11 September 1865 and arrived in England around 1881. On 14 December 1889, he appeared in court for allowing an unmuzzled dog in the street. His brother said the name was Abrahams. An elder brother, who arrived in England in 1872, used this name.[52] Kosminski said that the dog belonged to Jacobs and it was more convenient to use the name Abrahams. He was fined ten shillings plus costs and given two days to pay.[53]

Kosminski was admitted to the Mile End Workhouse Infirmary on 12 July 1890 and discharged three days later.[54] He was living at 3 Sion Square, given as the residence of his brother Wolf Kozminsky, really his brother-in-law Woolf Abrahams. He may have been living with Wolf in 1888, possibly at 25 Providence Square in the centre of Whitechapel and close to Berner Street. One of Wolf's daughters, Rebecca, was born at 38 Berner Street, next door to the club where Elizabeth Stride's body was found.[55]

196

On 7 February 1891, described as a Hebrew hairdresser, Kosminski was admitted to the Colney Hatch hospital suffering from mania. The admission book originally said the illness had lasted for six months and the cause was unknown, but this had been replaced with six years and self-abuse. His bodily state was fair, his main symptom was incoherence, and he was not considered dangerous.[56]

Kosminski was declared insane by Dr. Houchin who said that the man claimed to know the movements of all mankind, and was guided by an instinct, which controlled him. This instinct told him to refuse food and drink and eat out of the gutter.[57] A witness, Jacob Cohen, reported that Kosminski had not worked for years and wandered around the streets refusing to wash. He had threatened to kill his sister with a knife.[58] In January 1892, he attacked a hospital attendant with a chair. [59]In 1894, he moved to Leavesden asylum where he died, of gangrene, in 1919. At the time of his admission to Leavesden, his nearest relative was his mother whose address was 63 New Street, off New Road, Whitechapel.

His address at the time of death was given as 5 Ashcroft Road, Bow. This was the home of his brother-in-law. Shortly after Aaron's committal, the family moved to 63 New Street and changed their name to Cohen or Lubnowski-Cohen.

The seaside home where Swanson said the identification took place is assumed to be the police convalescent home in Clarendon Villas Hove. The home opened in March 1890, although other boarding houses were used for the same purpose from 1887. There was also a seaside home operated by Holloway Asylum in Brighton. Morley House.

In 1877, one of the Mitre Square witnesses Joseph Levy sponsored the naturalisation request of a furrier called Martin Kosminski.[60] No connection between Martin and Aaron Kosminski has been established but he is sometimes suspected. Joseph Levy was a butcher who moved from his shop around 1892, about the time that Kosminski was allegedly identified. Levy's wife, Amelia, appears to have died in Brighton in 1912 but the family were still in London in the 1901 and 1911 census.

On the retirement of Inspector Robert Sagar, the City Press of 7 January 1905 wrote that suspicion fell upon a man who was sent to a lunatic asylum. Identification was impossible, so he could not be charged.[61] Two days later the Morning Leader quoted Sagar as saying that the police had good reason to suspect a man working in Butchers Row, Aldgate. He was watched and was evidently insane. His friends chose to remove him to a private asylum and there were no more Ripper atrocities after that.[62]

In 1906 Thomson's news published a series of articles on the retired Chief Inspector Henry Cox. One was about Jack the Ripper.[63] Cox made it clear that the identity of the Ripper was unknown but described a suspect who was about five feet six inches tall with short black curly hair. He often walked about at night and occupied several shops in the East End but became insane at times and spent some time in an asylum in Surrey. During the Whitechapel murders, he lived in a certain street where Cox had him under surveillance for three months after the last killing. Cox and his colleagues told the local Jews that they were factory inspectors looking for people who employed underage children. This deception allowed them to disarm suspicion. Surveillance took place in a house directly opposite the man's shop. Cox described following him one night when he approached two prostitutes.

A press article from February 1892 may also relate to this suspect. It stated that the evidence had been completed except for a single link, which the police were endeavouring to supply. The criminal had, till within a month, been watched night and day and was aware of surveillance.[64] This does not fit Kosminski, who was already in the asylum.

A recent allegation is that the shawl allegedly belonging to Catherine Eddowes contained traces of Kosminski's semen. Doctor Jari Louhelainen copied traces of semen from the shawl and built a DNA profile, which matched a descendant of Kosminski's sister.[65] However, the provenance of the shawl is not ascertained, and semen had not previously been reported on it.

The Lady Aberconway version of the Macnaghten Memorandum expands on the description of the third suspect, Michael Ostrog:

"Michael Ostrog, a mad Russian doctor and a convict and unquestionably a homicidal manic. This man was said to have been habitually cruel to women, and for a long time was known to have carried about with him surgical knives and other instruments; his antecedents were of the very worst and his whereabouts at the time of the Whitechapel murders could never be satisfactorily accounted for. He is still alive."[66]

Michael Ostrog was born c.1830, possibly at sea.[67] A conman and thief he used various aliases. His first known crime was a series of petty thefts in Oxford, using the name Max Gosslar for which he received ten months in jail on 2 March 1863.[68] On 2 February 1864 under the name Max Sobieski, he was convicted as a rogue and vagabond and sentenced to three months. In December that year, he received a further eight months in Exeter for fraud and felony under the names Mutters Ostrogoc and John Sobieski. In January 1866, he was acquitted of a fraud charge in Gloucestershire where he posed as Knut Ostin.[69]

On 5 July 1866, he received a seven-year sentence for various thefts as Bertrand Ashley and Ashley Nabokoff in Kent, with three previous convictions being taken into consideration.[70] The 1871 census lists him in Dartmoor prison, under the name Bertrand Ashley, born 1836. He was released on 23 May 1873. During this period in jail, he encountered Michael Davitt who described him in a book, written in 1885. Davitt knew

199

him as Bertrand Victor, the son of a distinguished Russian. He had been educated at Oxford and served in the British Navy. Another convict told Davitt that the Russian had been imprisoned in Konigsberg and Mouilins in Paris before coming to England. [71]

Ostrog and Davitt met again at Chatham jail in 1874. Ostrog had been sentenced for ten years on 5 January that year. [72] During his arrest, he produced a revolver at the police station in Burton-on-Trent. [73] The 1881 census lists him in Portland prison as Michael Ostrog, a naturalised British subject born Poland 1834. His occupation was given as surgeon.

In 1883, he was released from Pentonville prison on a ticket of leave but failed to report. [74] In June 1886, he was deported from France. [75] A year later, he was in trouble for stealing a metal tankard and, despite pleading insanity, was sentenced to six months hard labour under the name Claude Cayton. [76] There was a secondary charge of attempting to commit suicide after he attempted to throw himself under a train on the way to Holloway prison. Subsequently the authorities moved him from Wandsworth prison to the Surrey pauper lunatic asylum. He was described as a 50-year-old married Jewish surgeon. [77] He was released on 10 March 1888.

In October 1888, the Police Gazette listed him as a failure to report with a comment that *"special attention is drawn to this dangerous man."* [78] Philip Sugden ascertained that he had been arrested in Paris, as Stanislas Lublinski, on 26 July 1888 for the theft of a microscope and sentenced on 15 November 1888 to two years imprisonment. [79] This absolves him entirely from involvement in the Ripper murders.

The British police were seemingly unaware of his detention. On 17 April 1891, he appeared in court, charged with a failure to report. [80] He was sent to the St Giles workhouse then to Banstead Lunatic asylum. On 7 May 1891, Macnaghten wrote to

Banstead, requesting that they inform Scotland Yard, if Ostrog was discharged.[81] This happened on 29 May 1893, but it is not known if the police were informed.

In 1894, Ostrog received a five-year sentence for thefts from Eton, where he had committed an earlier theft in 1873, on 13 October 1889 and 6 June 1893.[82]He was released after twelve weeks, with £10 compensation, after the French authorities confirmed his alibi for the 1889 theft. His next conviction was at Woolwich, under the name Henry Ray, for stealing books. He received six weeks hard labour.[83] His last known conviction was in December 1900, under the name John Evest, for the theft of a microscope.[84] Sentenced to five years, and partly paralysed, he was released early on 17 September 1904.[85] His final resting place is unknown.

Recollections

As time passed some individuals who knew, or thought they knew, about the crimes began to share their memories. In November 1889, a man named Thomas Molin who drove a sleigh on which a bridegroom died in Montreal in February that year, stated that he had to leave England because he was suspected of being Jack the Ripper. Detectives said that he was sane and had been arrested in London, Ontario, on suspicion of the Ripper murders.[1]

At Auckland police court on 29 November 1889, Henry Dalkin Robertson was sentenced for being drunk. He said he had been educated for a clergyman and had once been locked up in London for four hours under suspicion of being Jack the Ripper.[2] He may have been the showman Donald Robertson, professional name Harry Dalton, who appeared at Kinning Park Glasgow Police Court on 15 March 1896 charged with being drunk. He said he had only once previously been in a police court and that was in London on suspicion of being Jack the Ripper.[3]

On 10 June 1893 at the North London Police Court a 32-year-old shoeblack called John Norton was charged with begging at Clapton and given seven days hard labour.[4] He told police that he had once been charged as being Jack the Ripper and Constable 129 confirmed this.

In 1891, George Robert Sims wrote that his portrait on the cover of a sixpenny edition of his Social Kaleidoscope was taken to Scotland Yard by a coffee stall keeper. The keeper served a man, noticing bloodstains on his cuffs. The man told him that two bodies would be found in the morning. Seeing a resemblance between the man and Sims, the keeper showed the picture first to Doctor Forbes Winslow.[5] There is also a claim that the police stopped Sims when he carried a black bag in the East End.[6] This seems to be a distortion of Sims' own story that he once borrowed a knife and took it in a black bag to the Pavilion Theatre, Whitechapel.[7]

In a collection of Walter Sickert's writings, Sir Oswald Sitwell told a story about a young veterinary student who aroused the suspicion of his landlady, at the time of the murders. Sickert rented the student's former rooms at 6 Mornington Crescent. The landlady told him that the student would stay out all night, buy all the newspapers that told of the crimes and burn his clothes. He was in ill health. After the last murder, his mother took him to Bournemouth where he died three months later.[8] Sickert, who told this story to other people, apparently scribbled the name of the student in a copy of Casanova's memoirs belonging to Sitwell. The book was destroyed in the blitz.[9] In 1960, a notebook belonging to the painter Max Beerbohm was auctioned at Sotheby's. After Sickert's name, someone had written *"Extreme of refinement,"* followed by a long arrow then *"love of squalor. Lodged in Jack the Ripper's house."*[10] The 1891 census shows a medical student called Wuller living at 6 Mornington Crescent. He was born in Egypt, c. 1871.

In 1985, Stuart Hicks suggested that Sickert's student was John Hewitt, a doctor from Manchester who became mentally ill and went to Cotton Hill lunatic asylum.[11] Asylum records show that he was confined at the times of the murders. Hewitt married a nurse from the asylum and moved to Bournemouth, where he died in 1892.

The poet Ernest Dowson was born in August 1867. In March 1888, he abandoned his studies at Oxford to supervise Bridge Dock on the Thames at Limehouse, owned by his father. He resided in the East End at the time of the murders. In November 1889, he began courting eleven-year-old Adelaide Foltinowicz who served at her father's

203

restaurant in Sherwood Street, London. She married a tailor called August Noelte and died from a botched abortion on 13 December 1903.[12]

Dowson's father died from an overdose in August 1894 and his mother hanged herself six months later. He then spent some time in France and translated French texts. He died, from alcoholism in Catford on 23 February 1900.

Dowson was tentatively identified with a man described by journalist Robert Thurston Hopkins.[13] This man, who Thurston Hopkins called "Moring," was a poet and alleged friends with Mary Jane Kelly. He frequented various taverns and was addicted to opium, being disowned by his father for that reason. The father was a prosperous tradesman in the East End. Thurston-Hopkins read an old newspaper report about Hutchinson's sighting and saw similarities with the poet's description but could not imagine a man of such gentleness committing the crimes.[14] Martin Fido noted discrepancies between Hutchinson's sighting and the description of Mr Moring.[15] It is unclear where Thurston-Hopkins obtained his information about Mary Kelly's friends and he did not describe "Moring" as a suspect.

In an appendix to Dowson's published letters Thurston-Hopkins described how he and Dowson spent several evenings in a pub called The Bun House during the late 1890s when Hopkins was studying at University College. Dowson always carried a revolver. When walking the streets one night they were chased by a strange figure carrying a Gladstone bag.[16] Later Dowson's landlady reported that a lodger named Lazarus had been found dead in his bed, with a Gladstone bag that contained mounds of earth.

Thurston-Hopkins also claimed to have seen the poet John Barlas in the Bun House.[17] John Evelyn Barlas was born in Rangoon in 1860. His father died when he was one and his mother took him to Glasgow. He studied at Oxford and married Honoria Nelson Davies on 25 June 1881. He briefly studied law before becoming professor of languages at St Stanislaus College, Rahan, Tullamore, Ireland in 1884. Following the death of his three-year-old daughter, Evelyn, in June 1885 he returned to England and became assistant classical master at a grammar school in Chelmsford. In 1886, he moved to his family home in Crieff then to Englefield Green, Surrey.

He was 31 years old, when arrested on New Year's Eve 1891 for firing a revolver three times towards the Houses of Parliament. This resulted in him being bound over for £200 and having to find sureties of the same amount for his behaviour for two months. His friends, one of whom was Oscar Wilde, paid bail.[18] On 12 September 1892, he appeared at Crieff Police Court charged with assaulting a journalist, Reginald Booker, and a man named James Steward.[19] His friends placed him in Perth asylum. He was released in March 1893. A further charge of assault followed in July 1893, also at Crieff, when he resisted the police.[20] He was eventually sent to Gartnavel Royal asylum where the receiving doctor noted that he was dangerous to others and had many delusions.[21] He died in the asylum on 15 August 1914 of valvular disease of the heart.

At the time of the murders, Barlas was living with a prostitute in Lambeth at 44 Hercules Buildings.[22] David A Green connected him to a suspect mentioned in an article in the New York Times on 24 October 1897. The journalist, Rowland Strong, was informed by a perfectly trustworthy authority that the police knew the murderer as a lunatic confined in a Scottish asylum. The killer was an Oxford graduate and had a reputation ten years earlier as a minor poet. He bore a distinguished name, famous in Scottish history in connection with a young woman who saved a King's life in a heroic way. The suspect had a wife descended from a famous English Admiral and his latest delusion was that he was the grandson of Napoleon. Barlas wrote poetry under the name Evelyn Douglas, adopted in honour of his ancestor Kate or Catherine Douglas who was a lady in waiting to Joan Beaufort and used her arm to prevent assassins from entering the chamber of King James I of Scotland.

Robert Sherard, a drinking partner, and colleague of Strong's, knew Barlas. He wrote from Paris to the Pall Mall Gazette in 1892, saying that Barlas had been his best friend. He stated that Barlas gave away his fortune and was in one of General Booth's shelters the previous December.[23]

Francis Thompson was born in Preston on 16 December 1859, son of Charles Thompson, a homeopathic doctor. He studied for the priesthood between 1870 and 1877 at St Cuthberts College, Ushaw near Durham then failed medical examinations at Owens College, Manchester, in 1879 and 1882.[24] In 1885, he was dismissed from the military for failing a drill. He went to London to purse his ambition of being a writer but could only find employment as a shoemaker, shoeblack, matchbox seller, and porter. On 23 February 1887, he sent some poems to Wilfred Meynell, editor of a Catholic magazine called Merrie England. Meynell liked them but his response to Thompson was not delivered. In the autumn of 1887, Thompson attempted suicide, via an overdose, believing that the ghost of Thomas Chatterton saved him.[25] Chatterton was a poet who committed suicide in 1770.

Meynell published the poems in April 1888, hoping that the author would identify himself. Thompson wrote back, giving an address at a Chemist's shop. Meynell went there and settled a large debt for opium. In early 1889, he arranged for Thompson to be cared for at a monastery in Sturrington, West Sussex, and then, following his recovery, to live in London. Thompson's first book of poetry appeared in 1893. Two others followed in 1895 and 1897. He began taking drugs again in 1892 and went to a monastery in Wales for rehabilitation.

Thompson died at the age of 48 on 13 November 1907. G K Chesterton called him the greatest poet since Browning.[26] In 1913 Meynell's son, Everard, published a biography of Thompson. He stated that Thompson met a man supposed to be a murderer in a common lodging house and made several allusions to the murderer, describing him under the initials D.I.[27] Confirmation that Thompson used common lodging houses comes from Osbert Sitwell in his introduction to the poems of W.H.Davies.[28] He describes Davies seeing a stranger in a Lambeth doss house and later recognising him as Thompson. Davies (1871-1940) was a poet who also spent time on the streets.

One of Thompson's unpublished poems, "Nightmare of the Witch Babies," describes a knight disembowelling a woman he met in the fog. This was written prior to the Ripper murders. It included the phrase, ha ha, in several stanzas but samples of Thompson's handwriting did not match the Dear Boss Letter.[29]

Thompson befriended a prostitute during his time in the East End of London.[30] She disappeared from the Strand and an address in Chelsea and he was actively trying to find her in 1888. It is possible that he resided at the Providence Row Shelter at 272 Whitechapel Road, close to Dorset Street, in the autumn of 1888.[31] An obituary stated that he slept in the rubbish heap at Convent garden market.[32]

In an essay on Bunyan, Thompson wrote. "*He had better seek some critic who will lay his subject on the table, nick out every muscle of expression with light, fastidious scalpel and then call upon him to admire the neat dissection.*"[33] In a short story, he wrote about a future poet who murdered his lover and gave her body to Virgil in exchange for recognition of his talent.[34] In a letter, he stated that he had previously shaved with a dissecting scalpel.[35]

Richard Patterson suggested that Thompson was the suspect in Marie Belloc Lowdnes, The Lodger, which contains a scene where an inquest witness mentions a suspect reading poetry.[36] Belloc Lowndes lived in London from 1896 and described the Meynells as friends in her autobiography.[37] She was also a Catholic and acquainted with many writers and poets in the period but does not mention Francis Thompson. There are reports from fellow lodgers that Thompson behaved strangely, talking to himself in his room, and pacing up and down.[38]

In an interview given to John Blunts Monthly on 16 December 1929, a discharged Broadmoor patient alleged that a former inmate was known as Jack the Ripper. Said to have been caught after one of the murders he was immediately pronounced insane. Knowing that the public would demand his execution, which was not possible because of the madness, the authorities called him Mr Taylor. In captivity, he was quiet and well behaved, enjoying scientific books and diagnosing the ailments of fellow patients. He tried to escape by climbing a wall, but a chisel fell out of his pocket onto a glass frame and the noise attracted attention. Shortly afterwards, he died.[39] As he had been confined for thirty years his death must have occurred after 1918.

There was an inmate called William Taylor in Broadmoor until his death in 1925. He had killed his child and a police superintendent in Otley in February 1888, before the Ripper murders. A man called Frederick Taylor was admitted in 1891 and died in 1913.[40] The 1891 census for Broadmoor also shows a James Taylor, age 57, born London, and a William Joseph Taylor, age 56, born Limehouse. Neither were still there in 1911.

On 16 March 1931, the Daily Express published a letter from former Police Constable Robert Spicer who said that he arrested Jack the Ripper.[41] One night he came across a prostitute called Rosy and a doctor sitting on a bin in Heneage Street. The Doctor had bloodstains on his cuffs and carried a brown bag. Spicer took him to Commercial Street Police Station where an inspector asked why a respectable doctor had been arrested. The suspect gave an address in Brixton. He was allowed to leave, and his bag was not examined. He wore a high hat, black suit with silk facing and a gold watch and chain. He was about five feet, eight or nine inches tall and weighed twelve stone, with a fair moustache, high forehead, and rosy checks. Spicer saw him several times after the incident, usually accosting women. In particular, this happened near Liverpool Street station several months later. Spicer claimed to have been in trouble with his superiors because of the attempted arrest and chose to leave the police force. In reality, he was dismissed for being drunk on duty in April 1889.[42]

In 1972, B.E. Reilly discovered a man, who he called Doctor Merchant from Brixton, who died in December 1888 from a septic abscess of tubercular origin.[43] Riley suggested that this was the man arrested by Spicer. He was identified as Doctor Frederick Richard Chapman.[44] Born in Poona in 1851, Chapman qualified as a Doctor in Glasgow in 1874 and came to London, from Hull, in 1886. He lived in Brixton and died of septic tubercular abscesses on 12 December 1888.

Thomas Dutton, alleged author of the Chronicles of Crime, was the second of nine children born to George and Barbara Dutton. George was manager of the London and Westminster Bank in Whitechapel, before retiring to Ore. Thomas had a distinguished medical career, becoming a fellow of the Hunterian Society and vice chairman of the Pure Food Society. His books included the Kimpton Pocket Books for Medicine (1907), Indigestion Clearly Explained, Treated and Dieted (1892), and The Rearing and Feeding of Children (1895). He was noted as an expert on obesity. In later years, he became a recluse.

Following his death, the Empire News on 17 November 1935 claimed that he had been taken into protective custody a few days after the last Jack the Ripper murder because he was carrying a black bag.[45] In a letter printed in the Daily Mail six years earlier Dutton said that he was going home one night, after the murders, with a black bag that held a masonic apron when he was accosted by two women calling him "Jack the Ripper."[46]

A 67-year-old bootmaker from Wellingborough called Alfred Hinde died after being hit by an omnibus on 24 January 1936. The Times said that he was once detained by a detective who thought that he was Jack the Ripper. Hinde was assisting a woman who called for help and the real culprit had run off. He was injured in the struggle with the man and the police paid for his treatment.[47] He may be the Alfred T Hinde born Whitechapel who appears in the 1891 census living with his parents and siblings in Islington. An Alfred Hines gave evidence at the Old Bailey in 1896, after he helped a manslaughter victim.[48]

Griffith Salway, a broker who lived in London in 1888, claimed to know an Argentinian businessman called Alonzo Maduro. On the night of Emma Smith's murder Salway saw Maduro in Whitechapel and heard him say that all prostitutes should be killed. Afterwards Salway discovered that Maduro possessed surgical knives. This claim did not appear in print until 1949.[49] Researcher Juan Jose Delaney found people who had known Alfonso Maroni in Buenos Aires. In the early twentieth century, Maroni lived in the neighbourhood of the Bolsa, the stock exchange which he often frequented. He was known for dressing in a long dark overcoat and soft felt hat. He died in October 1929 in a hotel in the Paseo de Julio.[50]

In February 1959 George Edwards, who was aged 11 in 1888, accused his cousin Frank.[51] Frank visited George's family in Chichester after the double murder wearing gold pince-nez and carrying a razor and blood-stained shirt in his case. He was an accountant who frequently picked quarrels over women. George and another cousin read about the sighting of Leon Goldstein and believed that it matched Frank's description. George feared that he would be killed too. Another cousin, Mrs Bertha Parkhurst, aged

75, said that Frank was rumoured to have murdered a woman in London, but she could not remember the details. George and Bertha were brother and sister, children of Henry, a blacksmith, in Chichester. Henry's sister Eliza married Samuel Wilton in 1852 and gave birth to a son, Frank, in 1855. Frank became a policeman.

In the same year, Dr. Denis Halstead published a book in which he commented that staff at the London hospital were in the limelight. On more than one occasion, he found himself shadowed by plain-clothes detectives.[52] His own theory was that the Ripper suffered from syphilis and had joined a North Sea fishing fleet after Mary Kelly's death.

On 25 October 1959, the Sunday Times published a letter from the actor Bransby Williams (1870-1961), saying that the police stopped him on his way to a working man's club in Poplar.[53] He was asked to open his black bag, which contained a painted knife.

In 1969, former Police Inspector Lewis Henry Keaton gave a tape-recorded interview in which he revealed a theory that the Ripper was a doctor who collected infected wombs for research purposes. He appeared to name a suspect as either Dr Cohn or Koch, who used strychnine.[54] This might be a recollection of Dr Cream. Keaton joined the police force in 1891 and was not involved in the 1888 hunt for Jack the Ripper.

Clarence Simm was accused in 1989 by his widow, Betty in an article in the Weekly World News. The same newspaper reprinted the story three years later when Betty was 100.[55] Clarence made a deathbed confession in 1951 to having killed fourteen prostitutes as a teenager to free them from a life of sin. Betty met him in London 1905. She first made the allegation in a letter to her son, Walter. A lawyer found the letter after Walter's death. Betty said that Simm was a 36-year-old accountant when they met. The family moved to Yorkshire soon after the marriage. Polygraph operator Gerald Mevel, who conducted the test with a colleague, Jacques Clement, said there was less than 0.5%

211

chance that Betty was lying. No other record of Clarence and Betty's existence has been found.

In Section 185 of Brisbane's Toowong cemetery, a tombstone above plots nine and ten states "*Bessie died 25 June 1957 and her husband.*" Cemetery records identify Bessie as Eliza Porriott. Her husband was Walter Thomas Porriott, who died 29 August 1952. His age is given as 59, indicating that he was born in 1893, five years after the Ripper murders.

In 1997, an article appeared in "The Bulletin."[56] It alleged that Porriott was an alias of an international bigamist and conman, Andrew John Gibson, who was also Jack the Ripper. Gibson's descendant Steve Wilson suggested that the recorded age was incorrect and that Gibson/Porriott died in his eighties, meaning that he was just about old enough to have been Jack the Ripper. The date and place of Gibson's birth are unconfirmed. He lived in Sydney as Charles Ernest Chadwick from 1889 and served as a special constable during the Maritime strike in 1890. On 15 April 1891, age 20, he appeared in court, charged with delivering a false paper purporting to be a Supreme Court decree. A medical examination found that his sanity was questionable.[57]

On 15 October 1891, he married Frances Mary Skelly at St Matthews Church in the Windsor suburb. On 18 July 1893, he was convicted of fraud and sentenced to eighteen months in Goulburn Gaol. Prison records stated that he was born in 1867 and arrived in Australia on board the Ormuz in 1889.[58] He went on to serve a further three months for false pretences at Cootamundra and was released on 27 February 1895.[59]

Using the name Henry Westwood Cooper, he committed bigamy by marrying fifteen-year-old Helen Scott in June 1895. The Police Gazette of 7 August 1895 reported that there was a warrant against him for signing a certificate on 13 May as a medical practitioner, without being registered.[60] This gave his age as 28. He was found and sent

212

back to Goulburn, where his year of birth was given as 1868, and he claimed to have arrived on the Armosz in 1895. This record stated that he was a Doctor of Medicine born in England and gave the alias of Charles Ernest Chadwick.[61]

On 12 June 1896, he married seventeen-year-old Bertha Ethel Young under the name Dr Henry Irwin Llewellyn Cooper. They moved to America where he later abandoned her. Reverting to the name Henry Westwood Cooper, he married Ida Maud Campaign on 24 May 1897 in Toronto.

Arrested for fraud in San Francisco he told police that he was born in Ireland and educated in Oxford but did not graduate from the university. Instead in 1890, he received a diploma from the Royal College of Physicians and Surgeons and went to Australia, where he remained until 1893 when he obtained his M.D. He went to England where his diploma from the Royal College was cancelled for unprofessional conduct and he practised in Australia, using his Baltimore qualification before moving to Canada.[62]

The police found a receipt for a ladies watch from a London jeweller, in the name W. C. Joles and speculated that this was his real name. A W C Joles arrived in Australia from London on the Victoria on 22 September 1890. Another, or perhaps the same, person with this name arrived on the Carthage on 19 January 1889.[63] Two years later the Sydney Evening News reported that a woman was charged with stealing from William Charles Joles.[64] Gibson was then using the name Chadwick. There was a William Charles Joles born in Lewisham in 1862 and another in Corsham, Wiltshire on 9 February 1873. The first married a laundress named Mary Ann Tranter and stayed in England until his death in 1909. The fate of the second is unknown.

Gibson was jailed for fraud in San Francisco and, in 1899, told the authorities of an escape plot involving a guard and eight desperate inmates.[65] He married for a fifth time in California in 1901 and, for a sixth time in San Francisco jail in 1905. It was his second spell there, again for fraud. He remarried in February 1912, to Anna Millbraith, deserted her, and fled to England. The American authorities wanted him extradited on fresh charges of forgery, bigamy, obtaining money under false pretences and violating parole.[66]

In May 1912, he left England for South Africa and then returned to Australia. On 6 August, he was charged in Sydney with having unlawfully used the title of surgeon on 27 June 1912 as Swinton Home alias Dr James Boyd, 42 years old. He was also charged under the names Norman Ebenezer McKay, Dr Milton Abrahams, Ernest Moore Chadwick, Charles Ernest Chadwick, and Dr James Elingsworth Boyd, with having committed offences of forgery, falsity, and theft at Durban. The amount involved was about $1700.[67] He was sentenced to eighteen months imprisonment in Durban in March 1913. Oakland Police expected him to be deported from Natal on completion of his sentence.[68] Not much is known about the South African offences, but he could only have been in the country for a few weeks. Possibly, it matched his later pattern of presenting forged government documents to banks.

The Australian Police Gazette reported on 21 April 1915 that a warrant was issued at Johannesburg for his arrest in respect of frauds totalling $1,955. He was forty-eight and had left Johannesburg on 5 April 1915. [69] He was said to have been born in 1867 either in Maryland, New South Wales or Canterbury, England. Returned he was sentenced to life imprisonment on 17 or 19 October 1916 for frauds totalling $3,765.[70]

Wilson said that Gibson wrote a medical textbook, Health and Vigour, whilst in Australia in 1914. In it he claimed that prostitutes should be killed with an axe. The National Library of Australia has a copy of Health and Vigor by H.W. Cooper, and date it c. 1930. It contains two hundred and thirteen pages of text about many medical ailments. The author criticises marriages of convenience and states, "*Prostitution must go on until men, and women are wise and good enough to lay the axe at the very roots of this deadly evil.*" [71]

This appears to be a copy of an earlier textbook by Cooper. An undated reprint by Percy George Carte is also held by the National Library of Australia. On 2 April 1917, Carte was charged with unprofessional conduct. He admitted that he had written a pamphlet and replied to correspondence with copies of letters from Dr H.W. Cooper, dated 1914. He was struck off the medical register for the offence.[72] In 1918, he was fined for practicing as a medical practitioner without being registered.[73]

A medical practitioner called Henry Westwood Cooper appeared in a Sydney court on 9 September 1907 and lost a case over ownership of goods.[74] Gibson was not in the country then, having been sentenced to life imprisonment in South Africa six months before Carte's misconduct hearing. There was also a Henry Westwood Cooper sought by the police in Sydney in 1886, for fraud.[75] He was aged 35. On 10 May 1893, a doctor of this name, qualified in Baltimore, was registered in Australia with certificate number 1828.[76] He appears in subsequent lists up to 1899. Since Gibson was in jail, or in America during this time, it appears that he borrowed the identity of a real person. Consequently, he may not have been the author of Health and Vigor.

In November 1925, Andrew John Gibson was arrested for fraud in Bournemouth, where he had set up a medical practice and claimed to be the Deputy Agent-General for migration for the South Australian government. He was sentenced to seven years.[77] Almost certainly he was the Andrew John Gibson, age 61 of no fixed abode, prosecuted for obtaining money under false pretences in Bristol in 1932. It was alleged that he had placed advertisements offering to get medical positions for young men.[78]

In 1937 a wanted notice was again posted in the Australian Police Gazette, listing 29 aliases. He was wanted in London for fraud and was last seen there on 12 August 1937

215

accompanied by his wife, whose maiden name was Annie Gladys Tilston.[79] He was captured and, on 4 February 1938, jailed in Liverpool for a year for obtaining money with false pretences. He had used a forged Sydney Supreme Court certificate of probate on the will of his daughter, Nellie, claiming that she had died and left him a legacy.[80] His age was given as 72.

Mary Ellen Chadwick was the daughter from Gibson's marriage with Frances Mary Skelly. In 1912, she married Walter Thomas Perriott (Porriotte) at Woollahra in Sydney. Walter Thomas died in 1936, when the milk cart he was driving fell over a twenty-foot embankment.[81] It does seem likely that Gibson adopted the name Porriott, as his final alias. His death certificate gives his father's name as John and his mother's as Annie Bailey, which matches the names of his son-in-law's parents.

On 13 February 1940, Gibson was charged in England with unlawfully killing Gladys Ada Elizabeth Higginbotham.[82] His age was given as 72. Other charges included giving false death certificates, forging death certificates, uttering the forged certificates and obtaining money by false pretences. He said that his proper name was Henry Cecil Rutherford Darling. He had used that name, which belonged to a Sydney doctor, to obtain a position as locum at Stoke on Trent maternity hospital. On 20 December 1939, Mrs Higginbotham arrived at the hospital. Gibson told a nurse that it was a serious case but did not examine the patient who died the following morning.

Gibson told Chief Inspector Hobson that he was not qualified to issue a death certificate but had the necessary skill and knowledge. Inspector Thomas Sullivan of Liverpool said he had known the defendant as Arthur John Gibson, since 1935, and that the man had worked as a post-office sorter, labourer, and manager of an herbalist's business. Gibson used the name Henry Cecil Darling and was married under that name. An alderman confirmed that Gibson called himself Dr. Darling and claimed to be a gynaecologist. Judge Hallet asked Gibson if he had any evidence of his medical qualifications. He was unable to provide this and received a ten-year sentence for manslaughter.[83] Following the verdict a list of previous convictions was considered. A witness Charles Curtiss Hardy was called to identify Gibson as the man convicted in South Africa in 1916.[84]

On 3 June 1950, the press reported that all British and Irish airports had been asked to look out for Gibson, who had been working under the name Cecil Rutherford Darling at Sofala General Hospital, Sydney, for the last year. He disappeared a week earlier when a warrant was issued for his arrest. He was 83. This report states that he returned to Australia in 1946.[85] Another Australian newspaper states that the warrant concerned his lack of medical qualifications and that he was legally married under the name Gibson on 1 July 1914, in South Africa at the age of 44.[86]

Wilson said that Gibson gave a statement to Australian prison authorities that he left England on 9 November 1888, the day of Mary Kelly's murder, on the Liguita. Wilson also claimed that a bad cheque written by Gibson/Porriott in 1892 matched the handwriting in the Dear Boss letter. His third contention was that the marriage to a woman named Skelly suggested a link to Mary Kelly. Francis Mary Skelly was born in Goulborn in 1870.[87]

On his deathbed in 1935, Doctor Leonard Thornton apparently said to his granddaughter, Doreen, "*If you knew what I have done you would not come near me.*" Because of this and his preoccupation with fallen women, Doreen became convinced that he was the Ripper. Her half-brother, the journalist, Michael Thornton published details in the Daily Mail on Boxing Day 2006.[88] The police were hunting a modern-day killer of prostitutes in Ipswich and a television documentary about the Ripper prompted Thornton to come forward.

Leonard Thornton transported horses to the knacker's yard to fund his education. He studied anatomy at the London Hospital and would often walk home carrying a black bag with his surgical instruments inside. He qualified as a chemist and druggist at the age of 25 and married Hannah O'Sullivan in 1885. There were problems in the marriage and Hannah later told her granddaughter, Doreen, that Len was moody and came home at night with blood stained clothes. She also said that the police became suspicious of Len after Mary Kelly's death, asked him some searching questions, and followed him for a while. Michael claimed to have a diary of Leonard's, which gave insights into his troubled state of mind. Michael also said that Lady Aberconway told him in 1972 that Melville Macnaghten was convinced that Druitt was the Ripper. In 1992, he reported that Aberconway said the truth about the Ripper would cause the throne to totter.[89]

Littlechild's Letter

In 1913, Chief Inspector John Littlechild wrote a letter to George Sims stating:

"I never heard of a Dr. D. in connection with the Whitechapel murders but amongst the suspects and to my mind a very likely one was a Dr. T (which sounds very much like D). He was an American quack named Tumblety and was at one time a frequent visitor to London and on these occasions constantly brought under the notice of police, there being a large dossier concerning him at Scotland Yard. Although a "Sycopathia Sexualis" subject he was not known as a sadist (which the murderer unquestionably was) but his feelings towards women were remarkable and bitter in the extreme, a fact on record. Tumblety was arrested at the time of the murders in connection with unnatural offences and charged at Marlborough Street, remanded on bail, jumped his bail and got away to Boulogne. He shortly left Boulogne and was never heard of again. It was believed he committed suicide but certain it is that from this time the Ripper murders came to an end."[1]

The press reported that Tumblety was under suspicion in New York around 1888 for his connections to the Irish National Party.[2] This may explain Littlechild's interest and the dossier which is no longer extant.

Francis was the youngest of eleven children born to James and Margaret Tumblety in Ireland in 1830. He grew up in Rochester, New York and became a successful herb doctor, practising in several Canadian and American cities. His first confirmed brush with the law occurred in Montreal in September 1857. A detective posing as a client asked if he could procure a miscarriage. Tumblety agreed, for a fee of $20. The detective then

219

returned with a seventeen-year-old prostitute, Philomene Dumas. Tumblety gave her some medicine and took the money. Four hours later, he was arrested.[3] Due to conflicting evidence, the case was dismissed.[4] Tumblety's attorney sued him after he refused to pay a bill of $125. A court reduced the amount to $50.[5]

In September 1860, a Supreme Court judge in St Johns, Robert Parker, reversed a magistrate's view that Tumblety had fraudulently passed himself off as a doctor.[6] Tumblety donated the amount of the reimbursed fine, $20, to the poor. He was next in trouble when an inquest jury concluded that he was guilty of manslaughter, following the death of a patient, James Potmore.[7] Tumblety left town before the conclusion of the inquest.

In 1861, he sued the Chemical Bank in New York, claiming they had accepted a forged cheque on his account and accused a young man called Charles Whelpley of the fraud. Whelpley had previously cashed one legitimate cheque for Tumblety. Witnesses gave mixed evidence to Tumblety's character. The court found in favour of the defendant.[8]

The following year Tumblety was listed in the Washington City Directory as a physician. There are two extant allegations that he sold fake discharge papers to soldiers.[9] He filed an unsuccessful libel suit against a theatre that had ridiculed him in a sketch entitled "Dr. Tumblety's First Patient," performed on 7 March 1862. The theatre manager stated it was unintentional and promised not to use Tumblety's name in his program again.[10]

On 21 May 1863, Tumblety told the Philadelphia Police that a man named St. Clair had stolen a gold medal, worth $800, from him. He claimed that he received the medal from the citizens of Montreal. St Clair was released when the authorities of Montreal denied presenting the medal and Tumblety claimed to have found it. On 1 July, a warrant against Tumblety for perjury was issued.[11]

The following year Fenton Scully travelled from New York to Brooklyn to consult Tumblety about asthma. His health worsened, after taking the prescription, and he returned. Tumblety resented the request for a refund.[12] Scully's charge against the Doctor was dismissed.[13]

In St Louis, Tumblety was arrested for wearing the insignia of a federal officer.[14] He protested his right to freedom of dress. His next arrest was for a far more serious offence. John Wilkes Booth killed the American president, Abraham Lincoln, on 14 April 1865, and several people were taken into custody on suspicion of involvement. The link to Tumblety came through a boy who claimed to have been an errand boy for Booth. He said that Booth's accomplice, David Herold had lived in Brooklyn under the name Blackburn and had been an assistant to a physician.[15] Tumblety had an assistant called Mark Blackburn, known as J H Blackburn. The press reported that Tumblety had also been known by that name.[16]

A report of Tumblety's arrest by the Provost Marshall General of St Louis, Colonel Baker, stated that nothing was found amongst Tumblety's papers to implicate him in the assassination.[17] Despite this he spent three weeks in a Washington jail, before being released without charge. Later he wrote to several newspapers to clear his name.[18] He filed a claim for false imprisonment by the United States Army in March 1865 and, again, in May the same year. He also claimed for personal property and valuables taken by the army during the second arrest but subsequently withdrew this. His other claims were rejected.[19]

Tumblety visited Europe in 1869, going through Ireland to London. He claimed to have cured Louis Napoleon in France and to have stayed in the Royal Palace in Berlin.

221

His biographer pointed out that just eight days elapsed between 23 August 1868, when he wrote a letter from London, and 1 September when he sailed from Liverpool back to America. There was not enough time for him to complete the French and German trips.[20]

He returned to England four years later, arriving in Liverpool on 21 July 1873. In London, he persuaded seventeen-year-old Henry Carr to go to Liverpool and presented him with a gold chain. Carr left Tumblety and attempted to pawn the chain but was charged with theft. The magistrate dismissed the case.[21]

In 1874, Tumblety set up a business at 177 Duke Street Liverpool, as the Great American Doctor. One of his patients, Edward Hanratty, died. On 27 January 1875, an inquest attributed the death to natural causes. The jury strongly censured the conduct of Tumblety for administering treatment in ignorance of the patient's condition.[22] Tumblety did not attend the inquest, arguing through his solicitor that the jury was biased and that he had been stopped from attending the post-mortem.

At the same time, Tumblety faced a claim that he had used false testimony from William Caroll in one of his advertisements. The case was dismissed when neither party turned up to the hearing on 23 February 1875.[23] An advert for the Great American Doctor appeared in a Birmingham newspaper on 16 August 1875.[24] Tumblety was based in Union Passage in the city, but not for long as he arrived back in New York on 17 September 1875.[25]

In 1880, he attempted to sue Mrs Lyons after her son absconded with $7000 of bonds that Tumblety had left in his care. The case failed. On his return, Lyons sued Tumblety for "atrocious assault." On 24 July 1880, the New York Times reported that Judge Donohue granted the motion for Lyons v Sumblety.[26] Tumblety proceeded to sue the banker, William O'Connor, who took the bonds from Lyons. This case failed.[27]

On 14 October 1880, Tumblety was arrested in Toronto on a charge of indecent assault against a boy named Bulger. Convicted of common assault, he was fined a dollar, plus costs.[28] In New Orleans, in February 1881, he was accused of stealing a pocketbook containing $70 from Henry Govan who hired a private detective, Dominick O'Malley, to find him. O'Malley claimed that Tumblety had confessed and that burglar's tools were found in his room. The subsequent investigation led to O'Malley being charged with carrying a concealed weapon. Tumblety was freed.[29]

After visiting Liverpool in 1887, Tumblety returned to England the following June.[30] The Chicago Tribune of 7 October 1888 stated that an American, who used to live in New York, now kept a herb shop in Whitechapel.[31] If this is true and the man was Tumblety, it places him in the murder district. On 7 November 1888, two days before Mary Kelly's murder, he was arrested. A warrant was issued on 14 November, charging him with acts of gross indecency, with the following men on the given dates.

Albert Fisher, 27 July 1888.

Arthur Brice, 31 August 1888.

James Crowley, 14 October 1888.

John Doughty, 2 November 1888.

Tumblety received bail on 16 November and absconded to France then America on the steamer Bretagne, arriving in New York on 3 December 1888 under the name Frank Townsend. He is almost certainly the person referred to in press reports, which said, "*a certain person, whose name is known, has sailed from Le Havre to New York, who is famous for his hatred of women and who has repeatedly made threats against females of dissolute character.*"[32]

On 1 December 1888 William Smith, the Canadian Deputy Minister of Marine wrote to a friend saying that Tumblety was the man arrested in Whitechapel three weeks earlier as the murderer. He had been living in Birmingham and travelling to London on Saturday nights.[33] This may tie in with British Newspaper reports about the arrest of a man at Euston station on 17 November 1888.[34] Euston was the main terminal for trains from Birmingham, but this arrest was a day after Tumblety received his bail.

On Boxing Day 1888, the Dundee Courier said that Tumblety had been arrested on suspicion of the Whitechapel murders, but the police were unable to procure evidence and charged him with the other offences instead.[35]

An article in the Birmingham Daily Post on New Year's Day 1889 stated that Inspector Andrews had arrived in New York from Montreal with orders to look for the Whitechapel murderer. The suspect had left England three weeks earlier.[36] Andrews departed England on 29 November 1888. His role was to escort a prisoner called Roland Gideon Israel Barnett who was extradited to Canada. Ten days before this Scotland Yard had written to the Home Office offering to escort Barnett if the Canadian Government paid.[37] This was before the hearing at the Old Bailey on 20 November 1888, when Tumblety's trial date was set.

The press reported that the San Francisco Police were in contact with Scotland Yard and on 19 November 1888 offered to provide a sample of Tumblety's handwriting. Four days later Robert Anderson asked them to send any information that they had.[38] The New York Times claimed on 23 November 1888 that the Chief of the New York Police had contacted the British Police on 29 October offering to send samples of Tumblety's handwriting and had just received a response requesting them.[39]

On 25 June 1889 Tumblety was in a New York Court, indicted for assaulting George Davis on 4 June. He had failed to appear at the original hearing.[40]

On 20 November 1890, the Cardiff Mail reported that Tumblety had been sent to gaol in Washington as a suspicious character.[41] According to the Washington Post, he was

arrested for loitering in shadows. His possessions included several thousand dollars'
worth of valuables, some testimonials, and an article replying to the charges brought
against him in London. The judge dismissed the case.[42]

On 17 April 1891, he was the victim of a robbery at the Plateau Hotel in Hot Springs
Arkansas. Thieves took $2000 cash and diamonds valued between $5000 and $7000.[43] He
died in Rochester, New York, in 1903. His arrest on suspicion of being Jack the Ripper
was noted in reports of the death circulated in Britain.[44]

Evans and Gainey suggested that Tumblety was a man who lodged at 22 Batty Street
in 1888 and became a suspect after the discovery of a blood-stained shirt.[45] The German
landlady reported that she had been disturbed by the lodger's movements on the night of
the double event and he then went away, leaving her to wash the shirt. He was arrested.[46]
This was denied by the police who appeared to be preventing the landlady from
discussing matters with the press. It was then reported that the landlady was a laundress
and the man had deposited four shirts in a bundle to be washed. She discovered the blood-
stained shirt and handed it to the police who placed the house under observation and left
detectives posing as lodgers. The man returned on 13 October and was freed by the police
after an hour's interrogation.[47] He was a lady's tailor and the bloodstains came from an
accident to another man.[48]

Evans and Gainey argued that the story of the laundry was invented by the authorities
as a cover-up. They suggested that Tumblety killed Eddowes but not Stride and returned
to find the area around his lodgings crowded with police looking for Stride's killer. A
letter from one of the lodgers at the address, Carl Noun, was published in the Evening
News on 18 October 1888.[49] He said that a stranger brought the shirts and was arrested by
the police when he came to claim them.

Tumblety confirmed that he was arrested on suspicion of the murders. In an interview published in the New York World 29 January 1889, he stated that he had been visiting London since 1869 and, in common with others, visited Whitechapel at the time of the crimes. He felt that the police followed him because he had a slouch hat and carried diamonds which they wanted to procure. He said that he had been in prison for two or three days and was critical of the British police. In response to the suggestion that he was a woman-hater, he told a story about meeting a duchess in Torquay and recited a poem that she had devoted to him.[50] In 1889, Tumblety published a booklet about his travels, in which he referred to his reputation being blackened by hideous malice.[51]

According to Colonel Dunham, quoted in various newspapers, Tumblety showed him a collection of anatomical organs. This was soon after the pair met, a few days after the first battle of Bull Run on 21 July 1861. Dunham said that he and his Lieutenant Colonel went to a late dinner in Tumblety's rooms. There were eight diners. When asked why he had not invited any women Tumblety said, "No Colonel, I don't know any such cattle," and proceeded to denounce all women, especially fallen ones. He showed his guests a dozen or more jars containing the matrices of every class of women. By chance, he saw his wife entering a brothel one day and learnt that she had a history of prostitution. He then gave up on women.[52] Charles A Dunham was an alias of Sanford Conover who had a history of providing evidence to implicate officials of the Confederate Government in plots, including Lincoln's assassination. He was convicted of perjury and jailed in 1867. President Johnson pardoned him two years later.[53]

In 1905 Richard Norris testified that he met Tumblety around 1880. Tumblety carried a trunk with a tray containing large knives and said that, if he had his way, streetwalkers would be disembowelled. Norris said that Tumblety was arrested in a put-up job to find out who he was. Norris was working at the New Orleans Police Department in 1888, and

226

saw reports connecting Tumblety to Jack the Ripper. He told the chief of police, David Hennessey. Norris spoke to Tumblety who said that he was in Whitechapel when the women were killed. Tumblety then spent a lot of money on Norris, taking him to the theatre.[54] Testimony given in 1905 by J. H. Ziegler was that Tumblety discussed surgery with him in 1903, displaying a degree of medical knowledge.[55]

It is unclear if Tumblety was in custody at the time of Mary Kelly's murder. Trevor Marriott, a former police officer, argued that Tumblety was remanded after his arrest on 7 November until the committal hearing on 16 November when he was bailed.[56] Court records show that a warrant was issued on 14 November, and the general view is that he had police bail between his arrest and the issue of the warrant.

Lunatics

This chapter considers the other lunatics suggested as Jack the Ripper. On 19 September 1888, Sir Charles Warren wrote: "*A man named Puckeridge was released from an asylum on 4 August. He was educated as a surgeon – has threatened to rip people up with a long knife. He is being looked for but cannot be found as yet.*"[1]

Oswald Puckridge, sometimes spelt Puckeridge, was born on 13 June 1838 at Burpham in Sussex to John and Philadelphia (nee Holmes). He married Ellen Buddel in 1868. The marriage certificate gives his occupation as apothecary. The couple had a son, Edward born in 1869, but separated some time before the 1891 census.

As license of the Railway Inn in Deal, Puckridge appeared before magistrates on a charge of opening his premises for the sale of alcohol at 11:45 on Sunday 29 September 1872, forty-five minutes before the permitted time. Police Constable Seath gave evidence that Puckridge admitted people with a train ticket. There followed a legal argument about his right to do this. Railway passengers were exempt from the licensing requirements and allowed to request alcohol if they so wished. The court adjourned for a week then decided that there was no evidence to justify a conviction.[2] Puckridge asked the bench if he could supply refreshments to residents of Deal returning home by the last train on Sunday nights. The magistrates were unable to give advice. The following year Puckridge obtained permission to remain open until 01:00 on the morning of Friday 10 January.[3]

From 1874 he was license of the New Inn in Ramsgate. On 5 April 1880 described as a retired publican, he was sentenced to six months hard labour at Ramsgate for causing the death of his dog. He had painted it with the Liberal and Conservative colours, presumably for the general election won by the Liberals. The dog was poisoned through licking the paint off.[4] Puckridge obtained bail, on appeal, but fled, it appears, to Jersey. In August 1884, he was identified at Sandwich railway station on a surreptitious visit to friends and returned to prison to serve his sentence.[5]

Later that year, under the name Oswald Fussell and described as a student of medicine he was charged with being drunk and disorderly and using bad language. On 2 December 1884, he was preaching in Great Chapel Street wearing a red jersey embroidered "Salvation Army" and hitting people with his crutches. He was ordered to pay a fine or serve fourteen days in jail.[6]

Twenty days later, he appeared in the Jersey Police Court wearing a Salvation army uniform. He was charged with habitual drunkenness, and disorderly conduct and assaulting Mr and Mrs Lovett. He lodged in three rooms owned by Mrs Lovett. On 20 December, he caused a disturbance in the house and tried to kick the arresting police officer. He was well known to the Jersey courts, having been ordered to give bail of £5 for his future behaviour after an incident in the previous year. [7]

The day after his release, he approached Phillip Journeaux with a sheep and asked if he wanted to go drinking. Journeaux refused. Puckeridge knocked off his hat and kicked a hole in it. Puckeridge claimed that he had asked for assistance to move his furniture. He had a bag containing a turkey, which he intended sending to the magistrate, a goose, which he intended sending to Centenier Seymour, and a duck, which was a Christmas present for someone else. The magistrate ordered him to give £10 bail for future good and peaceable conduct and pay five shillings for the value of Journeaux's hat or spend fourteen days in prison.[8]

He appeared before the same court on 17 October 1885 on charges of insulting Albert Bernard Seymour. Puckridge lodged in a cottage with Trossle Carus Best. Seymour, who rented a stable nearby, claimed that he was unable to get his van out because of the conduct of the two men who used foul language towards him. Seymour said that he had brought Puckridge up before the courts before and had been receiving anonymous letters ever since. Puckridge gave an eccentric speech, described as usual for him by the newspaper. He said he had returned to the island to erect a tombstone to his mother and was collecting her tea cosy and broom when he met Seymour who remarked that he had handcuffed him before and would do so again. The magistrate said that Puckridge was a public nuisance. He now had to pay his bail from his last appearance and agree a sum of £5 for future good behaviour or go to jail for eight days. On his next appearance, a report was ordered so that he could be sent to his place of settlement. After leaving court, he was arrested by the St Helier police on another charge.[9]

Puckridge was admitted to the Hoxton House lunatic asylum on 6 January 1888, as a pauper and released on 4 August 1888. Sir Charles Warren was aware of this, but it is not known why he regarded Puckridge as a surgeon.

In July 1889, Puckridge was charged with violent assault after hitting Henry Frederick Orange on the head with a gun. The incident occurred in a coffee house on York Street, London Road. Puckridge, described as a dispensing chemist, claimed self-defence and that Orange had attempted to rob him.[10] Henry Frederick Orange appeared as a witness to a robbery at a coffee shop in October the same year.[11]

On 18 August 1893, the Morning Post reported that Puckridge, described as an apothecary of 6 Stanhope Street Euston Road had been charged with wandering, apparently of unsound mind. Ejected from the Salvation Army barracks in Queen Victoria Street by Police Constable Crossingham he ran at a passing hansom cab and climbed on the horse's back. He was taken, with difficulty, to the police station where Doctor Buncombe certified his removal to Bow Infirmary. It appeared that drink and the heat had affected him. Sergeant Mc'Vitty said that he known Puckridge for several months. Puckridge was in the habit of wearing a naval uniform and refusing to pay for hansom cabs. A lady claiming to be his nurse, said that she would take care of him and ensure that he avoided alcohol. He was discharged with a caution on the understanding that he would go back to his friends who, he said, were in Southampton.[12]

Shortly afterwards he was locked up on a charge of being disorderly and assaulting the landlord of the Lord Nelson in Stanhope Street. Smoke was seen coming from his cell and the police found his rug, pillow, and part of the woodwork alight. He could not explain how the fire started. Previously he injured his head in a tramway accident and was still under surgical treatment. [13] He was returned to Bow Infirmary on 5 February 1896, being discharged nine days later. He was then admitted to the City of London lunatic asylum at Stone, recorded in the register of lunatics as a danger to others, and released on 9 July 1896.[14]

On 8 April 1899, described as a gentleman of Southminster, he was convicted of driving without a lamp at Burnham on 23 March and fined.[15] On 26 May that year, he resided in Romford Workhouse infirmary and claimed an intimate acquaintance with the Prince of Wales. On arrival at the workhouse, he carried a bankbook with a balance of over £555, two purses containing £6 in gold and half a £5 note. It was said that he was a respected chemist before he became entitled to a large sum of money and developed a taste for strong drink. He had been a conspicuous figure in Essex towns and was returned to the county lunatic asylum.[16]

Puckridge was admitted to Holborn workhouse on 28 May 1900 and died there on 1 June. On 2 August, probate was granted to his son Edward, a grocer. He left effects worth

£300.[17] City of London Police records indicate that he was traced during the Whitechapel murders. Detectives Lawley and Child reported on 25 September 1888 that they had visited Mr W. Tolfree of the Imperial Coffee House, 50 Rupert Street who said that Puckridge had been lodging at the house for four weeks, was eccentric and given to drink but had ample means. He had slept every night in the house.[18]

Comments in a book by Major Smith, head of the City Police may refer to Puckridge. He wrote, "*After the second crime I sent word to Sir Charles Warren that I had discovered a man very likely to be the man wanted. He had been a medical student; he had been in a lunatic asylum; he spent all his time with women of loose character, whom he bilked by giving them polished farthings instead of sovereigns, two of these farthings having been found in the pocket of the murdered woman. Sir Charles failed to find him. I thought he was likely to be in Rupert Street, Haymarket. I sent up two men, and there he was; but, polished farthings and all, he proved an alibi without the shadow of doubt.*"[19]

Alternatively, Smith's suspect may be a man who entered King Street Police Station at 09:00 on 16 October 1888 and threatened to cut off the sergeant's head. He rambled about the Whitechapel murders and said he studied for the medical profession then gave it up for engineering. Doctor Bond said he was a dangerous lunatic with a homicidal tendency. Aged 67 he looked much younger. Detectives had been tracing his antecedents and movements. In July, he was sent to Lambeth infirmary and, since August 15, lodged at a coffee house in the Westminster Bridge Road. The keeper of the house stated that the man had slept there every night since his arrival.[20]

Contemporary press accounts accused Nikolay Vasiliev, also called Nicholas Vassili or Wassily. He was a Russian born at Tiraspol in 1847 and educated at the University of Odessa. At the age of 25, he became one of the heads of the Skoptsy, a sect of eunuchs known in England as the shorn. Sometime around 1872 he killed seven prostitutes, including his former girlfriend, in Paris, under the influence of religious fanaticism. He was released from an asylum, either Bayonne or Tiraspol, in January 1888.[21] Russian residents in London apparently believed that he was the killer.[22]

Research has uncovered no record of this person at Odessa University or any definitive proof of his existence.[23] According to an article in The Star on 17 November 1888, the French Police emphatically denied that there had been a series of murders such as the ones indicated. In 1875, a man did attack several women in Paris, but none died, and he was not Russian.[24] Press reports state that Vasiliev poured over religious books during the day but the Skoptsy had no books.

In 1918, William Le Queux wrote a book, "The Minister of Evil: The Secret History of Rasputin's betrayal of Russia". He referred to a rich banker from Tver who escaped detection for murdering a young girl.[25] Five years later, in his autobiography, Le Queux mentioned Doctor Alexander Pedachenko as a Ripper suspect. Following the death of Rasputin Le Queux was allegedly hired by the Russian Government to write about the monk's career and given documents from the safe in the cellar of Rasputin's house. Amongst these was a manuscript, dictated in French, entitled Great Russian Criminals. This purported to tell the truth about Jack the Ripper. One night in the Jubilee Street Club, which was a centre for Russian anarchists in London, Nicholas Zverieff told a man called Niderost that the Ripper was Alexander Pedachenko who had worked in the maternity hospital at Tver. He then lived with his sister in Westmoreland Road, Walworth. The Russian Secret Police, the Okhrana, commissioned the murders to embarrass the Metropolitan Police. Pedachenko had two accomplices. Levitski kept watch and a woman named Winberg engaged the victims in conversation.

After the murders, Pedachenko returned to Russia. There he killed a woman and was sent to an asylum. He died in 1908. Le Queux claimed to have found a doctor called

233

Pedachenko who lived in Tver and that Niderost was a member of the Jubilee Street Club. Levitski, supposed author of the Ripper letters, was exiled to Yaktusk.[26]

Rasputin's daughter told Colin Wilson that her father's house did not have a cellar, that he did not speak or write French and had no interest in criminals.[27] Niderost was Swiss not Russian and the surnames of most of the characters in Great Russian Criminals are found in a directory called the Address-Calendar of the Russian Empire for 1888 within a few pages of each other. These included the governor of Yenisei Province, Lieutenant General Ivan Pedachenko, the postmaster of Karginsky Post Office, Pavel Levitsky and the head of the Cheremkhovsky post office, Nikolay Zverev.[28]

In 1959, Donald McCormick claimed that Prince Serge Belloselski showed him a copy of the Ochrana Gazette from January 1909, which announced that Vassily Konovalov, alias Pedachenko, Alexey alias Luiskovo, Andrey was officially declared dead. [29] Konovalov was wanted for the murder of a woman in the Montmartre district of Paris in 1886, the murder of five women in the East Quarter of London in 1888 and the murder of a woman in Petrograd in 1891. Petrograd was not named until 1914. Prior to that, it was known, as it is now, as St Petersburg. In later works, after researchers discovered Michael Ostrog, McCormick added his name to those in the Ochrana Gazette article.[30]

Citing Doctor Dutton's Chronicles of Crime, McCormick said that Wolf Levisohn told Inspector Abberline that a more likely suspect than George Chapman was a barber's assistant from Walworth Road believed to be Dr Alexander Pedachenko who worked as a barber-surgeon for a hairdresser named Delhaye in Westmoreland Road, Walworth in 1888. William Leopold Frederick Delhaye was living at 1 Westmoreland Road at the time of the 1881 census. By 1891, he had moved to 30 Denmark Hills Lambeth. According to McCormick Dutton also alleged that Doctor Williams, who lived in Camberwell and attended the St Saviours Infirmary, said that a Russian barber-surgeon occasionally assisted him. The surgeon's name was Pedachenko.[31]

There was a St Petersburg doctor called Dimitri Panchenko, who was hired by Patrick O'Brien de Lacy to murder his wife's parents and brother. Panchenko injected the brother in-law, Captain Buturlin with diphtheria. He was overhead talking about the murder and arrested, receiving a fifteen-year prison sentence in February 1911.[32] A later newspaper report alleged that he had earlier sold prussic acid to a soldier for use in Ethiopia but the solider consumed it instantly and died.[33]

Prior to discovering Aaron Kosminski, Martin Fido searched asylum and other records for people with a similar sounding name. In the Whitechapel Workhouse Infirmary Admissions and Discharge Book for 1888, he discovered Nathan Kaminsky, a Polish bootmaker admitted on 24 March 1888. Kaminsky was 23, single, and diagnosed as syphilitic. He was discharged on 12 May [34] His address in Black Lion Yard was almost exactly at the centre point of the five canonical murders. The direct route there from Mitre Square crossed Goulston Street and the doorway where Eddowes' apron was abandoned would be the first open door passed.[35] The only other Nathan Kaminsky of the right age found died in Dalston in the 1920, after emigrating in 1905. By coincidence he lived in Hanbury street at the time of the 1911 census. A Nathan Karnsky was admitted to Bethlem asylum on 13 May 1899 then went to Bethnal Green workhouse on 21 December that year. He died there on 9 June 1908.

Fido suggested that Kaminsky was confused with another Jew who appeared at the Thames magistrate court on 7 December 1888 as a lunatic wandering at large under the name Aaron Davis Cohen. He was sent to the Workhouse infirmary. The records describe him as David Cohen, age 23, a single tailor. He was very violent, threatening other patients and refusing food. He tore down the leaden pipe in the ward and the wire guard.[36]

He was transferred to Colney Hatch where he died, on 20 October 1889, from exhaustion of mania and pulmonary phthisis.

Cohen was the only Polish Jew admitted to an asylum shortly after the death of Mary Kelly. Fido argued that he was Nathan Kaminsky and that Cohen was a name given to those who had no identification. He further argued that this man was Anderson's suspect and that the police confused him with Kosminski. In 2011, Fido stated that he did not make much of Kaminsky today, regarding him as a "coincidentally" fitting figure.[37] John Douglas who reviewed the main suspects as part of his criminal profile stated that the Ripper was David Cohen, or someone very much like him.[38]

Another Jew sent to an asylum was a 34-year-old cigar salesman called Hyam Hyams. He was arrested on 29 December 1888 as a wandering lunatic. Taken to the workhouse infirmary he was released on 11 January 1889, readmitted on 15 April, and transferred to Colney Hatch. He injured his mother's head with a chopper when attacking his wife. Unsurprisingly he was considered dangerous to the wife.[39]

He was discharged as recovered on 30 August 1889, then admitted to the City of London asylum at Stone nine days later. Records state that he had a terror of the police and believed that people were watching him. He had a delusion that his wife was unfaithful. [40]On 16 December 1889, he attacked the head attendant. On 4 January 1890, he was returned to Colney Hatch where he died on 22 March 1913. He was violent and destructive to staff and once attacked a medical officer with a sharp piece of steel.

Mark King postulated a family connection between Hyams and Joseph Levy, one of the three men who saw Catherine Eddowes with a man shortly before her murder.[41] This Hyam Hyams died in 1933 so was not the man confined in the asylum.[42]

Jacob Levy was a Jewish butcher who lived in Whitechapel and contracted syphilis from local prostitutes. Born in 1856 he married Sarah Abrahams in 1879. They had nine children. On 5 April 1886, he was convicted with another man of receiving stolen goods, namely fourteen pounds of beef. This was taken from the butcher's shop of Hyam Sampson at 35 Middlesex Shop. Levy lived next door. He was sentenced to a year's hard labour.[43] On 21 May, he was certified insane and transferred to the Essex County Asylum. This was due to a suicide attempt, a brother who committed suicide, and a family history of insanity. He was rambling and incoherent, spoke to imaginary people, and was violent. On 31 January 1887, he was discharged as cured.[44]

On 15 August 1890, he was admitted to Stone asylum. Doctor Sequeira, who had known Levy for several years as a shrewd businessman noted that he was now incapable and gave the wrong change. Levy said he felt something inside him, forcing him to take everything he saw. He complained of strange noises and felt that he would be violent, if left unrestrained. His wife, Sarah, said he had nearly ruined her business. He ordered things indiscriminately and was constantly taking other people's goods. He died in the asylum on 29 July 1891.[45]

Jacob Levy may have known Joseph Levy, as they had butcher's shops within sixty yards of each other. Joseph's parents, Hyam and Frances appear in the 1851, 1861, and 1871 census returns at 36 Middlesex Street, which became Jacob's shop.

On 18 November 1890, the press reported that a motion was brought before the sheriff's court in New York for the release of a man, alleged to be a London tobacco merchant. He was detained in a lunatic asylum and alleged by the authorities there to be Jack the Ripper.[46] Some newspapers named him as Charles Bruyn, but his real name was Cornelius. He was 26 years old. His father had been president of the Ulster County Bank.[47]

Cornelius studied law then moved to Britain where he set up business as a cigar and cigarette agent on Eyre Street, Piccadilly. He returned to America, under the delusion that the London police were after him for the Whitechapel murders. Alarmed by his behaviour his family arranged to have him committed to Bloomingdale asylum. A cousin, John Van Vleck, unconvinced that Bruyn was insane, brought a court case to challenge the decision, but changed his mind during the hearing. [48] On 7 January 1891, the judge returned Bruyn to the asylum. The 1900 census lists him as a patient in the Middletown State Homeopathic Hospital for the Insane.

George Hutchinson, not to be confused with the witness of the same name, was reportedly an inmate of the Elgin lunatic asylum in Illinois. Newspapers said that he used to visit the asylum slaughterhouse and make toys from bones. He escaped and was captured at Kankakee but escaped again and murdered a prostitute in Chicago. Her body was said to be mutilated in the same way as the Whitechapel murders. He was returned to Kankakee but escaped again in 1885.[49] Nobody of that name had killed a prostitute in Chicago or spent time at Kankakee in the period. There was a man called Billy Hutchinson who shot his mistress, Kitty Hall, in Chicago in 1885 and escaped from Kankakee in May 1888.[50] The Chicago Daily Tribune reported that he was quickly recaptured.[51]

Newland Francis Forester Smith was born in Cinderford, Gloucestershire on 15 September 1863. He received a third-class degree in Latin, from private study, in 1881.[52] In 1883, he married Sophia Dawes Swinhoe, the daughter of a Calcutta solicitor, in Bengal. At the time of the Whitechapel murders, he was a student at Lincoln's Inn.[53] He was called to the bar in June 1890.[54] Certified insane he was transferred to Holloway asylum and sanatorium at Virginia Walter in Surrey on 20 October 1890. Discharged in October 1891 he was immediately re-admitted, his case notes stating that he believed himself "*accused of being Jack the Ripper*." Transferred to Cane Hill Asylum on 9 February 1894 he died there on 23 July 1898 from organic brain disease and full degeneration of the heart. There was a legend that a room in the basement of Holloway asylum was known as Jack the Ripper's room.[55]

Another suspect in Holloway Asylum was John William Smith Sanders. He was born on 6 October 1860, the son of an Indian army surgeon. He entered the London Hospital Medical College in 1879 and was an outpatient dresser between 1880 and 1881. A note on the records states that he became ill and went to an asylum.[56] In 1887, he was sent to West Malling asylum, due to attacks of violence, unprovoked assaults on friends and tyranny in his household. He was transferred to Holloway and then to Heavitree Asylum in Exeter where he died on 1 April 1901. The police were looking for him at the time of the Whitechapel murders, unaware that he was in the asylum. Inspector Abberline reported that two officers went to Aberdeen Place, the last known address of the insane medical student named John Sanders. They ascertained that a lady named Sanders resided at number 20 but went abroad two years earlier.[57] Laura Tucker Sanders continued to be listed at 20 Abercon Place, a mistake in the transcription by Abberline is assumed, but there could have been a different Sanders living previously at 20 Aberdeen Place.

A Home Office Report in November 1888 referred to three insane medical students, two of whom had been traced and one went abroad.[58] Paul Begg suggested that one of the others was a student at the London Hospital accused of rape in April 1888.[59] This was George Goss Borrett who was accused by a servant girl called Emily Bevan and acquitted of indecent assault.[60] He qualified in 1889, and went on to have a career as a surgeon in the Royal Navy.[61]

On 23 October 1923, the Empire News reported a story from a student of criminology that the police knew Jack the Ripper had died in Morris Plains Lunatic Asylum in 1902.[62] He arrived there from Jersey City in 1899, briefly working in the asylum infirmary and suffering insane fits. The reporter knew him as a patient and gave information to the authorities. They sent a letter to Scotland Yard, without receiving a reply. He was a Norwegian sailor called Fogelma from Arendal. Two women visited him. One was Olga Storsjan and the other, a sister, gave the name Helen Fogelma. In periods when his brain worked, he talked about the murders. The reporter assured Helen that Fogelma was immune from the death penalty, as a lunatic. She revealed cuttings about the murders from the London and New York Press, found in her brother's trunk when he lived with her at 324, East 39th Street. The cuttings had been written on. In 1898, he appeared at the flat shared by her and Olga, who had been his sweetheart. She left him to go to Jersey City, but he followed her, and she gave information to the police that led to his committal. Before dying, Fogelma confessed to the Reverend J Miosen. One of his letters was sent to Carol Mackonvitch, talking of a need to leave London. The reporter believed that Mackonvitch had funded his departure. There is no record of Fogelma in the asylum and none of the other people mentioned have been traced.[63]

In 1915, the Nevada State Journal reported that a man named Bloomfein was suspected of being Jack the Ripper. He was detained in the Philadelphia hospital for the insane, after telling an incoherent story about cutting people up.[64] The Syracuse Daily Journal of the same day gave his name as George Bloombein. The Washington Post said that he had delusions at six weekly intervals and there were weeks between the killings.[65] He apparently lived on East Fifteen Street in the heart of the New York district where two children, Leonara Cohen (or Cohn) and Charles (Charlie) Murray had been killed, on 19 March and 4 May. Leonara's mother received letters signed by Jack the Ripper. Edward Richman was arrested, but a further letter arrived, signed H. B. Richmond, indicating that there would be another murder.[66] Bloomfein or Bloombein was one of several people questioned, but the murders were never solved.[67]

George Francis Miles, known as Frank, was born in 1852, the sixth son of Robert Miles rector of Bingham. He painted pictures of many notable figures, including Queen Victoria. In 1880, he won the Royal Academy Turner medal for landscape for *An Ocean Coast, Llangraviog, Cardiganshire.* He became friends with Oscar Wilde and lived with him between 1879 and 1881. He was confined in Brislington Asylum near Bristol on 27 December 1887, where he died on 15 July 1891. Toughill suggested that Miles might have temporarily escaped from the asylum and that Oscar Wilde had left clues in the Picture of Dorian Gray.[68]

Women

Lord Sidney Osborne wrote to the Times suggesting the killer was a woman in September 1888, before the name Jack the Ripper was coined.[1] Jill the Ripper is an alternative given by later researchers. Several women wrote letters purporting to be from the killer and, at least one, invoked the Ripper's name during acts of violence. On Boxing Day 1888, Elizabeth Ashworth stabbed George Taylor four times in the head in a public house in Peterborough. She said, "I am Jack the Ripper."[2] Convicted of malicious wounding she received nine months with hard labour.[3]

In 1893 some American newspapers named Elizabeth Halliday as the Ripper.[4] She was born Eliza Margaret McNally in Country Antrim in 1864 and moved to America at the age of three. In 1879, she married Charles Hopkin. Following his death, two years later, she remarried to Artemus Brewer, who died within a year. Her third husband was Hiram Parkinson, who deserted her, but she bigamously remarried to George Smith. After a failed attempt to poison him, she fled, with his possessions, to Vermont. There she married Charles Playstel and lived with him for a couple of weeks. She appeared next in Philadelphia, staying with the McQuillan family who had been neighbours in Ireland. She opened a small shop and burnt it for the insurance money, serving two years in jail at the Eastern State Penitentiary.[5]

She moved to Newburgh and married a widower called Paul Halliday. She ran away with a neighbour and some stolen horses but was arrested and sent to an asylum. Halliday accepted her back. She repaid him by burning his house, barn, and a mill, killing one of his sons. Halliday then disappeared. His body was found under the floorboards, along with those of Margaret and Sarah McQuillan.

In jail, Lizzie tried to strangle the sheriff's wife and attempted suicide. The press quoted Sherriff Harrison Beecher as saying that *"recent investigations show that Mrs Halliday is in all probability connected with the famous Whitechapel murders."*[6] He said that she was in Europe at the time and frequently referred to the crimes. She denied any involvement but also claimed to be innocent of the murders she had committed, sometimes saying that gypsies drugged her. In response to a direct question from the Sherriff about the Ripper murders, she said a man did them. Doctor Blumer, who examined her in jail, observed several hallucinations.[7]

Convicted of three murders, Elizabeth Halliday was the first woman sentenced to die in the electric chair. Reprieved, she lived in the Matteawan Home for the Criminally Insane until her death in 1918. In 1906, she stabbed and killed a nurse, Nellie Wicks, who was planning to leave the home.[8]

In 1937, Edwin T Woodhall told a story, allegedly published in an American newspaper before the war, that named Olga Tchkersoff as the Ripper.[9] Olga was a Russian immigrant whose sister, Vera, took up prostitution and died after an abortion. Olga blamed Mary Kelly for corrupting Vera. She embarked on a crusade of revenge, culminating in Kelly's death. The couple who looked after Olga's property discovered evidence of her involvement but destroyed it. No records of Olga's existence have been found.

William Stewart, writing in 1939, believed that only a midwife could have walked with bloodstains through the streets of Whitechapel without attracting attention.[10] He accused Mary Eleanor Pearcey, born Wheeler. She was executed on 23 December 1890 for the murder of Phoebe Hogg, who was married to her lover, and an infant of the same name. Stewart claimed that she wheeled the bodies of the Ripper victims to the locations where they were found, just as she did with the Hoggs.

In an unpublished essay Alastair Crowley wrote the cryptic comment, *'It is hardly one's first, or even one's hundredth guess that the Victorian worthy in the case of Jack the Ripper was no less a person than Helena Petrovna Blavatsky. "*[11] Blavatsky was a co-founder of the Theosophical Society in 1875 and wrote several esoteric works. She was born on 12 August 1831 in Ekaterinoslav, then in Southern Russia. After travelling to various countries, including a three-year-spell in Tibet, she settled in London in May 1887, and died there on 8 May 1891.

In 2006, E.J. Wagner suggested Constance Kent as a Ripper suspect.[12] Constance was sentenced to death for the murder of her half-brother in 1860. Four-year-old Francis Saville-Kent had his throat cut and a wound made in his chest. Constance was sixteen at the time. She confessed five years later. Granted a reprieve from the gallows she left prison in 1885.[13] She arrived in Sydney on board the Carisbrooke Castle on 27 February 1886.[14] In Australia she lived under the alias, Ruth Emilie Kaye, becoming matron of a home for lepers and later, Parramatta Industrial School for girls. She died on 10 April 1944.

A poster on Casebook Jack the Ripper suggested that Rose Mylett had been having an affair with Joseph Barnett. Discovering that he used prostitutes she killed all of them. When he found out, he killed her.[15]

In 2012, a book accused Lizzie Williams, the wife of Doctor John Williams, of being Jill the Ripper.[16] Lizzie, born Mary Elisabeth Hughes in 1850, was 38 at the time of the murders. She was said to be deranged, because of an inability to bear children and died, childless, of cancer of the rectum in 1915. Her husband was allegedly running an abortion clinic in Whitechapel and had an affair with Mary Kelly. The allegations against Lizzie followed a previous claim that he was the Ripper.

John Williams was born in Gwynfe, Carmarthenshire in 1840, and married Hughes in 1872. In 1883, he became obstetric physician at University College Hospital in London, having been assistant in that position for eleven years. He was appointed a court physician in 1886 and a baronet in 1894. From 1913 until his death in 1926, he was president of the University College of Aberystwyth and founded the National Library of Wales.

In 2005, he was accused by one of his descendants, Tony Williams and Humphrey Price.[17] The authors cited a letter sent to someone called Morgan, apologising for being unable to come to dinner, as he had to attend a clinic in Whitechapel on 8 September 1888. Williams allegedly performed an abortion on Mary Ann Nichols in 1884, and a knife found in the library archives was said to be the one used in the killings.

Jennifer Pegg noted that the original notebook documenting the operation on Nichols was different to the one printed in Uncle Jack and the handwriting did not match Sir John's.[18] Antonia Alexander who claimed to be a descendant of Mary Kelly also accused John Williams, copying almost verbatim some of the work in Uncle Jack and in a previous novel by Tony Williams. Jennifer Shelden, nee Pegg, demonstrated that Antonia Alexander was not a real person and suggested that Williams co-wrote the book with his daughter.[19]

Doctors and Surgeons

The belief that Jack the Ripper had surgical knowledge derives from Dr Phillips'
comments at the Chapman inquest. A man named Morford was described in the Star on
24 September 1888 as a former surgeon who had given way to drink and been absent
from his lodgings in Great Ormond Street since 10 September. He had pawned his
surgical instruments and someone representing himself as a detective had tried to find
him, believing that he might be able to throw light on the Whitechapel murders. The
pawnbroker reported him as a man of unsound mind.[1] Philip Sugden suggested that he
might have been a relative of John Orford, senior resident medical officer at the Royal
Free Hospital, and/or Henry Orford, a carter, of Rupert Street.[2] Nobody called Morford
has been found in medical directories, except a John Morford Cottle who died in 1873.

Thomas Barnardo was suggested as a Ripper suspect by Donald McCormick in the
second edition of his book published in 1970. Barnardo's charity is currently the largest
children's charity in the United Kingdom. Its founder was born in Dublin in 1845. He left
for London in 1866 and enrolled as a student at the London Hospital the following year.
Although known as a Doctor he never obtained medical qualifications. He became aware
of children sleeping rough in the East End of London and opened his first home for them
in 1868. By 1873, he had established a school, an employment agency, a church, and a
coffee house. His success led to allegations from other philanthropists, Frederick
Charrington and George Reynolds, that the homes were mismanaged, subjected the
inmates to cruelty, used fictitious photographs to generate income, and misappropriated
funds. Barnardo responded by writing, or at least commissioning, a personal attack on
Reynolds in the East London Advertiser on 28 August and 4 September 1875. The

investigation by the arbitrators began on 21 June 1877 and reported on 15 October that year. Barnardo's evidence took eighteen days. No evidence was found to support the allegations of fraud or cruelty, but the report commented that the use of artistic fiction was morally wrong.[3]

Barnardo appeared in court on 1 April 1888 on a charge of assaulting a girl and her sister in an argument about a barrier at 28 Stepney causeway, which opened onto Commercial Road.[4] He was sent to prison on 16 July 1889, by the court of appeal for not producing a child that he had taken in the belief that it had been ill-treated by its natural guardians.[5] This gives him an alibi for the murder of Alice McKenzie. It was one of 88 court appearances, due mostly to his habit of removing children from parents or guardians that he considered immoral and potentially able to harm the children. Barnardo died on 19 September 1905.

In a letter to The Times, published on 9 October 1888, Barnardo said that he visited 32 Flower and Dean Street, where Elizabeth Stride lodged, four days before her death. At the mortuary, he identified Stride as one of the women who had been present. [6] There are stories that he was under police surveillance.[7] It was later rumoured that he kept a diary, with the dates of the Ripper murders left blank.[8] One of his accusers informs us that shortly after Mary Kelly's death Barnardo had an accident that affected his hearing and suggests that this is why the murders stopped.[9] A biography indicates that the deafness began in 1885.[10]

Doctor John William Sanders was born in 1859. He practised as a gynaecologist and surgeon at the Croydon fever hospital, Guy's hospital, the Bethnal Green infirmary, and the St Georges in the East infirmary. He died of heart failure whilst under anaesthetic in January 1889. The East London Advertiser of 23 January 1889 reported that his death was hushed up. Jon Ogan suggested in 1993, that the police might have confused him with the student, John William Smith Sanders. [11]

In 1999, Martin Roberts suggested that Doctor James Cockburn Gloster was Jack the Ripper. [12] Gloster was born in Limerick in 1854. He qualified as a doctor in Dublin and obtained a licentiate in midwifery. In 1882, he was a student at the London Hospital. He practised at 15 Upper Phillmore Place, now part of Kensington High Street.

One of his patients, Eliza Jane Schummacher, died on 27 June 1888 after a failed abortion. Gloster and Dr Louis J Tarrico were charged in connection with her death on 2 July 1888. Tarrico was released on 17 July. [13] A month later, Gloster appeared at Westminster Police Court. A witness, Henry George Algernon Statham, who claimed to be a doctor from Pennsylvania University, produced a document purporting to be a confession from a Dr. Robertson. Statham admitted that he wanted to get the prisoner off and that he had requested out of pocket expenses. [14]

The trial was at the Old Bailey on 24 September 1888. The victim had been working as a dressmaker, a common cover for prostitutes, to earn some extra income. Two doctors independently dismissed the notion that she was pregnant. She visited Gloster who allegedly attempted an abortion at his premises in Pimlico a week later. She became ill and died.

The principal evidence for the prosecution was a statement made before the woman's death in which she accused Gloster. Given the number of deathbed confessions supposedly made by the Ripper the debate over the validity of her statement as evidence is interesting. The court ruled that it could not be presented, and Gloster was acquitted on 25 September 1888. [15] He continued to practise as a doctor in London and died there on 19 January 1916, still at 15 Upper-Phillmore Place.

In his biography of Montague Druitt John Leighton put forward Sir Arthur Conan Doyle as a possible suspect. Doyle was born in Edinburgh in 1859 and studied medicine at the university there. After a spell as a ship's surgeon, he set up a surgery in Southsea where he lived at the time of the Ripper murders. The first Sherlock Holmes novel, A Study in Scarlet, appeared in 1886. Doyle also created the character of Professor Challenger and wrote historical novels and works of non-fiction. On 30 August and 1 September 1888, he was playing cricket in Portsmouth.[16]

Doctor Septimus Swyer was born in Dorset in 1835 and moved to Whitechapel with his family in the 1850s. In 1861, he brought a court case against his neighbour, a German baker, whose cat had broken bottles in his shop. This was dismissed when he could not prove the identity of the cat.[17] On 23 April 1862, he was admitted to the Royal College of Surgeons. The following year he also obtained a licence from the society of apothecaries. On 2 December 1863, he was elected a fellow of the Obstetrical Society of London. On 20 July 1877, Swyer discovered that his surgical assistant, Joseph Frederick Castell, had absconded with money, a gold watch, chain, and locket. Castell received six months hard labour.[18]

In 1881, Swyer's second wife, Hannah Markin (nee Arons) was acquitted of bigamy. Her lawyer, Montagu Williams, stated that there was no evidence that Hannah knew her previous husband, Harold Markin, was alive at the time of her marriage to Swyer.[19] The Weekly Dispatch of 21 March 1886 reported that Swyer's watch was stolen, this time, by a gang. In the same year, Swyer's brother died in hospital, after being moved against his advice.[20]

In 1892, Swyer moved to Baltimore where he attempted to sue his landlord over the conduct of tenants in a nearby property.[21] He died in Manhattan on 10 December 1906. A poster on the Jack the Ripper casebook website used geographic profiling to pinpoint Swyer's address at the time of the murders, 23 Whitechapel Road. [22]

Stephen Herbert Appleford was a house surgeon at the London Hospital. Born in 1852 he became a member of the Royal College of Surgeons on 18 November 1880. On 2 May 1887, he applied for freedom of the City of London, from an address at 7 Finsbury Circus. He married in 1892 to Mary Annie Sergeant. Between 1903, and 1904 he was president of the Hunterian Society. On 29 February 1928, he proved the will of his brother-in-law, Dr Frederick Gordon Brown, who had conducted the post-mortem on Catherine Eddowes.[23] He died on 31 August 1940.

Eduardo Cuitino, a professor of mathematics at the University of Montevideo, accused Appleford as a left-handed surgeon working at the London hospital.[24] Cuitino used google maps to build a geographical profile of the killer and referred to an article by Appleford in the British Medical Journal about a small case to carry medical knives, which could be concealed on the body. Cuitino believed that Appleford began killing after his mother died and said that he was found near the scene where a woman was knifed in 1882.[25] In that year, Appleford gave evidence at the Old Bailey in a case of killing and another of wounding.[26] Both were in his professional capacity, and, apart from one comment, the evidence is that the Ripper was right-handed.

At the time of the murders, William Wynn Westcott was corner for Central London. He was born in Leamington on 17 December 1848. His parents died when he was ten. He obtained a medical degree from University College London in 1870 and went into practice with his uncle. He joined a Masonic lodge in 1875.He wrote many occult books and articles as well as publications on medical topics such as alcoholism and suicide. He retired in 1918 and died in Durban on 30 July 1925.

He was accused on the basis that the hermetic order of the Golden Dawn, which he founded with two other masons in 1887, was rumoured to have committed the murders as occult sacrifices.[27] In 1891, Westcott was accused of being the chief of the English Luciferans by a woman called Diana Vaughan. This was a hoax instigated by Leo Taxil, real name Gabriel Jorgand-Pages, who had made several critical attacks on Freemasonry.[28]

In 1996, an article in the Weekly World News said that workers tearing down an old bakery had found the bodies of Jack the Ripper and two female victims. The building was the home of Doctor Nigel Torme who disappeared in 1900. Doctor Jeanne Benot said that the overcoat worn by Torme exactly matched a piece, left at the scene of one of the murders. She felt that Torme had committed suicide, by poison due to his guilt.[29] There are no records of Torme's existence or other reports of the discovery.

In November 2012 Xanthe Mallet, a forensic anthologist, accused Doctor Charles Hebbert who worked on some of the Ripper and Thames Torso murders.[30] This preceded a conference in the Australian town of Armidale, which focused on how a modern town would cope with a Ripper like series of crimes. Hebbert died in Armidale and this connection, discovered by local historians, inspired the conference. Mallet commented that Hebbert's descendants found two mummified left hands in a secret compartment in his desk.

Charles Alfred Hebbert was born in Birmingham on 24 June 1856. He married Francis Helen Dilke on 22 January 1883 and they had three children, one of whom died in infancy. On 29 October 1885, he was given freedom of the city of London. His notes on the Torso victims were incorporated into a handbook in 1894.[31] The family appear to have separated by 1911, as Charles was not listed with his wife and two surviving children on the census at an address in Sheffield. He left England on the Borda for Sydney on 1 June

1922, sailing third class.[32] He died on 15 April 1925. A brief newspaper obituary noted that he had lectured in Boston.[33]

Dr. William Evans Thomas was born on the isle of Anglesey in 1856. At the time of the Whitechapel murders, he had a surgery in London at 190 Green Street, Victoria Park. He suffered a nervous breakdown and committed suicide by swallowing prussic acid on 12 June 1889 at his father's post office in Aberffraw.[34] An oral tradition in the village describes him as the Ripper and he was accused in a Welsh television programme, Helstaeon, on 31 October 1993 due to the timing of his breakdown, medical knowledge, location, and the fact that he was well dressed.

Frederick Treeves was born in Dorchester on 15 February 1853 and qualified as a member of the Royal College of Surgeons in 1875. In 1884, he became a full surgeon at the London Hospital. He demonstrated anatomy to students and wrote various textbooks. In 1898, he left the hospital to concentrate on his private practice. In 1902, he was made a baronet after draining an abscess on King Edward VII just before his coronation. He wrote books about his travels and experiences during the Boer War. His most famous work, *The Elephant Man and Other Reminiscences,* was published in 1923, the year of his death. There was a rumour that Treeves was under surveillance at the time of the Ripper murders.[35]

The Elephant Man was Joseph Carey Merrick. Born in Leicester with a disfiguring disease in 1862, he was exhibited as a freak in a shop opposite the London Hospital. When the shop closed, he was taken abroad but made his way back to England and was found with the card of Frederick Treeves, who had seen him in the shop. He had a private room at the London Hospital from January 1887 until he died in 1890.[36] Patricia Cornwell referred to a contemporary rumour linking him with Jack the Ripper.[37]

252

The idea that the British government and royal family were involved in the murders is a favoured theme of film and television producers. An oral tradition linked Albert Edward, later King Edward VII, to the killings but this is believed to be a confusion with his son, Prince Albert Victor, the Duke of Clarence, who was known as Eddy.[1] Some authors suggested that Albert Edward had an affair with Mary Kelly and made her pregnant.[2] Doctor Bond's post mortem notes on Kelly do not mention a pregnancy.[3]

A book by Philippe Jullian, in 1967, claimed that there were rumours linking Albert Victor to the Whitechapel murders. Jullian also said that others attributed the crimes to the Duke of Bedford.[4] In 1888, this was the ninth Duke, Francis Charles Hastings Russell. Born in 1819 he served in the Scots Fusilier Guards from 1838-44, He was elected as the Liberal MP for Bedfordshire in 1847, moving to the House of Lords in 1872. He was president of the Royal Agricultural Society in 1880 and became a Knight of the Garter in the same year. From 1884, he was Lord Lieutenant of Huntingdonshire. He died on 14 January 1891. The cause of death was reported as congestion of the lungs.[5] An inquest held on the morning of his funeral and cremation established that he had shot himself whilst of unsound mind.[6]

Two members of Parliament questioned the conduct of the inquest, and the lack of public awareness.[7] The Home Secretary replied that the press were informed of the inquest in the usual way but, when pressed, was unable to say if notice was given on the inquest on the coroner's lists and was not prepared to release the inquest depositions.[8] One of the MP's, Henry Cobb, suggested that he had information to prove the coroner's information was incorrect.[9] Mr Matthews subsequently clarified that the death was reported to the Coroner on 14 January and a jury summons issued the following day. The name of the deceased was given as Francis Charles Hastings Russell and the occupation given as Duke of Bedford. The title was not usually reported in the name.[10]

In his biography of Oscar Wilde, published in 1968, Jullian said that amongst the houses where Wilde stayed was one belonging to a Duke whose eccentricities were so marked that he was suspected of being Jack the Ripper.[11]

Stan Russo suggested that the Duke's son, and heir, George William Francis Sackville Russell was the Duke of Bedford referred to by Jullian, because of the elder Duke's age.[12] The tenth Duke of Bedford was born in 1852 and graduated from Balliol College, Oxford, in 1874. He was also MP for Bedfordshire from 1875 to 1885, deciding not to seek re-election when the electoral boundaries changed. He died of diabetes in 1893, leaving a wife Adeline, and at least one illegitimate child.

Jullian's source for accusing Prince Albert Victor appears to be Sir Harold Nicholson. In the introduction to his book, Jullian thanked Nicholson for providing previously unpublished anecdotes.[13] In 1973, Colin Wilson recalled that he told the story about Price Albert Victor being the killer to Nicholson on the day of his lunch with Thomas Stowell in 1960.[14]

Stowell was a surgeon who had been a friend and medical partner of Dr Theodore Dyke, the husband of Caroline Acland who was the daughter of Queen Victoria's physician, Sir William Gull. They married on 12 April 1888. Caroline died in 1929, two years before Theodore. Stowell contacted Wilson after reading his articles about Jack the Ripper in the Evening Standard.

Caroline Acland told Stowell that she had seen an entry in her father's diary, dated November 1889, saying, "*informed blank that his son was dying from syphilis of the brain.*" Stowell claimed that Prince Albert Victor had contacted syphilis, which caused him to commit the murders. Apprehended and taken to an asylum after the death of Catherine Eddowes, he escaped to kill Mary Jane Kelly. Recaptured he was placed under Gull's care and received treatment that allowed him to carry out some official duties prior to his death in 1892, exactly a year after the Duke of Bedford whom Stowell does not name. Stowell said that there was a cover-up enacted by the authorities.

Stowell wrote an article in the November 1970 edition of Criminology.[15] He called the suspect S, but the context leaves no doubt that he was referring to Prince Albert Victor. He appeared to confirm this in a television interview for the BBC programme, 24 Hours, on 4 November 1970. The Times said that contemporary evidence clearly placed Prince Albert Victor at Balmoral at the time of the double event and Sandringham on the day of Mary Kelly's murder.[16] A press report on 8 September 1888 stated that he had been in Yorkshire for the last ten days and left the previous day to join his regiment at York.[17]

On the day after the television programme Stowell wrote to the Times denying that he had accused the Prince.[18] He died on 8 November 1970, before the letter was published. He left a folder labelled Jack the Ripper which his son destroyed unread.[19]

Undeterred by Stowell's retraction and the Prince's alibi, Frank Spiering published a book in 1978.[20] He referred to papers, apparently in Gull's hand, which said that Gull told the Prince of Wales his son was dying from tertiary syphilis. Gull hypnotised the prince who confessed to the murders. He became aroused watching butchers in Aldgate High Street and took a knife from a firm of Horse Slaughters. No other researcher has seen these papers.

In his biography of Clarence, Michael Harrison demonstrated his subject's innocence then suggested that Stowell's suspect was James Kenneth Stephen who had been Prince Albert Victor's tutor for three months in 1883.[21] Stephen suffered a blow to the head in 1886, which caused brain damage. Harrison speculated that Clarence and Stephen had

255

been lovers and suggested that some of Stephen's poetry showed misogyny. Stephen chose the dates of the murders because they had some significance to Albert Victor. Harrison argued that Stephen was acting out a poem about the murder of ten prostitutes in Jerusalem. He counted ten Ripper victims as Emma Smith, Martha Tabram, Polly Nichols, Annie Chapman, Elizabeth Stride, and Catherine Eddowes as one, Mary Kelly, Annie Farmer, Rose Mylett, Alice McKenzie, and Frances Coles.

Stephen was born in 1859. He was a cousin of Virgin Woolf and the son of Judge Stephen who presided over the Maybrick trial. He was educated at Eton then Cambridge where his grandfather had once been professor of modern history. He was president of the Cambridge Union in 1880 and won various prizes including the Whewell Scholarship in 1881. He took a scholarship in international law in 1881. He was called to the bar on 25 June 1884 and elected to a fellowship at Cambridge in 1885.[22]

The blow to the head was caused by an accident at Felixstowe in the winter of 1886-87. Arthur Benson, who studied with Stephen and knew him well, said that it was caused by the sails of a windmill.[23] At the start of 1888, Stephen published a magazine, The Reflector, which ran for 17 issues. That summer he was appointed Clerk for the South Wales circuit having previously been Deputy-Clerk of the Peace for Glamorganshire.[24] He contributed to newspapers, including the Pall Mall Gazette. He resigned his clerkship of assizes in 1890 and lectured for two terms at Cambridge.

A biographer said that it appears that Lord Lytton, British Ambassador in Paris intervened to rescue Stephen from police custody in April 1891.[25] Lytton was a friend of the Stephens family. In November 1891, the month that Lytton died, Stephen's health deteriorated, and he left Cambridge. He died in Northampton on 3 February 1892.

Harrison appeared on the BBC series, Late Night Line-Up in 1972. He said that he had been preparing a biography of Albert Victor when Stowell's article appeared. He did not agree with the conclusions but felt that he had to find another likely candidate by looking for a man near the Duke who was a homicidal maniac.

On 16 February 1975, the Sunday Times published a letter from Mrs Marny Hallam of Newbury saying that her grandmother was told by her father, a barrister, that the authorities knew Stephen to be the Ripper.[26] Andy and Sue Parlour contacted Mrs Hallam in the 1990s, when she was in her eighties and unable to provide further information. A Howard Weaver used the same chambers as JK Stephen and his private address was across the road from Stephen's brother, Harry.[27] Marny's grandfather was Thomas Weaver, but no connection has been found between Harold and Thomas.

Marny was born Marjorie May Weaver on New Year's Eve 1911. Her parents were Roy and Sarah Jane, nee Thorntwaite. Their mothers were Edith Emily Weaver, nee Bartrum and Margaret Thorntwaite, nee Tiffin. Edith's father, Thomas Reynolds Bartrum died in 1856 and Margaret's father, William Tiffin, died in 1885. Neither of Marny Hallam's great-grandfathers could have known anything about Jack the Ripper, as they were both dead before 1888.

In 1972, a Scotland Yard detective advised BBC researchers, working on a series about Jack the Ripper, to talk to Joseph Sickert who knew of a clandestine marriage between Prince Albert Victor and a Catholic girl called Alice Mary Crook. Sickert, real name Joseph William Charles Gorman, claimed to be the son of the artist Walter Sickert and the grandson of Prince Albert Victor. He appeared in the final episode of the series, broadcast in 1973, to tell the following story, summarised from a BBC transcript.[28]

Joseph Sickert's mother told him that his grandmother had suffered terribly at the hands of the authorities and a servant had died. When older Joseph asked his father, Walter Sickert, for clarification and was told, what he described as "a sort of fairy story" about a prince, his lover, a baby girl, a nurse, and an artist. His father, after pressure, eventually elaborated.

When Albert Victor was twenty, he was introduced to Walter Sickert who, at that time, lived in the Cleveland Street area. The Prince met a shop girl called Ann Elizabeth Crook who modelled for Sickert and looked like Albert Victor's mother.[29] Albert Victor started a relationship with her, which resulted in pregnancy and a secret marriage at St Saviour's chapel in 1888.

The police raided a party in Cleveland Street and took Ann away to Guy's hospital. Later she was moved to a smaller hospital at 367 Fulham Road, where she died in 1921. Walter Sickert looked after the daughter, Alice Margaret, with the help of some friends. She grew up to have two children by Walter Sickert. One was Joseph and the other was Charles, who disappeared at the age of two in 1911.[30]

A servant girl called Mary Kelly disappeared at the time of the raid and went to an East End convent.[31] Worried that the pregnancy and marriage would become public knowledge the government decided to silence Kelly. They hired a coachman, John Netley and the Queen's surgeon, Sir William Gull, to kill other women so that Kelly's murder looked like the work of a random maniac.

A BBC researcher found an Elizabeth Cook who lived in the basement at 6 Cleveland Street in 1888. Martin Howells and Keith Skinner ascertained that 6 Cleveland Street was demolished in 1887 and that Elizabeth Cook lived on the site until 9 January 1893 when she died.[32] This disproves the statement by Sickert that she was abducted earlier from Cleveland Street.[33] In 1888 6 Cleveland Street was demolished so Cook must have lived on a new building on the same site.

Annie Elizabeth Crook was a confectionary assistant of 6 Cleveland Street who gave birth to a daughter, Alice Margaret Crook on 18 April 1885 at Marylebone workhouse.

The father's name was listed as unknown. When Alice married William Gorman, her father's name was given as William Crook (deceased). Her grandfather who died in 1891 had the same name. Joseph Gorman, born in 1925, was the son of William and Alice. There were rumours in the family that Walter Sickert was Alice's father.[34] Her conception occurred before the first of Sickert's three marriages and Joseph's was between the second and third.

Alice was baptised an Anglican, not a Catholic. Her conception occurred between July and 11 August 1884. Prince Albert Victor was in Germany from 18 June to 18 August 1884.[35] There is no record of the alleged marriage or of St Saviour's Chapel.

Joseph Sickert said that Joseph Netley drove a carriage, which tried to run Alice Crook down when she was walking with a woman friend in Drury Lane, at the age of seven, in 1892.[36] Stephen Knight claimed to have found evidence of an earlier attempt in a report in the Illustrated Police News, 6 October 1888.[37] This said that a hansom cab ran over a girl in Fleet Street on 1 October. She was taken in the cab to St. Bartholomew's hospital. Hospital admission registers record that a nine-year-old girl called Lizzie Madewell was admitted on 1 October, having been run over in Bridge Street off Fleet Street.[38]

Knight added detail to the second attempt on Alice's life. The woman friend became an elderly relative who described Netley to Walter Sickert. Alice was not badly injured, but the coach wheel was damaged. Unable to get it moving Netley jumped down and ran away. Sickert heard that he had thrown himself in the Thames from Westminster pier and drowned. Knight referred to a press report, which said that a respectably dressed man jumped in the Thames from Westminster pier and swam a few yards. He was rescued by the port master, Mr Douglas and taken to Westminster Hospital. He gave his name as Nickley but refused an address.[39] Knight checked birth registers and found nobody called Nickley, born between 1857 and 1875.[40] The 1891 census, not available to Knight, lists a

Thomas Nickley, born 1867 in St Giles, and serving as a solider in Dover. There was also a Francis Nickley, a Yorkshire man, living in Wolverhampton.

Melvyn Fairclough claimed to have information from an anonymous freemason that Netley was also a mason whose lodge met at The Gibraltar public house in Princes Yard opposite George's Yard. In 1888, the landlord was Netley's brother-in-law, John Percy Sutton.[41] Neither of Netley's sisters were married at that time.

John Charles Netley was born in Kensington in 1860, one of seven children. His father, John, was an omnibus conductor who later became a cab driver and groom. John Charles was described a carman in the census returns for 1871, 1881 and 1891. He died in 1903, when the wheel of his vehicle chipped a stone and he was thrown into the road to be kicked by a horse with the wheel running over him. A verdict of accidental death was returned. Melvyn Fairclough suggested it was murder, seeing significance in the body being found by Clarence gate.[42] It was also by the front door of a house owned by Michael Maybrick, although he lived on the Isle of Wight.[43]

Sir William Gull was born in Colchester on New Year's Eve 1816. In 1841, he graduated from London University with honours in physiology, comparative anatomy, medicine, and surgery and became a medical tutor at Guys hospital. He lectured at Guy's in Natural Philosophy from 1843 to 1847 and physiology and comparative anatomy from 1846 to 1856. From 1847 to 1849, he was Fullerian Professor at the Royal Institute. He resigned as a physician at Guys in 1865, to concentrate on private practice.

He treated Albert Edward for typhus in 1871. This led to a baronet the following year and he became Physician Extraordinary, then Physician in Ordinary in 1887. That autumn he suffered a minor stroke, leaving him slightly paralysed and forcing his retirement. After two more strokes, he died on 29 October 1890.

Thomas Stowell said that Gull was among surgeons named as suspects and had been seen more than once in Whitechapel on the night of a murder.[44] Caroline Acland told Stowell that her mother was annoyed by a visit from the police and a medium at her home one night. Gull apparently admitted to lapses of memory since his stroke, and once found blood on his shirt, which Stowell believed came from his patient "S."

In April 1895, some American newspapers claimed that the medium Robert James Lees had a psychic impression of the murderer then recognised him on a bus and led the police to his house. The man was a distinguished London Doctor committed to an asylum under the pseudonym Thomas Mason. He lived in the West End, was a former student at Guys and an advocate of vivisection. He was alive at the time of the article although the public were told that he was buried in Kensal Green cemetery. The story had been told by Doctor Howard in San Francisco to William Greer Harrison.[45] Melvyn Harris suggested that it was a fiction invented by the Whitechapel Club of Chicago. The club had about 90 members, including politicians, reporters, cartoonists, and writers. [46] Stephen Knight linked Thomas Mason to a retired bookbinder from Islington, but the name in the press articles was an alias.

After the story was published, Doctor Benjamin Howard, an American doctor who practised in London in the 1880s, denied any knowledge of Jack the Ripper and stated that he was nowhere near San Francisco at the time he was alleged to have made his drunken statement.[47] Gull supported vivisection but was buried in Thorpe-Le-Soken, not Kensal Green. Andy and Sue Parlour reported rumours from Thorpe-Le-Soken that the coffin contained bags of sand.[48]

Knight argued that Gull's 1887 stroke was relatively minor and did not stop him from participating in the murders.[49] Using information from Joseph Sickert, Knight implicated Gull, Sir Robert Anderson, Sir Charles Warren, and Lord Salisbury in a masonic

261

conspiracy designed to protect the throne from the revelation of Prince Albert Victor's marriage. A marriage that was illegal under the Royal Marriage's Act of 1772, which forbade heirs to the throne from marrying without the monarch's consent. Sickert now claimed that the victims knew each other and were attempting to blackmail the government. The conspirators killed Catherine Eddowes by mistake because she had used the name Mary Kelly.

Knight connected the Eddowes killing to an alleged masonic ritual, based on the murder of Hiram Abif by three apprentices, Jubela, Jubelo, and Jubelum. The murderers were killed with their breasts torn open and the heart and vitals cut out and thrown over the left shoulder.[50] Knight said that the word Juwes, in the Goulston Street graffiti, was the collective name for Jubela, Jubelo, and Jubelum. In England, the three assassins are unnamed in Masonic ritual and collectively known as ruffians.[51]

A crucial part of the theory was that Gull committed the murders in a coach with the help of Sir Robert Anderson. Netley disposed of the bodies. The evidence indicates that each murder was committed at the scene and no witnesses referred to hearing to seeing a coach. Melvyn Fairclough quoted Doctor Sequeira, as saying at Eddowes' inquest, that there was insufficient light in Mitre Square to enable the perpetrator to commit the deed there.[52] Sequeira said there was sufficient light.[53]

Robert Anderson was born in Dublin in 1841. He was a lawyer who came to London in 1867, as deputy head of an anti-Fenian intelligence branch. He was an advisor to the Home Officer on Political Crime and a spymaster, controlling the informant Thomas Miller Beach. In 1883, he worked as a liaison for the Home Officer and then as secretary of the Prison Commissioners. In 1887, he became assistant in secret work to James Monro, the Assistant Commissioner of CID. On 25 August 1888, he was appointed to succeed Monro but went on sick leave, to Switzerland on 8 September, the day of Annie

Chapman's murder, returning after the double-event. He could not have been the third man in the carriage. Sir Charles Warren confirmed Anderson's sick leave, in a letter dated 28th August 1888. This was sent from an address in France and Warren said that he expected to return on 7th September. [54] Warren was not in England when Mary Ann Nichols died.

Lord Salisbury was born Robert Arthur Talbot Gascoyne Cecil in 1830. He entered parliament as MP for Stamford in 1853. He was twice Secretary of State for India and entered the House of Lords after becoming the third Marquis of Salisbury in 1868. He was Foreign Secretary between 1878 and 1880 and became Prime Minister of a Minority Conservative Government in 1885. The following year the Conservatives obtained a majority and Salisbury served until 1892, returning for a third term between 1895 and 1902. He was not a mason.[55] In 1890, the Referee newspaper commented that there was no truth in the rumour that Lord Salisbury concealed Jack the Ripper at Hatfield House on the night of the last Whitechapel murder.[56] He was in the East End on the night of Alice McKenzie's murder, speaking at the new Conservative club in Commercial Road.[57]

At the end of his book, Stephen Knight postulated that the third killer was not Robert Anderson, but Walter Sickert. Joseph Sickert appeared to accept this in an afterword to the book.[58] On 18 June 1978, he confessed to the Sunday Times that most of his story was untrue but still insisted that he was the son of Walter Sickert. This may have some factual basis as Patricia Cornwell discovered that a literary agent sent Joseph a cheque for literary rights to one of Sickert's works.[59] One of Joseph Sickert's cousins told Paul Begg that elements of the story were circulating when Joseph was an infant.[60]

Walter Sickert was next accused by Jean Overton Fuller in 1990.[61] She was told the story by her mother, Violet, a friend of Florence Pash who knew Sickert and, so she claimed, Mary Jane Kelly. Pash said that Sickert had seen the bodies of the Ripper victims and assumed that this was at the murder sites. Pash did not believe that Sickert was the Ripper but felt that he painted clues into his paintings. In 1996, a study of Sickert's art by Anna Gruetzner Robins suggested an obsession with violence, perversion, and mutilation.[62]

Walter Richard Sickert was born in Munich in 1860. His father, Oswald, was a painter but it was to the stage that the young Sickert first turned. Between 1879 and 1881, he was an actor in London, using the pseudonym Mr Nemo. In 1882, he became a pupil to the artist James McNeil Whistler. His own artistic career had several phases, ranging from landscapes to intimate portraits.

A biography published a year before his death on 22 January 1942, said that he was once called Jack the Ripper by a party of young girls. After he was married and living in Broadhurst Gardens, Hampstead, he used to go to music halls and walk home. He wore a loud check coat, long to the ankles, and carried a little bag for his drawings. One night in Copenhagen Street, his appearance scared the girls who ran away.[63]

Marjorie Lilly, a friend and biographer of Sickert's told Stephen Knight that after a stroke in later life Sickert had Ripper periods in which he would dress up like the murderer and walk about like that for weeks.[64] Joseph Sickert showed Knight some of his alleged father's belongings, which included a Gladstone bag and a small metal case with a stain that appeared to be blood. The case contained three razor-sharp surgical knives.[65]

In 2002, Patricia Cornwell also accused Walter Sickert. She suggested that Sickert's paintings reflected the mutilations of the victims and that he was responsible for many of the letters claiming to be from the killer. Her researchers found matching samples of mitochondrial DNA from the front stamp of an envelope which contained a Jack the Ripper letter to Doctor Openshaw, an envelope used by Walter's wife Ellen, an envelope used by Walter Sickert, a stamp from a Walter Sickert envelope, and an envelope from a

Jack the Ripper letter. Cornwell said that about 1% of the UK population could have left the DNA on the Ripper letters and that the person who left DNA on Sickert's letters was one of those.[66] This would have been an estimated 40,000 people in London. Professor Ian Findlay used a different method of DNA testing to produce a partial profile from the same letter to Dr Openshaw. The results were inconclusive but suggested that the DNA on the stamp was female.[67]

Peter Bower, a forensic paper historian, discovered that two Ripper letters and three pieces of Sickert correspondence came from the same handmade batch containing just 24 sheets of paper. This implies that Sickert or someone close to him wrote those specific Ripper letters.[68] Cornwell and Robins connected Sickert with a sketchbook at the Lizard Hotel in Cornwall, which featured a sketch of a man, labelled Jack the Ripper, with graffiti and corrections.[69] Bower, and Robins, both distinguished experts in their field, formed the opinion that Sickert wrote much of the Ripper correspondence, including the Dear Boss letter.[70]

Cornwell believed that Sickert had a fistula on his penis, which made him infertile. He married three times. The first was to Ellen Cobden in 1885. She was twelve years his senior and they divorced in 1899. In 1911, he married again to Christine Angus, seventeen years his junior. She died in 1920. Six years later, he married the divorcee, Therese Lessore. None of the marriages produced any children.

Cornwell accused Sickert of several other murders including those of Percy Knight Searle in November 1888, John Gill in December 1888, Emily Dimmock in 1907, Jane Beadmoor in 1888, Emily Johnson in 1897, and Caroline Winter in 1889.

On 26 November 1888, the body of an eight-year-old boy, Percy Knight Searle, was found in Havant, Hampshire. His throat had been cut. A bloodstained pocketknife was found close by. Eleven-year-old Robert Husband was charged, following reports that he had played with a knife and said that he was Jack the Ripper. He claimed to have witnessed the murder, but the stated place did not command a good view of the scene. The knife was identified as his and he was alleged to have gone to wash his hands before summoning the Police.[71] He was acquitted, due to having no bloodstains on his clothes and because a witness who held his hand after the murder found it to be dry, without any trace of blood. It was also proved that his brother had lost the knife. [72]

The mutilated body of an eight-year old boy, John Gill, was found in a stable in Bradford on 29 December 1888. He had been missing for two days. The Divisional Police surgeon from Whitechapel was alleged to have met with the local surgeon and compared Gill's injuries with those of the Ripper murder victims. He concluded they were by a different hand.[73]

On 4 February 1889, the inquest jury returned a verdict of wilful murder against a milkman, William Barrett, seen with Gill by several witnesses. A magistrate had ruled that there was insufficient evidence against him, but the inquest heard from a new witness who said that he saw Barrett carrying a bundle out of a stable on the morning that Gill went missing.[74] When the case came to trial, the prosecution elected to bring no evidence.

Caroline Winter was an eight-year-old girl killed in Seaham, on 2 August 1889. A man approached her whilst she was playing with another girl, ten-year-old Ann Cowell. Claiming to be Winter's cousin the man offered her a shilling to buy sweets. She went with him. Later she was found dead with three jagged wounds on her face, possibly caused by stones. The man had raped her.[75] He was never caught.

Emily Johnson was a domestic servant who vanished in Windsor on 15 September 1897. Her body was found in a river. Someone had struck her on the head then cut her throat. Emily Dimmock was a prostitute killed in her home in Camden on 12 September 1907. Her throat was cut from left to right whilst she was asleep. An artist, Robert Wood, was tried and acquitted of her murder[76]. Sickert painted a group of pictures known as the Camden Town nudes. Following the murder, he gave some of them titles such as the Camden Town Murders and L'affair de Camden Town. In 1907, he painted "Jack the Ripper's bedroom" which may have been based on his story that his rented rooms were previously occupied by the killer.

Sickert was in the habit of spending time in Dieppe during the summer months.[77] Cornwell referred to a letter from Ellen Sickert, dated 21 September 88 saying that Walter would be in France for several weeks.[78] On 6 September 1888, Sickert's mother wrote to a friend saying that Sickert was having a happy time swimming and painting in France. The French artist Jacques Emilie Blanche, who painted Sickert in 1898, wrote from France to his father saying that Sickert visited him on 16 September 1888.[79] This suggests that Sickert was not in Whitechapel at the time of the murders but dated musical hall sketches place him in London on 28 September, 5 October and 8 October 1888.

Another twist to the royal conspiracy stories came when Joseph Sickert withdrew his retraction after Knight's death. He claimed that he had not trusted Knight and did not give the full story. The new confession was intended to stop a play, which blackened the name of his grandmother by portraying her as a common whore.[80] Melvyn Fairclough wrote a book based on Joseph Sickert's revised information and alleged diaries by Inspector Abberline. Sickert claimed that Abberline visited the family home on three occasions in 1926, 1927 and 1928. On the last visit, he gave the diaries to Joseph's alleged father, Walter Sickert.[81] The information, supposedly written in 1896 and repeated in 1915 contradicts Abberline's public comments.[82]

The conspirators accused by Fairclough were Sir William Gull, John Netley, Robert Anderson, Charles Warren, Lord Euston, Lord Arthur Somerset, John Courtenay, Randolph Churchill, Lord Blandford, and JK Stephen.

John Courtenay was described as a lieutenant commander in the Royal Navy or a naval attaché in the Diplomatic Corps. He was run over by a tram when his foot stuck in a tramline on the Hampstead Road. This was in 1936 but Fairclough found no records of such an accident between 1935 and 1937. Courtenay allegedly worked as a manservant for Lord Randolph Churchill.[83] He apparently visited Joseph Sickert at 195 Drummond Street and sometimes stayed in the spare room. He told people his name was Charles Grey.[84]

Randolph Churchill was born in 1849. Educated at Eton and Oxford he entered parliament in 1874. He became Chancellor of the Exchequer in 1886, resigning the same year but continuing as an MP. He died on 24 January 1895, at the age of 45, following several years of poor health. He was a freemason in the Churchill lodge. Reginald Hutchinson, alleged son of the witness, George Hutchinson, said that Jack the Ripper was someone like Lord Randolph Churchill. When interviewed by Fairclough and Sickert Reginald realised that his father knew all along it was Churchill and speculated that he received 100 shillings to keep quiet.[85]

Randolph Churchill's elder brother, Georges Charles Spencer Churchill, was the eighth Duke of Marlborough, a peerage created for the Churchill family. He was also Marquee of Blandford from 1857 to 1883. Born in 1844 he died in 1892, four years to the day after Mary Kelly. A freemason, he married twice with four legitimate children and, at least one that was illegitimate.

Henry James Fitzroy, the Earl of Euston, successfully sued the North London Press for libel in 1889 after it accused him of visiting a male brothel at 19 Cleveland Street. Inspector Abberline led the police enquiry into the brothel, discovered in July 1889. The newspaper, edited by Ernest Parke, said that Euston was allowed to leave the country for Peru because his prosecution would implicate others.[86]

Euston's defence was that he visited the brothel once, after receiving a card saying there were *poses plastiques* on display. He paid a sovereign but left when told the truth about the premises. Six witnesses testified that had he visited more than once. The jury accepted Euston's testimony, and Parke received a year in prison.[87] Chief Inspector Donald Swanson noted that Euston subsequently attended a "Bugger's ball."[88]

Several boys identified Lord Arthur Somerset as an attendee of the Cleveland Street brothel. He was the third son of the eighth Duke of Beaufort, head of stables for the Prince of Wales, and a Major in the Royal Horse Guards. The police interviewed him twice. He fled to Europe, settling in France where he died in 1926. His solicitor, Arthur Newton, received six weeks in jail for conspiring to prevent the cause of justice. There were allegations that the government, and Lord Salisbury, had allowed Somerset to escape. [89]

Fairclough ascribed the nickname Fingers Freddy to an Italian American footman, Frederico Albericci, who allegedly worked for Gull. This nickname had previously appeared in connection with the Ripper case in a series of articles written by ex-Superintendent Arthur Butler for The Sun in 1972. Butler believed that four of the victims died because of botched abortions by a midwife, who killed two others to keep them quiet.[90] Fingers Freddy was the name given to Emma Smith's pimp. Emma was killed because she was trying to blackmail the abortionist and Freddy then disappeared. Prior to the second edition of his book, in 2001, Fairclough told a newspaper that he no longer believed the theory.[91]

Andy and Sue Parlour felt that a line drawn between the sites of the four murders, excluding Eddowes, made an arrow pointing directly to the houses of Parliament.[92] They speculated that Salisbury, Warren, Gull, Netley, Fingers Freddy, JK Stephen and

Montague Druitt, were involved to hide the secret of Mary Kelly becoming pregnant by Prince Albert Edward.[93]

Karen Trenouth alleged that Mary Kelly stumbled on the secret of the Cleveland Street brothel, after working there, and shared this information with Inspector Abberline. Trenouth alleged that the aristocrats who used the brothel decided to kill prostitutes until they identified the "Mary" who had betrayed them. They were Lord Arthur Somerset, Henry James Fitzroy, Herbrand Arthur Russell, and William Humble Ward. Dr Alfred Pearson performed the mutilations and Prince Albert Victor killed Kelly.

Herbrand Arthur Russell was the eleventh Duke of Bedford, another son of Frances Charles Hastings Russell. Born in 1858 he married in India on New Year's Day 1888. In 1900, he declined an offer from Lord Salisbury to be under-secretary of state for war, preferring to concentrate on the management of his country estates. He became the first mayor of Holborn and served as president of the Royal Zoological Society from 1899 to 1936.

Alfred William Pearson was born on 22 May 1849 in Stourbridge. He studied medicine in Edinburgh. A petition for bankruptcy was made against him in 1882.[94] He was appointed medical officer of District 3, Stourbridge Union on 30 May 1884 with responsibility for midwifery. Following the death of his first wife, Elizabeth, in 1901 he remarried to Wilhelmina who was 26 years his junior. He died on 21 April 1920 in Wordsley.

William Humble Ward, the second Earl of Dudley was born in London on 25 May 1867. He married Rachel Gurney in 1891. He was parliamentary secretary to the board of trade between 1895 and 1902, with an interlude to fight in the Boer War. Between 1902 and 1905, he was Lord Lieutenant of Ireland and became the fourth Governor General of Australia in 1908. He returned to England in 1911 and commanded a Yeomanry unit in

Gallipoli and Egypt during World War I. He died on 29 June 1932. On the day of Mary Ann Nichol's murder, he was in Kidderminster, accepting an offer to be Lord High Steward of the borough.[95] The next day he travelled to Brechin in Scotland for a shooting party.[96]

An 1899 article in the Denver Evening Post alleged that Lord Harold De Walden had been using common prostitutes in Whitechapel, as well as being arrested for being drunk and disorderly.[97] His real name was Frederick George Ellis. Born on 9 August 1830 and educated at Eton, then Cambridge he became a major in the 4th Light Dragoons. In 1893, his divorce featured in the press as his wife Blanche made allegations of brutal and cruel behaviour, which were upheld by the court.[98] He died on 3 November 1899.

Jacquemine Charrot-Lodwidge accused King Leopold II, ruler of the Belgians between 1865 and 1909.[99] He has also been accused of presiding over the slaughter of four to eight million people in the Congo.[100] The suggestion that he was Jack the Ripper stems from a scandalous private life, allegations that he owed a house described by the daughter of R J Lees, as belonging to her father's suspect and a suggestion that he acquired sadistic tastes during visits to the Congo. Lees noted the house as belonging to a surgeon and Leopold never visited the Congo. In 1941 an article in a Canadian newspaper referred to a theory from an American detective that the killer was a member of a European royal family.[101]

William Ewart Gladstone was 79 at the time of the killings. He became prime minister for the fourth time in 1892 and died on 19 May 1898. In a letter published in the Sporting Times on 13 October 1888, he suggested that the acquisition of the organs was the objective of the murderer and that it was justified if used to advance medical science.[102] From the 1840s onwards, he tried to redeem fallen women, founding an association to assist them and spending time finding employment for them. His political enemies apparently used this against him.[103] Graham Norton accused him in a 1970 article in

Queen.[104] Norton observed that Gladstone always carried a black bag, and the Gladstone bag is named after him.

Other Men

The remaining suspects do not fit neatly into any of the earlier categories. George Robert Gissing was born on 22 November 1857, the son of a Wakefield chemist. While studying at Owens College, Manchester, he fell in love with a homeless girl, Marianne Helen Harrison known as Nell, and stole from other students to give her money. He spent a month doing hard labour in Bellevue prison in 1876. Later he moved to America but returned to marry Nell on 27 October 1879. She died in February 1888, six years after their separation.

On 25 February 1891, Gissing remarried to Edith Underwood. They had two children but separated in 1897. The following year he met Gabrielle Fleury and remained with her until his death, in France in 1903. The first of his 29 novels, Workers in the Dawn published in 1880, was about an idealistic young man trying to save a prostitute.

Richard Whittington-Egan first mentioned him as a suspect and later recalled that he read about the allegation around 1960 but could not remember his source.[1] Gissing travelled to France in the autumn of 1888 and then onto Italy. His diary records him buying a newspaper in Paris on 2 October 1888, two days after the double event, to read about the Whitechapel murders.[2]

Whittington-Egan also named Algernon Charles Swinburne as a prominent Victorian sometimes accused of the murders.[3] Born in London in 1837, Swinburne was educated at Oxford but left without obtaining a degree. His first book, *The Queen Mother and Rosamund* appeared in 1860. Six years later his *Poems and Ballards* contained verses that attacked many core Victorian beliefs and promoted decadent sexual feelings. Withdrawn by its first publisher it soon found another. In 1879, his health declined, due to alcoholism. He recovered in the house of his legal advisor, Theodore Watts Dunton, in Putney and continued to write poetry, plays, and novels until his death in 1909.

Thomas Vere Bayne was accused by Richard Wallace in 1996 of helping his friend Lewis Caroll commit the murders.[4] Born in 1829, Bayne was keeper of the archives at Oxford University at the time of the murders. He had serious back pain during the summer of 1888 and was in France from 1 September 1888 to 5 October 1888. Along with Caroll, he was in Oxford on the day of Mary Kelly's murder. The case against Caroll, real name Charles Lutwidge Dodgson, the writer of Alice in Wonderland, is based on anagrams in two of Caroll's books, which allegedly contained hidden clues about the murders and half-erased entries in his personal diaries. Karoline Leach demonstrated how to find similar anagrams in other literary works and said that Carroll was in Eastbourne from 31 August to 30 September 1888.[5]

In 2007, Sophie Herfort accused Sir Melville Macnaghten, suggesting that he committed the crimes to embarrass his rival, Sir Charles Warren.[6] Macnaghten was born in 1853. James Monro offered him the post of Assistant Chief Constable CID in 1887, but Warren rejected him.[7] He eventually took the post in June 1889, receiving a promotion the following year. In 1902, he became Assistant Commissioner, CID, and a knighthood followed in 1907.

A correspondent from Australia wrote to Robin Odell, suggesting that James Monro despised Sir Charles Warren and committed the murders to expose Warren's unsuitability for office.[8]

Tom Slemen alleged that a friend of Warren's, Colonel Claude Reignier Conder, was an assassin hired by the secret service because the victims had links to anarchist organisations.[9] Conder was born in Cheltenham on 29 December 1848 and is best known as an archaeologist. He joined the Royal Engineers and worked in Palestine with his friend, Lord Kitchener, enabling a complete survey of the topography to be completed.[10]

His explorations also identified several biblical places for the first time. In 1884, he worked for Warren on topography in South Africa. He translated some Hittite inscriptions in 1887, after four years work. That year he returned to England, going first to Plymouth and then Southampton where he oversaw the engraving department for Ordinance Survey. He retired, as a Colonel, in 1904 and died in Cheltenham on 16 February 1910.

On 9 March 2003, Slemen and his fellow writer, Keith Andrews gave a talk in Liverpool in which they repeated an earlier theory that Conder was a devil worshipper.[11] Both Abberline and Warren allegedly protected him. Annie Chapman worked for him as a cleaner and stole Masonic items, which she sold to Louis Diemschutz. Conder tried to kill Mrs Diemschutz but mistook Elizabeth Stride for her. He was also said to have known Mrs Buki, a former landlady of Mary Jane Kelly's.[12] Neal Shelden has since identified Buki, disproving this connection.[13]

In 2013, an eBook accused Sir Henry Wellcome[14]. Born in Wisconsin in 1853 he came to London in 1880. In conjunction with a fellow America, Silas Burroughs, he established a profitable pharmaceutical company. In 1885, he received a medal for life saving from the Royal Humane Society. He married one of Doctor Barnardo's daughters in 1901 but divorced her fourteen years later after she had a much-publicised affair with Somerset Maugham who subsequently married her. Following his death on 25 July 1936, the Wellcome Trust was established to administer his estate and is now the largest non-government source of funds for biomedical research in the UK. The grounds given for suspecting him of being Jack the Ripper are alleged cruelty in his home-life, experiences of battle at an early age during the Sioux Indian War, and a collection of medical artefacts. His wife is said to have alleged that he beat her with a cattle prod, whilst pregnant, and his native workers may have been beaten.[15]

275

In his biography of Vincent Van Gogh Albert Lupin suggested that the Ripper murders inspired the artist to remove his ear.[16] Dale Larner went further in alleging that Van Gogh was the Ripper. He claimed to have found clues in Van Gogh's painting, including the face of Mary Kelly in Irises. The supposed clues can be viewed on Mr Larner's website, Vincent Alias Jack, which is also the title of his book.

Larner suggested that Van Gogh committed other murders in London and that a gap between Ripper letters from 23 December 1888 to 8 January 1889 was due to Vincent cutting his ears off. In a letter to his sister in June 1888, Vincent noted that his straw hat in a self-portrait was like a hannekenmaaier, which means Little Jack Mower or Reaper.[17] Larner claimed that Vincent thus invented the name of Jack the Ripper. Letters that Vincent wrote from Arles, during the period of the Ripper murders, effectively give him an alibi.[18]

Another artist accused was Henri de Toulouse-Lautrec. He was born in France in 1864. At the age of thirteen, he fractured one knee bone and the other in the following year. They did not heal, and his legs ceased to grow, giving him an adult torso with juvenile legs. A Lambeth brasserie is named after him, but he is not known to have visited London, where he became friends with Oscar Wilde, before 1894.[19]

Greg Alexander suggested that Lautrec came to know Mary Kelly when she worked at a Parisian brothel and contracted syphilis from her. He cited an 1884 letter from the artist to his mother, which had the name Jeannette Hathway in the corner without an explanation. [20] Joseph Barnett said that Kelly told him she had worked in France at a gay house, but this is unconfirmed. Alexander, the only person to suggest Lautrec as a suspect, has since withdrawn this and claimed instead that a member of the artist's family may have sought revenge. He had previously suggested in posts on the Jack the Ripper Casebook website that Lautrec's doctor, Henri Bourges, was involved.[21]

Karen Trenouth mentioned the Filipino nationalist, Jose Protacio Rizal, as a suspect.[22] Born in the Philippines in 1861 Rizal studied medicine in Madrid. A poet and artist he formed a nationalist movement in the Philippines in 1891. The Spanish executed him on 30 December 1896. Trenouth claimed that the owners of Rizal's London flat found a jar containing a human kidney and a diary in January 1986, which contained a confession. She then accepted that, although Rizal was in London in 1888, he was visiting Paris at the time of Annie Chapman's murder. She suggested that his friend, Dr Antonio Regidor, could have killed Chapman and, later, mentioned Dr. Reinhold Rost. Both men were members of the International Association of Filipinologists, founded by Rizal in January 1889. Born in Germany in 1822, Rost was a librarian at the India Office. Regidor ran a law office in London that served as overseas correspondent for Spanish publications.

Robert Mann was an inmate of the Whitechapel workhouse who had charge of the mortuary. On the morning of the Nichols murder, the police came and told him that there was a body in the mortuary. He went there at 5 am. After breakfast he, and another man, James Hatfield, undressed the victim.[23] This contradicted the evidence of Inspector Helson who said that he saw the body with the clothes still on. Mann first said that Helson was not there then said that he could not say if he was there or not. Inspector Spratling told the inquest that he saw two workhouse men stripping the body and Detective Sergeant Enright said he gave instructions not to touch the body.[24] Hatfield denied receiving any such instructions. The corner said that Mann was subject to fits and his evidence was hardly reliable.

Mann was born in 1833. He lived in the workhouse from at least the age of fifteen, per the 1851 census. He went to the infirmary on 3 May 1873.[25] As Whitechapel lacked a public mortuary there was no paid mortuary attendant and Mann took on these duties. He died on 2 January 1896. Mei Trow accused him in 2009 on the basis that he knew the area and fitted profiles of the killer.[26] Trow suggested that the disregarding of the police instructions not to touch the body gave an opportunity for Mann to admire his handiwork.

The FBI profile suggested that the Ripper was 28-36, younger than Mann. It also said that he was employed during the week in a position where he worked alone and experienced his destructive fantasies. Possible occupations included butcher, mortician's helper, medical examiner's assistant, or hospital attendant.[27]

Edward Buchan was a marine store dealer who committed suicide on the day of Mary Jane Kelly's funeral and had been acting strange for some time previously. Roger Barber accused him in 1990, observing that the timing of his death coincided with the end of the murders.[28]

Another suicide later linked to Jack the Ripper was Police Constable Richard Brown. He resigned from the Metropolitan Police on 13 November 1888 and shot himself in Hyde Park three days later. The reason for his resignation was a failure to attend duty. Instead of being dismissed he was allowed to leave and keep his testimonial. Before joining the police, he had served in the army. In a blog Christopher T George reviewed Brown's life and asked if he could have been the Ripper.[29]

George Lusk was proposed as a suspect on Jack the Ripper Casebook website.[30] The poster suggested that the vigilante committee could have given a cover. Lusk was born in 1839. Susannah, his wife, died on 5 February 1888, leaving seven children. He was made bankrupt in 1891 and died in 1919.[31]

In 1999, Robert Graysmith accused Pastor John George Gibson.[32] From 1894, Gibson was pastor at Emmanuel Baptist Church in San Francisco. On 13 April 1895, the mutilated body of Minnie Williams was discovered in the library and that of Blanche Lamont in the bell-tower. Convicted of both murders Theodore Durrant was hanged on 7 January 1898. His lawyer's attempts to implicate Gibson were not believed.[33]

278

Gibson died in 1912. Thirteen years later, according to Graysmith, the San Francisco News reported that he had confessed the murders of Williams and Lamont on his deathbed to a man called Charlie Floyd. Graysmith contended that Gibson was the Ripper, assisted by the unrelated Jesse Gibson. This was on the basis that Gibson liked people to call him Jack, had a blotchy complexion when stressed and a small moustache like the man seen with Mary Jane Kelly. Graysmith noted that a man with a clerical collar asked for the address of George Lusk and may have sent the kidney. This refers to a statement made by Emily Marsh to the press. She was working in her father's shop at 218 Jubilee Street, Mile End, on 13 October 1888 when the man asked for Lusk's address. She gave it to him, without the house number, which is how the parcel containing the kidney was addressed. Marsh gave a full description of the man, estimating his age about 45, and said he spoke with an Irish accent.[34] The description does not match Gibson, who was 29 in 1888, based on the birth date of 14 August 1857 given on his gravestone.

In court, he said that he was educated in Edinburgh then went to London, back to St Andrews and came to America in 1881, proceeding to Red Bluff then Chico and finally Emmanuel.[35] Whilst there he wrote a short pamphlet, in which he spoke about living in different countries.[36] The date of his arrival in America is probably a misprint as records at Spurgeon's College show that he resigned his position in Scotland in 1888.[37] Various parishioners at Emmanuel described him for a newspaper article in 1902, some stating that they had known him for nearly 20 years.[38]

Samuel Barnett was the vicar at St Jude's Church in Whitechapel in 1888. The accusation against him came from Michael Straczynski, writer of an episode of Babylon 5 that featured Jack the Ripper. Straczynski outlined his reasons, following questions from fans of the show.[39] He claimed that police and church officials interviewed Barnett, without releasing the transcripts. He believed that the Ripper said, "You would say anything but your prayers" which meant he had to be a clergyman. Straczynski said that Barnett was the last person to see two of the victims, was related to Joseph Barnett and that his wife wrote to The Times saying the Ripper was trying to give a message and would stop if he was listened to. He also said that Barnett left England shortly after the murders.

Samuel Augustus Barnett was born in 1844. He became vicar of St Jude's, in 1873 and was involved in philanthropic work in the community. During the period of the Whitechapel murders, The Times published four of his letters, expressing ideas for reforms.[40] He became Canon of Bristol Cathedral in 1903 and was a sub-dean of Westminster from 1905 until his death in 1913. There are no records of Barnett being interviewed about the murders. He was not related to Joseph Barnett and there is no evidence that he knew the victims. Mrs Barnett drafted a petition to Queen Victoria, about the immorality of men.[41]

In 1996, Peter Fisher proposed the Reverend John Moses Eppstein.[42] Eppstein was born in Russia or Germany c.1827, the grandson of a Rabbi. He was baptised in 1844 and worked as a missionary in several countries. In London, he was involved with the London Society for the Spread of Christianity amongst the Jews.[43] He lectured frequently at the United Methodist Free Church directly opposite 29 Hanbury Street. His son, William Charles, was curate at St Marys, Spital Square, Whitechapel, between 1887 and 1889 and later, headmaster of Reading School. Eppstein died in Bristol on 10 May 1903.

In 2010, David Monaghan and Nigel Cawthorne wrote a book accusing the writer of "My Secret Life" of being Jack the Ripper. "My Secret Life" was published in eleven volumes between 1888 and 1894. It described the sexual practices of an anonymous Victorian gentleman, who used the pseudonym Walter. The unidentified author has been linked to several prominent individuals.[44] The experiences described may be autobiographical or fictitious or a combination of both.

Walter was a violent user of prostitutes, both adult and child, in London, including the East End. He carried knives for sex purposes. He was a serial rapist, obsessed with piercing the hymen, and had a blood fetish. He brought medical books and pretended to be a doctor, studying female sex organs. He was sexually aroused whilst hunting game.

One of his prostitutes was called Mary Davis. Walter met her when thinking of committing suicide by throwing himself in the canal. She was 19 and their relationship lasted for about three years. Monaghan saw similarities with Mary Jane Kelly, whose married name was allegedly Davies or Davis. Both were Irish and rented rooms in the East End. Both had allegedly worked in the West End.

Walter describes Mary Davies as short and plump, with grey eyes and nearly black hair.[45]Mary Kelly was believed to be twenty-five at the time of her death, a little stout, with blue eyes and blond hair. Mary Davies told Walter that she was the daughter of an under-game keeper who had a sexual relationship with a tradesman. Her father found out and she went to London where she lived in the brothel. This house was kept by an old man called Smith, a carpenter, and a woman. There were no other lodgers. Mary Kelly told Barnett that her husband Davies died in an explosion at a colliery and she went to an infirmary in Cardiff before going on the streets of London.

In 2015 Wynne Weston Davies argued that his ancestor Elizabeth was Mary Kelly and that her estranged husband, Francis Spurzheim Craig was Jack the Ripper. Spurzheim Craig, a journalist married Elizabeth Weston Davies in 1884 and filed for divorce two years later. He committed suicide by slitting his throat on 8 March 1903.

In 2013, a book accused William Belcher, a milkman who moved to Hartlepool and changed his name to Williams.[46] Research by Debra Arif showed that the family lived at

20 Grove Street, Marylebone not Whitechapel as claimed.[47] They continued to use the name Belcher into 1889.

A recent suspect is Albert Bachert. He appears throughout the series of murders, claiming to have seen a suspicious character prior to the murder of Elizabeth Stride and a man with Frances Coles. A week after the Mc Kenzie murder he apprehended a suspect with other members of the vigilante committee. He also claimed to have received letters from Jack the Ripper and said that a message was chalked on the outside of his house at 13 Newnham Street. In 1890, he told the press a variant of the lodger story.[48]

Bachert was probably the Albert Wilhelm Bachert baptised in Whitechapel on 7 September 1862. Some accounts give his name as Albert Edward. He worked as an engraver and became involved in political movements. He canvased for the Whitechapel Conservative candidate, Colonel Cowan, in 1885 complaining of threats by the opposition candidate.[49] In 1887 he complained about two constables, who allegedly harassed a woman and then assaulted him.[50] In 1888 he gave evidence when John Burns was charged with riotous assembly and assaulting the police.[51] The following year he was acquitted of trying to pass counterfeit coins.[52] In October 1890 he asked for advice at the Thames Magistrate Court, saying that he had been threatened after writing to the police about the Kingsland murders.

On 25 May 1891, he witnessed an alleged manslaughter outside the Great Eastern Hotel. Later that year he was convicted of disorderly conduct, after being ejected from a butcher's shop in Whitechapel High Street.[53] He made inquiries about charging a witness with perjury.[54] On 18 November 1891 he testified at the inquest of fourteen-year old Arthur Charles Puleston who was killed by a falling iron griffin whilst walking in front of Bachert during a gale.[55]

In 1892, he was prosecuted for stealing £300 from his father but this was dropped as a mistake.[56] In January 1893 he resigned as secretary of the Unemployed Investigation and Relief Committee, after writing to Mr. Gladstone without approval.[57] He was subsequently jailed for obtaining food under false pretences. On his release, he complained to the court, saying that he intended to emigrate. [58]

The Men who might have been the Ripper

At the end of the suspect list it is time to make some conclusions based on the known facts. The cornerstone of the legal system is that everyone is presumed innocent until proven guilty. We start then with 333 innocent people and must decide if that status should change for any of them.

First, we can rule out those who could not possibly have committed the crimes. These are those who were fictitious or have a confirmed alibi. James Carnac, Doctor Stanley, Walter and the American George Hutchinson are invented, although they may be based on real people. 42 suspects, including Prince Albert Victor, are known to have been elsewhere when at least one of the murders were committed.

For the remaining suspects we must consider if there is a reason to suspect them. Here we can dismiss those accused without a good reason. People who operated on horses, carried black bags, or just happened to live in Whitechapel need not detain us further. James Munro and Constance Kent are among the 71 cleared.

The next stage is to assess the evidence and remove the suspects accused without any. This requires some objectivity. Evidence is defined as the available body of facts or information indicating whether a belief or proposition is true or valid. If there is no information to support the accusation, then the suspect should be dismissed. The 92 cleared here include Albert Bachert, the Portuguese cattlemen and Doctor Strauss.

Where evidence exists, it needs to be evaluated for reliability. An effective way of doing this is to ask if it would be accepted by lawyers preparing a file for criminal prosecution. The answer is no if the evidence can easily be shown to be false. The 84 suspects cleared here, include most of those in the Royal Conspiracy, James Maybrick, and the drunks accused only by their own confessions.

The suspects left on the list are those who stand accused by evidence that might be reliable enough to withstand some scrutiny, but it may not be sufficient. Thirty can be cleared because there is not enough evidence to build a convincing case. They include Dick Austin, Francis Thompson, and Carl Feigenbaum. That leaves ten suspects. In alphabetical order they are William Bury, David Cohen, Thomas Cutbush, Montague Druitt, William Grainger, James Kelly, Seweryn Klosowski, Aaron Kosminski, Charles Le Grand, and Francis Tumblety.

Three were convicted of murder. Eight are known to have been violent. Four spent time in lunatic asylums. Nine were apparently considered suspects in the murders by the authorities. Nine were investigated for other offences. Eight are known to have been in London in the autumn of 1888.

On closer examination, the case against each of them is best described as inconclusive. The evidence against Druitt is the belief of a senior Police Officer and a vague story told by the Member of Parliament representing the constituency of the Druitt family. Macnaghten's comments, guided by his own belief that the suicide of the killer led to the cessation of the crimes, indicate a lack of knowledge about the suspect.

Macnaghten also accused Kosminski, and again did not know key facts about him. Chief Inspector Swanson fared little better when he put Kosminski's name to the Polish Jew that Robert Anderson identified as Jack the Ripper. It is not known why Kosminski became a suspect or what evidence, if any, was held. Martin Fido's theory of confusion between David Cohen and Kosminski is unproven. As a violent lunatic arrested shortly after the Mary Kelly murder and never again at liberty, Cohen remains on the suspect list but there is nothing else connecting him to the crimes.

James Kelly and William Bury both killed their wives with a knife and associated with prostitutes. The police did not regard either as a serious suspect. The half-hearted attempts to find Kelly indicates a lack of interest rather than a cover-up, perhaps mindful that a recaptured Kelly might lead to public revelations about his escape. Bury was apparently investigated and dismissed. The only indication that the police suspected Kelly is the raid on his mother in laws house shortly after the death of Mary Jane Kelly and this may have been routine rather than prompted by direct evidence against him. We can dismiss the unreliable thoughts of Bury's executioner but must reflect upon the enquiries of Ernest Parr, who claimed to have additional information.

Seweryn Klosowski killed three women. He is the only confirmed serial killer to remain on the suspect list. The fact that he used poison, rather than the knife, to despatch his known victims weakens the value of those murders argues against him, as does his relationship with those victims. He was accused belatedly by Chief Inspector Abberline, and the police investigated his movements from fifteen years earlier. They found nothing, beyond location.

William Grainger stabbed a prostitute in the abdomen. He was allegedly identified by an eyewitness to the Ripper murders, evidence diluted by a seven-year gap and the apparent use of the same witness on other occasions. A further accusation came later from his solicitor. We cannot tell if Mr Kebbell's comments were based on fact.

Thomas Cutbush was accused of stabbing women in the bottom and sent to a lunatic asylum. The case built by contemporary journalists can be dismissed as the hyperbole of Fleet Street and has not been enhanced by later studies. What remains is a deranged young man who showed signs of violence in captivity and was found with pictures of mutilated women, a feature it should be noted of the FBI profile. Macnaghten dismissed him as a viable suspect.

Francis Tumblety was mentioned as a suspect by Chief Inspector Littlechild. He is the only one of the nine arrested in connection with the Whitechapel murders. Littlechild's information is no longer extant and there was not enough evidence to bring charges.

Charles Le Grand was a violent pimp in Whitechapel at the time of the murders. There are suggestions that the police regarded him as a suspect, but the source of this information is unknown.

We can attempt to match these ten men against the three witness descriptions that are most likely to be of Jack the Ripper. These are the sightings by Mrs Long, Israel Schwartz, and Joseph Lawende. Lawende and Long saw the victim with a man shortly before they were killed. Schwartz saw a man assaulting the victim at the murder scene shortly before her body was found. Lawende and Schwartz described the man as about 30 years of age and Long's suspect was a decade older. A suspect fitting those descriptions would have been born between 1848 and 1858. Allowing five years on either side gives us birth range from 1843 to 1863. Bury (1859), Le Grand (c1850), Druitt (1857), Kelly (1860), and Grainger (1860) fit inside this range.

That is as far as we can go. It is not possible to identify Jack the Ripper from the list of current suspects. This may change in the future. The existence of the police suspects, Druitt, Kosminski, and Ostrog only became public knowledge after 1959, when Dan Farson discovered the Macnaghten memorandum. Research has since cleared Ostrog. Francis Tumblety was unknown to researchers until a chance discovery in the 1980s. Charles Le Grand, was not thought to be a suspect until researchers started exploring his background.

New evidence continues to be found in contemporary newspapers, archives, and personal records. Information that was previously difficult to access is slowly being digitised. Further research may ascertain the whereabouts of James Kelly during the

287

autumn of terror or fully explain the police identification at the seaside home. There is, undoubtedly, more material awaiting discovery on many other suspects. It may exonerate them or provide reasons for further inquiries.

Some cobwebs have been cleared, but others will weave fresh webs of deceit, entangling the gullible and sacrificing truth in the search for profit. Several prominent people in Victorian society have not yet been accused, and we can expect further attempts to blame the crimes on a long dead ancestor. It is possible that more artefacts, such as a knife, will surface.

Serious research cannot deliver results, whilst hindered by the inane. Writers and publishers have a duty to respect the facts without attempting to conceal or deny them. If the case against a preferred suspect does not add up, they should withdraw or honestly explain the pitfalls and refrain from misleading the public. It is a great shame that the libel law of the Victorians is no longer applied to the scoundrels and charlatans who deliberately publish fiction under the pretence of fact.

You may never know who the Ripper was but hopefully this book has helped you determine who he was not.

Alphabetical List of Suspects

This list of the suspects, alphabetically by surname also states the chapter in this book where they are featured, along with the source of the first known accusation against them or reason for suspicion and the author's classification of their current status as a suspect.

1. Abberline, Frederick.

False Confessions.

Accused by Jose Louis Abad, 2007.

No reason to suspect.

2. Akehurst, Charles.

Arrested on Suspicion.

Reported that he was arrested on 12 November 1888.

No evidence.

3. Alaska.

Accused during the Terror

Accused by George Dodge, c. 5 October 1888.

Unreliable evidence.

4. Albericci, Frederico (Fingers Freddy).

Aristocrats and Royals.

Accused by Melvyn Fairclough, 1992.

Unreliable evidence.

5. Albert Edward, Prince (King Edward VII).

Aristocrats and Royals.

Source of accusation unknown.

No reason to suspect.

6. Albert Victor, Prince.

Aristocrats and Royals.

Accused by Thomas Stowell 1970.

Cleared by alibi.

7. Anderson.

False Confessions.

Allegedly confessed to James Edward Brame in 1894, reported 1896.

Unreliable evidence.

8. Anderson, Robert.

Aristocrats and Royals.

Accused by Stephen Knight, 1975.

Cleared by alibi.

9. Andrews (Parnell).

Arrested on Suspicion.

Arrested c. 11 October 1888.

No evidence.

10. Appleford, Stephen.

Doctors and Surgeons.

Accused by Eduardo Cuitino, 2012.

Insufficient evidence.

11. Arthur, George Compton Archibald.

Arrested on suspicion.

Arrested, c. 11 November 1888.

No evidence.

12. **Ashworth, Elizabeth**.

Women.

Called herself Jack the Ripper, 26 December 1888.

Unreliable evidence.

13. **Austin, Dick.**

Accused during the Terror.

Accused by James Oliver, 5 October 1888.

Insufficient evidence.

14. **Avery, John.**

Mad confessions.

Confessed, 12 November 1888.

Unreliable evidence.

15. **Bachert, Albert.**

Other Men.

Accused by Mick Priestley, 2016.

No evidence.

16. **Barlas, John.**

Recollections.

Accused by Rowland Strong, 1897.

No evidence.

17. **Barnardo, Thomas.**

Doctors and Surgeons.

Accused by Donald McCormick, 1970.

No evidence.

18. Barnett, Daniel.

At the Scene.

Reported in the press, 10 November 1888, that he was with Mary Jane Kelly on the night of her murder.

No evidence.

19. Barnett, Joseph.

At the scene.

Accused by Bruce Paley, 1982.

No evidence.

20. Barnett, Samuel.

Other Men.

Accused by Michael Stracyznski, 1995.

No evidence.

21. Barrett, William.

Accused after the Terror.

Harriett Sinfield alleged that Barrett told her he was the Ripper, 31 January 1888.

Unreliable evidence.

22. Batterson, John.

Other Criminals.

Referred to as the Doncaster Jack the Ripper in the press, 1891.

No evidence.

23. Bayne, Thomas Vere.

Other Men.

Accused by Richard Wallace, 1996.

Cleared by alibi.

24. Belcher, William.

Other Men.

Accused by Diane Bainbridge and Norman J. Kirtlan, 2013.

No reason to suspect.

25. Benelius, Nikaner.

Arrested on suspicion.

Arrested 17 November 1888, and after the death of Elizabeth Stride.

No evidence.

26. Benjamin, Corporal.

Arrested on suspicion.

Arrested 9 September 1888.

Cleared by alibi.

27. Besley, Knightly (Knightley Bazeley).

Other Criminals.

Arrested 18 September 1889.

Insufficient evidence.

28. Bisgrove, William.

Contemporary killers.

Stated by Mark Stevens, 2013, that the police made enquiries about Bisgrove in

1891.

No reason to suspect.

29. Blanchard, Alfred Napier.

Mad Confessions.

Confessed, 5 October 1888.

Unreliable evidence.

30. Blandford, Lord (George Charles Spencer Churchill).

Aristocrats and Royals.

Accused by Melvyn Fairclough, 1992.

Unreliable evidence.

31. Blavatsky, Helena Petrovna.

Women.

Possible accusation by Alastair Crowley, 1943.

No reason to suspect.

32. Bond, Charles.

Mad Confessions.

Said that he was Jack the Ripper, 1890.

Unreliable evidence.

33. Bloomfein (Bloombein), George.

Lunatics.

Accused by the Press, 1915.

No evidence.

34. **Borret, George**.

Lunatics.

Suggested as a possible suspect by Paul Begg, 2015.

No evidence.

35. Boult, Willie.

Accused during the Terror.

Accused by W R Collett, 6 October 1888.

No reason to suspect.

36. Bourges, Henri.

Other Men.

Accused by Greg Alexander, 2012.

No reason to suspect.

37. Bowyer, Thomas (Harry).

At the Scene.

Accused by Robert Harris, 2013.

No evidence.

38. Britten, Charles.

At the scene.

Questioned by police, 31 October 1888.

No evidence.

39. Brodie (Broder), William.

Mad Confessions.

Confessed to the murder of Alice Mc Kenzie, 1889.

Cleared by alibi.

40. Brown, General.

Accused during the Terror.

Accused in a letter, October 1888.

No reason to suspect.

41. Brown, Richard (Police Constable).

Other Men.

Mentioned as a possible suspect by Christopher T George, 2013.

No reason to suspect.

42. Bruyn, Cornelius (Charles).

Lunatics.

Accused by the Press, 1890.

No evidence.

43. Buchan, Edward.

Other Men.

Accused by Roger Barber, 1990.

No reason to suspect.

44. Bull, William.

Mad Confessions.

Confessed to murder of Catherine Eddowes, 6 October 1888.

 Unreliable evidence.

45. Bure, Hans.

Accused during the Terror.

Accused by a mob, 7 October 1888.

No evidence.

46. Burrows, Edwin.

Arrested on Suspicion.

Arrested, 8 December 1888.

No reason to suspect.

47. Bury, William Henry.

Contemporary Killers.

Accused by the press, 1889.

Still suspected.

48. Carnac, James Willoughby.

False Confessions.

Alleged confession, c. 1920.

Did not exist.

49. Caroll, Lewis (Charles Dodgson).

Other Men.

Accused by Richard Wallace, 1996.

Cleared by alibi.

50. Castellano, Frank.

Accused during the Terror.

Accused by the Press, 1893.

No reason to suspect.

51. Chapman, Frederick.

Recollections.

Possibly accused by Robert Spicer, 1933.

Unreliable evidence.

52. Chatelle, Almeda.

Later Killers.

Accused by the press, 1894.

No reason to suspect.

53. Churchill, Mr (R).

Accused after the Terror.

Mentioned in the Chief Constable's Register 1888-1892.

Insufficient evidence.

54. Churchill, Randolph.

Aristocrats and Royals.

Accused by Melvyn Fairclough, 1992.

Unreliable evidence.

55. Cohen, David.

Lunatics.

Accused by Martin Fido 1987.

Still suspected.

56. Cohn (Koch, Dr).

Recollections.

Accused by Inspector Lewis Keaton, 1969.

Unreliable evidence.

57. Compton, George.

Arrested on Suspicion.

Arrested 10 November 1888.

No evidence.

58. Conder, Claude Reignier.

Other Men.

Accused by Tom Slemen, 2001.

No reason to suspect.

59. Connell, James (Jim).

Arrested on suspicion.

Arrested 22 November 1888.

No evidence.

60. Connors, John.

Arrested on suspicion.

Arrested, 1890.

No reason to suspect.

61. Conway, Thomas.

At the scene.

Accused in an anonymous letter, 1888.

No reason to suspect.

62. Corbett, Charles.

Mad Confessions.

Said he was Jack the Ripper, 1890.

Unreliable evidence.

63. Cornwall.

Accused after the Terror.

Accused by the press, 1889.

Cleared by alibi.

64. Courtenay, John.

Aristocrats and Royals.

Accused by Melvyn Fairclough, 1992.

Unreliable evidence.

65. Cow, Douglas.

Arrested on Suspicion.

Arrested, 21 November 1888.

No evidence.

66. Craig, Francis Spurzheim.

Other Men.

Accused by Wynne Weston Davies, 2013.

No reason to suspect.

67. Cream, Thomas Neil.

Contemporary Killers.

Allegedly suspected by James Billington, 1892.

Cleared by alibi.

68. Cross (Lechmere) Charles.

At the scene.

Accused by Michael Connor, 2006.

Insufficient Evidence.

69. Crossley.

Accused during the Terror.

Arrested 26 October 1888.

No evidence.

70. Cullen, George (Squibby).

Accused during the Terror.

Accused by a mob, 18 September 1888.

Cleared by alibi.

71. Cutbush, Thomas.

Other Criminals.

Accused by the press, 1894.

Still suspected.

72. Da Rocha, Joachim.

Accused after the Terror.

Accused by Edward Larkins, 1892.

No evidence.

73. Davidson, John.

Accused during the Terror.

Identified by police as a man who confessed to Thomas Ryan, 30 September 1888.

Unreliable evidence.

74. Davies, John (Jacky).

Accused during the Terror.

Accused by Sarah Franklin, 1888.

No reason to suspect.

75. Davies, John.

Mad Confessions.

Told women he was Jack the Ripper, 1889.

Unreliable evidence.

76. Davies, Morgan.

Accused after the Terror.

Accused by Robert D'Onston Stephenson, December 1888.

Unreliable evidence.

77. De Jong, Hendrick.

Later Killers.

Accused by the press, 1893.

Insufficient evidence.

78. De Walden, Lord Harold (Frederick George Ellis).

Aristocrats and Royals.

Accused by the press, 1899.

No evidence.

79. Deeming, Frederick.

Contemporary Killers.

Accused by Charles Barber and the press, 1892.

Unreliable evidence.

80. Denker, Henry.

Mad Confessions,

Called himself Jack the Ripper, 1889.

Unreliable evidence.

81. Denny, Joseph.

Arrested on Suspicion.

Arrested, 28 December 1888.

No evidence.

82. Diemschutz, Louis.

At the Scene.

Accused by Randy Williams, 2016.

Cleared by alibi.

83. Donkin, John George.

Accused during the terror.

Accused by William Wookey, October 1888.

No reason to suspect.

84. Donovan, Timothy.

At the scene.

Accused by Donald Rumbelow, 1975.

No evidence.

85. Dowson, Ernest.

Recollections.

Mentioned by Martin Fido, 1999.

No evidence.

86. Doyle, Arthur Conan

Doctors and Surgeons.

Mentioned by Jim Leighton, 2006.

No reason to suspect.

87. Druitt, Montague John.

Macnaghten's Memorandum.

Suspected by Sir Melville Macnaghten, 1894.

Still suspected.

88. Duberly.

False Confessions.

Allegedly accused by John Pavitt Sawyer, 1919.

Unreliable evidence.

89. Dutton, Thomas.

Recollections.

Claimed in 1929, that he had been stopped by the police.

No evidence.

90. Eagle, Morris.

At the Scene.

Accused on an internet forum, 2008.

No evidence.

91. Edwards, Frank.

Recollections.

Accused by George Edwards, 1959.

Unreliable evidence.

92. Eppstein, John Moses.

Other Men.

Accused by Peter Fisher, 1996.

No evidence.

93. Euston, Lord (Henry James Fitzroy).

Aristocrats and Royals.

Accused by Melvyn Fairclough, 1992.

Unreliable evidence.

94. Evison, Charles.

Arrested on Suspicion.

Arrested 17 July 1889.

No evidence.

95. Farley, James.

Other Criminals.

Reported by the press in 1893 that he was known as Jack the Ripper.

No evidence.

96. Farrow James (Police Constable).

Accused after the Terror.

Accused by Edward Smith, 5 January 1889.

No reason to suspect.

97. Feigenbaum, Carl (Anton Zahn).

Later Killers.

Accused by William Sanford Lawnton, 1896.

Insufficient evidence.

98. Fenwick, Collingwood Hilton.

Other Criminals.

Convicted of unlawfully wounding a prostitute in November 1888.

Insufficient evidence.

99. Fitzgerald, John.

Mad Confessions.

Confessed to police, 24 September 1888.

Unreliable evidence.

100. Fitzmaurice, John Alexander.

Accused after the Terror.

Arrested 16 March 1889.

Unreliable evidence.

101. Fleming, Joseph.

At the Scene.

Alleged by Julia Venturney to have ill-used Mary Kelly, November 1888.

No evidence.

102. Fogelma.

Lunatics.

Accused by the Press, 1923.

Unreliable evidence.

103. Forbes-Winslow, Lyttelton Stewart.

Accused during the Terror.

Accused in letter from C J Denny to the police, 3 October 1888.

No evidence.

104. Foster, William John.

Arrested on Suspicion.

Arrested 11 October 1888.

No evidence.

105. Foy, John.

Mad Confessions.

Told women he was Jack the Ripper, 21 October 1888.

Unreliable evidence.

106. Freund, Hebert Percy Edmund (Percy).

Accused during the Terror.

Source of accusation unknown.

No reason to suspect.

107. Friedman, Samuel.

At the Scene.

Accused by Randy Williams, 2016.

No reason to suspect.

108. Gavan, Daniel.

Other Criminals.

Linked by the press, March 1891.

Insufficient evidence.

109. Gee.

Mad Confessions.

Called himself Jack the Ripper, 1892.

Unreliable evidence.

110. George, Corporal.

Arrested on Suspicion.

Identified by Pearly Poll, 15 September 1888.

Cleared by alibi.

111. Gibson, John George.

Other Men.

Accused by Robert Graysmith, 1999.

No reason to suspect.

112. Gilbert, William.

Mad Confessions.

Several women testified that he called himself Jack the Ripper, 1889.

Unreliable evidence.

113. Gissing, George.

Other Men.

Source of accusation unknown, c. 1960.

Cleared by alibi.

114. Gladstone, William Ewart.

Aristocrats and Royals.

Accused by Graham Norton, 1970.

No reason to suspect.

115. Glen, James.

Mad Confessions

Called himself Jack the Ripper, 1889.

Unreliable evidence.

116. Gloster, James.

Doctors and Surgeons.

Accused by Martin Roberts, 1999.

No reason to suspect.

117. Goldstein, Leon.

At the Scene.

Walked down Berner Street around the time of the murder.

No evidence.

118. Graham, Benjamin.

Mad Confessions.

Confessed to police and another man, 17 October 1888.

Unreliable evidence.

119. Graham, Samuel.

Accused after the Terror.

Arrested c. 18 November 1888.

120. Grainger (Grant), William.

Other Criminals.

Accused by the press, 1895.

Still suspected.

121. Gray (Boxall), Alfred.

Other Criminals.

Arrested January 1889.

No evidence.

122. Greathead, William James Percy Beresford (Percy).

Other Criminals.

Arrested, August 1891.

No evidence.

123. Gull, William.

Aristocrats and Royals.

Accused by Stephen Knight, 1975.

Unreliable evidence.

124. Halliday, Elizabeth.

Women.

Accused by Sheriff Harrison Beecher, 1893.

Insufficient evidence.

125. Halstead, Denis.

Recollections.

Stated in 1959 that the police used to shadow him.

No reason to suspect.

126. Hamblar, Edward.

Accused after the Terror.

Accused by a mob, October 1889.

No reason to suspect.

127. Hanhart, Theophil (Theophile).

Mad Confessions.

Confessed to police, 21 December 1888.

Unreliable evidence.

128. Hardiman, James.

At the Scene.

Accused by Rob Hills, 2005.

No evidence.

129. Hardiman, William.

At the Scene.

Accused by Stanley Dean Reid, 2005.

No evidence.

130. Harding, Thomas.

Contemporary Killers.

Accused on an internet forum, 2009.

No reason to suspect.

131. Harting, Leonard (Carl Muller).

Other Criminals.

Acquitted of attacking Alice Seymour, 1891.

Insufficient evidence.

132. Hartley, Doctor.

Accused during the Terror.

Accused in a letter from John S Gordon, 3 October 1888.

No evidence.

133. Hebbert, Charles.

Doctors and Surgeons.

Accused by Xanthe Mallett, 2012.

No reason to suspect.

134. Henderson, George Richard.

Arrested on Suspicion.

Arrested 10 October 1888.

No evidence.

135. Hermann, Charles Y.

Mad Confessions.

Confessed to police, 1905.

Unreliable evidence.

136. Hertzberg, (Ladsburgh) Michael.

Mad Confessions.

Told five men that he was Jack the Ripper, 15 November 1888.

Unreliable evidence.

137. Hewitt, John.

Recollections.

Accused by Stuart Hicks, 1995.

Cleared by alibi.

138. Hill, John.

Mad Confessions.

Attacked Elizabeth Tilley, saying "Jack", 10 March 1891.

Unreliable evidence.

139. Hinde, Alfred.

Recollections.

The Press claimed in 1936 that he was once detained.

No evidence.

140. Hiron, Robert.

Accused after the Terror.

Known as "Mad Jack."

No reason to suspect.

141. Holmes, Henry Harold (HH) (Herman Webster Mudgett).

Later Killers.

Accused by Jeff Mudgett, 2011.

Unreliable evidence.

142. Holt, (William, Dr.).

Mad Confessions.

Allegedly said he was Jack the Ripper, 11 November 1888.

Unreliable evidence.

143. Hotham.

False Confessions.

Allegedly accused by John Pavitt Sawyer, 1919.

Unreliable evidence.

144. Hughes-Hallett, Francis Charles (Colonel).

At the Scene.

Accused by Simon D. Wood, 2013.

No evidence.

145. Hutchinson, George (American).

Lunatics.

Accused by the Press, 1889.

Did not exist.

146. Hutchinson, George.

At the Scene.

Accused by Bob Hinton, 1998.

Insufficient Evidence.

147. Hyams, Hyam.

Lunatics.

Accused by Mark King, 2001.

Insufficient evidence.

148. Irwin, Jack.

Accused after the Terror.

Accused by A H Skirving, 12 March 1889.

Cleared by alibi.

149. Isaacs, Benjamin.

Mad Confessions.

Confessed to Police Constable Coots, 22 November 1888.

Unreliable evidence.

150. Isaacs, Joseph.

Arrested on suspicion.

Arrested 5 December 1888.

Insufficient Evidence.

151. Isenschmid, Jacob.

Arrested on suspicion.

Arrested, 12 September 1888.

Cleared by alibi.

152. James, John (Henry).

Accused during the Terror.

Seen carrying a knife, 17 September 1888.

No evidence.

153. James, William.

Mad Confessions.

Confessed to Police Constable Sutherland, 7 December 1888.

Unreliable evidence.

154. Johnson, James.

Other Criminals.

Accused of assaulting Elizabeth Hudson, 27 September 1888.

Unreliable evidence.

155. Jones, William.

Mad Confessions.

Assaulted Annie Park, saying he was Jack the Ripper, October 1889.

Unreliable evidence.

156. Jones, Thomas.

Other Criminals.

Accused of threatening Annie Evans with a knife, October 1889.

Insufficient evidence.

157. Kaminsky, Nathan.

Lunatics.

Accused by Martin Fido, 1987.

No evidence.

158. Kelly, James.

Contemporary Killers.

Accused by John Morrison 1984.

Still suspected.

159. Kelly, John.

At the scene.

Questioned by Police, October 1888.

Cleared by alibi.

160. Kent, Constance.

Women.

Accused by D J Wagner, 2006.

No reason to suspect.

161. Kidney, Michael.

At the Scene.

Accused of murdering Elizabeth Stride by AP Wolf 1993.

No evidence.

162. Klosowski, Seweryn (George Chapman).

Later Killers.

Suspected by Inspector Abberline, 1903.

Still suspected.

163. Knutson, Bertram.

Accused during the Terror.

Found begging, 05 October 1888.

No evidence.

164. Kosminski, Aaron.

Macnaghten's Memorandum.

Suspected by Sir Melville Macnaghten 1894.

Still suspected.

165. Kosminski, Martin.

Macnaghten's Memorandum.

Mentioned by Scot Nelson, 2001.

No evidence.

166. Kozebrodski, Isaac.

At the Scene.

Accused by Randy Williams, 2016.

Cleared by alibi.

167. Kromschroeder, Christian Henry (HC).

Accused during the Terror.

Accused in a letter from W. Cunliffe to the City Police. October 1888.

Insufficient Evidence.

168. Kropotkin, Pyotr, Prince.

At the Scene.

Accused by Randy Williams, 2016.

No reason to suspect.

169. La Bruckman, Arbie (John Frenchy/Francis).

Arrested on Suspicion.

Claimed in 1891 that he had been arrested eighteen months earlier.

Insufficient Evidence.

170. Lampard, James David.

Accused during the Terror.

Accused by Mr. J. Beckett, 10 October 1888.

No evidence.

171. Langan, John.

Arrested on Suspicion.

Arrested, 10 October 1888.

No evidence.

172. Laurenco, Jose.

Accused after the Terror

Accused by Edward Larkins, March 1889.

No evidence.

173. Lautrec, Henri de Toulouse.

Other Men.

Accused by Greg Alexander, 2012.

No reason to suspect.

174. Law, Private.

Arrested on Suspicion.

Drinking with John Leary on the night of Martha Tabram's murder.

Cleared by alibi.

175. Le Grand (Grande), Charles.

Other Criminals.

Accused by the press, 1892.

Still suspected.

176. Leake, Henry Edward.

Accused after the Terror.

Accused by a man in a pub, November 1888.

No reason to suspect.

177. Leary, John.

Accused by Police Constable Thomas Barrett, 7 September 1888.

Cleared by alibi.

178. Leopold II, King.

Aristocrats and Royals.

Accused by Jacquemine Charrot-Lodwidge, c. 1970.

No reason to suspect.

179. Levisohn, Wolf.

Accused after the Terror.

Accused by two prostitutes, 15 November 1888.

No reason to suspect.

180. Levitski.

Lunatics.

Accused by William Le Queux, 1923.

Unreliable evidence.

181. Levy, Jacob.

Lunatics.

Accused by Mark King, 1999.

Insufficient evidence.

182. Lewis, John.

Mad Confessions.

Called himself Jack the Ripper, November 1888.

Unreliable evidence.

183. Lipman, Julius.

Arrested on Suspicion.

Press reports in 1900 claimed that he was known as Leather Apron.

No evidence.

184. Lis (Silver), Joseph.

Accused after the Terror.

Accused by Charles Van Onselen, 2007.

No evidence.

185. Lister.

False Confessions.

Allegedly accused by John Pavitt Sawyer, 1919.

Unreliable evidence.

186. Lock, John.

Accused during the Terror.

Accused by members of the public, 3 October 1888.

No reason to suspect.

187. Lott, Thomas.

Contemporary Killers.

Linked by the Press, October 1888.

Cleared by alibi.

188. Ludwig, Charles.

Arrested on Suspicion.

Arrested 18 September 1888.

Cleared by alibi.

189. Lusk, George.

Other Men.

Accused on an internet forum, 2009.

No reason to suspect.

190. Mac Donald, Donald.

Accused during the Terror.

Accused in a letter to the press, 03 October 1888.

No evidence.

191. Mac Sweeney.

Accused during the Terror.

Accused in a letter from W. J. Smith, 9 October 1888.

No reason to suspect.

192. Machado, Joao de Souza.

Accused after the Terror.

Accused by Edward Larkin, 1892.

No evidence.

193. Macnaghten, Melville.

Other Men

Accused by Sophie Herfort, 2007.

No reason to suspect.

194. Maduro, Alonzo.

Recollections.

Accused by Griffith Salway, 1949.

Unreliable evidence.

195. Malcolm, James.

Accused during the Terror.

Accused in a letter from John S. Gordon, 4 October 1888.

No reason to suspect.

196. Malone, James.

Mad Confessions.

Called himself Jack the Ripper, September 1891.

Unreliable evidence.

197. Mann, Robert.

Other Men.

Accused by Mei Trow, 2009.

No reason to suspect.

198. Mansfield, Richard.

Accused during the Terror.

Accused in an anonymous letter, October 1888.

No reason to suspect.

199. Mary.

Other Criminals.

Subject of police enquiries, September 1888.

Cleared by alibi.

200. Mason, Arthur Henry.

Arrested on Suspicion.

Accused by two men in a pub, 16 November 1888.

No evidence.

201. Matthews, Oliver.

Arrested on Suspicion.

Arrested 17 November 1888.

No reason to suspect.

202. Maurice.

Accused during the Terror.

Accused by the press, November 1888.

No evidence.

203. Maybrick, James.

False Confessions.

Accused by Shirley Harrison, 1993.

Unreliable evidence.

204. Maybrick, Michael.

False Confessions.

Accused by James Settler, 2009.

No reason to suspect.

205. Mc Grath (Magrath), William.

Accused after the Terror.

Mentioned in the Chief Constable's Register 1888-1892.

Insufficient evidence.

206. Mc Kenna, Edward.

Arrested on Suspicion.

Arrested, 14 September 1888.

Cleared by alibi.

207. Mc Carthy, John.

At the Scene.

Accused in a letter sent on 15 November 1888.

No evidence.

208. McClintock, Charles.

Mad Confessions.

Said he was Jack the Ripper, September 1890.

Unreliable evidence.

209. Mc Dermott, Jim (Red Jim).

Other Criminals.

Alleged contemporary drawing called him Jack the Ripper, reported on an

internet forum in 2010.

Insufficient evidence.

210. Merrick, Joseph (Elephant Man).

Doctors and Surgeons.

In 2017 Patricia Cornwell referred to a contemporary rumour that Merrick was

suspected.

No reason to suspect.

211. Miles, George Francis.

Lunatics.

Accused by Thomas Toughill, 2010.

No evidence.

212. Mills, John Larkin.

Arrested on Suspicion.

Arrested, 17 July 1889.

No evidence.

213. Mills, Thomas.

Arrested on Suspicion.

Accused by a mob, 19 September 1888.

No reason to suspect.

214. M'Kellick, William.

Accused after the Terror.

Antonio Brisighkali called him Jack the Ripper, 12 June 1889.

No reason to suspect.

215. Molin, Thomas.

Recollections.

Reported in the press, 1889.

No evidence.

216. Monro, James.

Other Men.

Accused in correspondence, c. 1966.

No reason to suspect.

217. Morford (Orford).

Doctors and Surgeons.

Accused by the press, 24 September 1888.

No evidence.

218. Morris, George.

At the Scene.

Accused by Rob Hills, 2007.

No evidence.

219. Moynihan, John (Henry Shaw).

Arrested on Suspicion.

Accused by Deputy Sheriff Wood, 1910.

Insufficient evidence.

220. Mumford, James.

At the Scene.

Questioned by the police, 31 August 1888.

No evidence.

221. Murphy, Thomas.

Arrested on Suspicion.

Arrested, 12 November 1888.

No evidence.

222. Murray, John.

Mad Confessions.

Told a ticket collector that he was Jack the Ripper, October 1888.

Unreliable Evidence.

223. Mylett, Rose.

Women.

Accused on an internet forum, 2009.

No reason to suspect.

224. Neating (Netting), George.

At the Scene.

Reported to police in 1901 by Mrs Clark.

No evidence.

225. Netley, John.

Aristocrats and Royals.

Accused by Joseph Sickert 1972.

Unreliable evidence.

226. Nochild, August (Augustus).

Mad Confessions.

Attacked a prostitute saying he had killed others, 2 October 1888.

Unreliable evidence.

227. Norton, John.

Recollections.

Told police in 1893 that he had been arrested on suspicion of the Whitechapel murders.

No evidence.

228. O'Brien, William.

Accused after the Terror.

Connected by Trevor Marriott in 2013 to the suspect O'Brien named in the Chief Constable's Register 1888-92.

No reason to suspect.

229. Onion, William.

Accused during the Terror.

Accused in an anonymous letter sent to the City Police, 13 November 1888.

Cleared by alibi.

230. Ostrog, Michael.

Macnaghten's Memorandum.

Suspected by Melville Macnaghten, 1894.

Cleared by alibi.

231. Parent, Alfred.

Arrested on suspicion.

Arrested, 25 November 1888.

No evidence.

232. Parnell, Charles Stuart.

Accused during the Terror.

Accused in an anonymous letter to the City Police, November 1888.

No reason to suspect.

233. Pearcey, Mary.

Women.

Accused by William Stewart, 1939.

No evidence.

234. Pearson, Alfred.

Aristocrats and Royals.

Accused by Karen Trenouth, 2006

Unreliable evidence.

235. Pedachenko, Alexander.

Lunatics.

Accused by William Le Queux, 1923.

Unreliable evidence.

236. Perryman, John Benjamin.

Mad Confessions.

Arrested, 14 November 1888.

Unreliable evidence.

237. Petitt, William.

Mad Confessions.

Said he was Jack the Ripper, 1889.

Unreliable evidence.

238. Pierilli, George.

Mad Confessions.

Called himself Jack the Ripper, December 1888.

Unreliable evidence.

239. Piggott, William.

Arrested on Suspicion.

Arrested, 9 September 1888.

Cleared by alibi.

240. Pizer, John.

Arrested on Suspicion.

Arrested, 10 September 1888.

Cleared by alibi.

241. Porriott, Walter Thomas (Andrew John Gibson, Henry Cecil Darling).

Recollections.

Accused by Steve Wilson, 1997.

No reason to suspect.

242. Pricha, Antoni.

Accused after the Terror.

Accused by Edward Larkin, 13 November 1888.

Cleared by alibi.

243. Puckridge (Puckeridge), Oswald.

Lunatics.

Mentioned by Charles Warren as a suspect, 19 September 1888.

Cleared by alibi.

244. Quinn, Edward.

Arrested on Suspicion.

Accused by a member of the public, 15 September 1888.

No evidence.

245. Raper, Frank.

Arrested on Suspicion.

Arrested 30 September 1888.

No evidence.

246. Regidor, Antonio.

Other Men.

Accused by Karen Trenouth, 2006.

No reason to suspect.

247. Richardson, John.

At the Scene.

Questioned by police, 8 September 1888.

No evidence.

248. Rizal, Jose Protacio.

Other Men.

Accused by Karen Trenouth, 2006.

No reason to suspect.

249. Robertson, Donald.

Recollections.

Told Police, 15 March 1896, that he was once under suspicion.

No evidence.

250. Robertson, George.

Later Killers.

Accused on an internet forum, 2010.

No reason to suspect.

251. Robertson, Henry Dalkin.

Recollections.

Told police, 29 November 1889, that he was once arrested as Jack the Ripper.

No evidence.

252. Robinson, Pierce John.

Arrested on Suspicion.

Accused by Richard Wingate, October 1888.

Cleared by alibi.

253. Rost, Reinhold.

Other Men.

Accused by Karen Trenouth, 2006.

No reason to suspect.

254. Royal, John.

Other Criminals.

Threatened to rip up Norah Brown, 20 July 1889.

Insufficient evidence.

255. Russell, George William Francis Sackville (Duke of Bedford).

Aristocrats and Royals.

In 1969 Philippe Jullian reported a rumour that the Duke was suspected.

No evidence.

256. Russell, Francis Charles Hastings (Duke of Bedford).

Aristocrats and Royals.

Accused by Stan Russo, 2011.

Insufficient evidence.

257. Russell, Herbrand Arthur (Duke of Bedford).

Aristocrats and Royals.

Accused by Karen Trenouth, 2006.

Unreliable evidence.

258. Sadler, James Thomas

At the Scene.

Arrested 14 February 1891.

Cleared by alibi.

259. Salisbury, Lord (Robert Arthur Talbot Gascoyne-Cecil).

Aristocrats and Royals.

Accused by Stephen Knight, 1975.

Unreliable evidence.

260. Salmon, Sampson Silas.

Later Killers

Accused on an internet forum, 2012.

No reason to suspect.

261. Sanders, John William Smith.

Lunatics.

Noted as a police suspect by Inspector Abberline, 1 November 1888.

Cleared by alibi.

262. Sanders, John William.

Doctors and Surgeons.

In 1993 Jon Ogan suggested that he was confused with John William Smith Sanders.

No reason to suspect.

263. Sanderson, John.

False Confessions.

Accused by John Long, 6 December 1897.

Unreliable evidence.

264. Sass, (Doctor, Edwin Etty).

Accused during the Terror.

Doctor Sass or Sassy was accused in a letter, 6 October 1888.

No evidence.

265. Saunderson, Reginald.

Later Killers.

Accused by the Press 1894.

Insufficient evidence.

266. Sawyer, John Pavitt.

False Confessions.

Alleged confession, 1919, reported by Frank Pearse 2012.

Unreliable evidence.

267. Scar, Samuel.

Mad Confessions.

Threatened to rip up a woman, August 1890.

Unreliable evidence.

268. Schulz, Ernest.

Later Killers.

Accused by the press, 1891.

No evidence.

269. Schumacher, Friedrich.

Arrested on Suspicion.

Arrested, 13 September 1891.

No reason to suspect.

270. Schwartz, Israel.

At the Scene.

Suggested by Gavin Bromley, 2007.

No evidence.

271. Shaw, James.

Arrested on Suspicion.

Accused by the press, 3 December 1888.

No evidence.

272. Sheals, William.

Mad Confessions.

Told women he was Jack the Ripper, 17 October 1889.

Unreliable evidence.

273. Sickert, Walter.

Aristocrats and Royals.

Accused by Stephen Knight, 1975.

Insufficient evidence.

274. Simm, Clarence.

Recollections.

Allegedly accused by Elizabeth Simm, 1999.

Unreliable evidence.

275. Sims, George Robert (GR).

Recollections.

Stated in 1891 that he had been accused.

No evidence.

276. Skinnerton, Henry.

Mad Confessions.

Told Henry Corney that he was Jack the Ripper, 21 October 1888.

Unreliable evidence.

277. Skipper.

Arrested on Suspicion.

Accused by Pearly Poll, 15 September 1888.

Cleared by alibi.

278. Smith, Newland Francis Forester.

Lunatics.

Asylum case notes state that he believed himself accused of being Jack the

Ripper, October 1891.

No evidence.

279. Solomon, Louis.

Accused during the Terror.

Accused by officials from Woking Prison, November 1888.

No evidence.

280. Somerset, Lord Henry Arthur George.

Aristocrats and Royals.

Accused by Melvyn Fairclough, 1992.

Unreliable evidence.

281. Somo, Gersie.

Accused after the Terror.

Accused by a mob, 18 November 1888.

No reason to suspect.

282. Stammer, Johann (John Kelly).

Accused during the Terror.

Accused by Jonas, 10 October 1888.

Unreliable evidence.

283. Stanley, Doctor.

False Confessions

Accused by Leonard Matters 1926.

Did not exist.

284. Stanley, Edward.

At the Scene.

Associate of Annie Chapman.

Cleared by alibi.

285. Stanley, William.

Mad Confessions.

Told Mary Ann Hill he was Jack the Ripper, 6 October 1888.

Unreliable evidence.

286. Stephen, James Kenneth (JK).

Aristocrats and Royals.

Accused by Michael Harrison, 1972.

Unreliable evidence.

287. Stephenson, Robert D'Onston.

Accused after the Terror.

Accused by George Marsh, 24 December 1888.

Cleared by alibi.

288. Stevenson, Robert Louis.

Accused during the Terror.

Suggested by Mrs Luckett, 1888.

Cleared by alibi.

289. Stewart (Ever).

Arrested on Suspicion.

Arrested, 30 November 1888.

No evidence.

290. Straus, (Doctor).

Accused during the Terror.

Accused by the Press, 1941.

No evidence.

291. Sullivan, John.

Arrested on Suspicion.

Arrested 17 July 1891.

No reason to suspect.

292. Swinburne, Algernon Charles.

Other Men.

Mentioned by Richard Whittington Egan, 1975.

No reason to suspect.

293. Swyer, Septimus.

Doctors and Surgeons.

Accused on an internet forum, 2012.

Insufficient evidence.

294. Szemerdy, Alois.

Contemporary Killers.

Accused by the press, 1892.

No evidence.

295. Taylor, Henry.

Arrested during the Terror.

Accused by a mob, 2 October 1888.

Cleared by alibi.

296. Taylor, Mr.

Recollections.

Anonymous accuser, 1929.

Unreliable evidence.

297. Tchkersoff, Olga.

Women.

Accused by Edwin T. Woodhall, 1937.

Unreliable evidence.

298. Thick, William (Police Sergeant).

Accused after the Terror.

Accused by W.T. Haslewood, 8 October 1889.

No reason to suspect.

299. Thomas, William Evans.

Doctors and Surgeons.

Accused in an oral tradition, reported 1993.

Insufficient evidence.

300. Thompson, John Henry.

Mad Confessions.

Said he was Jack the Ripper, 1890.

Unreliable evidence.

301. Thompson, Francis.

Recollections.

Accused by Richard Patterson, 1999.

Insufficient evidence.

302. Thornton, Leonard.

Recollections.

Accused by Michael Thornton, 2006.

Unreliable evidence.

303. Tomkins, Henry.

At the Scene.

Anonymous accuser, 3 October 1888.

No evidence.

304. Tomplier, Jean.

Accused after the Terror.

Accused by the press, 1894.

No reason to suspect.

305. Torme, Nigel.

Doctor's and Surgeons.

Accused by the press, 1996.

Unreliable evidence.

306. Totterman, Emil (Carl Neilson/Nilson).

Later Killers.

Accused by the press, 1903.

Insufficient evidence.

307. Treeves, Frederick.

Doctors and Surgeons.

Contemporary rumour noted by Richard Whittington Egan, 1975.

No reason to suspect.

308. Tumblety, Francis.

Littlechild's Letter.

Arrested 7 November 1888.

Still suspected.

309. Tyson, John.

Mad Confessions.

Said he was Jack the Ripper, 7 December 1888.

Unreliable evidence.

310. Van Burst, W.

Arrested on Suspicion.

Arrested, 25 November 1888.

No evidence.

311. Van Gogh, Vincent.

Other Men.

Accused by Dale Larner, 2011.

Cleared by alibi.

312. Vasiliev, Nikolay.

Lunatics.

Accused by the press, 15 November 1888.

Unreliable evidence.

313. Waddell, William.

Contemporary Killers.

Accused by the press, September 1888.

Cleared by alibi.

314. Walter.

Other Men.

Accused by David Monaghan and Nigel Cawthorne, 2010.

Did not exist.

315. Ward, Joseph Turner.

Accused after the Terror.

Suspected by tradesmen, 12 November 1888.

Cleared by alibi.

316. Ward, William Humble, Earl of Dudley.

Aristocrats and Royals.

Accused by Karen Trenouth 2006.

Cleared by alibi.

317. Warren, Charles.

Aristocrats and Royals.

Accused by Stephen Knight, 1975.

Cleared by alibi.

318. Watkins, Edward (Police Constable).

At the Scene.

Anonymous accuser, 13 October 1888.

No evidence.

319. Wellcome, Henry.

Other Men.

Accused by Joseph Busa, 2013.

No reason to suspect.

320. Wentworth, G Bell Smith (Henry Bellsmith).

Accused after the Terror.

Accused by Lyttelton Stewart Forbes-Winslow, 19 September 1889.

Unreliable evidence.

321. Westcott, William Wynn.

Doctors and Surgeons

Accused by Christopher S Smith, 1992.

No reason to suspect.

322. White, Frederick.

Mad Confessions.

Said he was Jack the Ripper, 10 October 1888.

Unreliable Evidence.

323. Williams, Bransby.

Recollections.

Said he was suspected, 1959.

No reason to suspect.

324. Williams, John.

Mad Confessions.

Called himself Jack the Ripper, 13 October 1888.

Unreliable evidence.

325. Williams, John (Dr.)

Women.

Accused by Tony Williams and Humphrey Price, 2005.

Unreliable evidence.

326. Williams, Lizzie (Elizabeth).

Women.

Accused by John Morris, 2012

No reason to suspect.

327. Wills, William Arthur.

Accused during the Terror.

Contemporary suspicion, noted by Nicholas Connell and Ruth Stratton, 2013.

No evidence.

328. Wilson (From Bushmills).

Accused after the Terror.

Mentioned in the Chief Constable's Register 1888-92.

No reason to suspect.

329. Wilson, James.

Accused after the Terror.

Said he was Jack the Ripper, 26 November 1888.

Unreliable evidence.

330. Winberg.

Lunatics.

Accused by William Le Queux, 1923.

Unreliable evidence.

331. Wirtkofsky, Julius.

Accused after the Terror.

Accused by Julius I Lowenheim, 11 December 1888.

Insufficient evidence.

332. Woods, Joseph.

Mad Confessions.

Said he was the Whitechapel murderer, 11 September 1888.

Unreliable evidence.

333. Xavier, Manuel Cruz.

Accused after the Terror.

Accused by Edward Larkin, 1889.

No evidence.

Bibliography

Ackroyd, P., <u>Thames, Sacred River</u>, Random House, 2008.

Adam, H. L., <u>Trial of George Chapman</u>, William Hodge & Co, 1930.

Alexander, G., "Suspects in Short, Henri deToulouse-Lautrec," <u>Ripperologist</u>, 134,

October

2013, 51-53.

Anderson, R., "Our Absurd System of Punishing Crime," <u>The Nineteenth Century</u>, 49,

1901, pp. 268-84.

Anderson, R, <u>Sidelights on the Home-Rule Movement</u>, Dutton, 1906

Anderson, R, <u>The Lighter Side of My Official Life</u>, Hodder and Stoughton, 1910.

Andrews, M, <u>The Return of Jack the Ripper</u>, Dorchester Publishing Company, 1977.

Arthur, G., <u>Life of Lord Kitchener</u>, Vol. 1, Cosimo, 2007.

Anon., <u>My Secret Life</u>, Kindle, 2012.

Aylmer, A., "The Detective in Real Life," <u>Windsor Magazine</u>, 1, May 1895, p. 499-510.

Bailey, J. A., "The Art of Profiling an Historical Case, The Whitechapel Murders,"

<u>Ripperology</u>, ed. Begg, P., Constable and Robinson, 2007, pp. 218-234.

Balfour, J. S., <u>My Prison Life</u>, Chapman and Hall, 1907.

Barbee, L., "An Investigation into the Carrie Brown Murder," Casebook<u>: Jack the Ripper</u>,

ed. Ryder, S. P., http://www.casebook.org. Dissertations accessed 1 September 2012.

Barnett, H., <u>Cannon Barnet, His Life, Work and Friends</u>, London, John Murray, Volume

2, Barber, J., "The Camden Town Murder", <u>Casebook: Jack the Ripper</u>, ed. Ryder, S. P.,

http://www.casebook.org., Dissertations accessed 11 June 2013.

Barber, R., "Did Jack the Ripper commit suicide?" <u>Casebook: Jack the Ripper</u>, ed. Ryder, S. P., http://www.casebook.org. Dissertations accessed 28 March 2012.

Baron, W., "Sickert, Walter Richard (1860–1942)", <u>Oxford Dictionary of National Biography</u>, Oxford University Press, 2004, online edition January 2011, accessed 30 January 2014.

Beadle, B, "The Real Rose Mylett," <u>Casebook: Jack the Ripper</u>, ed. Ryder, S. P., http://www.casebook.org, accessed 30 January 2013.

Beadle, W., "The Real Jack the Ripper," <u>The Mammoth Book of Jack the Ripper</u>, ed. Jakubowski, M., and Braund, N., Constable and Robinson, 2008, 111-130.

Beadle, W., <u>Jack the Ripper Unmasked</u>, John Blake, 2009.

Beadle, W., "Suspects: The Best (or Worst) of the Rest", <u>Jack The Ripper, The Suspects</u>, Whitechapel Society, 2011, pp. 86-92.

Begg, P., ed., <u>Ripperology</u>, Constable and Robinson, 2007.

Begg, P., "Did Leather Apron Exist?" <u>Ripperologist</u>, 109, December 2009, 24-35.

Begg, P., <u>Jack the Ripper: The Facts</u>, Kindle, 2013.

Begg, P., and Bennett, J., <u>The Complete and Essential Jack the Ripper</u>, Kindle, 2013.

Begg, P., Fido, M., and Skinner, K., <u>The Complete Jack the Ripper A to Z</u>, John Blake, 2010.

Bell, D., "Jack the Ripper – The Final Solution," <u>Criminologist</u>, 9, 1974, 40-51.

Bell, N., and Clack, R., "City Beat: PC 881 Edward Watkins", <u>Ripperologist</u>, 105, August 2009, 25-37.

Belloc Lowndes, M., <u>The Merry Wives of Westminster</u>, MacMillan, 1946.

Bellsmith, H.W., <u>Henry Cadavere: A Study of Life and Death</u>, Read Books, 2009.

Bennett, J., "Letters to the City Police, Part 3, J'Accuse," <u>Ripperologist</u>, 114, May 2010, 18 27.

Bennett, J., "The Autobiography of James Carnac," Ripperologist, 124, February 2012, 59-67.

Benson, A. G., The Leaves of the Tree, Studies in Biography, G. P. Putnam and Sons, 1911.

Berry, J., My Experiences as an Executioner, Percy Lund, 1882.

Berry, S., "John Barlas, (Evelyn Douglas), Sweet Anarchist and Schizophrenic?" William Morris Society in the United States Newsletter, Winter 2007, 13-18.

Bew, P., "Parnell, Charles Stewart (1846–1891)." ed. Goldman, L., Oxford Dictionary of National Biography, Oxford University Press, 2004, online edition January 2011, accessed 30 November 2013.

Blake, V., Mrs Maybrick, National Archives, 2006.

Bloomfield, J., "Gallows Humour: The Alleged Ripper Confession of Dr. Cream", Ripper Notes, 23, June 2005, 50-58.

Blunt, W. S., Francis Thompson, Burns, and Oates, 1907.

Boardman, B., Poems of Francis Thompson, Continuum, 2002.

Boardman, B. M., 'Thompson, Francis Joseph (1859–1907)', Oxford Dictionary of National Biography, Oxford University Press, 2004, online edition January 2011, accessed 19 Jan 2014.

Bondeson, J., "Two Contemporary Swedish Pamphlets on Jack the Ripper", Ripperologist, 155, April 2017, 7-8.

Bondeson, J., and Droog, B. F. M, "The Dutch Jack the Ripper, New Light on Hendrik de Jong, the 'Continental Suspect,'", Ripperologist, 159, February 2018, 2-24.

Brinley Jones, R., 'Williams, Sir John, baronet (1840–1926)', Oxford Dictionary of National Biography, Oxford University Press, 2004, online edition January 2011, accessed 26 Jan 2014.

Brode, P., <u>Death in the Queen City: Clara Ford on Trial 1895</u>, Natural Heritage, 2005.

Bromley, G., "The Other Side of the Fence," <u>Casebook: Jack the Ripper</u>, ed. Ryder, S. P., http://www.casebook.org, Dissertations, accessed 21 January 2013.

Bromley, G., "Mrs Kuer's Lodger," <u>Ripperologist</u>, 81, July 2007, 2-42.

Brown, H., "The Cremers Memoirs, Another Crumpled Pillar," <u>Ripperologist</u>, 98, December 2008, 2-8.

Brown, N., and Brown, H., "The Men who would be Ripper, 1. Theophile Hanhart", <u>Ripperologist</u>, 127, August 2012, 50-52.

Brown, N. and Brown, H., "The Men who would be Ripper: An American Suspect", <u>Ripperologist</u>, 131, April 2013, 38-46.

Browne, D. G., <u>The Rise of Scotland Yard</u>, Putnam, 1956.

Browning, C., "The Mind of Jacob Isenschmid," <u>Ripperologist</u>, 118, January 2011, 2-18.

Buddle, N., "The Cable Street Dandy: Severin Klosowski aka George Chapman", <u>Ripperologist</u>, 102, May 2009, 4-20.

Bull, P., "O'Brien, William (1852–1928)", <u>Oxford Dictionary of National Biography</u>, Oxford University Press, 2004, online edition, Jan 2008, accessed 3 Jan 2014

Bullock, D., <u>The Man Who Would be Jack</u>, The Robson Press, 2012.

Busa, J., Wellcome<u> to Hell. Was Sir Henry Wellcome Jack the Ripper?</u> Kindle 2013.

Carey, J., "Jack the Ripper's Room and Newland Francis Forester Smith," <u>Ripperana</u>, 24, April 1998, 1-5.

Carnac, J., <u>The Autobiography of Jack the Ripper</u>, Bantam Press, 2012.

Cates, L., "The Case Against Jacob Isenschmid", <u>Ripperologist</u>, 125, 8-27.

Charles, G., <u>Gallows Parade</u>, Jarrold and Sons, 1951.

Chetcuti, J., "The Canterbury Encore," <u>Ripperologist</u>, 64, February 2006, 3-6.

Chetcuti, J., "Doctor Francis Tumblety," Jack the Ripper, The Suspects, Whitechapel Society, 2011, pp. 70-78.

Chetcuti, J., "A Nuns Letter", Ripperologist, 158, 2017, 2-5.

Clack, R., "Death in the Lodging House," Ripper Notes, 24, October 2005, 48-79.

Clutterbuck, L., An Accident of History? The Evolution of Counter Terrorism Methodology in the Metropolitan Police from 1829 to 1901, with Particular Reference to the Influence of Extreme Irish Nationalist Activity, University of Portsmouth, PhD thesis, 2002.

Cohen, P. K., John Evelyn Barlas, A Critical Biography: Poetry, Anarchism, and Mental Illness in Late-Victorian Britain, Rivendale, 2012.

Conlon, M., "A tale of two Frenchys," Casebook: Jack the Ripper, ed. Ryder, S. P., http://www.casebook.org, Dissertations, accessed 1 September 2012.

Conlon, M., "Ripper Redux," Casebook: Jack the Ripper, ed. Ryder, S. P., http://www.casebook.org, Dissertations, accessed 10 September 2012.

Conlon, M., "The Ripper in America," Ripperology, ed. Begg, P., Constable and Robinson, 2007, 1-13.

Conlon, M., "The Carrie Brown Murder Case: New Revelations", Ripperology, ed. Begg, P., Constable and Robinson, 2007, 20-32.

Connell, N., "Ostrog, An Adventurer at Eton," Casebook Jack the Ripper, ed. Ryder, S. P., http://www.casebook.org, Dissertations, accessed 21 June 2014.

Connell, N., and Evans, S. P., The Man Who Hunted Jack the Ripper, Amberley, 2009.

Connell, N., and Stratton, R., Hertfordshire Murders, Sutton, 2003.

Conway, J., Remembering the Sullivan County Catskills, History Press, 2008.

Cook, A., Jack the Ripper, Amberley, 2009.

Cooke, G. A., Topographical and Statistical Description of the County of Worcester,

Sherwood, Neely and Jones, 1820.

Connor, M, "Did the Ripper work for Pickfords," Ripperologist, 72, October 2006, 25-30.

Connor, M., "Charles Cross was Jack the Ripper," Ripperologist, 78, April 2007, 21-23.

Connor, M., "AKA Charles Cross," Ripperologist, 87, January 2008, 14-19.

Connor, M., "Lechmere- the Man in Buck's Row," Ripperologist, 94, August 2008, 40-41.

Connor, M. "Jack the Ripper: The Prime Suspect", Quadrant Online, 27 April 2010,

http://www.quadrant.org.au, accessed 14 June 2014.

Cooper, H. W., Health and Vigor, Milton House, n.d.

Corcoran, M., "Rediscovering Austin's Jack the Ripper," Casebook: Jack the Ripper, ed.

Ryder, S. P., http://www.casebook.org, Dissertations, accessed 15 March 2014.

Cornwell, P., Portrait of a Killer, Little, Brown, 2003.

Cornwell, P., The Secret Life of Walter Sickert, Kindle Edition, 2017.

Coustillias, P., "Gissing, George Robert (1857–1903)", Oxford Dictionary of National

Biography, Oxford University Press, 2004, online edition, accessed 5 Feb 2014.

Covell, M., "Robert D'Onston Stephenson: Dissecting the Incident off Flamborough

Head.",

Ripperologist, 89, March 2008, 12-22.

Covell, M., "D'Onston Stephenson From Robert to Roslyn", Ripperologist, 98. December

2008, 9-14.

Covell, M., Frederick Bailey Deeming- Jack the Ripper or Something Worse, Kindle,

2014.

Coville, G., and Luciano, P., Jack the Ripper: His Life and Crimes in Popular

Entertainment, McFarland & Co, 1999.

Covell, M., Jack the Ripper: The Black Magic Myth, Kindle, 2016.

Cullen, T., Autumn of Terror, Fontana Books, 1966.

Cumming, C., "The American Connection: Sandford Conover aka Charles A Dunham and Dr Francis Tumblety", Ripperology, ed. Begg, P., Constable and Robinson, 2007, 66-73.

Cunneen, C., "Dudley, second Earl of (1867–1932)", Australian Dictionary of Biography, National Centre of Biography, Australian National University, online edition, accessed 5 February 2014.

Crowley, A., The Confessions of Alastair Crowley, hermetic.com, http://www.hermetic/com, accessed 16 November 2013.

Dahahay, M. A., and Chisholm, A., Jekyll and Hyde Dramatized, Mc Farland, 2005.

Daniel, M, "How Jack the Ripper saved the Whitechapel Murderer," The Mammoth Book of Jack the Ripper, ed. Jakubowski, M., and Braund, N., Constable and Robinson, 2008, pp. 131-149.

Davis, D., "Jack the Ripper-The Hand-Writing Analysis," Criminologist, 9, 1974, 62-9.

Davitt, M., The Fall of Feudalism in Ireland, Harper & Brothers, 1904.

Deer, B., Sir Henry Wellcome, thy will be done, 19 September 1993, http://briandeer.com, accessed 14 October 2013.

Dew, W., "The Hunt for Jack the Ripper," 1938, Casebook: Jack the Ripper, ed. Ryder, S. P., http://www.casebook.org, accessed 27 October 2013.

Dimolianis, S., Jack the Ripper and Black Magic, Kindle, 2011.

Donkin, J. G., Trooper and Redskin in the Far Northwest, Sampson Low, Marston, Searle and Rivington, 1889.

Douglas, J., E., and Olshaker, M., The Cases that Haunt Us, Simon and Schuster 2001.

Douglas, J., A Criminal Investigative Analysis of Jack the Ripper, Kindle, 2011.

Dowson, E. C., The Letters of Ernest Dowson, Fairleigh Dickinson University Press, 1968.

Earp, S., "Identifying William Bury as Jack the Ripper," Ripperologist, 139, August 2014, 2-9.

Eddleston, J., Jack the Ripper, An Encyclopedia, ABC-Clio, 2001.

Edwards, I., Jack the Ripper's Black Magic Rituals, John Blake, 2003.

Edwards, I. J., "Tumblety- the Patsy? The Truth, the Whole Truth and Nothing but the Truth," Ripperologist, 88, February 2008, 2-30.

Edwards, R., Naming Jack the Ripper, Lyons, 2014.

Emmons, R., The Life and Opinions of Walter Richard Sickert, Lund Humphries, 1992.

Evans, S. P., "On the origins of the Royal Conspiracy Theory," Casebook: Jack the Ripper, ed. Ryder, S. P., http://www.casebook.org, Dissertations, accessed 17 March 2013.

Evans, S. P., "A Slouch-Hatted Yank, A Few Thoughts on the Newly Found Interview with Dr. Tumblety," Ripperologist, 82, August 2007, 14-16.

Evans, S. P., "My life and Jack the Ripper," The Mammoth Book of Jack the Ripper, ed. Jakubowski, M., and Braund, N., Constable and Robinson, 2008, pp. 150-172.

Evans, S. P., and Gainey, P., Jack the Ripper First American Serial Killer, Arrow Books, 1996.

Evans, S. P., and Rumbelow, D., Jack the Ripper, Scotland Yard Investigates, Kindle, 2013.

Evans, S. P., and Skinner, K., The Ultimate Jack the Ripper Sourcebook, Robinson 2001.

Evans, S.P., and Skinner, K., Letters from Hell, Sutton, 2001.

Fairclough, M., The Ripper and the Royals, Gerald Duckworth, 1992.

Farson, D., Jack the Ripper, Sphere Books, 1973.

Feldman, P. H., Jack the Ripper, the Final Chapter, Virgin Books, 2002.

Fido, M., The Crimes, Detection, and Death of Jack the Ripper, Barnes and Noble, 1993.

Fido, M., "Ernest Dowson as Mr Moring," Ripperana, 29, July 1999, 1-6.

Fido, M., "David Cohen and the Polish Jew theory," The Mammoth Book of Jack the Ripper, ed. Jakubowski, M., and Braund, N., Constable and Robinson, 2008, pp. 173-195.

Fido, M., "Rethinking Cohen and Kosminski," Ripperologist, 129, December 2012, 3-12.

Fisher, P., An Illustrated Guide to Jack the Ripper, P&D Riley, 1996.

Forbes Winslow, L., Recollections of Forty Years, John Ouseley, 1910.

Forester, K., Inside Broadmoor: Secrets of the Criminally Insane Revealed by the Chief Attendant, Kindle, 2016.

Forshaw, B., "Patricia Cornwell names the Ripper", The Mammoth Book of Jack the Ripper, ed. Jakubowski, M., and Braund, N., Constable and Robinson, 2008, pp. 433-444.

Fox, R. K. The history of the Whitechapel murders: A full and authentic narrative of the above murders, with sketches, New York, Richard K. Fox, 1888.

Frank, S. J., "The Conspiracy to Implicate the Confederate Leaders in Lincoln's Assassination," The Mississippi Valley Historical Review, 40, 4, March 1954, 629-656.

Freeman Sharp, E., "Francis Thompson, A Psychoanalytical Study," The British Journal of Medical Psychology, Vol. V. 4, 1927, 81-4.

Fuller, J. O., Sickert and the Ripper Crimes, Mandrake, 2001.

George, C. T., "Letter from the Sickbed: D'Onston writes to Police", Casebook: Jack the Ripper, ed. Ryder, S. P., http://www.casebook.org, Dissertations, accessed 24 September 2012.

George, C. T., "Black Magic and the Ripper," Ripperology, ed. Begg, P., Constable and Robinson, 2007, 59-65.

Gibson, J. G, Outlooks from the Zenith, Blumberg, 1898.

Goodman, J., Bloody Versicles, Kent State University Press, 1993.

Gray, D. D., London's Shadows, Continuum 2010.

Graysmith, R., The Bell Tower: The Case of Jack the Ripper Finally Solved in San Francisco, Regnery Publishing, 1999.

Green, D. A., "In the Shadow of Red Desire, John Barlas and the Scottish Lunatic Suspect," Ripper Notes, 26, 2006, 10-14.

Griffiths, A, Mysteries of Police and Crime Volume 1, Cassell and Company, 1898

Griffiths, I., D., ed. Phillips, R., "Memories of Morgan Davies, MD, F.R.C.S. (1854-1920), Transactions of the Honourable Society of Cymmrodorion, 1976, 208-215.

Hainsworth, J., "Druitt's Ghost," Ripperologist, 99, January 2009, 5-23.

Hainsworth, J., "The Drowned Doctor Red Herring," Ripperologist, 103, June 2009, 3-23.

Hainsworth, J., "Clerical Sphinx, Did Jack the Ripper Confess to a Priest," Ripperologist, 105, August 2009, 13-24.

Hainsworth, J., "Safely Caged, Should Kosminski still be a Prime Suspect," Ripperologist, 111, February 2010, 5-32.

Hainsworth, J., "A Pair of Jacks," New Independent Review, 1, September 2011, p. 1-51.

Halstead, D. G., Doctor in the Nineties, Casebook Jack the Ripper, ed. Ryder, S. P., http: www//casebook.org, Ripper Media, Ripper Preservation Society, accessed 24 January 2013.

Harries, K., Mapping Crime: Principle and Justice, National Institute of Justice, 1999.

Harris, M, Jack the Ripper, The Bloody Truth, Columbus Books, 1987.

Harris, M., "The Maybrick Will- The Crucial Key to a Shabby Hoax," Casebook: Jack the Ripper, ed. Ryder, S. P., http://www.casebook.org, Dissertations, accessed 15 July 2012.

Harris, M., "The Maybrick Hoax, Donald McCormick's Legacy," Casebook: Jack the Ripper, ed. Ryder, S. P., http://www.casebook.org, Dissertations, accessed 15 July 2012.

Harris, M., "The Maybrick Hoax, A Guide through the Labyrinth," ed. Ryder, S. P., Casebook: Jack the Ripper, http://www.casebook.org, Dissertations, accessed 28 September 2012.

Harris, R, The New Suspect, Indian Harry and the Jack the Ripper Case, CreateSpace, 2013.

Harrison, M., Clarence, Was he Jack the Ripper, WH Allen, 1972.

Harrison, P, Jack the Ripper: The Mystery Solved, Robert Hale, 1991.

Harrison, P, "Catch me when you can," The Mammoth Book of Jack the Ripper, ed. Jakubowski, M., and Braund, N., Constable and Robinson, 2008, pp. 196-212.

Harrison, S., The Diary of Jack the Ripper, Hyperion, 1993.

Harrison, S., "The Diary of Jack the Ripper," The Mammoth Book of Jack the Ripper, ed. Jakubowski, M., and Braund, N., Constable and Robinson, 2008, pp. 213-36.

Hawley, M. L., The Ripper's Haunts, Kindle Edition, 2016.

Hayes, V., Revelations of the True Ripper, Lulu, 2006.

Herfort, S., Jack L'Eventruer Demasque, Talandier, 2007.

Hermann, C. H., Recollections of Life and Doings in Chicago from the Haymarket Riot to the End of World War 1, Normadic House, 1945.

Hills, R., "From the Bars of the Cradle," Ripperologist, 62, December 2005, 19-25.

Hills, R., "Cat's Cradle", Ripperologist, 75, January 2007, 35-47.

Hills, R., and Stockton, A., "Cousin Jack," Ripperologist, 68, June 2006, 17-21.

Hinton, B., From Hell, Old Bakehouse, 1998.

Hochschild, A., King Leopold's Ghost: A story of Greed, Terror, and Heroism in Colonial Africa, Mariner, 1999.

Hodgson, P., Jack the Ripper: Through the Mists of Time, Minerva Press, 2002.

Hoffler, Benjamin, "Portrait of a Killer, case closed," Casebook: Jack the Ripper, ed. Ryder, S. P., http://www.casebook.org, Dissertations, accessed 29 March 2013.

Holgate, M., Jack the Ripper: The Celebrity Suspects, Kindle, 2013.

Holmgren, C., "An Affair of the Heart: The Case Against Joseph Fleming", Ripperologist, 97, November 2007, 37-46.

Holmgren, C., "Two Murders in Bucks Row," Ripperologist, 126, June 2012, 13-20

Horrall, S.W., "Donkin, John George," Dictionary of Canadian Biography, vol. 11, University of Toronto, 2003, online edition, accessed 4 February 2013.

House, R., Jack the Ripper and the case for Scotland Yard's Prime Suspect, Kindle, 2010.

Howells, M., and Skinner, K., The Ripper Legacy, Sphere Books, 1988.

Huddleston, T., Annihilation in Austin, Kindle, 2013.

Hudson, S. E., Leather Apron or the Horrors of Whitechapel, Town Printing House, 1888.

I'Anson, N., and I'Anson, T., "Jacob the Ripper," Ripperologist, 124, February 2012, 68-90.

Irving, J., Supplement to the Annals of Our Time, Macmillan, and Co, 1875.

Jakubowski, M, and Braund, N., ed., The Mammoth Book of Jack the Ripper, Constable and Robinson, 2008.

Jones, B. O., "Deeming, Frederick Bailey (1853–1892)", Australian Dictionary of Biography, National Centre of Biography, Australian National University, online edition, accessed 9 December 2013.

Jones, C., "James Maybrick, Ripper Suspect," Jack the Ripper, The Suspects, Whitechapel Society, 2011, pp. 55-62.

Jullian, P., trans. Dawnay, P., Edward and the Edwardians, Viking, 1967.

Julian, P., trans. Wyndham, V., Oscar Wilde, Viking, 1969.

Keith, A., "Treves, Sir Frederick, baronet (1853–1923)", rev. Gibbs. D. D., Oxford Dictionary of National Biography, Oxford University Press, 2004; online edition, May 2006, accessed 26 Jan 2014.

Kelly, A., Jack the Ripper, a bibliography and review of the literature, Association of Assistant Librarians, 1973.

Kendell, C., Jack the Ripper, The Theories and the Facts, Kindle, 2010.

Keppel, R. D., Weis, J. G, Brown, K, M, and Welch, K, "The Jack the Ripper Murders: A Modus Operandi and Signature Analysis of the 1888-91 Whitechapel Murders", Journal of Investigative Psychology and Offender Profiling, 2, 2005, 1-25.

King, M., "Hyam Hyams, the overlooked lunatic," Ripperana, 21, 1997, 18-20.

King, M., "Jacob Levy," Casebook: Jack the Ripper, ed. Ryder, S. P., http://www.casebook.org, Dissertations, accessed 19 June 2013.

King, M., "Hyam Hyams," Casebook: Jack the Ripper, ed. Ryder, S. P., http://www.casebook.org, Dissertations, accessed 10 June 2013.

Kirtlan, N., J., and Bainbridge, D., Jack the Ripper: In My Blood, Stone Boy Books, 2013

Knight, S., The Final Solution, Panther, 1980.

Kobek, J., ed., "Crowley's Ripper: The Collected Writings of Roslyn D'Onston, 2005", ed. S. P. Ryder, Casebook: Jack the Ripper, Dissertations, accessed 24 September 2012.

Krishnamurti, G., 'Barlas, John Evelyn (1860–1914)', Oxford Dictionary of National Biography, online edition, accessed 22 July 2013.

Larson, E., The Devil in the White City, Kindle, 2010.

Laurence, J., A History of Capital Punishment with Special Reference to Capital Punishment in Great Britain, Sampson Low, 1932.

Leach, K., "Jack Through the Looking-Glass (or Wallace in Wonderland", ed. Ryder, S. P., Casebook: Jack the Ripper, http://www.casebook.org, Dissertations, accessed 10 October 2013.

Leeson, B., Lost London: The Memoirs of an East-End Detective, Chapter 5, Casebook: Jack the Ripper, ed. Ryder, S. P., http://www.casebook.org, Ripper Media, Ripperological Preservation Society, accessed 01 March 2013.

Le Queux, W., The Minister of Evil, Casell & Company, 1918.

Lupin, A.J., Stranger on the Earth, a Psychological biography of Vincent Van Gogh, Da Capo, 1996.

MacDonald, D., The Prince, his Tutor and the Ripper, McFarland, 2007.

MacPherson, E, The Trial of Jack the Ripper, Mainstream, 2005.

MacPherson, E., "The Case of William Bury," The Mammoth Book of Jack the Ripper, ed. Jakubowski, M., and Braund, N., Constable and Robinson, 2008, pp. 267-278.

Newton, M., The Encyclopedia of Unsolved Crimes, Infobase, 2009.

Magellan, K., "Cut-throat: A detailed Examination of the Neck Wounds sustained by the Whitechapel Murder Victims", Ripperology, ed. Begg, P., Constable and Robinson, 2007, p. 208-217.

Majoribanks, E., For the Defence: The Life of Sir Edward Marshall Hall, MacMillan, 1930.

Marquis, P., "The Mysteries of Aaron Kosminski," Jack the Ripper, The Suspects, Whitechapel Society, 2011, pp. 48-54.

Marriott, T., Jack the Ripper: The 21st Century Investigation, Kindle, 2007.

Marriott, T, "Carl Feigenbaum-aka Jack the Ripper," The Mammoth Book of Jack the Ripper, ed. Jakubowski, M., and Braund, N., Constable and Robinson, 2008, pp. 390-407.

Marriott, T., "Doctor at Sea," Ripperologist, 127, August 2012, 34-45.

Marriott, T., The Evil Within, Kindle, 2013.

Marriott, T., Jack the Ripper, The Secret Police Files, Kindle, 2013.

Macnaghten, M., Days of My Years, Edward Arnold, 1914.

Marshall, P., and Phillips, C., "New Light on Aaron Kozminski," Ripperologist, 128, October 2012, 59-69.

Martin, J. B, Call it North Country, The Story of Upper Michigan, Wayne State University Press, 1986.

Matters, L., The Mystery of Jack the Ripper, Arrow, 1964.

Mayhew, M., "The Beatification of Joseph Barnctt," Jack the Ripper, The Suspects, Whitechapel Society, 2011, pp. 12-18.

McCormick, D., The Identity of Jack the Ripper, Jarrolds, 1959.

McKenna, D., "The Tales of the Twos," Ripper Notes, 23, June 2005, 69-71.

McKenna, J., The Irish-American Dynamite Campaign, McFarland, 2012.

McLaren, A., A Prescription for Murder, University of Chicago Press, 1993.

Mehew, E., "Stevenson, Robert Louis (1850–1894)." ed. Goldman, L., Oxford Dictionary of National Biography, Oxford University Press, online edition, accessed 29 November 2013.

Meynell, E., The Life of Francis Thompson, Charles Scribner's Sons, 1913.

Michael Gordon, R., Alias Jack the Ripper, McFarland, 2001.

Monaghan, D., and Cawthorne, N., Jack the Ripper's Secret Confession, Kindle, 2010.

Morley, C., "Jack the Ripper: A Suspect Guide", Casebook: Jack the Ripper, ed. Ryder, S. P., http://www.casebook.org, Ripper Media, Book Reviews, Non-Fiction, accessed 21 October 2012.

Morris, A., "More likely than Cutbush: Montague John Druitt", Jack the Ripper, The Suspects, Whitechapel Society, 2011, pp. 35-41.

Morrison, J., <u>Jimmy Kelly's Year of Ripper Murders</u>, J.B. Printers, 1990.

Morton, J. and Lobez, S., <u>Kings of Stings: The Greatest Swindles from Down Under</u>, Victory, 2011.

Muggett, J., <u>Bloodstains</u>, Kindle, 2011.

Murphy, D., "A Ripping Yarn," <u>The Bulletin</u>, 116, 30 December 1997, 22.

Murray, J. W., ed. Speer, V., <u>Memoirs of a Great Detective</u>, The Baker and Taylor Company, 1905.

Neil, A. F., <u>Forty Years of Man-Hunting</u>, Jarrolds, 1932.

Nelson, S., "David Cohen, Talking Points of a Storyline," <u>Ripperologist</u>, 130, February 2013, 3-17.

Nelson, S., "Coles, Kosminski and Levy, was there a victim/suspect/witness connection", <u>Casebook: Jack the Ripper</u>, ed. Ryder, S. P., http://www.casebook.org, Dissertations, accessed 2 January 2014.

Nelson, S., "The Butcher's Row Suspect- was he Jack the Ripper," <u>Ripperologist</u>, 84, October 2007, 2-19.

New York State Government, <u>Public Papers of Frank W Higgins</u>, J.B. Lyon Company, 1906.

Newton, M., <u>Encyclopedia of Unsolved Crimes</u>, Infobase, 2008.

Niven, J., <u>Gideon Welles, Lincoln's Secretary of the Navy</u>, Oxford University Press, 1973.

Nixon, G., "Le Grand of the Strand," <u>Ripperology</u>, ed. Begg, P., Constable and Robinson, 2007, p. 110-114.

Odell, R., "Jack the Redeemer," <u>Ripperology</u>, ed. Begg, P., Constable and Robinson, 2007, pp. 170-81.

Odell, R., "Jack in the Box', Casebook: Jack the Ripper, ed. Ryder, S. P., http: www.casebook.org, Dissertations, accessed 26 January 2014.

Odell, R., Ripperology, A Study of the World's First Serial Killer and a Literary Phenomenon, Kent State University Press, 2006.

O'Connor, T. P, Mrs, I Myself, Brentanos, 1911.

O'Connor, T. P., Memoirs of an Old Parliamentarian, Appleton, 1929.

O'Donnell, B., "This Man was Jack the Ripper," JacktheRipperForums, http://www.jtrforums.com, accessed 12 September 2012.

O'Donnell, K., Andy & Sue Parlour's Research of The Jack the Ripper Whitechapel Murders, Ten Bells, 1997.

O'Flaherty, D., "The Smart Talk of Alfred Blanchard," Casebook Jack the Ripper, ed. Ryder, S. P., http://www.casebook.org, Suspects, accessed 12 July 2012.

Ogan, J., "The Third Man," Casebook: Jack the Ripper, ed. Ryder, S. P., http://www.casebook.org, accessed 2 October 2012.

Ogan, J., "Martha Tabram: The Forgotten Victim", Ripperology, ed. Begg, P., Constable and Robinson, 2007, p. 36-43.

Oldridge, M. W., "Prince Albert Victor," Jack the Ripper, The Suspects, Whitechapel Society, 2011, pp. 79-85.

Osborne, D. F., "The Man Who Shielded Jack the Ripper," Casebook: Jack the Ripper, ed. Ryder, S. P, http://www.casebook.org, accessed 31 October 2013.

Overton-Fuller, J., Sickert and the Ripper Crimes, Mandrake, 2003.

Paley, B., "The Facts Speak for themselves," The Mammoth Book of Jack the Ripper, ed. Jakubowski, M., and Braund, N., Constable and Robinson, 2008, pp. 237-266.

Paley, B., Jack the Ripper, The Simple Truth, Kindle, 2011.

Palmer, R. J., "Tumblety Talks," Ripperologist, 79, May 2007, 2-6.

Parry, S., "Severin Klosowski, alias George Chapman," <u>Jack the Ripper, The Suspects,</u> Whitechapel Society, 2011, pp. 26-34.

Patterson, R., A., <u>The Story of Jack the Ripper, A Paradox</u>, 2012, http://www.richard-a-patterson.com, accessed 19 January 2014.

Pearse, F., <u>Secret Witness, The Whitechapel Murders</u>, Kindle, 2012.

Pegg, J., "Uncle Jack under the microscope," <u>Ripper Notes</u>, 24, October 2005, 12-22.

Pegg, J. D., "Robert James Lees, the Facts," <u>Ripperologist</u>, 96, October 2008, 63-74.

Pegg, J. D., "Robert D'Onston Stephenson: A Jack the Ripper suspect", <u>Casebook: Jack the Ripper</u>, ed. Ryder, S. P., http://www.casebook.org, accessed 24 September 2012.

Perry Curtis, Jr, L., "The Irish Dimension of the Ripper Saga," <u>Ripperology</u>, ed. Begg, P., Constable and Robinson, 2007, p.197-207.

Phillips, C, and Ruffels, J., "Dandenong Revisited." <u>Ripperologist</u>, 127, August 2012, 21-33.

Pittman, Q. L., "The Case for Re-canonizing Martha Tabram," <u>Casebook: Jack the Ripper</u>, ed. Ryder, S. P., http://www.casebook.org, accessed 17 January 2013.

Plarr, V., <u>Ernest Dowson, 1888-1897: reminiscences, unpublished letters, and marginalia</u>, L. J. Gomme, 1914.

Plimmer, J. F., <u>Whitechapel Murders-Solved, Jack the Ripper revisited</u>, House of Stratus, 2010.

Poberowski, S., "Pedachenko Revisited: The British Secret Service and the Assassination of Rasputin", <u>Ripperology</u>, ed. Begg, P., Constable and Robinson, 2007, p.74-87.

Poberwoski, S., "Nikolay Vasiliev: The Ripper from Russia", <u>Ripperology</u>, ed. Begg, P., Constable and Robinson, 2007, p. 88-97.

Pollard, H. B.C., <u>The Secret Societies of Ireland</u>, Philip Allan, 1922.

Porter, I., "Walter Sickert," Jack the Ripper, The Suspects, Whitechapel Society, 2011, pp. 63-69.

Powles, J., "The Most Extraordinary Ancestral Enquiry Ever? Or the Strange Case of Jack the Ripper and Spurgeon's College," Bulletin of the Association of British Theological and Philosophical Libraries, 21.1, March 2014, 8.

Priestley, M., One Autumn in Whitechapel, Flower and Dean Street Ltd, 2016.

Ramsland, K, "Servant Girl Annihilator," True Crime Library, http://www.trutv.com, accessed 15 August 2013.

Ransom, J. B., "Shall Insane Criminals be Imprisoned or Put to Death", Transactions of the Medical Society of the State of New York, 1895, pp. 233-34.

Rappoport, A., Leopold the Second, King of the Belgians, Hutchinson, 1910.

Reid, S. D., "Mr Ripper or Master Ripper," Ripperologist, 62, December 2005, 26.

Richardson, F., The Worst Man in the World, Evelyn Nash, 1908.

Richardson, F., The Other Man's Wife, Evelyn Nash, 1908.

Riordan, T. B., "The Nine Lives of Dr. Tumblety, Lies, Damned Lies and Biography," Ripperologist, 94, May 2008, 3-8.

Riordan, T. B., Prince of Quacks: The Notorious Life of Dr. Francis Tumblety, Charlatan, and Jack the Ripper Suspect, Kindle, 2009.

Roberts, M, "Doctor Who?" Ripperana, 30, October 1999, 1-12.

Robins, A. G., Walter Sickert Drawings-Theory and Practice, Word and Image, Scolar Press, 1996.

Robinson, B., They All Love Jack: Busting Jack the Ripper, Kindle, 2015.

Roland, P., The Crimes of Jack the Ripper, Arcturus, 2007.

Rooksby, R., "Swinburne, Algernon Charles (1837–1909)", Oxford Dictionary of National Biography, Oxford University Press, 2004; online edition, May 2009, accessed 6 Feb 2014.

Rowlands, G., "The Mad Doctor," The Mammoth Book of Jack the Ripper, ed. Jakubowski, M., and Braund, N., Constable and Robinson, 2008, pp. 279-301.

Rumbelow, D., The Complete Jack the Ripper, Penguin, 2004.

Russo, S., "The Suspect Series, Pizer's Problem," Ripperologist, 95, September 2008, 55-9.

Russo, S., "The Suspect Series, Sanders, Suspect or Scapegoat?" Ripperologist, 96, October 2008, 75-9.

Russo, S., "The Suspect Series, Tumblety Murderer or a Means to a Solution," Ripperology, 97, November 2008, 53-6.

Russo, S., "The Russian Quadrangle," Ripperology, 101, April 2009, 4-16.

Russo, S., The Jack the Ripper Suspects, Persons Cited by Investigators and Theorists, McFarland, 2011.

Russo, S., "The Strange Case of Doctor John Hewitt," Casebook Jack the Ripper, ed. Ryder, S. P., http://www.casebook.org, Dissertations, accessed 18 January 2014.

Salway, G. S..., "I knew Jack the Ripper," True Detective, October 2012, 40-44.

Savage, J., "The Early Life of Roslyn D'Onston Stephenson aka Sudden Death," Ripperologist, 102, May 2009, 22-36.

Scarsi, J. L, "Jack el Destripador: una pista en la Argentina", Historias de la Ciudad, 4, 31, 2005. Trans. Zinna, E., "On the Trail of Jack the Ripper, Szemeredy in Argentina," Ripperologist, 63, January 2006, 6-12.

Scott, C., Jack the Ripper, A Cast of Thousands, 2004, ed. Ryder, S. P., Casebook: Jack the Ripper, http://www.casebook.org, accessed 01 October 2012.

Scott, C., Will the Real Mary Kelly, Publish and Be Damned, 2005.

Senise, S., "Terror Australis: Whatever Happened to George Hutchinson", Ripperologist, 146, 2015, 3-14.

Settipani, C., "Ameer Ben Ali," Northwestern University School of Law, Bluhm Legal Clinic, Centre on Wrongful Convictions, http://www.law.northwestern.edu, accessed 1 September 2013.

Sharp, A., "A Ripper Victim that Wasn't: The Capture of Jane Beadmore's Killer", Casebook: Jack the Ripper, ed. Ryder, S. P., http://www.casebook.org, accessed 5 November 2013.

Shelden, J., "The Fifth Victim: The Hands of a Woman?" Ripperologist, 134, October 2013, 15-28.

Shelden, N., Mary Jane Kelly and the Victims of Jack the Ripper, Kindle, 2013.

Sherard, R. H., Oscar Wilde, The Story of an Unhappy Friendship, Greening and Co, 1905.

Sims, G. R., My Life, Sixty Years Recollection of Bohemian London, Eveleigh Nash Company, 1917.

Simons, J. G., "10:18 from Gravesend; William Henry Piggott," Ripperologist, 120, May 2011, 15-23.

Sitwell, O., ed., A Free house! Or the artist as craftsman: Being the writings of Walter Richard Sickert, Macmillan, 1947.

Sitwell, O., Noble Essences: A Book of Characters, Grosset & Dunlap, 1950.

Slemen, T., Jack the Ripper Secret Service, Kindle, 2011.

Smith, H., From Constable to Commissioner, Chatto & Windus, 1910.

Smith, K. J. M, "Stephen, Sir James Fitzjames, first baronet (1829–1894)", Oxford Dictionary of National Biography, Oxford University Press, 2004; online edition, Jan 2012, accessed 27 Jan 2014.

Smith, N., "Professor Findlay and the Ripper's DNA," Ripperologist, 66, 37-42.

Souden, D., "Time is on my Side," Ripper Notes, 26, September 2006, 39-46.

Spallek, A., "John Henry Lonsdale, A Possible Source of Macnaghten's Private Information," Ripperologist, 85, November 2007, 3-10.

Spallek, A., "The West of England MP Identified", Ripperologist, 88, February 2008. 31-4.

Spallek, A., "Young Montie, Montague John Druitt at Winchester," Ripperologist, 96, October 2008, 2-9.

Spallek, A. J., "Montague John Druitt: Still Our Best Suspect", Ripper Notes, 23, 2005, 4-21.

Spallek, A. J., "Sifting the Druitt Archives," Ripperologist, 106, September 2009, 57-62.

Spicer, G., "The Thames Torso Murders of 1887-89," Casebook: Jack the Ripper, ed. Ryder, S. P., http://www.casebook.org, accessed 20 June 2012.

Spiering, F., Prince Jack, Doubleday, 1978.

Stettler, J., The Diary of Jack the Ripper, Another Chapter, Area 9 Publishing, 2009.

Stevens, M., A., Broadmoor Revealed, Kindle, 2013.

Stewart, P., and McGovern, B. P., The Fenians: Irish Rebellion in the North Atlantic World, 1858-1876, University of Tennessee Press, 2013.

Stocks, D., "Freemasonry and the Ripper," Casebook: Jack the Ripper, ed. Ryder, S. P., http: www://casebook.org, Dissertations, accessed 29 January 2014.

Stocks, D., "The Anti-Freemason Movement," Casebook: Jack the Ripper, ed. Ryder, S. P., http://www.casebook.org, accessed 29 March 2013.

Storey, N., R., East End Murders, The History Press, 2008.

Stowell, T., "Jack the Ripper – A Solution", The Criminologist, Vol. 5. 18, November 1970, 40-51.

Sugden, P., The Complete History of Jack the Ripper, Constable and Robinson, 2002.

Tautriadelta, "A Modern Magician: An Autobiography", Casebook: Jack the Ripper, ed. Ryder, S. P., http://www.casebook.org, accessed 24 August 2013.

Thompson, B., My Experiences at Scotland Yard, Doubleday, Page and Company, 1923

Thompson, B, The Story of Scotland Yard, Literary Guild, 1936.

Thompson, C. J. S., Poison Mysteries in History, Romance and Crime, Forgotten Books, 2012.

Thompson, F., Collected Poems, Hodder and Stoughton, 1913.

Thompson, F., A Renegade Poet and Other Essays, Books for Libraries Inc., 1965.

Thomson, G. S., "Russell, Herbrand Arthur, eleventh duke of Bedford (1858–1940)", rev. Pimlott Baker, A., Oxford Dictionary of National Biography, Oxford University Press, 2004; online edition, May 2011, accessed 3 Feb 2014.

Thompson, J., Francis Thompson: The Preston Born Poet, Simpkin Marshall, 1913.

Thurston-Hopkins, R., Life and Death at the Old Bailey, Herbert Jenkins, 1935.

Toughill, T., The Ripper Code, The History Press, 2008.

Trow, M.J., The Many Faces of Jack the Ripper, Summersdale, 1997.

Trow, M. J., "The Way to Hell," The Mammoth Book of Jack the Ripper, ed. Jakubowski, M., and Braund, N., Constable and Robinson, 2008, pp. 302-316.

Trow, M., "Robert Mann- the non-starter," Ripperologist, 113, April 2010, 5-7.

Trow, M J., Jack the Ripper: Quest for a Killer, Kindle, 2011.

Trow, M.J., "Sir William Gull," Jack the Ripper, The Suspects, Whitechapel Society, 2011, pp. 42-47.

Tully, J., The Secret of Prisoner 1167, Constable, 1998.

Tully, J., "Was James Kelly Jack the Ripper?" The Mammoth Book of Jack the Ripper, ed. Jakubowski, M., and Braund, N., Constable and Robinson, 2008, pp. 317-41.

Tumblety, F., "A Few Passages in the Life of Francis Tumblety," 1866, Casebook: Jack the Ripper, ed. Ryder, S. P., http://www.casebook.org, accessed 7 August 2012.

Tumblety, F., Narrative of Dr. Tumblety, Russell's American Steam Printing House, 1872.

Tumblety, F., A Sketch of the Life of the Gifted, Eccentric, and World-Famed Physician, Press of Brooklyn Eagle, 1889.

Turnbull, P., "Jack the Ripper: Man or Myth", The Mammoth Book of Jack the Ripper, end Jakubowski, M., and Braund, N., Constable and Robinson, 2008, pp. 342-360.

Turgoose, S. A., "Report on Engravings on Watch, 10 August 1993", Casebook Jack the Ripper, ed. Ryder, S. P., http://www.casebook.org, Dissertations, Maybrick Diary, Maybrick Watch, Scientific Analysis accessed 14 January 2014.

Twohig, P. L., "The "Celebrated Indian Herb Doctor": Francis Tumblety in Saint John, 1860", Acadiensis, 39, 2, Summer/Autumn 2010, 70-88

Vanderlinden, W., "Considerable Doubt and the Death of Annie Chapman," Casebook: Jack the Ripper, ed. Ryder, S. P., http://www.casebook.org, accessed 21 January 2013.

Vanderlinden, W., "The New York Affair, Part II," Casebook: Jack the Ripper, ed. Ryder, S. P., http://www.casebook.org, accessed 28 April 2013.

Vanderlinen, W., "On the Trail of Tumblety? Part 1", Ripper Notes, 23, June 2005, 34-49.

Vanderlinden, W., "On the Trail of Tumblety, Part 2," Ripper Notes, 24, October 2005, 23-47.

Vanderlinden, W., "Carl Ferdinand Feigenbaum: An Old Suspect Resurfaces", <u>Casebook: Jack the Ripper</u>, ed. Ryder, S. P., http://www.casebook.org, Suspects, accessed 28 May 2013.

Vanderlinden, W., "Hyam Hyams: Portrait of a Suspect", <u>Casebook: Jack the Ripper</u>, ed. Ryder, S. P., http://www.casebook.org, accessed 10 June 2013.

Van Onselen, C., <u>The Fox and the Flies: The Criminal World of the Whitechapel Murderer</u>, Kindle, 2011.

Vetch, R. H., "Conder, Claude Reignier (1848–1910)". rev. Butlin, R. A., <u>Oxford Dictionary of National Biography</u>, Oxford University Press, 2004, online edition, accessed 11 Feb 2014.

Wagner, E. J., <u>The Science of Sherlock Holmes</u>, John Wiley and Sons, 2006.

Wagner, G., "Barnardo, Thomas John (1845–1905)", <u>Oxford Dictionary of National Biography</u>, Oxford University Press, 2004; online edition, Sept 2010, accessed 24 Jan 2014.

Wallace, R., <u>Jack the Ripper: Light Hearted Friend</u>, Gemini Press, 1996.

Walsh, J. E, ed., <u>The Letters of Francis Thompson</u>, Hawthorn, 1969.

Warman, C., "William Henry Bury", <u>Jack the Ripper, The Suspects</u>, Whitechapel Society, 2011, pp. 19-28.

Warren, N., "The Great Conspiracy, <u>The Mammoth Book of Jack the Ripper</u>, ed. Jakubowski, M., and Braund, N., Constable and Robinson, 2008, pp. 363-380.

Warren, N., P., "The Asylum at Ascot", <u>Ripperana</u>, July 1992, p. 8-10.

Westcott, T., "Exonerating Michael Kidney," <u>Casebook: Jack the Ripper</u>, ed. Ryder, S. P. http://www.casebook.org, accessed 20 October 2013.

Westcott, T., "Thomas Bulling and the Myth of the London Journalist," <u>Casebook: Jack the Ripper</u>, ed. Ryder, S. P., http://www.casebook.org, accessed 3 November 2012.

Westcott, T. "The Ripper in Oxford Street?" <u>Ripper Notes</u>, 23, June 2005, 71-5.

Westcott, T., "The McCarthys of Dorset Street," <u>Ripper Notes</u>, 26, September 2006, 32-38.

Westcott, T., <u>The Bank Holiday Murders, The True Story of the First Whitechapel Murders</u>, Kindle, 2014.

Westcott, T., <u>Ripper Confidential</u>, Kindle, 2017.

Whittington-Egan, R., <u>Jack the Ripper, The Definitive Casebook</u>, Amberley, 2013.

Wood, S. D., <u>Deconstructing Jack the Ripper</u>, Kindle, 2015.

Wild, R. K., "Surface Analysis of a Gold Watch, Comparison of Original and Surface and Scratch Marks", Bristol University, Interface Analysis Centre, 31 January 1994, <u>Casebook: Jack the Ripper</u>, ed. Ryder, S. P., http://www.casebook.org, accessed 28 September 2012.

Williams, M., <u>Later Leaves, Being the Further Reminiscences of Montagu Williams QC</u>, Macmillan and Co, 1891.

Williams, P., "Suicide of a Shoemaker, Robert Hiron," <u>Ripperologist</u>, 127, August 2012, 46-49.

Williams, P., "The Mountie and the Cabman's Shelter," <u>Ripperologist</u>, 131, April 2013, 19-21.

Williams, P., "The Violence of Spring Onion", <u>Ripperologist</u>, 142, February 2015, Kindle edition, loc. 1211-1722.

Williams, P., "Thomas Cutbush: His Crimes and Kin", <u>Ripperologist</u>, 154, February 2017, 2-13.

Williams, R., "The Theotokos Murders: Mother Mary and the Four Jacks", <u>Ripperologist</u>, 142, 7-20.

Williams, T., and Price, H., <u>Uncle Jack</u>, Orion, 2005.

Wilding, J., Jack the Ripper Revealed, Constable and Company, 1993

Wilson, C., "A Lifetime in Ripperology," The Mammoth Book of Jack the Ripper, ed. Jakubowski, M., and Braund, N., Constable and Robinson, 2008, pp. 408-432.

Wilson, C. and Odell, R., Jack the Ripper: Summing Up and Verdict, Corgi, 1988.

Wolf, A. P., Jack the Myth, Chivers Press, 1994.

Wood, A., "From Buenos Aires to Brick Lane: Were Alois Szemeredy and Alonzo Maduro the same man?" Casebook: Jack the Ripper, ed. Ryder, S. P., http://www.casebook.org, accessed 1 October 2012.

Wood, A., Swanson: The Life and Times of a Victorian Detective, Kindle Edition, 2020.

Wood, S. D., "Smoke and Mirrors, Francis Tumblety, The Times and the Parnell Commission," Ripperologist, 106, September 2009, 26-56.

Wood, S. D., "The Macnaghten Memorandum and Other Fictions," Ripperologist, 109, December 2009, 3-23.

Wood, A, and Skinner, K., "Red Lines and Purple Pencil," Ripperologist, 128, October 2012, 3-58.

Wood, S., D., "One Lone Maniac Too Many Part Two," Ripperologist, 133, August 2013, 29-50.

Woodhall, E. T., Jack the Ripper or When London Walked in Terror, P & O Riley, 1987.

Wojtczak, H., Jack the Ripper at Last? The Mysterious Murders of George Chapman, Kindle, 2014.

Wroe, G., "Jack the Ripper. Person or Persons Unknown," Casebook: Jack the Ripper, ed. Ryder, S. P., http://www.casebook.org, accessed 13 January 2012.

Zinna, E., "The Search for Jack el Destripador," ed. Begg, P., Ripperology, Constable and Robinson, 2007, p. 128-39.

Zinna, E., "The Ripper People: William Le Queux", ed. Begg, P., <u>Ripperology</u>, Constable and Robinson, 2007, p. 154-69.

Notes

The Murders

[1] The Times, 9 April 1888, p. 7.

[2] Report by Inspector Edmund Reid, S. P. Evans, and K. Skinner, The Ultimate Jack the Ripper Sourcebook,

Constable and Robinson, 2001, p. 4.

[3] The Times, 24 August 1888, p. 4.

[4] The East London Advertiser, 11 August 1888, Casebook: Jack the Ripper, ed. S. P. Ryder,

http://www.casebook.org, Press Reports, accessed 10 June 2014.

[5] Ibid. See also The Times, 10 August 1888, p. 12.

[6] The Daily Telegraph, 4 September 1888, p. 2. The Times, 4 September 1888, p. 8, refers to her as Jane

Oram.

[7] The Times, 3 September 1888, p. 12.

[8] Report by Inspector Joseph Chandler, 8 September 1888, Evans and Skinner, Sourcebook, p. 56.

[9] The Daily Telegraph, 14 September 1888, p. 3.

[10] The Lancet, 29 September 1888, p. 637.

[11] The Times, 13 September 1888, p. 5.

[12] The Times, 20 September 1888, p. 4.

[13] The Times, 2 October 1888, p. 6.

[14] The Times, 3 October 1888, p.10.

[15] The Times, 4 October 1888, p. 10.

[16] The Times, 6 October 1888, p.6.

[17]. Distance stated by Frederick William Foster, an Architect and surveyor who appeared at the inquest

with the relevant street plans, written statement,4 October 1888, Evans and Skinner, Sourcebook, p. 225.

[18.] Written statement of Police Constable Edward Watkins, 4 October 1888, Evans and Skinner, Sourcebook, p. 224.

[19.] Written Statement of Frederick Gordon Brown, 4 October 1888, Evans and Skinner, Sourcebook, p. 228-32.

[20.] The Times, 12 October 1888, p. 4.

[21.] Written Statement of George William Sequeira, 11 October 1888, Evans and Skinner, Sourcebook, p. 232.

[22.] Written Statement of William Sedgwick Saunders, 11 October 1888, Evans and Skinner, Sourcebook, p. 232.

[23.] Written Statement of Joseph Lawende, 11 October 1888, Evans and Skinner, Sourcebook, p. 237.

[24.] Inquest Papers, 12 November 1888, Evans and Skinner, Sourcebook, p. 409.

[25.] Ibid, p. 415-416.

[26] Report by Dr Bond, 10 November 1888, Evans and Skinner, Sourcebook, p. 400-2

[27.] Inquest Papers, 12 November 1888, Evans and Skinner, Sourcebook, p. 417.

[28.] Statement of Mary Ann Cox, 9 November 1888, Evans and Skinner, Sourcebook, p. 405.

[29.] Statement of Elizabeth Prater, Evans and Skinner, Sourcebook, p. 405. In her inquest testimony, she said she spoke to nobody, Inquest Papers, 12 November 1888, Evans and Skinner, Sourcebook, p. 413.

[30.] Statement of Sarah Lewis, 9 November 1888, Evans and Skinner, Sourcebook, p. 406.

[31.] Statement of Caroline Maxwell, 9 November 1888, Evans and Skinner, Sourcebook, p. 405-6.

[32.] The Times, 22 December 1888, p. 5.

[33.] The Times, 10 January 1889, p. 12.

[34.] The Times, 22 December 1888, p. 5.

[35.] The Times, 3 January 1889, p. 12.

[36.] Report by James Monro, 26 December 1888, Evans and Skinner, Sourcebook, p. 470, mentions that both doctors examined the body and notes McKellar's view. He had not seen Hebbert's report but the inquest testimony of Dr. Bond, The Times, 3 January 1889, p. 12, states that Hebbert attributed the death to strangulation.

[37.] The Times, 3 January 1889, p. 12.

[38.] The Times, 10 January 1889, p. 12.

[39.] The Times, 22 December 1888, p. 5.

[40] Report by Robert Anderson, 11 January 1889, Evans and Skinner, Sourcebook, pp. 482-84.

[41.] The Times, 18 July 1889, p. 11.

[42.] The Times, 19 July 1889, p. 11.

[43.] The Times, 18 July 1889, p.11. The Times 15 August 1889, p. 5.

[44.] The Times, 18 July 1889, p.11.

[45.] The Times, 15 August 1889, p. 5.

[46] Report by Dr Phillips, 22 July 1889, Evans and Skinner, Sourcebook, pp. 505-510.

[47.] Report by Dr Bond, 17 July 1888, Evans and Skinner, Sourcebook, pp. 503-04.

[48.] The Times, 12 September 1889, p. 4.

[49.] The Times, 25 September 1889, p. 5.

[50.] Ibid.

[51.] Ibid.

[52.] The Times, 16 February 1891, p. 12

[53] The Times, 21 February 1891, p. 12.

[54.] The Times, 24 February 1891, p. 3.

[55.] The Times, 28 February 1891, p. 13.

[56] Doctor Phillips noted that the Pinchin Street torso showed strong evidence of prostitution in a report dated 12 September 1889, Evans and Skinner, Sourcebook, p. 559.

[57] Report by Melville Macnaghten, 23 Feb 1894, Evans and Skinner, Sourcebook, pp. 645-49.

[58.] P. Sugden, The Complete History of Jack the Ripper, Constable and Robinson, 2002, p. 359.

[59] R. D. Keppel, J.G. Weis, K.M. Brown, M. Katherine, and K. Welch, "The Jack the Ripper Murders: A modus operandi and signature analysis of the 1888-91 Whitechapel murders", <u>Journal of Investigative Psychology and Offender Profiling</u>, 2, January 2005, 1-25.

[60] T. Westcott, <u>The Bank Holiday Murders. The True Story of the First Whitechapel Murders</u>, Kindle, 2014, loc. 1770-1798. See also R. House, <u>Jack the Ripper and the case for Scotland Yard's Prime Suspect</u>, Kindle, 2010, loc. 1286.

The Evidence

[1.] The Times, 20 September 1888, p.4

[2.] The Times, 12 October 1888, p. 4.

[3] Ibid.

[4] Written Statement of Frederick Gordon Brown, Evans and Skinner, <u>Sourcebook</u>, p.231-32.

[5] The Independent on Sunday, 19 October 2014, 18-19.

[6] Sugden, <u>Complete History</u>, p. 369-70.

[7.]The Times, 27 September 1888, p. 5.

[8] Chicago Tribune, 7 October 1888, states that the physician was American, <u>Casebook</u>, Press Reports, accessed 07 March 2014.

[9] British Medical Journal, 6 October 1888, posted by Chris Scott, <u>Casebook,</u> Forums, Ripper Discussions, Motive Method and Madness, Lessons of the Murders, British Medical Journal, 1, accessed 25 October 2013.

[10.]The Times, 5 October 1888, p. 4.

[11] Daily Telegraph, 14 September 1888, p. 3.

[12] Report by Dr Bond, 10 November 1888, Evans and Skinner, <u>Sourcebook</u>, p. 401-402.

[13.]The Times, 4 October 1888, p. 10.

[14.]The Times, 6 October 1888, p. 6.

[15.] The Times, 24 February 1891, p. 3.

[16] H. B. C. Pollard, The Secret Societies of Ireland, Phillip Alan, 1922.

[17] The Times, 5 February 1883, p. 7.

[18] N. Warren, "The Great Conspiracy", The Mammoth Book of Jack the Ripper, ed. M. Jakubowski, and N. Braund, Constable and Robinson, 2008, pp. 377-80.

[19] D. G. Browne, The Rise of Scotland Yard, Greenwood, 1973, p. 207, n1.

[20] An entry in the register of the Swedish Church for 30 September 1888 notes the death of Liz Stride and comments (Murdered by Jack the Ripper?). This suggests that the name was in circulation prior to the publication of the letter on 1 October, K O'Donnell, Andy & Sue Parlour's Researches of The Jack the Ripper Whitechapel Murders, Ten Bells, 1997, p. 40.

[21] Report by Chief Inspector Swanson, 6 November 1888, Evans and Skinner, Sourcebook, p.209.

[22] Report by Chief Inspector Moore, 18 October 1896, Evans and Skinner, Sourcebook, p. 723.

[23] The Times, 19 October 1888, p.5.

[24] The Star, 19 October 1888, p. 3.

[25]. Report by Chief Inspector Swanson, 6 November 1888, Evans and Skinner, Sourcebook, p. 209

[26.] The Times, 20 September 1888, p. 4.

[27.] Report by Chief Inspector Swanson, 19 October 1888, Evans and Skinner, Sourcebook, p. 75.

[28.] The Times, 6 October 1888, p. 6.

[29.] Ibid.

[30.] Ibid.

[31.] Report by Chief Inspector Swanson, 19 October 1888, Evans and Skinner, Sourcebook, pp. 136-140.

[32.] Report by Inspector Abberline, 1 November 1888, Evans and Skinner, Sourcebook, p. 141.

[33] Ibid.

[34.] Report by Chief Inspector Swanson, 19 October 1888, Evans and Skinner, Sourcebook, pp. 137-38.

[35.] The Times, 12 October 1888, p. 4.

[36.] Report by Chief Inspector Swanson, 19 October 1888, Evans and Skinner, Sourcebook, p. 138.

[37.] The Times, 12 October 1888, p. 4.

[38.] Report by Chief Inspector Swanson, 19 October 1888, Evans and Skinner, <u>Sourcebook</u>, p. 138.

[39.] Inquest Papers, 12 November 1888, Evans and Skinner, <u>Sourcebook</u>, p.412.

[40.] Witness Statement of Sarah Lewis, 9 November 1888, Evans and Skinner, <u>Sourcebook</u>, p. 406.

[41.] Inquest Papers, 12 November 1888, Evans and Skinner, <u>Sourcebook</u>, p. 414.

[42.] Statement of George Hutchinson, 12 November 1888, Evans and Skinner, <u>Sourcebook</u>, pp. 418-19.

[43.] Report by Inspector Abberline, 12 November 1888, Evans and Skinner, <u>Sourcebook</u>, p. 420.

[44.] The Times, 28 February 1891, p. 13.

[45] Report by Dr Bond, 10 November 1888, Evans and Skinner, <u>Sourcebook</u>, pp. 400-402.

[46] J. Douglas, <u>A Criminal Investigative Analysis of Jack the Ripper</u>, Kindle, 2011.

At the Scene

[1.] M. Connor, "Did the Ripper work for Pickfords," <u>Ripperologist</u>, 72, October 2006, 25-30.

2. The Times, 4 September 1888, p. 8.

[3.] Ibid.

[4.] The Times, 3 September 1888, p. 12.

[5.] The Times, 18 September 1888, p. 8.

[6] The address was given in The Star, 3 September 1888, p. 3.

[7.] For example, The Daily Telegraph, 4 September 1888, p. 2.

[8.] M. Connor, "Jack the Ripper: The Prime Suspect", <u>Quadrant Online</u>, 27 April 2010,

http://www.quadrant.org.au, accessed 14 June 2014.

[9.] Daily Telegraph, 4 September 1888, p. 2.

[10.] Marriage Certificate posted by Edward Stow, <u>JTRforums</u>, http://www.jtrforums.com, The

Witnesses+Evidence, Full Notes on Charles Cross/Lechmere, 30, 09 October 2013, accessed 15 October

2013.

[11.] Dockland and East London Advertiser, 4 September 2012, http://www.eastlondonadvertiser.co.uk, accessed 18 January 2013.

[12.] The Times, 4 September 1888, p.8.

[13.] S. P. Evans, and D. Rumbelow, Jack the Ripper Scotland Yard Investigates, Kindle, 2013, loc.3266.

[14.] Report from Chief Inspector Swanson, 19 October 1888, Evans and Skinner, Sourcebook, p. 32.

[15.] The Times, 13 September 1888, p. 5.

[16] Report by Chief Inspector Swanson, 19 October 1888, Evans and Skinner, Sourcebook., p. 76,

[17] S.D. Reed, "Mr Ripper or Master Ripper", Ripperologist, 62, December 2005, 26.

[18] Daily Telegraph, 13 September 1888, p. 3.

[19.] Post by Stan Reid, JTRforums, Suspects and Theories, William Hardiman, 21 October 2013, accessed 14 June 2014.

[20] William Hardiman', Mapping the Practice and Profession of Sculpture in Britain and Ireland 1851 1951, University of Glasgow History of Art and HATII, online database 2011,

[http://sculpture.gla.ac.uk/view/person.php?id=msib2_1211193473, accessed 21 Jan 2013.

[21] R. Hills, "Cat's Cradle", Ripperologist, 75, 43.

[22] Letter to Sir Charles Warren, 24 September 1888, Evans and Skinner, Letters from Hell, p. 218. Letter to the Supt, 16 November 1888, Evans and Skinner, Letters from Hell, pp. 256-7.

[23.] The Times, 11 September 1888, p. 6.

[24] Rumbelow, The Complete Jack the Ripper, Penguin, 2004, p. 262-64

[25] Evans and Rumbelow, Scotland Yard Investigates, loc. 6103.

[26] East London Observer, 13 October 1888, Casebook, Press Reports, accessed 13 November 2014.

[27] Details from death certificate posted by Debra A, 16 October 2009, Casebook, Casebook Forums, Ripper Discussions, Suspects, General Suspect Discussion, Timothy Donovan, The Real Crossingham's Timothy Donovan, 1, accessed 27 June 2013.

[28.] The Times, 11 September 1888, p. 6.

[29.] Report by Inspector Abberline, 19 September 1888, Evans and Skinner, Sourcebook, p. 71.

[30] The Times, 20 September 1888, p. 3.

[31] Report by Inspector Abberline, 19 September 1888, Evans and Skinner, Sourcebook, p. 71.

[32] S.D. Wood, "One Lone Maniac Too Many Part Two," Ripperologist, 133, August 2013, 41-43. For more on Hughes Hallett see S. D. Wood, Deconstructing Jack the Ripper, loc. 6306-6758.

[33] Pall Mall Gazette, 20 September 1887, p. 8.

[34] Atlanta Constitution 7 October 1888, reprinted Casebook, Press Reports, accessed 2 October 2016.

[35] Pall Mall Gazette, 1 October 1888, p. 3.

[36] Report by Chief Inspector Swanson, 19 October 1888, Evans and Skinner, Sourcebook, p. 137.

[37] W. Dew, "The Hunt for Jack the Ripper," Casebook, Ripper Media, Ripperological Preservation Society, The Hunt for Jack the Ripper, accessed 27 October 2013.

[38] Casebook, Forums, Ripper Discussions, Suspects, General Suspect Discussion, Morris Eagle the Ripper, 1-18, accessed 25 March 2014.

[39] R. Williams, "The Theotokos Murders: Mother Mary and the Four Jacks", Ripperologist, 152, 7-20.

[40] Derby Daily Telegraph, 9 April 1889, p. 4.

[41] Morning Post, 26 April 1889, p.2

[42] G. Bromley, "Mrs Kuer's Lodger", Ripperologist, 81, July 2007, 41.

[43] Post by Diana, Casebook, Message Boards, Witnesses, Schwartz Israel, Who was Schwartz? 26 March 2003, accessed 9 November 2015.

[44] Report by Inspector Abberline, 1 November 1888, Evans and Skinner, Sourcebook, 141.

[45] The Star, 1 October 1888, p. 2.

[46] Report by Chief Inspector Donald Swanson, 19 October 1888, Evans and Skinner, Sourcebook, 136.

[47] Sugden, Complete History, p. 196.

[48] P. Begg, M. Fido and K. Skinner, The Complete Jack the Ripper A-Z, John Blake, 2010, p. 262.

[49] The Times, 4 October 1888, p. 10.

[50] The Times, 2 October 1888, p. 6.

[51] The Times, 3 October 1888, p. 10.

[52] Whitechapel Infirmary Records, posted by Chris Scott, 22 December 2008 and 23 December 2008, Casebook, Casebook Forums, Ripper Discussions, Victims, Elizabeth Stride, Michael Kidney and the Whitechapel Infirmary, 1, 3, accessed 31 October 2013

[53] Report by Chief Inspector Donald Swanson, 19 October 1888, Evans and Skinner, Sourcebook, pp. 138-39.

[54] Evans and Rumbelow, Scotland Yard Investigates, loc. 3643.

[55] N. Bell and R. Clack, "City Beat: PC 881 Edward Watkins," Ripperologist, 105, August 2009, 28.

[56] Evans and Rumbelow, Scotland Yard Investigates, loc. 3196.

[57] Evans and Skinner, Letters from Hell, p. 236.

[58] The Morning Advertiser, 1 October 1888, Casebook, Press Reports, accessed 10 November 2014.

[59] "England Marriages, 1538–1973," index, FamilySearch (https://familysearch.org/pal:/MM9.1.1/N6XZ-2G1: accessed 23 Feb 2014), Thomas Morriss and Ann Hannah Tabram, 13 Aug 1854.

[60] Hills, "Cat's Cradle," 36-41.

[61] Evans and Rumbelow, Scotland Yard Investigates, loc. 3602-14.

[62] The Times, 12 October 1888, p. 4.

[63] Report by Inspector James McWilliam, 27 October 1888, Evans and Skinner, Sourcebook, p. 201.

[64] Evans and Rumbelow, Scotland Yard Investigates, loc. 3614-24

[65] The Times, 5 October 1888, p. 4.

[66] B. Paley, Jack the Ripper, The Simple Truth, Kindle, 2011.

[67] P. Harrison, Jack the Ripper: The Mystery Solved, Robert Hale, 1991.C. Scott, Will the Real Mary Kelly? Publish and Be Dammed, 2005, p. 111-20, explains why Harrison was incorrect.

[68] H. Smith, From Constable to Commissioner, Chatto and Windus, 1910, p. 153 and 161.

[69] Statement of Julia Venturney, 9 November 1888, Evans and Skinner, Sourcebook, pp. 406-407.

[70.] Lloyds Weekly Newspaper, 11 November 1888, p. 3.

[71.] Daily Telegraph, 10 November 1888, Casebook. Press Reports, accessed 25 March 2014.

[72] The Star, 10 November 1888, p. 2.

[73] Illustrated Police News, 17 November 1888, Casebook, Press Reports, accessed 10 November 2013.

[74.] Records posted by Chris Scott, JTRforums, Forums, The Victims, Mary Kelly, 1-4, 05 January 2011, accessed 9 February 2013. Also, Scott, Will the Real, 109-111.

[75.] Records provided by Rob Clack and posted by Chris Scott, Casebook, Ripper Discussions, Suspects, Fleming Joseph, The Records from Stone Asylum for Joseph Fleming transcription, 1, 25 January 2009, accessed 26 March 2014.

[76.] Admissions Register for Whitechapel Union Infirmary, cited by Chris Scott, Casebook, Ripper Discussions, Suspects, Fleming, Joseph, Where does Joseph Fleming fit into the equation, 524, 16 July 2013, accessed 26 March 2014.

[77.] Inquest Papers, 12 November 1888, Evans and Skinner, Sourcebook, p. 411.

[78.] The Standard, 12 November 1888, p. 3.

[79] Written Statements of Thomas Bowyer and John McCarthy, 9 November 1888, Evans and Skinner, Sourcebook, p. 403, compared with Inquest Papers, 12 November 1888, Evans and Skinner, Sourcebook, p. 412.

[80] D. Souden, "Time is on my side," Ripper Notes, 26, September 2006, 42-46.

[81] The Echo, 14 November 1888, p. 3.

[82] The Echo, 14 November 1888, p. 3.

[83] Bristol Mercury and Daily Post, 13 November 1888, p. 8.

[84] Daily Telegraph, 10 November 1888, p. 5.

[85] Ancestry.com. UK, Naval Medal and Award Rolls, 1793-1972 [database on-line]. Provo, UT, USA: Ancestry.com Operations, Inc., 2010. Class: ADM 171; Piece: 29.

[86] Dew, "The Hunt for Jack the Ripper"

87. Evans and Rumbelow, Scotland Yard Investigates, loc. 4414-25.

88. Inquest Testimony, Evans and Skinner, Sourcebook, p. 412.

89 Daily Telegraph, 13 November 1888, p. 5.

90. Birmingham Post, 29 March 1882, p. 6.

91. Illustrated Police News, 22 November 1890, p. 3.

92. See T. Westcott, "The McCarthys of Dorset Street," Ripper Notes, 26, September 2006, 32-38.

93 Report from Inspector Thomas Divall, 28 May 1901, R. Clack, "Death in the Lodging House," Ripper Notes, 24, October 2005, 49-50.

94. Report from Sergeant John Gill, 10 June 1901, Clack, "Death in the Lodging House," p. 58.

95 Letter from Cardiff Police to Scotland Yard, 25 August 1901, Clack, "Death in the Lodging House," p.72-4.

96 Letter from Cardiff Police to Scotland Yard, 25 August 1901, Clack, "Death in the Lodging House," p.72-4.

97 D. Osborne, "Line of Enquiry", Ripperana, 42, January 2002.

98. Report by Inspector Abberline, 12 November 1888, Evans and Skinner, Sourcebook, p. 420.

99. M. Fairclough, The Ripper and the Royals, Gerald Duckworth, 1992, p. 246.

100 S. Senise, "Terror Australis: Whatever Happened to George Hutchinson", Ripperologist, 146, 2015, 3-14.

101. Report by Inspector Moore, 2 March 1891, Evans and Skinner, Sourcebook, p. 626.

102. Statement of James Thomas Sadler, 14 February 1891, Evans and Skinner, Sourcebook, pp. 612-16.

103 Crew Agreement posted by JerryD, Casebook, Casebook Forums, Ripper Discussions, Victims, Non-Canonical Victims, Frances Coles, Crew Agreement/SS Winestead, 11 February 2014, 1, accessed 15 July 2014.

104. Report by Sergeant Kuhrt, 3 March 1891, Evans and Skinner, Sourcebook, p. 627.

105. Daily Telegraph, 18 February 1891, Evans and Skinner, Sourcebook, 616-7.

106. The Times, 21 February 1891, p. 12.

107. The Times, 24 February 1891, p. 3. Also, The Times, 28 February 1891, p. 13.

108. Report by Sergeant Kuhrt, Evans and Skinner, Sourcebook, p. 626.

109. The Times, 24 February 1891, p. 3.

110. Report by Sergeant Boswell, 16 May 1892, Evans and Skinner, Sourcebook, pp. 635-6.

Arrested on Suspicion

1 Report by Chief Inspector Swanson, September 1888, Evans and Skinner, Sourcebook, p. 17-18.

2 Report by Inspector Edmund Reid, 24 September 1888, Evans and Skinner, Sourcebook, pp. 14-16.

3 Report by Inspector Edmund Reid, 16 August 1888, Evans and Skinner, Sourcebook, p. 12.

4 Report by Inspector Edmund Reid, 24 September 1888, Evans and Skinner, Sourcebook, pp. 14-16.

5. The Times, 24 August 1888, p. 4.

6. The Star, 4 September 1888, p. 3.

7. The Star, 6 September 1888, p. 3.

8. Report by Acting Superintendent W. Davis, 7 September 1888, Evans and Skinner, Sourcebook, p. 23.

9. Report by Inspector Joseph Helson, 7 September 1888, Evans and Skinner, Sourcebook, p. 27.

10. The Times, 8 July 1887, p. 4.

11. Sugden, Complete History, p. 146.

12. Report by Inspector Frederick Abberline, 19 September 1888, Evans and Skinner, Sourcebook, p. 70.

13. The Times, 13 September 1888, p. 5.

14. Daily News, 5 October 1888, p. 7. Lloyds Weekly Newspaper, 14 October 1888, p. 1.

15. B. Leeson, Lost London: The Memoirs of an East-End Detective, Chapter 5, Casebook, Ripper Media,

Ripperological Preservation Society, Lost London, accessed 01 March 2013.

16. Sheffield and Rotherham Independent, 17 October 1900, p.4.

17 C. Scott, Jack the Ripper: A Cast of Thousands, 2004, Casebook, Ripper Media, Book Reviews, Non-

Fiction, A Cast of Thousands, Julius Lippman, accessed 15 August 2014.

18. Report by Inspector Frederick Abberline, Evans and Skinner, <u>Sourcebook</u>, p. 65. Also, Lloyds Weekly Newspaper, 9 September 1888, p. 7.

19. The Times, 11 September 1888, p. 6.

20. The Times, 14 September 1888, p. 4.

21. Whitechapel Infirmary Records, posted by Debra Arif, <u>Casebook</u>, Message Boards, Suspects, Pigott, William, What is Known about Pigott, 21 February 2005, accessed 13 August 2013.

22. Report from Acting Superintendent John West, 13 September 1888, Evans and Skinner, <u>Sourcebook</u>, p. 59.

23. Report from Detective Inspector John Styles, 11 September 1888, Evans and Skinner, Sourcebook, 57-9.

24. Police report, in the handwriting of Sergeant Thick, 19 September 1888, Evans and Skinner, <u>Sourcebook</u>, pp. 66-67.

25. Report by Inspector Frederick Abberline, 18 September 1888, Evans and Skinner, <u>Sourcebook</u>, p. 65.

26 Colney Hatch Asylum records, C. Browning, "The Mind of Jacob Isenschmid", <u>Ripperologist</u>, 118, January 2011, 5-7.

27. Report by Sergeant Thick, 17 September 1888, Evans and Skinner, <u>Sourcebook</u>, p. 64.

28. Report by Inspector Helson, 19 September 1888, Evans and Skinner, <u>Sourcebook</u>, pp. 67-68.

29. Report by Inspector Abberline, 19 September 1888, Evans and Skinner, <u>Sourcebook</u>, p.72.

30. <u>Hansard</u>, HC Debate 12 November 1888, v.330, c.888.

31. Report by Inspector Abberline, 14 September 1888, Evans and Skinner, <u>Sourcebook</u>, p.61.

32. The Times 19 September 1888, p. 5.

33. The Standard, 19 September 1888, p. 2.

34. The Times, 19 September 1888, p. 3.

35. The Echo, 19 September 1888, <u>Casebook</u>, Press Reports, accessed 14 November 2013.

36 The Times, 3 October 1888, p. 3.

[37] The arrest was noted by Martin Fido, posted by Howard Brown, JTRforums, Suspects Theories, Martin Fido's Asylum Notes, 4, 22 July 2011, accessed 13 March 2014.

[38] The Morning Post, 18 September 1888, p. 3.

[39] Manchester Times, 6 October 1888, p. 2.

[40] Letter from E. W. Bonham, British Consulate Boulogne to Commissioner of Police, 11 October 1888, Evans and Skinner, Sourcebook, pp. 342-45

[41] The Times, 10 October 1888, p.3.

[42] Belfast Newsletter, 13 October 1888, p. 8.

[43] Aberdeen Weekly Journal, 20 October 1888, p. 5.

[44] Liverpool Mercury, 23 October 1888, p. 3.

[45] The Star, 12 October 1888, p. 3.

[46] Morning Post, 12 November 1888, p. 8.

[47] Morning Advertiser, 12 November 1888, Casebook, Press Reports, accessed 28 March 2014.

[48] New York World, 18 November 1888, Casebook, Press Reports, accessed 14 November 2013.

[49] Morning Post, 14 November 1888, p. 8.

[50] Report from Superintendent H Jones, 18 January 1889, Evans and Skinner, Sourcebook, p. 666.

[51] Report from Kingston Police Station, 18 December 1888, Evans and Skinner, Sourcebook, p. 656.

[52] The Standard, 19 November 1888, p. 3.

[53] Letter from Nikaner Benelius to the Mayor of London, 4 October 1888, Evans and Skinner, Letters from Hell, p. 207.

[54] Report from Superintendent Sheppard, 18 January 1889, Evans and Skinner, Sourcebook, p. 664-65.

[55] The Star, 19 November 1888, p.3.

[56] Report from D Fairey, Inspector, 18 January 1889, Evans and Skinner, Sourcebook, pp. 663-64.

[57] British Medical Journal, 30 July 1921, 173-4, has an obituary for Douglas Vernon.

58. Report from Inspector J. Bird, 18 January 1889, Evans and Skinner, Sourcebook, p. 664.

59. Report from H Jones, Superintendent, 18 January 1889, Evans and Skinner, Sourcebook, p. 666-67.

60. Ibid. p. 665.

61. Leeds Mercury, 3 December 1888, p. 5.

62. York Herald, 4 December 1888, p. 5.

63. Frederick Times, 24 November 1888, Casebook, Press Reports, accessed 23 August 2012.

64. Sheffield and Rotherham Independent, 8 April 1889, p. 5.

65. Los Angeles Herald, 3 December 1910, p. 8.

66. Los Angeles Times, 30 October 1910, N. Brown, and H. Brown, "The Men who would be Ripper,"

Ripperologist, 131, April 2013, 41-3.

67. Daily Capital Journal, 3 December 1910, p. 2.

68. Los Angeles Herald, 3 December 1910, p. 8.

69. Los Angeles Herald, 7 December 1910, p. 11.

70. Los Angeles Times, 8 July 1911, Brown and Brown, "Men who would be", 44-5.

71. Ogden Evening Standard, 29 July 1911, p. 3.

72. Brown and Brown, "Men who would be," 45.

73. Lloyds Weekly Newspaper, 2 December 1888, p.7

74. The Standard, 1 December 1888, p.5.

75. Lloyds Weekly Newsletter, 9 December 1888, p. 7.

76. Manchester Times, 8 December 1888, p. 5.

77. Begg, Fido and Skinner, A-Z, p. 220.

78. Lloyds Weekly Newspaper, 23 December 1888, p. 7.

79. Old Bailey Proceedings Online, (t18871024-1118), accessed 10 August 2013.

[80] Minutes of the Court of General Sessions of the Peace, Manhattan, The People vs Joseph Liss, 10 Oct. 1889, C. Van Onselen, <u>The Fox and the Flies: The Criminal World of the Whitechapel Murderer</u>, Kindle, 2011, loc. 1680, n.18.

[81] Ibid., loc. 1361-71 and 1417.

[82]. Ibid, loc. 1231-43 and 1393-1405.

[83] Report from Inspector G. Rutt, 18 January 1889, Evans and Skinner, <u>Sourcebook</u>, p. 662.

[84] Report from Superintendent H Jones, 18 January 1889, Evans and Skinner, <u>Sourcebook</u>, p. 665.

[85] He pleaded guilty to bigamy on 27 February 1888 and received four months hard labour, Old Bailey Proceedings Online (t18880227), accessed 26 August 2013.

[86] Evans and Skinner, <u>Sourcebook</u>, pp. 660-61

[87] Report by Superintendent Arnold, 17 July 1889, Evans and Skinner, <u>Sourcebook</u>, p. 503.

[88] Trewmans Exeter Flying Post, 18 July 1889, p. 4.

[89] Pall Mall Gazette, 18 July 1889, p. 4.

[90] North Eastern Daily Gazette, 18 July 1889, p. 2.

[91] LMA, Saint Barnabas, Finsbury, Register of marriages, P76/BAN, Item 009. LMA, Saint Mark, Myddelton Square, Register of marriages, P76/MRK, Item 023. LMA, Saint Mary, Spital Square, Register of marriages, P93/MRY2, Item 008.

[92] New York Herald, 25 June 1889, p.4

[93] Reading Times, 4 May 1891, p. 1.

[94] New York World, 29 April 1891, p.1.

[95] M. Conlon, "The Ripper in America", <u>Ripperology</u>, ed. Begg, Paul, Constable and Robinson, 2007, 1-13.

[96] C. Settipani, "Ameer Ben Ali," Northwestern University School of Law, Bluhm Legal Clinic, Centre on Wrongful Convictions, http://www.law.northwestern.edu, accessed 1 September 2013.

Accused During the Terror

[1] The Times, 18 September 1888, p. 12.

[2] The Times, 24 September 1888, p. 3.

[3] Lloyds Weekly Newspaper, 9 September 1888, p. 12.

[4] Morning Post, 21 September 1888, p. 2.

[5] Morning Advertiser, 4 October 1888, p. 5.

[6] N. Connell and R. Stratton, Hertfordshire Murders, Sutton, 2003, pp. 158-9.

[7] Daily Telegraph, 5 October 1888, Casebook, p. 3.

[8] Evans and Rumbelow, Scotland Yard Investigates, loc. 3346-51.

[9] Aberdeen Journal, 12 August 1874, p. 6.

[10] London Gazette, 12 September 1876, p. 4964.

[11] Register of Lunatics, 1885 Sep – 1891 Feb, LMA, STPBG/154/002

[12] Leavesden Asylum admission orders, H26/LEA/B/01/033, case no 5350.

[13] Newcastle Chronicle, 2 October 1888, Evans and Skinner, Sourcebook, pp. 333-334.

[14] Evans and Rumbelow, Scotland Yard Investigates, loc. 6968.

[15] Letter from William Wookey to the Home Office, Evans and Skinner, Sourcebook, pp. 336-37. Wookey's name is incorrectly transcribed.

[16] S. W. Horrall, "Donkin, John George," Dictionary of Canadian Biography, vol. 11, University of Toronto/Université Laval, 2003, http://www.biographi.ca, accessed 4 February 2013. Obituary, Monthly Chronicle of North-Country Lore and Legend, February 1890, p. 93.

[17] London Gazette, 15 February 1876, p. 748.

[18] Obituary, Monthly Chronicle of North-Country Lore and Legend, February 1890, p. 93.

[19] For a fuller account of Donkin's life see P. Williams, "The Mountie and the Cabman's Shelter", Ripperologist, 131, April 2013, 19-21.

[20] Report by Inspector Abberline, 10 October 1888, Evans and Skinner, Sourcebook, pp. 338-339.

[21] Ibid, loc. 3301.

[22] Ibid. loc. 3336.

[23] Old Bailey Proceedings Online, (t18850914-848) and (t18851019-982), accessed 10 September 2013.

[24] Birmingham Post, 6 January 1888, p. 5.

[25] Dundee Courier and Argus, 14 July 1893, p. 7.

[26] Birmingham Post, 6 October 1888, p. 5.

[27] Huddersfield Daily Chronicle, 8 October 1888, p. 3.

[28] Glasgow Herald, 8 October 1888, p.7

[29] The Times, 6 October 1888, p. 6.

[30] Atchison Daily Globe, 19 November 1888, Casebook, Press Reports, accessed 21 March 2013.

[31] T. Huddleston, Annihilation in Austin, Kindle, 2013, loc. 491-541 gives an account of the trial.

[32] K. Ramsland, Servant Girl Annihilator, True Crime Library, http://www.crimelibrary.com, accessed 15 August 2013 gives a summary of the Austin axe murders.

[33] Austin Statesman, 5 September 1888, Casebook, Press Reports, accessed 15 August 2013.

[34] . Liverpool Mercury, 8 October 1888, p. 5.

[35] Evans and Rumbelow, Scotland Yard Investigates, loc. 3351.

[36] E. Mehew, "Stevenson, Robert Louis (1850–1894)." Oxford Dictionary of National Biography, Online ed. Ed. Lawrence Goldman, Oxford: OUP, http://www.oxforddnb.com/view/article/26438, accessed 29 November 2013.

[37] Begg, Fido and Skinner, A-Z, p. 335.

[38] . Evans and Rumbelow, Scotland Yard Investigates, loc. 3265-3275.

[39] D. McCormick, The Identity of Jack the Ripper, Jarrolds, 1959, p. 84.

[40] Letter from L.R. Burnett to Scotland Yard, 5 October 1888, Evans and Skinner, Sourcebook, p. 657-58.

[41] Letter from L. R. Burnett to Scotland Yard, 19 October 1888, Evans and Skinner, Sourcebook, p. 659.

[42] British Army Service Records 1760-1915, Attestation, 2nd Quarter 1886,

[43] Chelsea Pensioners, Discharge Documents, 17 May 1884.

[44] Chelsea Pensioners, British Army Service Records, WO97, 224, 100.

[45] National Archives, ADM 188/54/69961 and ADM 139/728/32786

[46] National Police Gazette, 3 January 1876, p. 8.

[47] Letter from W R Collett to City Police, 6 October 1888, posted by Howard Brown, JTRforums, A Suspicious Sort, Willie Boult, accessed 7 October 2013.

[48] The Times, 2 October 1888, p. 6.

[49] The Times, 1 October 1888, p. 6. Also, Evans and Skinner, Letters from Hell, p. 99-100.

[50] . Evans and Rumbelow, Scotland Yard Investigates, loc. 3395.

[51] Daily News, 24 December 1858, p. 3.

[52] The Morning Post, 21 July 1860, p. 7.

[53] Daily News, 8 November 1884, p. 7.

[54] The Times, 14 March 1894, p. 12 notes an adjudication order. Journal of the Canadian Bankers Association, 4, 1, October 1896, p. 108-109, reports on an appeal by the National Provincial Bank of England against the partial rejection of their proof by the official receiver, trustees in Sass's bankruptcy.

[55] Winnipeg Free Press, 12 April 1941, posted by Howard Brown, JTRforums, Suspects and Theories, Doctor Strauss: Is he Leonard Matter's Suspect, 27 February 2013, 1, accessed 09 June 2014.

[56] The Times, 9 October 1888, p. 3.

[57] Evans and Rumbelow, Scotland Yard Investigates, loc. 3565.

[58] Letter from J. Beckett to the City of London Police, posted by Chris Scott, 23 November 2011, JTRforums, Suspects and Theories, J D Lampard, 29, accessed 23 August 2013.

[59] There is a reference to a James David Lampard in Ramsgate in 1879, Thanet Advertiser, 16 August 1879, p.3.

[60.] Information posted by John Bennett, 22 June 2011, JTRforums, Suspects and Theories, J D Lampard, 17, accessed 23 August 2013.

[61.] Letter from Sir Augustus Paget, 10 October 1888, Evans and Skinner, Sourcebook, pp.353-356.

[62.] Letter from Sir Augustus Paget, 4 November 1888, Evans and Skinner, Sourcebook, p. 359.

[63.] Letter from Sir Augustus Paget, 29 December 1888, Evans and Skinner, Sourcebook, pp. 362-63.

[64.] Letter from James Monro, 2 January 1889, Ibid. p. 362.

[65] Connell and Stratton, Hertfordshire Murders, p. 159-60.

[66] Sheffield and Rotherham Independent, 28 October 1889, p. 5.

[67] Evans and Rumbelow, Scotland Yard Investigates, loc. 3514-34.

[68] Letter from Charles Warren, 17 October 1888, Evans and Skinner, Sourcebook, p. 368.

[69]. Evans and Rumbelow, Scotland Yard Investigates, loc. 3475-67.

[70] T. P. O'Connor, I Myself, Brentanos, 1911, p. 213-14.

[71] Truth, 18 August 1906, P. Bew, "Parnell, Charles Stewart (1846–1891)", ed. L. Goldman, Oxford Dictionary of National Biography, online edition, accessed 30 November 2013.

[72] R. Anderson, Sidelights on the Home-Rule Movement, Dutton, 1906, p. 145.

[73] L. Perry Curtis, Jnr., "The Irish Dimension of the Ripper Saga," Ripperology, ed. P. Begg, p. 203.

[74] Begg, Fido and Skinner, A-Z, p. 279.

[75] Cover Page to destroyed home office letter, received 15 November 1888, Evans and Skinner, Sourcebook, p. 426.

[76] Old Bailey Proceedings Online, (t18790915-818), accessed 19 August 2013. This gives his name as Lewis Solomons. The prison records give as Louis Solomon, PCOM2, Woking Prison Register, p 171.

[77] Evans and Rumbelow, Scotland Yard Investigates, loc.4388.

[78] The Standard, 25 June 1866, p. 6. Also, The Times, 25 June 1866, p. 11

[79] The Standard, 4 July 1866, p. 7. England and Wales Criminal Registers, HO 27, Piece 144, p. 210.

[80] Morning Post, 7 June 1870, p. 7.

[81] The modern address is 128 the Highway. The pub closed in 2011.

[82] Old Bailey Proceedings Online, (t18740713-478), accessed 4 December 2013.

[83] The Times, 1 July 1875, p. 13.

[84] The Times, 4 Jan 1873, p. 4, gives an account of one of the thieves' suppers organised by Wright.

[85] Pall Mall Gazette, 3 October 1877, p. 4.

[86] The Standard, 31 December 1878, p. 2.

[87] Daily News, 27 March 1879, p. 2.

[88.] Sheffield and Rotherham Independent, 10 April 1879, p. 3.

[89.] Morning Post, 8 December 1879, p. 8.

[90] Morning Post, 10 August 1881, p. 7.

[91.] Morning Post, 11 November 1881, p. 7.

[92] The Standard, 11 November 1881, p. 2.

[93] The Morning Post, 12 November 1881, p. 6. Lunacy Patients Admission Registers, MH 94, 26, 75997,

[94] London Evening News, 18 May 1882, p. 2

[95] The Standard, 23 August 1882, p. 3.

[96] Lunacy Patients Admissions Register, MH 94, 26, 94363.

[97] London Evening News, 14 September 1883, p. 3.

[98] Morning Post, 27 December 1883, p. 7.

[99] Illustrated Police News, 22 March 1884, p. 4.

[100] Reynolds Newspaper, 27 March 1887, p. 8.

[101.]Berrows Worcester Journal, 12 November 1887, p. 2.

[102] *Old Bailey Proceedings Online* (www.oldbaileyonline.org, version 7.0, 29 December 2014), January

1888, trial of ROBERT GALLINGAD BONTINE CUNNINGHAME GRAHAM JOHN BURNS (t18880109-223).

[103] T. Cullen, Autumn of Terror, Fontana, 1966, p. 17, n. 1.

[104] The Star, 20 November 1888, p.3.

[105] The Times, 21 December 1888, p. 14.

[106.] The Standard, 12 August 1891, p. 3.

[107] The Standard, 1 November 1895, p.7.

[108] The Standard, 15 January 1896, p. 2.

[109] Sheffield Daily Telegraph, 21 January 1896, p. 7.

[110] Hansard, HC Deb 04 April 1898, vol. 56, c.101.

[111] The Standard, 17 November 1888, p. 4.

[112] Dundee Courier and Argus, 18 November 1888, p. 4.

[113] The Times, 21 November 1916, p. 5.

Accused after the Terror

[1] Home Office Report, 10 January 1889, Evans and Skinner, Sourcebook, p. 443.

[2] Reynolds Newspaper, 21 February 1892, p.1

[3] M. Williams, Later Leaves, Being the Further Reminiscences of Montagu Williams QC, Macmillan and Co, 1891, pp 253-54.

[4] Letter from Robert Anderson to the Home Office, 6 February 1893, Evans and Skinner, Sourcebook, p. 461.

[5] Report from Inspector Rutt, 18 January 1889, Evans and Skinner, Sourcebook, pp. 661-62.

[6] Leeds Mercury, 17 November 1888, p. 9.

[7] Evening News, 16 November 1888, Casebook Press Reports, accessed 6 December 2013.

[8] R. Michael Gordon, Alias Jack the Ripper: beyond the usual Whitechapel suspects, McFarland, 2001, p. 24, 214, and 294.

[9] H. Wojtczak, Jack the Ripper at Last: The Mysterious Murders of George Chapman, Kindle, 2014, loc. 4362-4465 gives a critical appraisal of Levisohn's testimony about Chapman.

[10] Guernsey Star, 22 November 1888, p. 4.

[11] Daily News, 20 November 1888, p. 2.

[12.] Morning Advertiser, 20 November 1888, Casebook, Press Reports, accessed 9 December 2013. Poor Law Removal Records, Poplar, POBG/128/03, Ancestry.com. London, England, Selected Poor Law Removal and Settlement Records, 1828-1930 [database on-line]. Provo, UT, USA: Ancestry.com Operations, Inc., 2013, accessed 16 March 2014.

[13.] Statement of George Marsh, 24 December 1888, Evans and Skinner, Sourcebook, pp. 671-2.

[14] Report by Inspector Roots, 26 December 1888, Evans and Skinner, Sourcebook, pp. 672-3.

[15] Letter from Roslyn D'O.Stephenson, 26 December 1888, Evans and Skinner, Sourcebook, pp. 669-71.

[16] Tautriadelta, A Modern Magician: An Autobiography, ed. J. Kobek, Casebook, Dissertations, Crowley's Ripper: The Collected Writings of Roslyn D'Onston, accessed 24 August 2013.

[17] Biographical notes on Stephenson and his family posted by Mike Cowell, Casebook, Casebook Forums, Ripper Discussions, Suspects, Stephenson Robert Donston, Stephenson and Family Chronology, 17 February 2008, accessed 16 March 2014.

[18] S. Dimolianis, Jack the Ripper and Black Magic, Kindle, 2011, loc. 2139.

[19] Letter from Roslyn D'O.Stephenson, 16 October 1888, Evans and Skinner, Sourcebook, pp. 668-69.

[20] Pall Mall Gazette, 1 December 1888, pp. 1-2.

[21] Dimolianis, Black Magic, loc. 2498-2507.

[22] Pall Mall Gazette, 3 December 1888, p, 7.

[23.] Hospital records posted by Mike Covell, http://blog.casebook.org/mcebe, accessed 24 April 2013.

[24] Pall Mall Gazette, 3 January 1889, p. 1-2.

[25.]W. T. Stead's Introduction to Tautriadelta, Part 6, Casebook, Dissertations, Crowley's Ripper: The Collected Writings of Roslyn D'Onston   accessed 08 April 2013.

[26] B. O'Donnell, This Man Was Jack the Ripper, JTRForums, JTR Studies, The O'Donnell Manuscript, accessed 15 November 2013, p. 216.

[27] Ibid. pp. 225-26.

[28.]Ibid. p. 227.

[29] Begg, Fido and Skinner, <u>A-Z</u>, p. 342.

[30] O'Donnell, <u>This Man</u>, p. 229-31.

[31.] A. Crowley, <u>The Confessions of Alastair Crowley</u>, p. 690, <u>hermetic.com</u>,

http://hermetic.com/crowley/confessions, accessed 16 November 2013.

[32] Ibid. p. 690-1.

[33] O'Donnell, <u>This Man</u>, pp. 258-60

[34] Crowley, <u>Confessions</u>, p. 691-2.

[35] A. Crowley, "Jack the Ripper," <u>Casebook</u>, Dissertations, Crowley's Ripper: the collected writings of Roslyn d'Onston, accessed 04 April 2014.

[36] M. Harris, <u>Jack the Ripper: The Bloody Truth</u>, Columbus, 1987, <u>The Ripper File</u>, WH Allen, 1989, The <u>True Face of Jack the Ripper,</u> Caxton, 2001.

[37] I. Edwards, <u>Jack the Ripper's Black Magic Rituals</u>, John Blake, 2003.

[38] Mike Covell's blog, http://blog.casebook.org/mcb, accessed 23 August 2013. Dimolianis, <u>Black Magic</u>, loc. 2314, notes that Stephenson would have needed to persuade night and gate porters to record false details and the inattention or cooperation of nursing staff in order to leave the hospital at night.

[39] Dimolianis, <u>Black Magic</u>, loc. 2232-2241.

[40] I., D. Griffiths, ed. R. Phillips, "Memories of Morgan Davies, MD, F.R.C.S. (1854-1920), <u>Transactions of the Honourable Society of Cymmrodorion</u>, 1976, 213.

[41]. Obituary, <u>British Medical Journal</u>, 11 September 1920, 416.

[42] Letter from Foreign Office to Home Office, 14 December 1888, Evans and Skinner, <u>Sourcebook</u>, p. 433-34.

[43] Van Onselen, <u>The Fox and the Flies</u>, loc. 3442-3454.

[44.]The Standard, 1 January 1889, p. 2.

[45] J. J. Eddleston, <u>Jack the Ripper An Encyclopedia</u>, ABC-Clio, 2001, p. 215.

[46] Lloyds Weekly Newspaper, 5 May 1889, p. 4.

[47] Inquest Papers, London Metropolitan Archive, MJ/SP/C/LAN/355.

[48.] Lloyds Weekly Newspaper, 11 August 1889, p.4

[49] The Times, 14 June 1889, p. 3.

[50] Possibly the Truss society, Begg, Fido and Skinner, A-Z, p. 475.

[51.] Birmingham Daily Post, 20 September 1889, p. 8.

[52] Report by Chief Inspector Donald Swanson, 23 September 1889, Evans and Skinner, Sourcebook, 595-98.

[53] Post by Dave Knott, JTRforums, Suspects and Theories, The Lodger(s), G Wentworth Bell Smith, 8, 19 May 2007, accessed 16 March 2014.

[54] L. Forbes Winslow, Recollections of Forty Years, John Ouseley, 1910, pp. 267-76.

[55] Ibid, pp. 273-77.

[56]. Galveston Daily News, 19 October 1884, posted by AP Wolf, JTRforums, Suspects and Theories, The Prince of Israel, 4 September 2007, accessed 30 September 2013.

[57] Pall Mall Gazette, 31 May 1882, p. 10.

[58.]The Standard, 27 March 1883, p. 4.

[59] The Standard, 12 June 1883, p. 4 and 23 October 1883, p. 4.

[60]. The Times, 27 December 1884, p. 9.9

[61] Morning Post, 20 April 1885, p. 4.

[62] Morning Post, 30 September 1887, p. 6. The Standard, 14 October 1887, p. 4.

[63] Birmingham Post, 25 October 1887, p. 5.

[64] Daily News, 23 April 1889, p. 7.

[65] Daily News, 30 April 1889, p. 4.

[66] The letter was reported in various newspapers, such as Birmingham Post, 18 July 1889, p. 8,

[67] "False Clues," The Spectator, 27 July 1889, p. 11. Albert Bachert was a witness to an alleged manslaughter outside The Great Eastern Hotel on 25 May 1891, Old Bailey Proceedings Online, (t18910629-525), accessed 06 April 2014.

[68] The Standard, 15 October 1889, p. 2.

[69] Letter from M. T. Haslewood to the Home Office, 10 September 1889, Evans and Skinner, Sourcebook, pp. 576-79.

[70] T. Westcott, The Bank Holiday Murders: The True Story of the First Whitechapel Murders, Kindle, 2014, loc. 2278-2286. Dew, "The Hunt for Jack the Ripper."

[71] Research by Nina Brown, posted by Howard Brown, JTRforums, Letters from Hell or Thereabouts, H. T. Haslewood & the Poison Pen, 4 April 2014, 1, accessed 6 April 2014.

[72] Salt Lake Herald, 22 March 1893, p. 1.

[73] Bristol Mercury, 2 June 1894, p. 3.

[74] L. Clutterbuck, An Accident of History, The Evolution of Counter Terrorism Methodology in the Metropolitan Police from 1829 to 1901, With Particular Reference to the Influence of Extreme Irish Nationalist Activity, PhD Thesis, University of Portsmouth, June 2002, p. 69.

[75.] Ibid. p. 65.

[76.] Ibid. p. 263-64.

[77] Post Office Directory, 1889, p. 177.

[78] Passenger list (Microfilm roll: M237_528; line: 47; list number: 1690).

[79] T. Marriott, Jack the Ripper, The Secret Police Files, Kindle, 2013, loc. 4800-4823.

[80.] Marriot, Secret Police, loc. 4783-4800. Belfast Newsletter, 28 November 1888, p.5.

[81] Birmingham Post, 18 March 1889, p. 6. Western Mail, 18 March 1889, p. 3.

Mad Confessions

[1] Reynolds News, 30 September 1888, p. 6.

[2.] Birmingham Post, 28 September 1888, p. 8.

[3] Morning Post, 28 September 1888, p. 6.

[4] J. Bondeson, "Two Contemporary Swedish Pamphlets about Jack the Ripper", Ripperologist, 155, 7.

[5] Reynolds Newspaper, 7 October 1888, p. 7.

[6] The Star, 2 October 1888, p. 3.

[7] The Times, 4 October 1888, p. 3.

[8] Birmingham Post, 6 October 1888, p. 5.

[9] Birmingham Post, 8 October 1888, p. 8.

[10] D. O'Flaherty, "The Smart Talk of Alfred Blanchard," Casebook, Suspects, accessed 12 July 2013.

[11] Birmingham Post, 10 October 1888, p. 7.

[12] Morning Advertiser, 12 October 1888, Casebook, Press Reports, accessed 28 November 2013.

[13]. Huddersfield Daily Chronicle, 16 October 1888, p. 3.

[14]. Weekly Guardian, 19 October 1888, posted by Howard Brown, JTRForums, Suspects and Theories, The Men who would be the Ripper, 70, 03 February 2013, accessed 16 February 2014.

[15] Morning Advertiser, 24 October 1888, Casebook, Press Reports, accessed 15 February 2012.

[16] Cheshire Observer, 27 October 1888, p. 7.

[17] Cheshire Observer, 3 November 1888, p. 3.

[18] The Times, 19 October 1888, p. 10.

[19] The Times, 26 October 1888, p. 3.

[20] Birmingham Post, 12 November 1888, p. 8.

[21] Medical Register, 1887, p. 530.

[22] E. T. Woodhall, Jack the Ripper or When London Walked in Terror, P & O Riley, 1987, pp. 76-79.

[23] P. Ackroyd, Thames Sacred River, Random House, 2008, p. 380. Commenting on the retirement of the police officer responsible for Waterloo Pier a journalist referred to thirteen attempted suicides in the first twelve days of April 1896, Lloyds Weekly Newspaper, 12 April 1896, p. 3.

[24] Report by Acting Superintendent H Jones, 19 January 1889, Evans and Skinner, Sourcebook, p. 666.

[25] The Standard, 16 November 1888, p. 6.

[26] Aberdeen Weekly Journal, 15 November 1888, p. 6.

[27] London Metropolitan Archives, Clerkenwell St Paul, Register of Baptism, p.76/pau2, Item 033.

[28] The National Archives of the UK; Kew, Surrey, England; Court for Divorce and Matrimonial Causes, later Supreme Court of Judicature: Divorce and Matrimonial Causes Files; Reference: J 77/322/9659.

[29] Old Bailey Proceedings Online, (t18881119-50), accessed 12 January 2013.

[30] Bristol Mercury and Daily Post, 27 November 1888, p. 3.

[31] City Press, 24 November 1888, Casebook, Press Reports, accessed 16 February 2013.

[32] Lloyds Weekly Newspaper, 16 December 1888, p. 3.

[33] Old Bailey Proceedings Online, (t18870912-976), accessed 24 July 2012.

[34] The Standard, 8 December 1888, p. 3.

[35] The Times, 12 December 1888, p. 11.

[36] The Times, 19 December 1888, p. 13.

[37] Old Bailey Proceedings Online, (t18890107-178), accessed 19 December 2013.

[38] The Morning Post, 24 December 1888, p. 7.

[39] Sunday Times, 23 December 1888, Casebook, Press Reports, accessed 15 August 2014.

[40] The Courier, 5 January 1889, posted by Howard Brown, JTRForums, Suspects and Theories, The Men who would be the Ripper, 71, 3 March 2013, accessed 16 February 2014.

[41]. Sheffield and Rotherham Independent, 1 July 1889, p. 3.

[42] Old Bailey Proceedings Online, (t18770507-436), accessed 08 June 2014. See also report from Inspector Thomas Haines, 19 July 1889, Evans and Skinner, Sourcebook, pp. 511-12.

[43] Report by Sergeant Eugene Bradshaw, 23 July 1889, Evans and Skinner, Sourcebook pp. 516-7.

[44] Reynolds Newspaper, 21 July 1889, p.5.

[45] Ipswich Journal, 2 August 1889, p. 6.

[46] The Sun, 20 October 1889, posted by Howard Brown, JTRForums, Suspects and Theories, The Men who would be Ripper, 13, 6 December 2012, accessed 4 April 2014.

[47] Yorkshire Herald, 10 October 1891, p. 3.

[48] The Sun, 14 August 1889, posted by Howard Brown, JTRForums, Suspects and Theories, The Men who would be Ripper, 14, 6 December 2012, accessed 16 February 2014.

[49] Glasgow Herald, 13 November 1889, p. 6.

[50]. Glasgow Herald, 27 December 1889, p. 3.

[51] Sheffield and Rotherham Independent, 30 December 1889, p. 5.

[52] Cheshire Observer, 22 March 1890, p. 6.

[53] Morning Post, 4 April 1890, p. 6.

[54] Fresno Republican Weekly, 11 April 1890, posted by Howard Brown, JTRForums, Suspects and Theories, Brutal Charles Bond, 1, 11 June 2013, accessed 15 February 2014.

[55] Morning Post, 27 August 1890, p. 2.

[56] Royal Cornwall Gazette, 11 September 1890, p.7.

[57] The Times, 9 April 1891, p. 14.

[58] The Times, 23 April 1891, p. 4.

[59] Liverpool Mercury, 15 September 1891, p. 6.

[60] Birmingham Daily Post, 7 June 1892, p. 8.

[61] Syracuse Post Standard, 10 April 1905, Casebook, Press Reports, accessed 17 March 2014.

[62] Grey River Argus, 14 July 1905, posted by Dave James, JTRforums, Other Ripper Notables, Forbes Winslow, Dr L S Forbes Winslow Charlatan, 32, 19 April 2012, accessed 18 March 2014.

False Confessions

[1] Trewman's Exeter Flying Post, 22 August 1896, p. 5.

[2.]Lloyds Weekly Newspaper, 18 October 1896, p. 11.

[3] Canberra Times, 20 December 1927, p. 2.

[4]. Galveston Daily News, 6 December 1897, Casebook, Press Reports, accessed 7 October 2012.

[5] L. Matters, The Mystery of Jack the Ripper, Arrow, 1964.

[6] E. Zinna, "The Search for Jack el Destripador", ed. Begg, Paul, Ripperology, Constable and Robinson, 2007, p. 128-39.

[7] Salt Lake Herald, 25 August 1901, p. 10.

[8] Farson, Jack the Ripper, p. 81.

[9] A. Las Heras, Jack, El destripador y la pista de Buenos Aires, http://drantoniolasheras.wordpress.com/2013/08/29/jack-el-destripador-y-la-pista-de-buenos-aires/, accessed 10 June 2014.

[10] Darwin Northern Standard, 1 May 1925, p. 4. Richmond River Herald and Northern Districts Advertiser, 3 April 1925, p. 3.

[11] Medical Register, 1891, p. 776. The last entry found is in 1903, p. 1035. There was also an artist called William Maris (1843-1910).

[12] C. Wilson, and R. Odell, Jack the Ripper, Summing Up and Verdict, pp. 132-3.

[13] A facsimile of the diary is in S. Harrison, The Diary of Jack the Ripper, Hyperion, 1993, p.205-69, followed by a transcript, p.273-92.

[14] Ibid. p. 4-7.

[15] . Sunday Times, 3 July 1994, pp. 1-3.

[16] Affidavit by Michael Barrett, 5 January 1995, Casebook, Suspects, James Maybrick, Michael Barrett's Confessions, January 5, 1995, accessed 9 June 2014. Affidavit by Michael Barrett, 25 January 1995, Ibid.,

[17] P. Feldman, Jack the Ripper: The Final Chapter, Virgin Books, 2002, p. 170-2.

[18] K. W. Rendell, "Report on the Diary of Jack the Ripper," September 1993, The Diary, pp. 305-312.

[19] Ibid, p. 311.

[20] Ibid, p. 312.

[21] Sunday Times, 19 September 1993, pp. 4-6.

[22] Harrison, The Diary, Original Diary, p. 217 and p. 241. Transcript, p. 275 and 284. Dr Bond's Post Mortem report notes the position of the breasts, Evans and Skinner, Sourcebook, p. 383.

[23] Harrison, The Diary, Original Diary, p. 208, Transcript, p. 273.

[24] R. Wilkes, Appendix to M. Harris, "The Maybrick Hoax, A Guide Through the Labyrinth," Casebook, Dissertations, accessed 25 November 2013.

[25] Harrison, The Diary, p. 202.

[26] S. A. Turgoose, "Report on Engravings on Watch, 10 August 1993," Casebook, Dissertations, Maybrick Diary, Maybrick Watch, Scientific Analysis accessed 14 January 2014. R. K. Wild, "Surface Analysis of a Gold Watch, Comparison of Original and Surface and Scratch Marks", Bristol University, Interface Analysis Centre, 31 January 1994, Casebook, accessed 28 September 2012

[27] Feldman, Jack the Ripper, p. 240-1.

[28] Ibid, p. 237-51.

[29] J. Stettler, The Diary of Jack the Ripper, Another Chapter, Area 9 Publishing, 2009.

[30] B. Robinson, They All Love Jack: Busting Jack the Ripper, Kindle, 2015.

[31] Feldman, p. 347-70.

[32] Daily Mail, 6 August 2011, online edition, www.dailymail.co.uk, accessed 9 June 2014.

[33] Feldman, Jack the Ripper, p. 347.

[34] The Sun, 6 August 2011, p. 8.

[35] F. Pearse, Secret Witness, The Whitechapel Murders, Kindle 2012.

[36] Petition from Samuel Montagu, MP, Evans and Skinner, Sourcebook, p. 309.

[37] J. Carnac, The Autobiography of Jack the Ripper, Bantam Press, 2012.

Contemporary Killers.

[1] M. A. Stevens, Broadmoor Revealed, Kindle, 2013, loc. 2658.

[2] His confession dated 16 December 1868 was published in The Bristol Mercury, 19 December 1888, p. 3.

[3] The Daily Gazette, 24 September 1873, p. 3.

[4] London Metropolitan Archives, Mile End Old Town St Peter, Register of Baptism, p93/pet1, Item 006. Sadler was baptised on 18 October 1840.

[5.]Old Bailey Proceedings Online, (t18830730-724), accessed 09June 2014.

[6.] An account of Kelly's stated movements is given in J. Tully, The Secret of Prisoner 1167, Robinson, 1998, pp. 70-94

[7] Anonymous letter to Detective Sergeant Pierpoint, 25 January 1906, Tully, Prisoner 1167, p. 86-87.

[8] Report by Chief Inspector Chas. Arrow and Superintendent A. Hare, undated, Tully, Prisoner 1167, p. 88-89.

[9] J. Morrison, Jimmy Kelly's Year of Ripper Murders, J.B. Printers, 1990.

[10] Evans and Skinner, Sourcebook, p. 389-95.

[11] Letter from James Monro to Superintendent, Broadmoor, 23 February 1888, Tully, Prisoner 1167, pp. 68-9.

[12] Belloc Lowdnes, Marie, The Merry Wives of Westminster, MacMillan, 1946, p. 171.

[13] Minute by CET on James Kelly file, 12 November 1888, Tully, Prisoner 1167, p. 328.

[14] Letter from Dr Nicholson to Mrs Brider, 13 November 1888, Tully, Prisoner 1167, p. 328.

[15] Letter from Thomas O Evans Solicitors to Dr Nicholson, 14 November 1888, Tully, Prisoner 1167, p. 329.

[16] Western Mail, 25 October 1888, p. 3.

[17] The Penny Illustrated Paper and Illustrated Times, 27 October 1888, p. 263.

[18] Western Mail, 20 December 1888, p. 4.

[19] A. Sharp, "A Ripper Victim that Wasn't: The Capture of Jane Beadmore's Killer", Casebook, Dissertations, accessed 5 November 2013.

[20] Dundee Courier, 29 March 1889, p. 5.

[21] Dundee Courier, 12 February 1889, p. 3. E. MacPherson, The Trial of Jack the Ripper: The Case of William Bury, Kindle, 2005, loc. 1101-1111.

[22] Dundee Courier, 29 March 1889, p. 5.

[23] McPherson, The Trial of Jack the Ripper, loc. 362.

[24] Birmingham Post, 12 February 1889, p.8.

[25] Dundee Courier, 29 March 1889, p. 5.

[26] Washington Post, 17 November 1907, Casebook, Press Reports, accessed 26 August 2013.

[27] Dundee Courier and Argus, 25 April 1889, p. 2.

[28] Thompsons News, 12 February 1927, Begg, Fido and Skinner, A-Z, p. 57.

[29] J. Berry, My Experiences as an Executioner, Percy Lund, 1882.

[30] Letters from Ernest Parr, 28 March 1908, and 4 April 1908, posted by Boogles at Casebook, Forums, Ripper Discussions, Suspects, Bury W. H., So What did Parr Know, 1 and 3, 15 November 2012, accessed 26 August 2013.

[31] Letter from William Bury to Reverend Gough, 22 April 1889, Evans and Skinner, Letters from Hell, p. 208.

[32] S. Earp, "Identifying William Bury as Jack the Ripper", Ripperologist, 139, August 2014, 2-9.

[33] . Old Bailey Proceedings Online, (t18900623-521), accessed 12 February 2014.

[34] Post by Captain Jack, Casebook, Forums, Ripper Discussions, General Suspect Discussions, The Compelling Case of Mad Tom, 1, 24 July 2009, accessed 12 February 2014.

[35] A. McLaren, A Prescription for Murder: The Victorian Serial Killings of Dr Thomas Neill Cream, University of Chicago Press, 1995, pp. 36-7.

[36] Ibid. pp. 37-40.

[37] Ibid. p. 40.

[38] Old Bailey Proceedings Online, (t18921017-962), accessed 02 September 2013.

[39] J. Laurence, A History of Capital Punishment with Special Reference to Capital Punishment in Great Britain, Sampson Low, 1932, pp. 125-26.

[40] D. Bell, "Jack the Ripper – The Final Solution," Criminologist, 9, 1974, 40-51.

[41] Aberdeen Weekly Journal, 16 November 1892, p. 5

[42] D. Davis, "Jack the Ripper-The Hand-Writing Analysis," Criminologist, 9, 1974, 62-9. Also Montreal Gazette, 6 January 1875, p. 3, and The Times, 12 March 1985, p. 12.

[43] McLaren, A Prescription for Murder, p. 43.

[44] E. Majoribanks, <u>For the Defence: The Life of Sir Edward Marshall Hall</u>, MacMillan, 1930, pp. 35-6.

[45] The Ubssey, Vancouver, 2 February 1979, <u>Casebook</u>, Press Reports, accessed 9 January 2013.

[46] The Spy, 16 April 1892, Evans and Skinner, <u>Sourcebook</u>, pp. 640-1.

[47] Ibid, p. 640-2. Letter from Charles Barber to the Home Office, 6 May 1892, Evans and Skinner, <u>Sourcebook</u>, pp. 642-3.

[48] Ancestry.com, Criminal Registers, 1791-1892, Class: HO 27; Piece: 149; Page: 86, accessed 2 September 2013.

[49] M.Covell, <u>Frederick Bailey Deeming- Jack the Ripper or Something Worse</u>, Kindle, 2014, loc. 8076-94.

[50] New South Wales Police Gazette, 30 November 1881, p. 426.

[51] New South Wales Police Gazette, 26 April 1882, p. 161 and 8 March 1882, p. 91.

[52] Covell, <u>Deeming</u>, loc. 8094

[53] State Records Authority of New South Wales; Series: 5264; Reel: 2674.

[54] Report by Sergeant Considine and Sergeant Cawsey, 5 May 1892, Public Record Office Victoria, Bigamy, Theft & Murder, The Extraordinary Tale of Frederick Bailey Deeming, http://www.prov.vic.gov.au, accessed 20 July 2014.

[55] Rockhampton Morning Bulletin, 25 August 1883, p. 1, 28 August 1883, p.1, 1 October 1883, p. 4. A further advert on 19 September 1883, p.1 uses the name P.S.Deeming.

[56] Rockhampton Morning Bulletin, 21 November 1883, p. 2.

[57] Rockhampton Morning Bulletin, 12 March 1884, p.1. Rockhampton Morning Bulletin, 14 March 1884, p. 3. This advert was repeated several times to 29 March 1884.

[58] Sydney Evening News, 2 November 1887, p. 4.

[59] Sydney Morning Herald, 3 December 1887, p. 3.

[60] Sydney Morning Herald, 16 December 1887, p. 4.

[61] Sydney Morning Herald, 15 June 1888, p. 4.

[62] Report by Sergeant Considine and Sergeant Cawsey, 5 May 1892.

[63] Western Australian, 24 March 1892, p.4

[64] Belfast News Letter, 24 March 1892, p. 5.

[65] Bristol Mercury, 28 March 1892, p, 8. The Dunkeld left Cape Town for Natal on 20 September 1889, Glasgow Herald, 9 October 1889, p. 10.

[66] Covell, Deeming, loc. 794-810.

[67] Testimony of John William Stringthorpe, Covell, Deeming, loc. 5558, and 5576.

[68] Ibid. loc. 899.

[69] Ancestry.com. England & Wales, Criminal Registers, 1791-1892, Class: HO 27; Piece: 217; Page: 236.

[70] Belfast Newsletter, 21 March 1892, p. 5. Hampshire Advertiser, 23 March 1892, p. 4.

[71] Aberdeen Weekly Journal, 8 April 1892, p. 5.

[72] Western Mail, 2 April 1892, p. 5.

[73] Sheffield and Rotherham Independent, 5 April 1892, p. 5.

[74] Pall Mall Gazette, 12 April 1892, p. 4.

[75] Sheffield and Rotherham Independent, 13 April 1892, p. 5.

[76] Sheffield and Rotherham Independent, 23 April 1892, p. 5. A novel called Jacks Secret by Lovett Cameron was published in 1891.

[77] Bury and Norwich Post, 17 May 1892, p. 8.

[78] Royal Cornwall Gazette, 14 April 1892, p. 7.

[79] Pall Mall Gazette, 26 March 1892, p. 4.

[80] Dundee Courier and Argus, 30 March 1892, p. 3.

[81] Pall Mall Gazette, 20 April 1892, p.5.

[82] Aberdeen Weekly Journal, 29 April 1892, p.5.

[83] Dundee Courier and Argus, 29 April 1892, p.2

[84] The Times, 4 April 1892, p. 6.

[85] Manchester Evening Times, 8 April 1892, p. 4.

[86] Cullen, Autumn of Terror, p. 202, n1.

[87] Scarsi, J. L, "Jack el Destripador: una pista en la Argentina", Historias de la Ciudad, 4, 31, 2005. Trans. E. Zinna, "On the Trail of Jack the Ripper, Szemeredy in Argentina", Ripperologist, 63, January 2006, 6-12.

[88] Brisbane Courier, 5 November 1892, p. 7.

[89] Scarsi, "On the Trail."

[90] The Standard, 29 September 1892, p. 5.

[91] The Standard, 1 October 1892, p.5.

[92] C. Muusmann, trans. A. Wood, Hvem Var Jack the Ripper? En Dansk Forhorsdommers Undersogelse, A. Christiansens Forlag, 1999.

Later Killers

[1] Pall Mall Gazette, 2 October 1893, p. 3.

[2] Huddersfield Chronicle, 11 October 1893, p. 3.

[3] Newcastle Weekly Courant, 9 June 1894, p.3.

[4] Morning Post, 27 April 1894, p. 5.

[5] Liverpool Mercury, 15 September 1897, p. 7.

[6] J. Bondeson and B.F.M Droog, "The Dutch Jack the Ripper, New Light on Hendrik de Jong, the Continental Suspect", Ripperologist, 159, 19.

[7] National Police Gazette, 86, 16 May 1896, http://www.policegazette.us, accessed 25 May 2013.

[8] Ibid.

[9] Ibid.

[10] New York World, 9 November 1894, p. 1.

[11] New York Times, 28 April 1896, Casebook, Press Reports, accessed 16 September 2013.

[12] T. Marriott, Jack the Ripper: The 21st Century Investigation, Kindle, 2007.

[13] Ibid, loc. 4713-4862

[14] Ibid, loc. 5638.

[15] Ibid. loc. 5385.

[16] Marriott, Secret Police, loc. 3193-3233

[17] Daily News, 13 April 1863, p. 6.

[18] The Times, 31 January 1873, p. 7.

[19] The Times, 18 February 1889, p. 9.

[20] Belfast Newsletter, 19 October 1889, p. 8.

[21] W. Vanderlinden, "Carl Ferdinand Feigenbaum: An Old Suspect Resurfaces", Casebook, Suspects, accessed 28 May 2013.

[22] J.B. Martin, Call it North Country: The Story of Upper Michigan, Wayne State University Press, 1986, p. 180-81.

[23] Marriott, Secret Police, loc. 3234-3243

[24] Vanderlinden, "Carl Feigenbaum"

[25] Birmingham Post, 4 December 1890, p. 4.

[26] Blackburn Standard, 31 October 1891, p. 7.

[27] Birmingham Post, 7 November 1891, p. 8.

[28] Newark Daily Advocate, 30 October 1891, Casebook, Press Reports, accessed 13 April 2014.

[29] Morning Post, 16 December 1892, p. 5.

[30] Vanderlinden, "Carl Feigenbaum",

[31] Syracuse Daily Journal, 3 February 1892, p. 3. See also Vanderlinden, "Carl Feigenbaum"

[32] Vanderlinden, "Carl Feigenbaum"

[33] Reynolds Newspaper, 28 October 1894, p. 4.

[34] P. Brode, Death in the Queen City: Clara Ford on Trial 1895, Natural Heritage, 2005, p. 61.

[35] J. W. Murray, ed. V. Speer, Memoirs of a Great Detective, The Baker and Taylor Company, 1905, pp. 385-90.

[36.] Belfast Newsletter, 4 January 1896, p. 5-6.

[37] The Standard, 5 December 1894, p. 4.

[38] Leeds Mercury, 10 December 1894, p.6.

[39] Pall Mall Gazette, 10 December 1894, p. 8.

[40] Old Bailey Proceedings Online, (t18950128-199), accessed 16 December 2013.

[41.] E. Larson, The Devil in the White City, Kindle, 2010, loc. 924-937.

[42] Ibid. loc. 2364.

[43] Ibid, loc. 2610 to 2754.

[44] Daily Mail, 1 December 2012, http://dailymailonline, accessed 13 January 2013.

[45] In practice, US courts will accept relevant testimony from qualified document examiners. Margaret Webb is a graphologist who states that she has qualifications in forensic document examination, http://www.graphologist.co.uk/, accessed 27 February 2014.

[46] Old Bailey Proceedings Online. (t18990306-230), accessed 15 February 2014.

[47] Ibid.

[48] Posted by Uncle Jack, Casebook, Ripper Discussions, Suspects, General Suspect Discussion, George Robertson Possible Suspect, 1, 01 March 2010, accessed 15 February 2014.

[49] Posted by Harry Poland, Casebook, Ripper Discussions, Suspects, General Suspect Discussion, Sampson Silas Salmon, 1, 29 December 2012, accessed 15 February 2014.

[50] H. L. Adam, Trial of George Chapman, William Hodge & Co, 1930, pp. 219-223.

[51] Old Bailey Proceedings Online, (t19030309-318), accessed 21 June 2014.

[52] Wojtczak, loc. 1241-1270, gives an account of the fire.

[53] Ibid. loc. 13417-1463.

[54] Pall Mall Gazette, 24 March 1903, Casebook, accessed 19 September 2013.

[55] Old Bailey Proceedings Online, (t19030309-318), accessed 14 April 2014.

[56] A. F. Neil, Forty Years of Man-Hunting, Jarrold, 1932, p. 26.

[57] McCormick, The Identity, p. 164-65.

[58] Sunday Chronicle, 17 November 1935, Evans and Skinner, Letters from Hell, 189-90.

[59] Ancestry.com, London, England, Electoral Registers, 1832-1965, accessed 25 October 2013.

[60] Daily Express, 12 November 1935, posted by John Savage, 25 September 2003, Casebook, Message Boards, Notable Persons, Dr. Thomas Dutton, Archive through September 29, 2003, accessed 24 January 2014.

[61] Letter from Donald McCormick, 5 May 1995, Evans and Skinner, Letters from Hell, pp. 192-3.

[62] Daily Mail, 14 May 1929, R. Whittington-Egan, Jack the Ripper, The Definitive Casebook, Amberley, 2013, p. 12.

[63] Sugden, Complete History, pp. 439-66

[64] R. Michael Gordon, R., Alias Jack the Ripper, pp. 88-9.

[65] Ibid, p. 14.

[66] Begg, Fido and Skinner, A-Z, p. 439-40.

[67] Evening World, 14 June 1892, p. 1.

[68] Bluefield Daily Telegraph, 22 December 1903, Casebook, Press Reports, accessed 18 December 2013.

[69] New York Times, 28 February 1904, p. 5.

[70]. New York Globe and Commercial Advertiser, 2 March 1904, p. 2.

[71] Monroe County Mail, 24 December 1903, p. 1.

[72]. New York State Government, Public Papers of Frank W Higgins, J.B. Lyon Company, 1906, pp. 229-230.

[73]. New York Times, 22 August 1916, p. 6.

Other Criminals

[1] Letter from Sergeant F. Kuhrt, 27 September 1888, Evans and Skinner, Sourcebook, p. 654-55

[2] Daily News, 29 September 1888, p. 7.

[3] Morning Post, 16 November 1888, p.6

[4] Morning Post, 22 November 1888, p.6.

[5] Ancestry.com, England & Wales Criminal Registers, 1791-1892, Piece 211, Page 141. The Proceedings of the Old Bailey state that he was not guilty, Proceedings of the Central Criminal Court, Second Session 1888-89, p. 163. Prison records confirm that he was sent to Wandsworth for twelve months.

[6] Ancestry.com, England & Wales, National Probate Calendar (Index of Wills and Administrations), 1858-1966, accessed 5 August 2012.

[7] Dundee Courier and Argus, 29 January 1889, p. 3.

[8] The Standard, 22 July 1889, p. 3.

[9] Morning Post, 19 September 1889, p. 2.

[10] Birmingham Post, 28 October 1889, p. 5.

[11] The Yorkshire Herald, 29 January 1891, p.3.

[12] Sheffield and Rotherham Independent, 29 January 1891, p. 3.

[13] The Yorkshire Herald, 14 January 1891, p. 5.

[14] The Yorkshire Herald, 31 August 1891, p. 3.

[15] Old Bailey Proceedings Online, (t18910309-277), accessed 13 April 2013.

[16] Birmingham Daily Post, 24 February 1891, p. 5.

[17] Belfast Newsletter, 28 March 1892, p. 5.

[18] East London Advertiser, 13 October 1888, Casebook, Press Reports, accessed 19 December 2013.

[19] Report from Sergeant Stephen White, 4 October 1888, Evans and Skinner, Sourcebook, p. 145.

[20] Ibid. pp. 144-5, White notes that Packer originally said he saw nothing suspicious when asked on 30 September 1888.

[21] The Times, 6 October 1888, p.6.

[22] Report by Chief Inspector Swanson, 19 October 1888, Evans and Skinner, Sourcebook, p. 139.

[23] Illustrated Police News, 26 March 1887, p.4.

[24] Lloyds Weekly Newspaper, 20 March 1887, p. 12.

[25] The Standard, 29 May 1897, p.6.

[26] The Standard, 30 May 1897, p. 3.

[27.] The Times, 8 June 1889, p. 6.

[28] Old Bailey Proceedings Online, (t18890624-563), accessed 12 January 2013.

[29] The Times, 29 September 1891, p.2.

[30] Morning Post, 13 October 1891, p. 2.

[31] Old Bailey Proceedings Online, (t18911116-27), accessed 12 January 2013.

[32] Old Bailey Proceedings Online (t18911116-56), accessed 12 January 2013.

[33] Huddersfield Chronicle, 21 November 1891, p. 8.

[34] Birmingham Post, 20 October 1891, p. 5.

[35] Evans and Rumbelow, Scotland Yard Investigates, loc. 2366.

[36] York Herald, 7 April 1876, p. 5.

[37] Answers, 5 March 1907, p.1.

[38] Old Bailey Proceedings Online, (t19080623-49), accessed 13 April 2013.

[39] MEPO 6/29 (1917), posted by Rob Clack, Casebook, Discussions, Le Grand Charles, Le Grand Conspiracy, 14 July 2011, 109, accessed 12 July 2013.

[40] Post by Kattrup, Casebook, Forums, The End of the Road: Le Grande's death, accessed 11 April 2016.

[41] England, Dreadnought Seamen's Hospital Admissions and Discharges, 1868-1871, p. 7.

[42] Posted by Debra Arif, JTRforums, Suspects and Theories, Le Grand of the Strand, Is this Le Grand's Marriage Certificate? 24 October 2012, 1, accessed 15 April 2014.

[43] England, Cheshire, Marriage Bonds and Allegations, 1606-1900, FamilySearch, index, FamilySearch (MM9.1.1/F16Z-M9G), accessed 19 Apr 2014.

[44] Report by Melville Macnaghten, 23 February 1894, Evans and Skinner, Sourcebook, pp.645-649.

[45] The Sun 13 February 1894, Casebook, Press Reports, accessed 17 July 2013.

[46] The Sun, 15 February 1894, Casebook, Press Reports, accessed 17 July 2013.

[47] Lloyds Weekly Newspaper, 3 May 1891, p. 2.

[48.] Lloyds Weekly Newspaper, 19 April 1891, p. 9.

[49] The Sun, 17 February 1894, Casebook, Press Reports, accessed 17 July 2013.

[50] Report by Melville Macnaghten, 23 February 1894, Evans and Skinner, Sourcebook. p. 647.

[51.] Lloyds Weekly Newspaper, 19 April 1891, p. 9.

[52] Lloyds Weekly Newspaper, 3 May 1891, p. 2.

[53] Ibid. pp. 279-84.

[54] D. Bullock, The Man Who Would be Jack, Robson Press, 2012, p. 243.

[55] The Sun, 17 February 1894, Casebook, Press Reports, accessed 17 July 2013.

[56] Western Mail, 14 February 1894, p. 6.

[57] Begg, Fido and Skinner, A-Z., p. 428.

[58] Report by Melville Macnaghten, Evans and Skinner, Sourcebook, p. 647.

[59] A. P. Wolf, Jack the Myth, Chivers Press, 1994, p. 140-45.

[60] Morning Post, 22 January 1891, p. 2.

[61] Morning Post, 21 March 1891, p. 2.

[62] Northern Echo, 4 March 1891, p. 3.

[63] Belfast Newsletter, 6 March 1891, p. 5.

[64] Trenton Times, 6 March 1891, Casebook, Press Reports, accessed 20 February 2013.

[65] Daily News, 24 August 1891, p. 7.

[66] Daily News, 31 August 1891, p. 7.

[67] Greathead.org, http://www.greathead.org, William James Percy Beresford Greathead, accessed 12 November 2013.

[68] Aberdeen Weekly Journal, 16 August 1893, p. 8.

[69] Dundee Courier and Argus, 16 August 1893, p. 3.

[70] Old Bailey Proceedings Online, (t18950325-318), accessed 16 September 2013. The evidence is noted as unfit for publication.

[71] The Times, 27 February 1895, p. 13.

[72.] Pall Mall Gazette, 7 May 1895, p. 7.

[73] The Morning Post, 12 February 1895, p. 7.

[74] Pall Mall Gazette, 7 May 1895, p. 7.

[75] Weekly Dispatch 1906, posted by Debra Arif, Ibid. 1, 24 June 2011, accessed 17 April 2014.

[76] J. S. Balfour, My Prison Life, Chapman and Hall, 1907. For Balfour's prior interest in the Ripper murders see Westcott, Bank Holiday Murders, loc. 1413-1423.

[77] MEPO, 6/18.

[78] Pall Mall Gazette, 16 April 1910, p. 1.

[79] Pall Mall Gazette, 19 April 1910, posted by Chris, Casebook, Forums, Ripper Discussions, General Suspect Discussion, William Grant Grainger, and Censorship, 20 August 2008, 24, accessed 17 April 2014.

[80] Pall Mall Gazette, 20 April 1910, posted by Chris, Casebook, Forums, Ripper Discussions, General Suspect Discussion, William Grant Grainger, and Censorship, 20 August 2008 25, accessed 17 April 2014.

[81] Pall Mall Gazette, 23 April 1901, posted by Chris, Casebook, Forums, Ripper Discussions, General Suspect Discussion, William Grant Grainger, and Censorship, 20 August 2008 30, 21 August 2008, accessed 17 April 2014.

[82] Forbes Winslow, Recollections, pp. 278-80.

[83] Ibid, p. 282.

[84] Sydney Morning Herald, 28 July 1910, p. 7.

[85] Freemans Journal, 13 November 1878, p. 7.

[86] Posted by Debra Arif, JTRforums, Suspects and Theories, William Grant Grainger, Previous Convictions and another alias, 16, 26 September 2012, accessed 19 April 2014.

[87] Pall Mall Gazette, 7 May 1895, p. 7.

[88] Monmouthshire Beacon 31 January 1891, p. 3.

[89] Post by Rob Clack, JTRforums, Suspects and Theories, William Grant Grainger and Jabez Balfour, 58, 30 June 2011, accessed 21 July 2014.

[90] Picture and comment posted by MKLHawley, reposted by Chris, Casebook, Forums, Ripper Discussions, Suspects, General Suspects, J. McDermott, 03 August 2010, 1, accessed 27 December 2013.

[91] Irish World, 18 October 1890, posted by Chris, Casebook, Forums, Ripper Discussions, Suspects, General Suspects, J. McDermott, 03 August 2010, 1, accessed 27 December 2013.

[92] Testimony of Robert B. Lynch, in Queen v Daniel Whelan, Correspondence Respecting the Recent Fenian Aggression on Canada, Harrison and Sons, 1867, p. 63.

[93] Brooklyn Daily Eagle, 29 October 1880, p. 2.

[94] M. Davitt, The Fall of Feudalism in Ireland or the Story of the Land League Revolution, Harper & Brothers, 1904, pp. 432-33.

[95] Ibid. p. 429.

[96] Ibid. p. 430-1.

[97] The Times, 10 August 1883, p. 10.

[98] McKenna, The Irish, p. 66.

[99] Ibid. p. 67.

[100] The Tablet, 8 August 1883, p. 1.

[101] Davitt, Fall of Feudalism, p. 431.

[102] Clutterbuck, An Accident of History, pp. 205-06.

[103] Pall Mall Gazette, 26 January 1885, p. 2.

[104]. Birmingham Post, 24 August 1885, p. 3.

[105] The Times, 29 October 1887, p. 7.

[106] Posted by Chris, Casebook, Ripper Discussions, Suspects, General Suspect Discussion, J. McDermott, 16 June 2010, 13, accessed 20 April 2014.

[107] Reynolds Newspaper, 10 March 1895, p.5.

Macnaghten's Memorandum

[1] Report by Melville Macnaghten, 23 February 1894, Evans and Skinner, Sourcebook, p. 645-49.

[2] A. Griffiths, Mysteries of Police and Crimes, Cassels and Company, 1898, pp. 34-35.

[3] Cassell's Family Magazine, April 1896, posted by SPE, JTRforums, Suspects and Theories, Major Arthur Griffiths, 1, 17 May 2010, accessed 21 June 2014.

[4] B. Thompson, The Story of Scotland Yard, Literary Guild, 1936, p. 335.

[5] Begg, Fido and Skinner, A-Z, p. 328.

[6] On 4-5 May 1877 Druitt and Ruggles-Brise played for Oxford University against the University's second eleven, Cricket Archive, http://www.cricketarchive.com, accessed 1 January 2014. Druitt played with WG Grace against Wiltshire, on 10-11 August 1885, Ibid. He also played against Ruggles-Brise on at least two occasions.

[7] Acton, Chiswick & Turnham Green Gazette, 5 January 1889, Casebook, Press Reports, accessed 10 January 2013.

[8] Ibid.

[9] Scorecard of Blackheath v The Christophersons, 8 September 1888, CricketArchive, accessed 01 January 2014.

[10] Sugden, Complete History, p. 382.

[11] Hampshire Advertiser, 23 June 1888, p.7.

[12] Old Bailey Proceedings Online, (t18880917), accessed 01 June 2013.

[13] Law Journal, Vol. 23, 1888, p. 150. The Times 29 November 1888, p. 13, incorrectly states that the appeal was dismissed. The Times, 30 November 1888, p. 14, corrects this.

[14] Information posted by Chris Scott, Casebook, Message Boards, General Discussion, Newspaper Articles, Lloyds News 22 September 1907 Article by George R Sims, 26 May 2004, accessed 28 April 2014.

[15] M. Fido, The Crimes, Detection and Death of Jack the Ripper, Barnes & Noble, 1993, p. 204.

[16] The Referee, 13 July 1902, Casebook, Press Reports, accessed 12 September 2013.

[17] The Referee, 22 January 1899, Casebook, Press Reports, accessed 12 September 2013. G. R. Sims, My Life, Sixty Years Recollection of Bohemian London, Eveleigh Nash Company, 1917, p. 142.

[18] Albury Banner and Wodonga Express, 31 December 1915, p. 40.

[19] Gloucestershire Citizen, 9 January 1905, posted by Jonathon H., Casebook, Casebook Forums, Ripper Discussions, Suspects, Druitt Montague John, Druitt Disguised by accident or design?, 5 March 2014, 1, accessed 19 April 2014.

[20] McCormick, Identity, p. 156.

[21] Pall Mall Gazette, 14 February 1891, p. 5. Bachert was banned from the inquest jury by the coroner, Mr Baxter.

[22] North Eastern Daily Gazette, 18 February 1891, p.2.

[23] Western Mail, 26 February 1892, p. 5.

[24] North Eastern Daily Gazette, 18 January 1899, p. 3. Dundee Courier and Argus 19 January 1899, p.5.

[25] Ancestry.com, UK, Clergy List, 1897. See also http://www.wraysbury.net/history/standrews.htm, which states that Hake was vicar of the parish for forty years.

[26] F. Richardson, The Worst Man in the World, Evelyn Nash, 1908, p. 59.

[27] F. Richardson, The Other Man's Wife, London, Evelyn Nash, 1908, p. 330.

[28] Whittington-Egan, Definitive Casebook, p. 31.

[29]. Farson, Jack the Ripper, p. 109.

[30] Ibid., 119-123,

[31] Research by Adam Went, JTRForums, JTR Studies, Dissertation: The Infamous East End Murderer, I Knew Him Revealed, 10 October 2013, 1, accessed 01 January 2014.

[32] Farson, Jack the Ripper, p. 121-2.

[33] Ibid, p. 149-50.

[34] Brown, Rise of Scotland Yard, p. 208.

[35] Evans and Rumbelow, Scotland Yard Investigates, loc. 5387-5399.

[36] The Times, 14 December 1887, p. 9.

[37] M. Macnaghten, Days of My Years, Edward Arnold, 1914, p. 54.

[38] Sugden, Complete History, p. 399.

[39] Begg, Fido and Skinner, A-Z, p. 305.

[40]. Macnaghten, Days of my Years, p. 59-60.

[41] Begg, Fido and Skinner, A-Z, p. 547-49.

[42] Rumbelow, Complete Jack the Ripper, p. 176.

[43] Fido, Crimes, p. 117.

[44] The Referee, 22 September 1907, Casebook, Press Reports, accessed 12 September 2013.

[45] J. Overton Fuller, Sickert and the Ripper Crimes, Mandrake, 1990, p. 179.

[46] R. Anderson, "Our Absurd System of Punishing Crime", The Nineteenth Century and After, ed. J. Knowles, Vol. 49, January-June 1901, Leonard Scott, p. 269.

[47] Begg, Fido and Skinner, op. cit., p. 25.

[48] A. Aylmer, "The Detective in Real Life," Windsor Magazine, 1, May 1895, p. 507.

[49] Evans and Skinner, Sourcebook, p. 701.

[50] Pall Mall Gazette, 7 May 1895, p. 7.

[51] Fido, Crimes, p. 225.

[52] House, Jack the Ripper, loc. 789.

[53] Lloyds Weekly Newsletter, 15 December 1889, p. 12.

[54] Begg, Fido and Skinner, A-Z, pp. 268-9.

[55] P. Marshall, and C. Phillips, "New Light on Aaron Kosminski," Ripperologist, 128, October 2012.

[56] Begg, Fido and Skinner, A-Z, p. 270-1.

[57] Colney Hatch Register of Admissions, Begg, Fido and Skinner, A-Z, 271.

[58] Ibid.

[59] Case Notes from Colney Hatch, Ibid, p. 272.

[60] Begg, Fido and Skinner, A-Z, p. 297-98.

[61] City of London Press, 7 January 1905, Casebook, Press Reports, accessed 13 January 2013.

[62]. Morning Leader, 9 January 1905, Casebook, Press Reports., accessed 14 February 2013.

[63]. Thompson's News, 1 December 1906, Evans and Skinner, Sourcebook, pp. 703-9.

[64] Western Mail, 26 February 1892, p. 5.

[65] Daily Mail, 7 September 2014, Daily Mail Online, http: www.dailymail.co.uk, accessed 9 September 2014.

[66] Begg, Fido and Skinner, A-Z, pp, 385-7

[67] Reading Gaol, Entry Book of Pardons and Prisoners, Piece 393, findmypast.com.

[68]. Jacksons Oxford Journal, 7 March 1863, posted by Chris Scott, Casebook, Forums, Ripper Discussions, Suspects, Ostrog Michael, The Criminal Career of Ostrog-Press Accounts, 28 September 2009, 1, accessed 14 September 2013.

[69] Sugden, Complete History, p. 426-9.

[70]. Daily News, 28 July 1866, p. 6.

[71] M. Davitt Leaves from a Prison Diary, Vol. 1, 1885, Chapman and Hall, Lecture X, posted by Robert Charles Linford, Casebook, Message Boards, Suspects, Ostrog Michael, Davitt on Ostrog, 27 August 2005, accessed 4 January 2014.

[72] Pall Mall Gazette, 6 January 1874, p. 6.

[73] P. Begg, Jack the Ripper: The Facts, Kindle, 2013, loc. 6413-21 describes the arrest.

[74]. Sugden, Complete History, p. 431.

[75]. Ibid. p. xx.

[76]. Old Bailey Proceedings Online, (t18870912-961), accessed 14 September 2013.

[77] Begg, The Facts, loc. 6446.

[78] Police Gazette, 26 October 1888, cited by Sugden, Complete History, p. 433.

418

[79] Sugden, <u>Complete History</u>, p. xi.

[80] Daily News, 18 April 1891, p. 7.

[81]. Sugden, <u>Complete History</u>, p. xviii.

[82] N. Connell, "Ostrog, An Adventurer at Eton," <u>Casebook</u>, Dissertations, accessed 21 June 2014.

[83] Sugden, <u>Complete History</u>, p. xix.

[84]Morning Post, 20 December 1900, p. 8.

[85] Sugden, <u>Complete History</u>, p. xix-xx.

Recollections

[1]. Blackburn Standard and Weekly Express, 16 November 1889, p. 3.

[2]. North Eastern Daily Gazette, 30 November 1889, p.3

[3]. Aberdeen Weekly Journal, 16 March 1896, p. 3.

[4]. Reynolds Newspaper, 11 June 1893, p. 8.

[5] The Referee, 1 March 1891, Dagonet and Jack the Ripper, <u>Casebook,</u> Press Reports, accessed 22 April 2014.

[6] Gloucestershire Citizen, 9 January 1905, posted by Jonathon H., <u>Casebook</u>, Forums, Ripper Discussions, Suspects, Druitt Montague John, 5 March 2014, accessed 20 April 2014.

[7] The Referee, 31 July 1904, Dagonet and Jack the Ripper, <u>Casebook</u>, Press Reports, accessed 22 April 2014.

[8] Howells and Skinner, <u>Ripper Legacy</u>, p. 41.

[9] O. Sitwell, <u>Noble Essences: A Book of Characters</u>, Grosset & Dunlap, 1950, pp. 211-13.

[10] Cullen, <u>Autumn of Terror</u>, p. 154.

[11] Begg, Fido and Skinner, <u>A-Z</u>, p. 205.

[12] The Times, 25 March 1904, p. 2.

[13] M. Fido, "Ernest Dowson as Mr Moring", <u>Ripperana</u>, 29, July 1999, 1-6.

[14] R. Thurston-Hopkins, Life and Death at the Old Bailey, Chapter VIII, Casebook, Ripper Media,

Ripperological Preservation Society, accessed 18 January 2014.

[15] Fido, "Ernest Dowson", 1-2.

[16] R. Thurston-Hopkins, Appendix to E. C. Dowson, The Letters of Ernest Dowson, Fairleigh Dickinson

University Press, 1968, pp. 441.

[17.] Ibid. p. 440.

[18.] Pall Mall Gazette, 16 January 1892, p.5.

[19.] Dundee Courier and Argus, 13 September 1892, p. 3.

[20.] Glasgow Herald, 23 July 1894, p. 4.

[21] S. Berry, "John Barlas, (Evelyn Douglas), Sweet Anarchist and Schizophrenic?" William Morris Society in

the United States Newsletter, Winter 2007, 17.

[22] D. A. Green, "In Hours of Red Desire", Ripper Notes, 26, September 2006, 11

[23] Pall Mall Gazette, 7 January 1892, p. 3. Sherard refers to the arrest in his biography of Oscar Wilde, R. H.

Sherard, Oscar Wilde, The Story of an Unhappy Friendship, Greening and Co, 1905, p. 104-05.

[24] R. A. Patterson, The Story of Jack the Ripper, A Paradox, 2012, http://www.richard-apatterson.com,

accessed 19 January 2014, p. 27-29.

[25] B. M. Boardman, "Thompson, Francis Joseph (1859–1907)", Oxford Dictionary of National Biography,

Oxford University Press, 2004; online edn, Jan 2011, accessed 19 Jan 2014.

[26] Patterson, Paradox, p. 31-32.

[27] E. Meynell, The Life of Francis Thompson, Charles Scribner's Sons, 1913, p. 64-65.

[28] Patterson, Paradox, p. 46.

[29] Ibid. p. 9.

[30.] Meynell, Francis Thompson, p. 81-3.

[31] One of Thompson's biographers, John Walsh, stated that Thompson gravitated to the Catholic shelter in

Providence Row during a discussion of his whereabouts as a vagrant, cited by Richard Patterson,

Casebook, Ripper Discussions, Suspects, Francis Thompson, Proof that Thompson was Living in

Whitechapel just off Dorset Street, 1, 3 February 2015, accessed 4 February 2015.

[32] Sheffield Evening Telegraph, 22 November 1907, p. 8.

[33] F. Thompson, A Renegade Poet and Other Essays, Books for Libraries Inc., 1965, p. 215.

[34] Ibid. pp. 309-46.

[35] Letter from Francis Thompson to Wilfrid Meynell, February 1889, J. E. Walsh, The Letters of Francis

Thompson, Hawthorn, p. 25.

[36] Patterson, Paradox, p. 11.9

[37] Belloc Lowndes, Merry Wives of Westminster, p. 10.

[38]. Meynell, Francis Thompson, p. 280.

[39] John Blunts Monthly, 16 December 1929, Casebook, Press Reports, accessed 11 November 2012.

[40.] Broadmoor Case File 1527.

[41] Daily Express, 16 March 1931, Casebook, Press Reports, accessed 22 October 2012.

[42] Begg, Fido and Skinner, A-Z, 481.

[43] B. E. Reilly, "Jack the Ripper – The Mystery Solved", City, February 1972, cited by Begg, Fido and Skinner,

A-Z, p. 90.

[44] Whittington-Egan, Definitive Casebook, p. 296.

[45] Empire News, 17 November 1935, Feldman, The Final Chapter, p. 371.

[46] Daily Mail, 14 May 1929, posted by Howard Brown 10 April 2003, JTRforums, accessed 24 January 2014.

[47] The Times, 27 January 1936, p. 7.

[48] Old Bailey Proceedings Online, (t18961019-792), accessed 15 February 2014.

[49] G. S. Salway, "I knew Jack the Ripper," True Detective, October 2012.

[50] E. Zinna, "The Search for Jack el Destripador"

[51] San Mateo Times, 9 February 1959, reprinted Casebook. Edwards gave his story to the Worthing

Gazette.

[52] D. G. Halstead, Doctor in the Nineties, Chapter 3, Casebook, Ripper Media, Ripper Preservation Society, accessed 24 January 2013.

[53] Sunday Times, 25 October 1959, posted by Howard Brown, JTRForums, 03 June 2012, accessed 22 January 2014.

[54] Begg, Fido and Skinner, A-Z, p. 267.

[55] Weekly World News, 20 June 1988, p. 11 and 1 September 1992, p. 2.

[56] D. Murphy, "A Ripping Yarn," The Bulletin, 30 December 1997, 22.

[57] Sydney Morning Herald, 21 April 1891, p. 3.

[58] State Archives NSW; Kingswood, New South Wales; Gaol Description and Entrance Books, 1818-1930; Series: 2232; Item: 3/5971; Roll: 5119.

[59] New South Wales Police Gazette, 21 August 1895, p. 295.

[60] State Archives NSW: State Records Authority of New South Wales, Police Gazettes 1862-1930, Roll 3142, Year 1895, Page 283.

[61] State Archives NSW; Kingswood, New South Wales; Gaol Description and Entrance Books, 1818-1930; Item: 4/8515; Roll: 2363.

[62] San Francisco Call, 2 September 1897, p. 5.

[63] New South Wales Government. Inward passenger lists. Series 13278, Reels 399-560, 2001-2122, 2751. State Records Authority of New South Wales. Kingswood, New South Wales, Australia.

[64] Sydney Evening News, 31 January 1891, p. 3.

[65] Salt Lake Herald, 5 March 1899, p. 6.

[66] Tacona Times, 17 April 1912, p. 7. See also The Day Book, 17 February 1912, 1-2.

[67] The Perth West Australian, 7 August 1912, p. 7. See also New South Wales Police Gazette, 18 December 1912, p. 515.

[68] Bisbee Daily Review, 27 April 1913, p. 1.

[69] State Archives NSW: State Records Authority of New South Wales, Police Gazettes 1862-1930, Roll 3598, Year 1915, Page 186.

[70] Adelaide Advertiser, 20 October 1916, p. 9.

[71] H.W. Cooper, Health and Vigor, Milton House, n.d. p. 46.

[72] Ballarat Courier, 25 April 1917, p. 5. See also Australasian Journal of Pharmacy, April 1917, 161.

[73] Tamworth Daily Observer, 9 February 1918, p. 2.

[74] Sydney Morning Herald, 10 September 1907, p. 4.

[75] New South Wales Police Gazette, 14 April 1886, p.115.

[76] New South Wales Government Gazette, *1853–1899,* p. 548.

[77]. Perth Daily News, 19 November 1925, p.7.

[78] Western Daily Press, 18 October 1932, p.5.

[79] South Australia Police Gazette, 29 September 1937, p. 1.

[80] Sydney Morning Herald, 5 February 1938, p. 12.

[81] Adelaide Advertiser, 11 August 1936, p. 18.

[82] The Times, 14 February 1890, p. 5.

[83] The Times, 12 July 1940, p.2.

[84] Staffordshire Advertiser, 13 July 1940, p. 7.

[85] Launceston Examiner, 3 June 1950, p. 6.

[86] Barrier Miner, 29 May 1950, p. 1.

[87] Ancestry.com. Australia Birth Index, 1788-1922, accessed 10 January 2013.

[88] Daily Mail, 2 December 2006, Ripperologist, 134, October 2013, loc. 2498-2640.

[89] Begg, Fido, and Skinner, A-Z, p. 12.

Littlechild's Letter

[1] Letter from John Littlechild to G R Sims, Evans and Skinner, Sourcebook, p. 674-75.

[2] Brooklyn Eagle, 27 April 1890, p. 12.

[3] Montreal Pilot, 23 September 1857, Casebook, Press Reports, accessed 12 August 2012.

[4] T. B. Riordan, Prince of Quacks: The Notorious Life of Dr. Francis Tumblety, Charlatan and Jack the Ripper Suspect, Kindle, 2009, loc. 520-642.

[5] Ibid. loc. 671-7.

[6] Morning Freeman, 13 September 1860, Casebook, Press Reports, accessed 12 August 2012

[7] P. L. Twohig," The "Celebrated Indian Herb Doctor": Francis Tumblety in Saint John, 1860", Acadiensis, 39, 2, Summer/Autumn 2010, 82-86. See also O'Riordan, Prince of Quacks, loc. 1012-89.

[8] O'Riordan, Prince of Quacks, loc. 1129-82.

[9] Ibid. loc.1357-68.

[10] Ibid. loc. 1409-26.

[11] Ibid. loc. 1511-23.

[12] Brooklyn Daily Eagle, 6 May 1864, Casebook, Press Reports, accessed 5 January 2014.

[13] Brooklyn Daily Eagle, 10 May 1864, Casebook, Press Reports, accessed 5 January 2014.

[14] O'Riordan, Prince of Quacks, loc. 1658-65.

[15] New York Times, 5 May 1865, Casebook, Press Reports, accessed 5 January 2014.

[16] Brooklyn Daily Eagle, 10 May 1865, Casebook, Press Reports, accessed 5 January 2014.

[17] Letter from Colonel Baker, O'Riordan, Prince of Quacks, loc. 1724-30.

[18] For example, Brooklyn Daily Eagle, 19 June 1865, Casebook, Press Reports, accessed 4 January 2014.

[19] List of Claims of British subjects against the United States and American Citizens Against Great Britain: before the Mixed Commission under the twelfth article of the Treaty of Washington of May 8, 1871, Washington, 1873, pp. 44-45.

[20] O'Riordan, Prince of Quacks, loc. 2092-2109.

[21] The Times, 1 December 1873, p. 11.

[22] Liverpool Mercury, 28 January 1875, p. 3. See also British Medical Journal, 5 Feb 1875, p. 184.

[23] Liverpool Mercury, 24 February 1875, p. 3.

[24] Birmingham Post, 16 August 1875, p. 5.

[25] O'Riordan, Prince of Quacks, loc. 2402-13.

[26] New York Times, 24 July 1880, O'Riordan, Prince of Quacks, loc. 2467.

[27] O'Riordan, Prince of Quacks, loc. 2473.

[28] Ibid. loc. 2491-7.

[29] O'Riordan, Prince of Quacks, loc. 2503-2550. Also, Daily Picayune, 25 March 1881, p. 12.

[30] W. Vanderlinden, "On the Trail of Tumblety? Part 1", Ripper Notes, 23, June 2005, 41.

[31] Chicago Tribune, 7 October 1888, p. 13.

[32] Birmingham Post, 4 December 1888, p. 5.

[33] Vanderlinden, "On the Trail, Part 1," 41.

[34] The Times, 19 November 1888, p. 6.

[35] Dundee Courier and Argus, 26 December 1888, p. 3.

[36] Birmingham Daily Post 1 January 1889, p.3.

[37] W. Vanderlinden, "On the Trail of Tumblety, Part Two," Ripper Notes, 24, October 1888, p. 25.

[38] The Daily Alta California, 23 November 1888, Casebook, Press Reports, accessed 8 August 2012.

[39] New York Times, 23 November 1889, Ibid, accessed 20 September 2013.

[40] Decatur Saturday Herald, 26 June 1889.

[41] Western Mail, 20 November 1890, p. 5.

[42] Washington Post, 19 November 1890, Casebook, Press Reports, accessed 10 June 2013.

[43] Arkansas Gazette, 19 April 1891, Casebook, accessed 8 August 2012

[44] Whitstable Times, 4 July 1903, p. 2.

[45] S. P. Evans, and P. Gainey, Jack the Ripper, First American Serial Killer, Arrow, 1996, pp. 219-20.

[46] Bristol Mercury, 17 October 1888, p. 8.

[47] Daily News 18 October 1888, p. 3.

[48] The Standard, 18 October 1888, p. 2.

[49] Evening News, 18 October, Casebook, Press Reports, accessed 15 April 2014.

[50] New York World, 28 January 1889, R. J. Palmer, "Tumblety Talks," Ripperologist, 79, May 2007, 3-5.

[51] F. Tumblety, A Sketch of the Life of the Gifted, Eccentric, and World-Famed Physician, Press of Brooklyn Eagle, 1889.

[52] Willamsport Sunday Grit, 9 December 1888, Casebook, Press Reports, accessed 20 September 2013.

[53] J. Niven, Gideon Welles, Lincoln's Secretary of the Navy, Oxford University Press, 1973, p. 547. See also S. J. Frank, "The Conspiracy to Implicate the Confederate Leaders in Lincoln's Assassination", The Mississippi Valley Historical Review, 40, 4, March 1954, 629-656.

[54] Mike Hawley read the extract on a podcast, Casebook, Ripper Media, Audio Visual, Rippercast, Tumblety the hidden truth.

[55] J. Chetcuti, "A Nuns Letter", Ripperologist, 158, 3-4.

[56] T. Marriott, "Doctor at Sea," Ripperologist, 127, August 2012, pp. 34-45.

Lunatics

[1] Report by Sir Charles Warren, 19 September 1888, Evans and Skinner, Sourcebook, p. 132.

[2] Deal, Walmer and Sandwich Mercury, 12 October 1872, p. 1.

[3] Deal, Walmer and Sandwich Mercury, 4 January 1873, p. 1.

[4] Daily News, 7 April 1880, p. 3.

[5] Daily News 23 August 1884, p. 3.

[6] Morning Post, 4 December 1884, p. 6.

[7] The Guernsey Star, 25 December 1884, p. 2.

[8] The Guernsey Star, 3 January 1885, p. 2.

[9] The Guernsey Star, 20 October 1885, p. 2.

[10] Illustrated Police News, 6 July 1889, p.3.

[11] Old Bailey Proceedings Online, (t18891021-882), accessed 29 January 2013.

[12] Morning Post, 18 August 1893, p. 6.

[13] Reynolds Newspaper, 10 September 1893, p. 2.

[14] Begg, The Facts, loc. 8906.

[15] The Essex County Standard, 15 April 1899, p. 7.

[16] Western Mail, 26 May 1899, p. 5.

[17] Ancestry.com, Probate Calendar, accessed 29 January 2013.

[18] London Metropolitan Police Archives, posted by Chris, Casebook, Forums, Ripper Discussions, Suspects, General Suspect Discussion, Puckeridge, 14, accessed 26 January 2013.

[19] Smith, From Constable to Commissioner, p. 147

[20] The Times, 18 October 1888, p. 7.

[21] Huddersfield Daily Chronicle, 15 November 1888, p.3,

[22] Bury and Norwich Post, 4 December 1888, p.3

[23] S. Poberowski, "Nikolay Vasiliev: The Ripper from Russia", ed. P. Begg, Ripperology, Constable and Robinson, 2007, pp. 90-2.

[24] The Star, 17 November 1888, p. 3.

[25] W. Le Queux, The Minister of Evil, Casell & Company, 1918, pp. 103-12.

[26] Le Queux's text was reprinted by Melvin Harris, Jack the Ripper, pp. 57-8.

[27] C. Wilson, "A Lifetime in Ripperology," in Jakubowksi and Braund, The Mammoth Book, p. 412.

[28] S. Poberowski, "Pedachenko Revisited: The British Secret Service and the Assassination of Rasputin", Ripperology, ed. P. Begg, Constable and Robinson, 2007, pp. 84-85.

[29] McCormick, Identity, p. 174-75.

[30] Begg, Fido and Skinner, A-Z, p. 217-8.

[31] McCormick, Identity, p. 177-8.

[32] Brisbane Courier, 25 March 1911, p. 12.

[33] The Milwaukee Sentinel, 9 April 1937, p. 13.

[34] *STBG/WH/123/020.*

[35] Fido, Crimes, p. 217

[36] Infirmary records, Begg, Fido and Skinner, A-Z., pp. 97-8.

[37]. Post by Martin Fido, JTRForums.com, Suspects and Theories, Martin Fido's Asylum Research: The Notes, 5, 22 July 2011, accessed 27 April 2014.

[38] Douglas, Cases that Haunt, p. 180.

[39]. W. Vanderlinden, "Hyam Hyams: Portrait of a Suspect", Casebook, Dissertations, accessed 28 June 2014.

[40] City of London Lunatic Asylum, Case Book, Male Patients No. 7' Reference CLA/001/B/02/007, posted by Rob Clack, Casebook, Forums, Ripper Discussions, Suspects, Hyam Hyams, 66, 8 April 2011, accessed 29 June 2014.

[41] M. King, "Hyam Hyams," Casebook, Dissertations, accessed 10 June 2013.

[42] Posts by TJ and Chris, Casebook, Forums, Ripper Discussions, Suspects, Hyam Hyams, 43-45, accessed 01 August 2014.

[43] Old Bailey Proceedings Online, (t18860405-419), accessed 16 January 2014.

[44] Asylum Records, posted by TJI, Casebook, Casebook Forums, Ripper Discussions, Suspects, Levy Jacob, Jacob Levy Asylum Records, 1, 23 June 2013, accessed 14 January 2014.

[45] Ibid. 9, posted 24 June 2013.

[46] Reynolds News, 11 January 1891, p. 5.

[47] Aurora Daily Express, 15 November 1890, p. 3.

[48] New York Sun, 8 January 1891, p. 3.

[49] Pall Mall Gazette, 12 January 1889, p. 5.

[50] Maysville Evening Bulletin, 17 May 1888, p.4.

[51] Chicago Daily Tribune, 15 May 1888, posted by Simon Wood, Casebook, Forums, Ripper Discussions, Suspects, General Suspect Discussion, George Hutchinson (American), 2, 20 January 2009, accessed 01 July 2014.

[52] The Times, 27 August 1881, p. 6.

[53] J. Carey, "Jack the Ripper's Room and Newland Francis Forester Smith," Ripperana, 24, April 1998, 2.

[54]. The Times, 19 June 1890, p. 4.

[55] N.P. Warren, "The Asylum at Ascot," Ripperana, July 1992, p. 8-10.

[56] Begg, The Facts, loc. 2091.

[57] Report by Inspector F. G. Abberline, 1 November 1888, Evans and Skinner, Sourcebook, p. 142.

[58] Home Office Report, Evans and Skinner, Sourcebook, p. 142-3.

[59] Begg, The Facts, loc. 2078-86.

[60] Lloyds Weekly Newspaper, 22 April 1888, p. 4. Also, Old Bailey Proceedings Online, (t18880423), accessed 27 April 2014.

[61] Ancestry.com, UK, Navy Lists, 1888-1970, accessed 8 January 2013.

[62] Empire News, 23 October 1923, Casebook, Press Reports, accessed 21 February 2013.

[63] Research by Stephen P. Ryder, Casebook, Message Boards, Suspects, Fogelma (Norwegian Sailor), Morris Plains Asylum, 2 March 2005, accessed 19 July 2012.

[64] Nevada State Journal, 3 June 1915, Casebook, Press Reports, accessed 21 February 2013.

[65] Washington Post, 23 June 1915, p. 2.

[66] New York Tribune, 6 May 1915, p. 1.

[67] Another man questioned was Lewis Stemler, a 29-year-old Austrian waiter. He is sometimes accused of being Jack the Ripper but would have been seven at the time of the murders, Indiana Evening Gazette, 8 May 1915, Casebook, accessed 18 January 2014. See also M. Newton, The Encyclopedia of Unsolved Crimes, Infobase, 2009, pp. 188-90.

[68] T. Toughill, Thomas, The Ripper Code, The History Press, 2008.

Women

[1] The Times, 11 September 1888, p. 11.

[2] Birmingham Post, 4 January 1889, p. 3.

[3] Ancestry.com. England & Wales, Criminal Registers, 1791-1892, HO 27; Piece: 213; Page: 333, accessed 12 February 2014.

[4] Marion Daily Star, 19 December 1893, Casebook, Press Reports, accessed 8 September 2013.

[5] J. Conway, Remembering the Sullivan County Catskills, History Press, 2008, p. 39.

[6] Middletown Daily Times, 4 December 1893, Casebook, Press Reports, accessed 03 July 2014.

[7] J. B. Ransom, "Shall Insane Criminals be Imprisoned or Put to Death", Transactions of the Medical Society of the State of New York, 1895, pp. 233-34.

[8] Conway, Remembering the Sullivan, p. 41.

[9] Woodhall, Jack the Ripper, p. 47-58.

[10] W. Stewart, Jack the Ripper a New Theory, London, Quality Press, 1939.

[11] Casebook, Dissertations, Crowley's Ripper, The Collected Writings of Roslyn D'Onston, accessed 14 January 2014.

[12] E.J Wagner, The Science of Sherlock Holmes, Wiley, 2007, p. 206.

[13] This was earlier than anticipated and several newspapers in 1890 note that she was released that year.

[14] New South Wales Government. Inward passenger lists. Series 13278, Reels 399-560, 2001-2122, 2751. State Records Authority of New South Wales. Kingswood, New South Wales, Australia.

[15] Post by Blood Rose, Casebook, Casebook Forums, Ripper Discussions, Suspects, General Suspect Discussion, Rose Mylett- Jill the Ripper, 1 March 2009, accessed 15 February 2009.

[16] J. Morris, Jack the Ripper, Hand of a Woman, Seren, 2012.

[17] T. Williams, Uncle Jack, Orion, 2006.

[18] J. Pegg, "Uncle Jack Under the Microscope," Ripper Notes, 24, October 2005, p. 16.

[19] J. Shelden, "The Fifth Victim: The Hands of a Woman", Ripperologist, 134, October 2013, 15-28.

Doctors and Surgeons

[1] The Star, 24 November 1888, Casebook, Press Reports, accessed 26 January 2013.

[2] Sugden, Complete History, pp. 156-67.

[3] The Times, 19 October 1877, p.6. Also see "Dr Barnardo's Case," The Spectator, 27 October 1877, p. 9.

[4] The Times, 1 August 1888, p. 3.

[5] The Times, 17 July 1889, p. 3.

[6] The Times, 9 October 1888, p. 4.

[7] Whittington Egan, Definitive Casebook, p. 27.

[8] Begg, Fido and Skinner, A-Z, p. 43.

[9.] G. Rowlands, "The Mad Doctor," ed. Jakubowski and Braund, The Mammoth Book, p. 301.

[10] G. Wagner, "Barnardo, Thomas John (1845–1905)", Oxford Dictionary of National Biography, Oxford University Press, 2004; online edn, Sept 2010,

[11] J. Ogan, "John William Smith Sanders – A Problem of Identity", Ripperana, 5, July 1993.

[12] M. Roberts, "Doctor Who?" Ripperana, 30, October 1999.

[13] Reynolds Newspaper, 22 July 1888, p.2.

[14] The Times, 17 August 1888, p. 10.

[15] Old Bailey Proceedings Online, (t18880917-864), accessed 14 January 2013.

[16] Scorecard Portsmouth Borough v Southampton, Hampshire Challenge Cup, 30 August 1888. Scorecard, Portsmouth Borough v Dorset Regiment, 1 September 1888.

[17] Lloyds Weekly Newspaper, 6 October 1861, p. 12.

[18] Lloyds Weekly, 27 August 1871, p. 4.

[19] Old Bailey Proceedings Online (t18810110-180), accessed 31 March 2013.

[20] The Times, 21 May 1886, p. 10.

[21] Baltimore Sun, 1 August 1893, p. 6.

[22] Posted by mic_ads, 01 April 2012, Casebook, Forums, Ripper Discussions, General Suspect Discussion, Dr Septimus Swyer, 04January 2012, accessed 31 March 2013.

[23] London Gazette, 6 March 1928, p. 1647

[24] Daily Mail, 30 October 2012, online edition, http://www.dailymail.co.uk, accessed 30 March 2013.

[25] Daily Mirror, 31 October 2012, p. 24.

[26] Old Bailey Proceedings Online (t18820327-414) and (t18820911-873), accessed 25 January 2013.

[27] This argument was put forward by Christopher S Smith in three articles in Criminologist, 1992-3, Begg, Fido and Skinner, A-Z, p. 545.

[28] D. Stocks, "The Anti-Freemason Movement," Casebook, Dissertations, accessed 29 March 2013.

[29] Weekly World News, 30 July 1996, Ripperologist, 122, September 2011, 41.

[30] Armidale Express, 16 November 2012, http://www.armidaleexpress.com.au, accessed 29 March 2013.

[31] A. M. Hamilton and L. Godkin, A System of Legal Medicine, E.B. Treat, 1894, p. 75-87.

[32] Ancestry.com. UK, Outward Passenger Lists, 1890-1960.

[33] Northern Star, Lismore, 18 April 1925, p. 4.

[34] Carnarvon and Denbigh Herald, 21 June 1889, p. 3.

[35] Whittington Egan, Definitive Casebook, p. 27.

[36]. The Times, 5 January 1887, p. 10

[37] P. Cornwell, The Secret Life of Walter Sickert, Kindle Edition, 2017.

Aristrocrats and Royals

[1] Begg, Fido and Skinner, A-Z, p. 14.

[2] O'Donnell, Researches, p. 200-2.

[3] Dr Bond's post mortem notes on Mary Jane Kelly, reprinted in Evans and Skinner, Sourcebook, p. 383-84.

[4] P. Jullian, trans. P. Dawney, Edward and the Edwardians, Viking, 1967, pp. 143-44.

[5] The Times, 15 January 1891, p. 15.

[6] Birmingham Post, 21 January 1891, p. 5.

[7] Hansard, HC Debates, 23 January 1891, vol. 349, cc. 893-5.

[8] Hansard, HC Debates, 26 January 1891, vol. 349, cc. 1024-5.

[9] Hansard, HC Debates, 2 February 1891, vol. 349, cc1518-9.

[10] Hansard, HC Debates, 26 February 1891, vol. 350, cc1686-7.

[11] P. Jullian, trans. V. Wyndham, Oscar Wilde, Viking, 1969, p. 189.

[12] S. Russo, The Jack the Ripper Suspects, Persons Cited by Investigators and Theorists, McFarland, 2011, p. 131.

[13] Jullian, Edward and the Edwardians, p. v.

[14] A. Kelly, Jack the Ripper, A Bibliography and Review of the Literature, Association of Assistant Librarians, 1973, pp. 12-14.

[15] T. E. A. Stowell, "Jack the Ripper: A Solution", The Criminologist, Vol.5, November 1970, 40-51.

[16] The Times, 4 November 1970, p. 12.

[17] Morning Post, 8 September 1888, p. 5.

[18] The Times, 9 November 1970, p. 9.

[19] The Times, 14 November 1970, p. 12

[20] F. Spiering, Prince Jack, The True Story of Jack the Ripper, Jove, 1978.

[21] M. Harrison, Clarence, Was he Jack the Ripper, WH Allen, 1972.

[22] The Times, 16 March 1885, p. 8.

[23] A. G. Benson, The Leaves of the Tree, Studies in Biography, G. P. Putnam and Sons, 1911, pp. 134-35.

[24] York Herald, 30 June 1888, p. 4.

[25] J. M. K. Smith, 'Stephen, Sir James Fitzjames, first baronet (1829–1894)', Oxford Dictionary of National Biography, Oxford University Press, 2004; online edn, Jan 2012, accessed 27 Jan 2014.

[26] Sunday Times, 16 February 1975, posted by Howard Brown, JTRforums, Suspects and Theories, Inside Information on Stephen's Candidacy dating back to the LVP, 1, 6 September 2012, accessed 2 May 2015.

[27] O'Donnell, Researches, p. 189.

[28] M. Howells and K. Skinner, The Ripper Legacy, Sphere, p. 37-40.

[29] In a later version, J K Stephen introduced them. Stephen and Annie were said to be second cousins, Fairclough, The Ripper and the Royals, p. 148.

[30] Howells and Skinner, Ripper Legacy, pp. 38-40. It was later alleged that Charles was abducted in 1905 and exchanged for John Charles Francis, fifth son of Prince George who became King George V and was the young brother of Prince Albert Victor, Fairclough, Ripper and the Royals, pp. 99-103.

[31] Curiously the 1871 census contains a Mary Kelly working as a nursemaid to a family in Cleveland Street.

[32] Howells and Skinner, Ripper Legacy, p. 44.

[33] Knight places the abduction in 1888. Fairclough, noting the demolition, suggested the abduction may have occurred as early as 1885, Fairclough, Ripper and the Royals, p. 8-9.

[34] Begg, Fido and Skinner, A-Z, p. 466.

[35] Howells and Skinner, Ripper Legacy, p. 45.

[36] Howells and Skinner, Ripper Legacy, p. 39.

[37] Reprinted by S. Knight, Jack the Ripper: The Final Solution, Granada, 1980, p. 214.

[38] Howells and Skinner, Ripper Legacy, p. 47.

[39] The Observer, 7 February 1892, Knight, Final Solution, p. 214-5. Also, Lloyds Weekly Newspaper, 7 February 1892, p. 2.

[40] .Knight, Final Solution, p. 215.

[41] Fairclough, Ripper and the Royals, pp. 123-4.

[42] Ibid. p. 176.

[43] Feldman, Final Chapter, p. 223.

[44] Stowell, "Jack the Ripper," 40-51.

[45] Fort Wayne Sentinel, 24 April 1895, Casebook, Press Reports, accessed 14 August 2014.

[46] C. H. Hermann, Recollections of Life and Doings in Chicago from the Haymarket Riot to the End of World War 1, Normadic House, 1945, p. 128-29.

[47] Letter from Dr Benjamin Howard, The People, 26 January 1896, Whittington-Egan, Definitive Casebook, p. 210-11.

[48] O' Donnell, Researches, p. 177-78.

[49] Knight, Final Solution, p. 180-85.

[50] Knight, Final Solution, p. 168

[51] Evans and Rumbelow, Scotland Yard Investigates, 2811-2821.

[52] Fairclough, Ripper and the Royals, p. 38.

[53] Statement of George William Sequeira, 11 October 1888, Evans and Skinner, Sourcebook, p. 232.

[54] Letter from Charles Warren to Robert Anderson, 23 August 1888, Evans and Skinner, Sourcebook, p. 122.

[55] Fairclough suggests otherwise, although he was unable to find any evidence, Fairclough, Ripper and the Royals, p. 50.

[56] Evans and Skinner, Sourcebook, p. 397-8.

[57] Morning Post, 17 July 1889, p. 3.

[58] Knight, Final Solution, pp. 236-4.

[59] Cornwell, Secret Life.

[60] Begg, The Facts, loc. 7538-46.

[61] J. O. Fuller, Sickert and the Ripper Crimes, Mandrake, 2001.

[62] A.G. Robins, Walter Sickert, Drawings Theory and Practice, Word and Image, Scolar Press, 1996.

[63] R. Emmons, The Life and Opinions of Walter Richard Sickert, Lund Humphries, 1992, pp. 48-49.

[64] Knight, Final Solution, p. 254.

[65] Ibid. p. 262.

[66] P. Cornwell, <u>Portrait of a Killer; Jack the Ripper, Case Closed</u>, Little Brown, 2002, p. 166-74.

[67] The Times, 19 December 2005, p. 3.

[68] Unpublished research, Begg, Fido and Skinner, <u>A-Z</u>, p. 467-8.

[69] Cornwell, <u>Portrait of a Killer,</u> p. 277-83.

[70] Begg, <u>The Facts</u>, loc. 7737-62.

[71] Daily News, 29 November 1888, p. 3.

[72] The Standard, 21 December 1888, p. 2.

[73]. Nottinghamshire Guardian, 5 January 1889, p. 5.

[74] Illustrated Police News, 19 January 1889, p. 2

[75] North Eastern Daily Gazette, 3 August 1889, p. 3.

[76] Old Bailey Proceedings Online (t19071210-29), accessed 28 July 2014

[77] Emmons, <u>Life and Opinions</u>, p. 73.

[78] Cornwell, <u>Portrait of a Killer</u>, p. 214.

[79] W. Vanderlinden, <u>Casebook</u>, Suspects, Walter Sickert, A New Sickert Clue, Archive, 30 January 2004, accessed 8 May 2014.

[80] Fairclough, <u>Ripper and the Royals</u>, p. viii-ix.

[81] Ibid. pp. 145-6.

[82] Pall Mall Gazette, 24 March 1903, <u>Casebook</u>, Press Reports, accessed 8 April 2014.

[83] Fairclough, pp. 76-7.

[84] Ibid. pp. 114-5.

[85] Ibid. pp. 245-6.

[86] North London Press, 16 November 1889, p. 5.

[87] Old Bailey Proceedings Online, (t18900113-139), accessed 08 January 2013.

[88] Begg, Fido and Skinner, <u>A-Z</u>, p. 172.

[89] Hansard, HC Debate 28 Feb 1890, vol. 341, cc1523-611.

[90] The Sun, 29 August 1972, p, 13-6. Also, 30 August 1972, p. 14-5, 31 August 1972, p. 15 and 1 September 1972, p. 19.

[91] Daily Express, 15 December 2001, Newsbank, accessed 26 November 2013.

[92] O'Donnell, Researches, 186-7.

[93] Ibid. p. 200-9.

[94] Liverpool Mercury, 20 September 1882, p. 6.

[95] Pall Mall Gazette, 1 September 1888, p. 6.

[96] Birmingham Post, 4 September 1888, p. 4.

[97] Denver Evening Post, 23 August 1899, posted by A. P, Wolf, JTRForums, Suspects and Theories, Funny Ripper Theories, Lord Harold de Walden, 14 April 2007, accessed 15 February 2014.

[98] The Times, 3 March 1893, p. 14, 4 March 1893, p. 16, 6 March 1893, pp. 13, 11 March 1893, p. 15, 13 March 1893, p. 13.

[99] Begg, Fido and Skinner, A-Z, p. 293.

[100] A. Hochschild, King Leopold's Ghost: A story of Greed, Terror and Heroism in Colonial Africa, Mariner, 1999.

[101] Winnipeg Free Press, 12 April 1941, posted by Howard Brown, JTRForums, Suspects and Theories, Doctor Strauss: Is he Leonard Matter's Suspect, 27 February 2013, 1, accessed 09 June 2014.

[102] Sporting Times, 13 October 1888, posted by Chris Scott, Casebook, Forums, Ripper Discussions, General Discussion, William Gladstone's Thoughts on the Murderer, accessed 10 October 1888.

[103] Cullen, Autumn of Terror, p. 233.

[104] G. Norton, "Was Gladstone Jack the Ripper," Queen, September 1970, cited by P. Hodgson, Jack the Ripper: Through the Mists of Time, Minerva Press, 2002, p. 181-182.

Other Men

[1] Whittington-Egan, Definitive Casebook, p. 28.

[2] M. Holgate, Jack the Ripper: The Celebrity Suspects, Kindle, July 2013, loc. 1683.

[3] Whittington-Egan, Definitive Casebook, p. 28.

[4] R. Wallace, Jack the Ripper: Light Hearted Friend, Gemini Press, 1996.

[5] K. Leach, "Jack Through the Looking-Glass (or Wallace in Wonderland", Casebook, Dissertations accessed 10 October 2013.

[6] S. Herfort, Jack L'Eventruer Demasque, Talandier, 2007.

[7] Begg, Fido and Skinner, A-Z, p. 321. Macnaghten claimed that he refused the position when first offered, Days of My Years, p. 58.

[8] Wilson and Odell, Summing Up and Verdict, pp. 242-3.

[9] T. Slemen, Jack the Ripper Secret Service, Kindle, 2011.

[10] There are references to Conder in the biography of Kitchener, written by Sir George Arthur who was himself briefly a Ripper suspect, G. Arthur, Life of Lord Kitchener, Vol. 1, Cosimo, 2007, especially Chapters 1 and 2.

[11] D. Mc Kenna, "The Tales of the 'Twos'", Ripper Notes, 23, June 2005, 69-70.

[12] Begg, Fido, and Skinner, Jack the Ripper, A-Z, p. 105.

[13] N. Shelden, Mary Jane Kelly and the Victims of Jack the Ripper, Kindle, 2013, loc. 576.

[14] K. Busa, Wellcome to Hell: Was Sir Henry Wellcome Jack the Ripper? Kindle, 2013.

[15] B. Deer, "Sir Henry Wellcome, thy will be done," Brian Deer's Website, http://www.briandeer.com, 19 September 1993, accessed 14 October 2013.

[16] A. J. Lupin, Stranger on the Earth, a Psychological biography of Vincent Van Gogh, Da Capo, 1996, p.159-60.

[17] Letter from Vincent Van Gogh to Wilhelmina Van Gogh, 22 June 1888, WebExhibits.org, http://www.webexhibits.org, Van Gogh Letters, accessed 16 February 2014.

[18] For translations of Van Gogh's letters, see Ibid.

[19] Chronology at Henri De Toulouse Lautrec, http://www.toulouselautrec.free.fr, accessed 16 February 2014.

[20] G. Alexander, "Suspects in Short, Henri deToulouse-Lautrec," <u>Ripperologist</u>, 134, October 2013, 53.

[21] Post by Galexander, <u>Casebook</u>, Message Boards, General Discussion, New Theory on the Identity of Jack the Ripper, 11 March 2012, 1, accessed 10 January 2013.

[22] The theory was posted online but is no longer available. It was summarised in The Philippine Daily Inquirer, 22 February 2006, posted by Howard Brown, <u>JTRforums</u>, Ripper Media, Ripper Books, Ripper Fiction, Ripper Fiction Mentioned/Produced in Asian Sources, 6, 18 March 2011, accessed 7 July 2014.

[23] The Times, 12 September 1888, p. 12.

[24] The Times, 4 September 1888, p. 8.

[25] Whitechapel Infirmary Registers, posted by Chris Scott, <u>Casebook</u>, Forums, Ripper Discussions, Scene of the Crimes, Whitechapel Infirmary Registers 1885-87, 1 October 2008, 8, accessed 18 October 2013.

[26] M. J. Trow, <u>Jack the Ripper: Quest for a Killer</u>, Kindle, 2011.

[27] Douglas, <u>Criminal Investigative Analysis</u>

[28] R. Barber, "Did Jack the Ripper commit suicide?" <u>Casebook</u>, Dissertations, accessed 28 March 2012.

[29] Blog by Christopher T. George, 22 September 2011, <u>blog.casebook.org/chrisgeorge</u>, accessed 1May2016.

[30] Post by Uncle Jack, Casebook, Forums, Ripper Discussions, Suspects, General Suspect Discussion, George Lusk as a Suspect, 18 September 2009, accessed 14 February 2014.

[31] The Times, 29 April 1891, p. 12.

[32] R. Graysmith, <u>The Bell Tower: The Case of Jack the Ripper Finally Solved in San Francisco</u>, Regnery Publishing, 1999.

[33] San Francisco Call, 26 September 1895, p. 4.

[34] Daily Telegraph, 20 October 1888, p. 3.

[35] San Francisco Call, 25 April 1895, p. 5.

[36] J. G. Gibson, <u>Outlooks from the Zenith</u>, Blumberg, 1898.

[37] J. Powles, "The Most Extraordinary Ancestral Enquiry Ever? Or the Strange Case of Jack the Ripper and Spurgeon's College, <u>Bulletin of the Association of British Theological and Philosophical Libraries</u>, 21.1, March 2014, 8.

[38] San Francisco Call, 16 March 1902, p. 6.

[39] Email from John Michael Stracyznski to Ray Pelzer, 29 October 1995, Google Groups, https://groups.google.com, Babylon Five, accessed 11 February 2014. Also email from John Michael Stracyznski to Brian Walsh, 26 July 1998, http://www.am-utils.org/pipermail/b5jms/1998-July/002965.html, accessed 10 February 2014.

[40] The Times, 19 September 1888, p. 3. The Times, 29 September 1888, p. 4. The Times, 11 October 1888, p. 5. The Times, 16 November 1888, p. 4.

[41] Henrietta Barnett wrote a biography of her husband, which briefly discussed his use of the murders to promote reform, H. Barnett, <u>Cannon Barnett, His Life, Work and Friends</u>, London, John Murray, Vol. 2, pp. 302-09.

[42] P. Fisher, <u>An Illustrated Guide to Jack the Ripper</u>, P&D Riley, 1996.

[43] The Times, 27 April 1889, p. 5.

[44] D. Monaghan, and N. Cawthorne, <u>Jack the Ripper's Secret Confession</u>, Kindle, 2010, loc. 4474-4650, discusses the various candidates including Robert D'Onston Stephenson.

[45] Anon, <u>My Secret Life</u>, Kindle Edition, 2012, loc. 5911-5915.

[46] N. J. Kirtlan and D. Bainbridge, <u>Jack the Ripper: In My Blood</u>, Stone Boy Books, 2013.

[47] Posted by Debra A, <u>JTRForums</u>, http://www.jtrforums.com, Ripper Books, Non-Fiction, Jack the Ripper in My Blood, 06 June 2013, accessed 12 February 2014.

[48] Dundee Advertiser, 14 October 1890, p.7.

[49] St James Gazette, 24 November 1885, p 8.

[50] Morning Post, 16 August 1887, p. 6.

[51] Morning Post, 18 January 1888, p.2.

[52] Calendar of prisoners tried at the Essex Assizes, 30 November 1889, no. 16.

[53] Cheltenham Chronicle, 04 July 1891, p. 3.

[54] Derby Daily Telegraph, 03 July 1891, p. 3.

[55] The Times, 19 November 1891, p.7.

[56] Lloyds Weekly, 18 December 1892, p. 4.

[57] Reynolds Newspaper, 22 January 1893, p. 8.

[58] Lloyds Weekly Newspaper, 18 June 1893, p. 16.

Printed in Great Britain
by Amazon